APM Best Practices

Realizing Application Performance Management

Michael J. Sydor

D1502680

Apress·

APM Best Practices: Realizing Application Performance Managment

Copyright © 2010 by CA Technologies. All rights reserved. All trademarks, trade names, service marks and logos referenced herein belong to their respective companies.

The information in this publication could include typographical errors or technical inaccuracies, and the authors assume no responsibility for its accuracy or completeness. The statements and opinions expressed in this book are those of the authors and are not necessarily those of CA Technologies. ("CA"). CA may make modifications to any CA product, software program, method or procedure described in this publication at any time without notice.

Any reference in this publication to third-party products and websites is provided for convenience only and shall not serve as the authors' endorsement of such products or websites. Your use of such products, websites, any information regarding such products or any materials provided with such products or on such websites shall be at your own risk.

To the extent permitted by applicable law, the content of this book is provided "AS IS" without warranty of any kind, including, without limitation, any implied warranties of merchantability, fitness for a particular purpose, or non-infringement. In no event will the authors or CA be liable for any loss or damage, direct or indirect, arising from or related to the use of this book, including, without limitation, lost profits, lost investment, business interruption, goodwill or lost data, even if expressly advised in advance of the possibility of such damages. Neither the content of this book nor any software product referenced herein serves as a substitute for your compliance with any laws (including but not limited to any act, statute, regulation, rule, directive, standard, policy, administrative order, executive order, and so on (collectively, "Laws") referenced herein or otherwise. You should consult with competent legal counsel regarding any such Laws.

All rights reserved. No part of this work may be reproduced or transmitted in any form or by any means, electronic or mechanical, including photocopying, recording, or by any information storage or retrieval system, without the prior written permission of the copyright owner and the publisher.

ISBN-13 (pbk): 978-1-4302-3141-7
ISBN-13 (electronic): 978-1-4302-3142-4

Printed and bound in the United States of America (POD)

Trademarked names may appear in this book. Rather than use a trademark symbol with every occurrence of a trademarked name, we use the names only in an editorial fashion and to the benefit of the trademark owner, with no intention of infringement of the trademark.

President and Publisher: Paul Manning
Lead Editor: Jeffrey Pepper
Editorial Board: Steve Anglin, Mark Beckner, Ewan Buckingham, Gary Cornell, Jonathan Gennick, Jonathan Hassell, Michelle Lowman, James Markham, Matthew Moodie, Duncan Parkes, Jeffrey Pepper, Frank Pohlmann, Douglas Pundick, Ben Renow-Clarke, Dominic Shakeshaft, Matt Wade, Tom Welsh
Coordinating Editor: Laurin Becker
Copy Editor: Mary Behr
Compositor: Mary Sudul
Indexer: BIM Indexing & Proofreading Services
Artist: April Milne
Cover Designer: Anna Ishchenko

Distributed to the book trade worldwide by Springer Science+Business Media, LLC., 233 Spring Street, 6th Floor, New York, NY 10013. Phone 1-800-SPRINGER, fax (201) 348-4505, e-mail orders-ny@springer-sbm.com, or visit www.springeronline.com.

For information on translations, please e-mail rights@apress.com, or visit www.apress.com.

Apress and friends of ED books may be purchased in bulk for academic, corporate, or promotional use. eBook versions and licenses are also available for most titles. For more information, reference our Special Bulk Sales–eBook Licensing web page at http://www.apress.com/info/bulksales.

The information in this book is distributed on an "as is" basis, without warranty. Although every precaution has been taken in the preparation of this work, neither the author(s) nor Apress shall have any liability to any person or entity with respect to any loss or damage caused or alleged to be caused directly or indirectly by the information contained in this work.

Contents

About the Author

Michael J. Sydor is a software solution architect who has invested 20 years in the mastery of high performance computing technology. He has significant experience identifying and documenting technology best practices and has designed programs to mentor and realize client performance management teams. With a broad combination of software and systems architecture experience, as well as critical situation and traditional performance analysis, Michael is well positioned to influence and guide major initiatives within client IT organizations, for both distributed and mainframe architectures, and across Telco, Cable, Financial Trading, Media, Banking, Insurance, and Utilities industries.

Acknowledgments

This book is possible only through the efforts and interests of a large number of people who have supported the project, contributed to this body of experience, or helped in the refinement of the message. There are three teams:

Team A—My wife Jill and daughter Natasha, who had to endure my constant distraction and long hours devoted to this project over a very difficult year. Their support and patience helped keep it going.

Team B—The collaborators: Karen Sleeth (CA Press) and Jeff Cobb at CA. Jeffrey Pepper (editor) and Lauren Becker at Apress, along with the Apress production team. This is my first book. I needed a lot of help. These folks helped get it done right.

Team C—The extended team who bring APM to the marketplace: sales, technical and management.

A number of sales people directly contributed to this project by getting me in front of the real problems in the industry, primarily Ron Berkovits, who had (and maintains) a great enthusiasm for the best practices approach. Kristine Chamberline commissioned the first discussion paper introducing the best practice value proposition which lead to the vendor-neutral, Center of Excellence program. Kristine also committed Ron, Sam Terrell and Fran Rempusheski to the initial rollout of the sales-facing side of this story to further refine business propositions.

I am of course indebted to my direct and executive management who have kept me entertained, challenged and employed. This includes Mike Measel, Tom Bertrand, Kenton Siekman and Chris Cook. Chris has been guiding the APM business for many years, effectively commissioned this book, and made sure it survived the nuances of the business. It is exceptionally rare to be able to talk about what really leads to customer success and see it through.

In order to reach this current level of technical maturity I needed to draw from many other practitioners including Dave Martin, Ki Allam, Jason Collins, Mark Addleman, Mike Measel, Carl Seglum, Don Darwin,

Haroon Ahmed, Andreas Reiss, Gil Rice, Paul Jasek, Sylvain Gilbassier, David Barnes, Omar Ocampo, Mike Risser, Ben Tan, Tom Krupta, Shubra Kar, Matt LeRay, Prabhjot Singh, and Hal German. All of these folks contributed experiences, often beyond my own skills, and frequent cross-fertilization of ideas as the best practices were established and refined.

These varied experiences would not have been possible without the seasoned guidance of Dick Williams, who shepherded Wily Technology from startup to acquired company. Dick was a great inspiration who helped deliver some of the earliest APM messages as we all helped the marketplace mature. None of which was possible without a solid, capable product by Lew Cerne, Jeff Cobb, John Bley and many others. Their innovations made it possible for the extended team to focus on how to employ the tool, rather than being distracted with how to get it functioning. It just worked.

Finally, I'd like to thank two folks at the very beginning of my adventure with APM: Dave Martin for my first demo of Introscope, now long years ago, and putting up with my many uncomfortable questions. And Brian Meehan who persisted, over a few months, in inviting me to interview, after I initially declined. You were right. This stuff is cool.

Introduction

Application Performance Management (APM) is the name given to the use of technology to initiate, deploy, monitor, fix, update and/or optimize systems within an organization. Application management software employs measurements of response times, and other component and resource interactions, to help manage the overall stability and usability of the software within its purview. This book, presented in three parts, is intended to take you from the first discussions about planning and assessing your monitoring needs, through the details and considerations of an APM technology implementation, and onto the types of skills, processes and competencies that you will need to be completely successful in the utilization of APM. And it is not simply a discussion of ideas for you to consider. The approach used is largely metrics-based. I have included the appropriate artifacts so that you may conduct these activities exactly the same as I would if I were working with you.

My role as an APM practitioner is to guide stakeholders through every phase of the journey to APM excellence and the discussions in this book are taken directly from my presentations, engagement artifacts and training materials. In particular, I lead client teams through a comprehensive program of best practices that allow them to establish and staff an APM discipline. What is unique about this collection of best practices is that they are vendor-neutral, which is an enormous consideration when you reflect on the reality that your IT tools are selected from many different vendors. For my work, and especially my credibility in defining these practices as essential, they have to work for every vendor technology. I have included specific exercises which you can use to track your progress in establishing an APM discipline.

For a wide variety of reasons, folks have difficulty getting the full measure of usefulness from their investments in APM. There is often a disconnect between the APM technology capabilities and the organizatioal capabilities in actually understanding and employing the technology. I developed many of these APM best practices by helping clients recover from any number of missteps in selecting and employing APM technology. APM can be complex as much as it is easy to use. While a good part of what I do might be considered brainstorming (discussing new techniques and approaches), an equal part is gut-wrenching and frustration-laden. This is the hard part—figuring out how to get your organization to reliably adopt APM.

My motivation in writing this book is to show you what many users of APM miss and also how powerful the technology and processes can be. When I began in this industry there were no meaningful references nor texts from which to get some useful ideas. Even today I really don't find anything substantial to address APM education across planning, implementation and best practices – especially with a vendor-neutral tone. So I'm going to put a stake in the ground with a bold and ambitious statement: APM starts here.

Vendor Neutrality

Yes, I am employed by a monitoring solution vendor. And you can figure out who by looking on the book cover. It is not the goal of this book to highlight or recommend any particular vendor or technology. Instead, we will focus on the processes that are applicable to any vendor solution, especially in a multi-vendor or heterogeneous monitoring environment. We will also pay particular attention to when it makes sense to employ a particular technology. When it is necessary to illustrate how a tool presents data, or otherwise how a tool might be employed to support one of these processes, you may reliably assume that *any* vendor of the underlying technology may provide that capability. And if I simply cannot avoid mentioning a specific type of tool then I will use a freely available or open source technology as the example.

Any monitoring tool is appropriate—provided you understand its application and limitations. We will address that as well. In general, any visibility is better than "no visibility". However, you cannot simply drop in a tool without considering some framework of processes to support and utilize the tool appropriately. This process gap is what many organizations fail to address and so their monitoring initiatives are less effective. My goal is simply to take whatever system you have today and reliably increase its capabilities and value to your organization – as far as you may want to advance it.

Conveniently, the guideline of vendor neutrality also fits in with our first and most important objective for a monitoring initiative: it is not the time to talk about specifics of a specific vendor technology solution. It is time to talk about the process of realizing an APM initiative.

APM Starts Here

This book is about how to do APM 'right'. APM means different things to different people and this quickly becomes a fantastic gap between reality and expectation. My professional role is to jump into this gap and get things back on track. Maybe you want my job? Maybe you want to avoid seeing me turn up? Maybe you want to get this right the first time. Nothing available today is going to help you do it right the first time – save for this book. The single biggest gap in understanding APM is this:

APM is not simply an end-user monitoring application. It is part of the IT infrastructure and the use of the tool will be divided over many stakeholders. Fail to accommodate and empower these stakeholders and your APM initiative will follow.

APM is much more than a monitoring technology. It is a *collaboration* technology. Through the techniques in this book you are going to educate your stakeholders in the language of APM. You are going to harness their capabilities and tear down the barriers to cooperation. It is how your organization is going to finally get control of the application life cycle and improve software quality, without excuse or exception.

Organization of this Book

This book is presented in three parts: Planning, Implementation and Practitioner's Guide.

Introduction to Part 1: Planning

Planning for an APM initiative is a course of action that will balance the capabilities of the IT team, the demands of the business and the alignment with corporate objectives. It is advantageous to move quickly from establishing the overall goals of the initiative, to formulate and present (sell internally) a tactical plan that will have a high degree of success. Successful management and execution of this planning activity sets the stage for a successful deployment of the technology and implementation of the supporting processes. Failure to plan will result in an uneven or failed initiative.

We are concerned with five major themes:

- Establishing the business justification (Chapter 2)
- Assessing your current monitoring capabilities (Chapter 3)
- Understanding staffing requirements (Chapter 4)
- Defining the catalog of services that will track the progress of the initiative (Chapter 5)
- Executing a successful pilot evaluation leading to selection of a suitable technology (Chapter 6)

Each of these themes will be handled in its own chapter and each needs to be addressed prior to the deployment phase, which is covered in the second part of this book: Implementation.

Of these themes, staffing is probably the most controversial as this exposes the organization's understanding of impact of APM and how it should be leveraged. Frankly put, while the greatest potential for APM initiative failure is inadequate scope, the second greatest has to do with staffing: who does the work of using APM technology and processes? You should not really be concerned with total manpower but more about who will fulfill the various APM roles, where the monitoring initiative will sit in the organization, and how it will interact with other stakeholders.

An important aspect of the APM best practices presented here is the focus on an early and detailed assessment of existing skills, processes and competencies. This is specifically targeted to address the looming staffing/ownership question but also may be extended to survey the strengths/weaknesses of existing tools and groups within the IT organization and how they may be leveraged to help support and continue the pace of the APM initiative while avoiding any immediate increase in headcount. Doing more with less is always a theme in modern IT management and I find that any APM initiative will be under significant pressure to do exactly this.

Some discussion of the service catalog, and how we use these defined capabilities as milestones to manage the evolutions of an APM discipline, is important because this topic is a frequent point of confusion. A catalog of services is a popular IT feature, and one that is directly descended from the ITIL descriptions of service management. I find while many organizations believe that this work is already done; few can quickly point to precisely what this catalog currently includes. This is another gap which can significantly impair the progress of the APM initiative. We focus on this *service catalog* concept because this is the area where we will need the greatest degree of tracking, that in fact, these services are actually being achieved.

Because many organizations have already been initiated to this service catalog concept, much of my planning response is to make up for the earlier gaps, so I needed an efficient way to measure exactly what was missing from the existing service catalog. Very often a client will have a comprehensive set of services defined but no corresponding implementation roadmap is specified. And after some months, attention wanes and other priorities come to the fore, and the service catalog fades from view. I will show you how to successfully manage the realization of the APM service catalog by aligning with an evolution of staff skills and demonstrable competencies. This results in a more manageable job of tracking and reporting progress towards realizing the service catalog.

The final discussion topic in this planning part of the book: how to define a pilot of a new technology, is also a point where the IT team can easily fail. The IT organization has probably been evaluating a variety of technologies for many years. However, the current crop of economic pressures, down-sizing and transition of responsibilities off-shore have eliminated much of the hard-earned experience in defining and executing a pilot evaluation. I see the pilot evaluation as an important validation of the overall objectives of the monitoring initiative. Failing to do a thorough and timely job here will of course cripple any chance of a successful deployment and ongoing use of the technology. I will take the opportunity here to simply address that gap and present a successful best practice for doing a solid evaluation of a prospective technology.

Introduction to Part 2: Implementation

In this Implementation part, chapters 7-9, we want to look at the implementation of APM from the perspective of a project manager tasked with bringing the initiative to realization. With a small scope, it is rare that you will have a project manager role assigned, but whomever has to oversee the progress of the initiative will benefit from the project management perspective that will be discussed here. For large initiatives, especially those with multiple and recurring monitoring deployments, you should considering moving to an APM-specific project manager, along the lines of what was outlined in Chapter 4 – Planning – Staffing and Responsibilities.

First, a word of caution. Implementation is often used interchangeably with deployment. Deployment of software does not include getting the software to do what you want. This is the largest point of confusion and dissatisfaction with performance monitoring software—IT thought their responsibility was to deploy the monitoring solution while the business expected an implementation that would help them identify performance problems. Part of this confusion has to do with who "owns" the software. IT deploys lots of applications on behalf of the application owners, why is APM different? Often, an initial APM deployment is limited to a single stakeholder and the reality of APM being more of an infrastructure choice is lost. Here we mean *implementation* to cover the initial physical deployment, developing essential processes for employing the tool and how these processes are assembled into service capabilities. These processes are the difference in establishing a meaningful APM discipline.

Implementation of an APM solution is surprisingly quick, compared to other IT initiatives: usually on the order of weeks. Sometimes in just a day or two for a small environment. The overall coordination however can be large, depending on the scope. Such coordination is required for any re-testing of applications and also for integration of alerts with existing Trouble Management systems. The scope (level of effort) will increase proportionally to the number of applications. For 1-2 applications, all of these implementation considerations can be discussed in a 1-2 hours planning session. For 20-30 applications, this might take 2-3 months before consensus and approval of the plan is achieved.

This section will review each of the topics that the implementation plan needs to consider. Traditionally, this task is managed by a project manager who will build the project schedule and then work to coordinate the resources to achieve the deployment. Smaller initiatives may want to forgo the project manager role, which incurs some risk (which we expect that an understanding of this section will help you to avoid). Even the smaller initiatives will benefit from the implementation considerations that are presented here.

I also know that there will be a number of other goals and activities that the monitoring initiative needs to accomplish that are outside the traditional definition of deployment: getting the technology up and running. For the project manager, these are simply additional objectives which they will schedule and resource accordingly. You will need to provide the project manager with a model or template concerning how these non-traditional requirements will be achieved. I call this template the *Phased Deployment Model*.

In the event that your APM initiative planning will involve multiple phased deployments leading to a dedicated APM team, then you will also want to consider using the service catalog approach to set goals and track the progress of your APM Service Bureau or Center of Excellence for the enterprise. At minimum you will want to document capabilities from the service catalog that you are *not* pursuing as part of you implementation. Often, a smaller initiative does not have the latitude to address these enterprise considerations but you can do a much better job in managing expectations if you fully understand and fully communicate to your stakeholders what you are setting aside.

The bottom line for the APM implementation is to show you how to scale the available resources in advance of dedicated staff for APM, spread out the workload and focus on what is important for your organization.

Introduction to Part 3: Practioner's Guide

This section introduces a variety of techniques for how to employ the tools that are important in realizing the best possible value from your APM investment. This has always been a controversial topic because the motivation for investing in monitoring software is that it "does stuff."

APM software is simply a tool that does monitoring. The trick is in how you employ the tool to realize IT and business objectives. Earlier generations of users were focused on the acquiring the tool. The current generation is focused on employing the tool with appropriate process.

My favorite analogy is the common hammer. The hammer comes with guidelines for safe use and typical applications. It does not include instructions on how to build a house or a condominium complex. For that you need an architect and a general contractor who will guide you in how and when to use that hammer.

The format for the chapters in this Practitioner's Guide is as if I were delivering a best practice module, to your team as part of a mentoring session. Each chapter addresses topics in roughly the same order. The first topic is a kickoff meeting, which is used to both gather specifics about your environment and processes, as well as a lecture on the topic. The second is to define the process or cookbook for conducting the best practice. This is frequently tailored to the client environment. The third section is a definition of the competency exercises that you will need to demonstrate before you may go confidently forth with a new badge of APM prowess. I will also summarize any artifacts that would typically be developed and any references that are appropriate.

To be frank, much of what I have defined as best practices is a result of trial and error, with a strong dose of step-wise refinement. I have depended as much on my own experiences as those of my peers who may have delivered these service capabilities first, or sometimes better than me. My role has always been to collect them, create a framework to organize them, and through frequent client interactions, innovate to fill any gaps. The fact is that there has been simply next to nothing freely available for the industry to really show you how to be successful with APM. I trust you will now find this situation much improved.

Michael J. Sydor

Getting Started with APM

The second mouse gets the cheese.

The Challenge

Software systems, the applications and strategies on which your business depend today have become extraordinarily complex. For many organizations, the wide array of applications and tools to develop this software results in application architectures that can overwhelm the capabilities of many organizations to manage them.

Not so long ago, how you implemented your software was hidden deep within your organization. Typically, your interactions consisted of exchanges of data representing inventory, orders, debits, and credits that were transferred across private networks. These interactions involved a limited number of other corporations, loosely called *trading partners*, who themselves also had hidden software capabilities and assets. The number of trading partners, as well as the variety of interactions, was constrained but easily managed. These types of transactions were conducted daily and often took days to resolve.

With the growth of internet computing, these private networks became public thoroughfares, increasing access to trading partners as well as creating new opportunities to interact directly with the consumers of your products and services. As consumers migrated all of their interactions to the web, the ability to manage the underlying software systems simply did not keep pace. Somehow, every aspect of the software life cycle—development, delivery, management, and ultimately, innovation—had become unpredicatable and unstable.

Whatever the current state of your application software and IT management practices, I have a shockingly simple observation: you can't expect to manage what you can't measure. Often the fundamental gap is that you lack meaningful visibility into the nature and causes of your performance issues, other than the fact that trading partners and consumers may be complaining.

Application Performance Management[1] (APM)consists of processes and technologies to enable you to get these measurements. Visibility into performance issues at every stage of the software life cycle is how to best restore manageability and predictability.

The challenge is that if your *software life cycle management* process is already broken, you may have a really tough time getting APM to work reliably. It would be nice if you could simply procure an APM tool that just makes everything better. That is an empty dream. There is no quick fix for a set of problems that have developed over years. It is really *processes* for APM—how you use the technology in your daily procedures—that are going to have the most significant impact on your performance management. And it is these same processes that will establish a new foundation upon which you can bring the whole of the software life cycle under control.

The first challenge is to assess your corporate system's maturity, which includes a number of dimensions. Your *organizational maturity* is reflected in how you monitor, test, deploy, and operate the infrastructure and software that comprise the applications or *services* that you manage. In order to measure maturity, I use a maturity model that addresses the skills, processes, and competencies that will need to be established in order to obtain consistent benefits from APM. This model, which I call "APM best practices," will be presented so that you can freely incorporate it within your APM discipline.

Reference Architecture

My challenge is to talk about APM without explicit mentioning anything about a vendor implementation of APM. This is going to result in an occassional oversimplification. There is very little available on the web that explores APM in a vendor-neutral fashion that I can reference, but I'll give you those links when appropriate.

Part of this reference architecture is language and terminology, which is where I'll start. And then I'll build toward a diagram of what an APM solution can look like.

Life Cycles

I will be concerned with three varieties of life cycles: software, application, and APM.

---

[1] http://en.wikipedia.org/wiki/Application_performance_management

The Software Development Life Cycle

The root of all of these is the Software Development Life Cycle (SDLC),[2] which describes the cycle of activities for a software system including planning, analysis, design, implementation, and maintenance. No one realistically expects to get a system exactly right the first time, so after the first iteration is delivered, the life cycle process begins anew, using previous experience as an input plus additional requirements that have been uncovered as a result of the earlier iteration. This can result in rapid protyping, which is one possible model of a SDLC that focuses on short iterations of development, testing, and validation. When a particular system undergoes multiple interations of a life cycle, I call this an *evolution*. A working system arises from the evolution of multiple rapid-protyping cycles.

The Application Life Cycle

An *application life cycle* is the evolution of a software system after its initial deployment and regardless of the development strategy that was employed. I make this distinction because much of what you have to deal with are applications that are already "cooked." They have been deployed for years; while they may undergo periodic maintenance or upgrades in capabilities, the majority of the systems do not experience any significant redesigns. The stages in the application life cycle include development, functional tests, performance tests, user acceptance tests (UAT), production, and triage. These stages appear to overlap with the SDLC life cycle but become more critical after the initial release. Functional and performance testing are often lumped together at the Quality Assurance (QA) stage. I make particular emphasis on triage as a stage of the application life cycle because I want to distinguish well-behaved applications from problematic ones, and triage activity— the frequency and manner that you conduct triage—is the most direct way to gain this perspective. For a mature application, triage is also the most expensive activity, in terms of personnel, that you have to contend with. This offers the possibility for tracking savings as the APM initiative is realized by tracking the frequency and duration of triage activities.

Triage, in the APM context, is the process of determining and addressing which IT systems are the likely contributor to a performance incident. Usually undertaken during a bridge call (conference call), triage typically involves dozens of stakeholders working to prioritize restoration efforts for the affected systems. Reducing the time and personnel spent in triage is an important management goal. You will find three chapters devoted to growing your triage capabilities as this is a primary benefit of APM technology. Related to triage is the concept of *root-cause*[3]. I treat root-cause analysis as something outside of APM. I look to APM to provide the raw data, or *metrics*, upon which to base a root-cause analysis. APM tells you where the problem lies. Root-cause tells you why. Your goal for triage is to make sure that everyone is looking at the most likely contributor to the problem and not spending any effort on less-profitable concerns.

---

[2] Wikipedia, "systems development life cycle," http://en.wikipedia.org/wiki/Systems_Development_Life_Cycle

[3] Systems Thinking, "Root Cause Analysis," www.systems-thinking.org/rca/rootca.htm

The APM Life Cycle

The third type of life cycle is APM itself. It has characteristics of SDLC in that it expects an interative evolution until the full capabilities of the tool are realized. And it follows the application life cycle with tailored techniques for each stage in order to meet the specific needs of the *stakeholders*[4] at each stage.

Each APM iteration involves the following activities:

- Identify gaps.
- Establish (or increase) triage.
- Leverage (or establish) QA activities.
- Enhance the deployment mechanism.
- Enhance (or establish) collaboration.

In my experience, three iterations should get the job done. So this yields 15 separate activities. This discussion has significance for the next topic, maturity models, because in order to establish what APM potential your current organization has, you need to quickly identify any gaps in your current practices. These 15 activities allow for a reasonable amount of detail to be collected without requiring in-depth interviews. Much more detail on skills assessments is found in Chapter 3.

Organizational Maturity

The breadth of your IT infrastructure—managing projects and technology while aligning them with strategic goals across the life cycle—is examined to develop a score representing current capabilities and gaps. You will look first at the organizational capabilities in general and then focus on the management (monitoring) capabilities. Maturity increases as capabilities increase. Management maturity improves as you first respond to events in production (reactive management) and ultimately avoid those production events by detecting them pre-production (proactive management). Figure 1-3 illustrates the relationship between the application life cycle and the management capabilities of your existing system, which are the primary mechanisms of tracking management maturity.

---

[4] *Stakeholders* are the parties interested in the health of the application. Most notable is the business sponsor—the group that "owns" or commissions development or purchase of a software system.

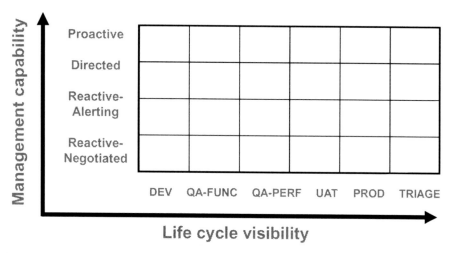

Figure I-I. Management capabilities vs. life cycle visibility

As monitoring visibility is enhanced, shown as moving up the management capability axis on Figure 1-1, the management capability is extended from reactive to directed and proactive. I distinguish between *reactive-negotiated,* when you have to ask for alerts, and *reactive-alerting,* when you automatically receive alerts, as the first example of how to separate what is perceived from what are the actual capabilities of monitoring the system. Every IT organization today has well-developed availability alerting, so you might conclude that their monitoring is mature. But because many organizations are still heavily partitioned internally, in what is called an IT silo[5], those alerts are often not shared. The fact that someone may be monitoring the system is not really helpful if you are not notified of the alert. When you no longer have to ask for that alert or negotiate to get access to that alert, then your management capability is enhanced.

Earlier in the life cycle, you will often find a complete absence of monitoring. As applications become more complex, the integration and testing likewise become complex. How do you know, prior to a test, that all of the contributing systems are functioning? This is a basic monitoring question, and without the answer you have little chance of conducting your testing correctly.

To address these potential gaps, the two other levels of management maturity from Figure 1-1 are:

- **Directed**, when availability and performance information are collected during development and QA testing in order to direct remediation of issues as they occur.

---

[5] M. R. Nelson, "Breaking out of the IT Silo: The Integration Maturity Model," http://net.educause.edu/ir/library/pdf/ERB0506.pdf, March 15, 2005.

- **Proactive**, when availability and performance information are used to limit the deployment to production of problematic applications or otherwise prepare for incidents before they occur in the production environment.

Both of these management maturity levels require a pre-production use of monitoring technology.

Along with the initial assessment of an organization's maturity, another reason for assessments is to support an ongoing measurement of the progress of your APM initiative. You will need to make a measurement after each iteration of your APM initiative in order to document the progress and goals achieved. This is often overlooked for small initiatives but is always present with larger efforts.

The root concept for this maturity measurement is the Capability Maturity Model Integration (CMMI)[6]. This model was developed for assessing software engineering maturity in terms of the processes that should be part of your business practices. It defines five maturity levels:

- Initial
- Managed
- Defined
- Quantitatively managed
- Optimized

However, while this is a well-supported maturity model, it does not have enough flexibility to accommodate the multiple stakeholders and activities that an APM initiative involves[7].

To address this, this book presents a number of *capability dimensions* within the maturity model to allow for the variety of levels of organizational maturity that are typically encountered today. These additional dimensions include the addition of evaluating capabilities for alerts, technology, reporting, testing, support, deployment (change control), operations, and incident management. Each of these will have a minimum of three increasing maturity/capability levels, up to a maximum of 24 levels when each of the processes are taken into account. For example, the alerting dimension of the organizational maturity model is scored as illustrated in Figure 1-2.

---

[6] Wikipedia, "Capability Maturity Model Integration," http://en.wikipedia.org/wiki/Capability_Maturity_Model_Integration

[7] In February 2009 the Software Engineering Institute (SEI) made an initial release of CMMI-SVC 1.2 to provide this missing guidance on establishing, managing, and delivering services in a business environment. This CMMI-SVC also defines 24 process areas, similar to the 24 capability dimensions that I use for assessing APM maturity, which dates to 2006. Other than this unforeseen correspondence, there is currently no mapping between CMMI-SVC and the APM Best Practices. For more details on CMMI-SVC model see www.sei.cmu.edu/cmmi/tools/svc/download.cfm

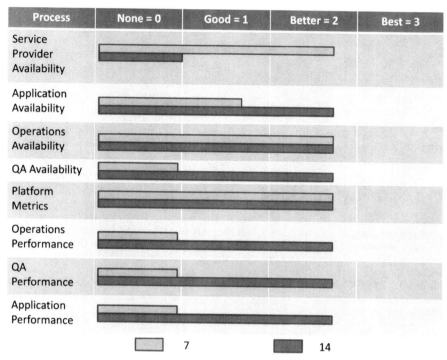

Figure 1-2. Alerting dimension of the organizational maturity model

As shown in Figure 1-2, if you consider planning a move to more web-enabled (on-demand) services for a typical batch operation without much of a QA system in place, you would get a score of 7. This type of application is often unsuited for performance measurements of any kind. In contrast, in a more mature organizational framework with greater experience in web-enabled apps, including a QA performance system, the result will be a higher score. You will find more detail on these additional maturity dimensions when I introduce assessment and artifacts in Chapter 3.

The real benefit from these additional maturity dimensions is that you may easily articulate exactly where you are and what you have yet to accomplish in order to establish a mature APM system. You can then rationalize training and technology investments, as well as track the overall progress of the initiative.

The Five APM Competencies

I have given a lot of thought as to what a performance engineer should be able to do. This has resulted in five APM competencies that I consider the minimum for a "certified" performance engineer to be able to master.

These APM competencies include:

- Rapid deployment
- Solution sizing
- Application audit
- Triage
- Assessments

You will find examples for most of these competencies (rapid deployment is omitted) in Chapters 3, 10, and 13-17. These are exactly what I use to evaluate the progress of the APM teams that I mentor.

Monitoring Architectures

APM is a superset of earlier monitoring techniques. When assessing an organization's capabilities, the fact that they are not yet using APM technology does not automatically result in a poor score. Instead, if they have the appropriate processes or inclination, any monitoring technology can be used to enhance visibility overall. This often results in a better situation, even if they do not undertake a full APM initiative. It is helpful to establish some nomenclature about those earlier technologies so that you can understand how APM technology enhances monitoring capabilities.

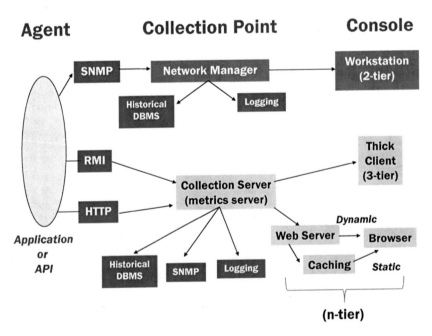

Figure 1-3. Metrics collection architectures

Figure 1-3 illustrates the two basic metrics collection architectures. The top architecture is the classic SNMP-based monitoring. A collection point called the network manager would poll the connected SNMP devices. Alerts would be logged and the various metrics would be stored in a relational database. A workstation would connect to the collection point to receive alert status updates or to navigate among the connected devices to collect metrics and issue queries for the current status directly from the attached devices.

While the network manager architecture is completely capable for SNMP activities, it does not scale well to the metrics volumes that you are likely to incur in support of APM.

I prefer to refer to any measured quantity as a *metric*, consistent with definitions you can find on the web.[8] This makes the collection point a *server of metrics* or *metrics server*. Regardless of capability, the basic function is to collect metrics. What is important about metrics is that there will be a lot of them to manage. This in itself is not a problem, but as you can see from Figure 1-4, the number of potential metrics grows significantly as you get closer to the internals of the application or service.

Metrics can represent any type of data. In general, there are three primary *metric types*: counts, response times, and invocation rates. Metrics are measured at varying rates from real-time (each and every invocation) all the way up to 15 minute intervals. The actual *measurement frequency* depends on the type of measurement point (see Figure 1-4) that is in use. And some measurement points operate with a combination of measurement frequencies. For example, a logfile can record every transaction processed, in near real-time, but the logging agent may only process the new log entries every 10 minutes. In another system, the log may not be processed until after business hours. Both log agents can contribute metrics to APM but they will have vastly different measurement frequencies.

The number of metrics that you can expect varies as you traverse the *monitoring stack*, illustrated in Figure 1-4. The visibility into the monitoring stack, which is another measure of management capability, is directly proportional to the number of metrics that may be available.

---

[8] Wikipedia, "metrics," http://en.wikipedia.org/wiki/Metrics

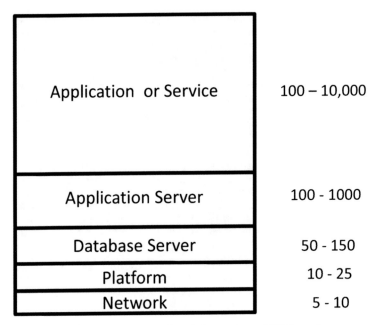

Figure 1-4. The monitoring stack and the number of APM metrics

To manage this new level of metrics and to provide greater capabilities with the agents and console devices, monitoring architectures simply evolved much the same as the applications they were being tasked to monitor: from 2-tier to 3-tier to n-tier architectures.

APM Architecture

In addition to the availability monitoring via SNMP that is ubiquitous in IT today, there are a number of other technologies that may be present in an APM solution. These break down along five major *measurement points*, indicated in Figure 1-5 and summarized as follows:

1. Logfiles
2. Appliance or dedicated applications (often homegrown for a specific system)
3. Synthetic transactions,[9] also called *robots*
4. Real transactions, often called *probes*
   - Transaction filtering or pattern matching
   - Protocol capture and analysis

---

[9] Wikipedia, "operational intelligence," http://en.wikipedia.org/wiki/Operational_intelligence#Systems_management

5. Instrumentation

- JMX/PMI or other measurement frameworks
- Byte-code instrumentation

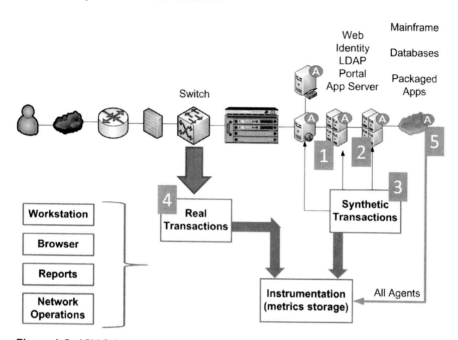

Figure I-5. APM Solution architecture and the five measurement points

You can also break the technologies down as agent-based (indicated by the "A") or agent-less. I don't see the need for these distinctions because all the metrics can end up in the metrics server at some point. I have not indicated availability monitoring as a measure point because it is almost certainly there, and all of the other measurement points will provide the availability status redundantly anyway.

	Good	Better	Best
Transaction	Log **1**	Synthetic **3**	Real **4**
Application	Log **1**	Instrumentation JMX/PMI **5**	Instrumentation BCI **5**
Platform	Availability Monitoring	Instrumentation JMX/PMI **5**	Instrumentation BCI **5**
Network	Availability Monitoring	Appliance and Homegrown **2**	Packet Tracing **4**

Increasing Utility (vertical axis)

Increasing Performance Visibility

Figure 1-6. Visibility Summary

There are a number of monitoring contexts, each with their own particular utility. Within each context, you survey what technologies you may bring to bear in order to get visibility into that context. This results in the graphic in Figure 1-6 which lists all of the currently available technology choices to support APM. I have overlayed the *measurement points* that were illustrated in Figure 1-5. A mapping of the technologies in current use, as with Figure 1-6, shows what visibility gaps may be present and where APM technology will help the situation. Ultimately, organizational maturity will limit the ability to incorporate the new data streams into existing processes. There isn't much point in trying to implement more capable monitoring technologies if the process infrastructure is not first established and viable.

My point is that all of the APM technologies are useful. If you have solid practices for managing and using logfiles, you are likely going to have a good experience with synthetics. If your synthetics practices are solid, you are going to appreciate working with real transactions.

But if you are struggling with synthetics, for example, then you should delay moving to instrumentation until you understand and resolve the process gaps that are impeding your progress. Organizational maturity is not additive. Instead, the weakest link is what will hold back the APM initiative.

Application Characteristics

Depending on the software architecture of the application, you can make a quick assessment of what APM technologies might be useful by determining the component types present and the transaction profiles.

Software components are reusable elements of an application. The coarsest component is a process,[10] which has reusability limited to multiple invocations, each as a separate process. The next level of reuse is through component-based languages[11], such as Java, .NET, CORBA, SOAP, and COM. These allow for multiple invocations of the same object within a single process. Each object is associated with a thread to manage its execution.

Transaction profiles are characteristics of individual or collections of applications. A *business transaction,* such as a new_customer transaction, can visit one or more applications in the course of being completed, resulting in an *application transaction* (transaction with an application server). Each application transaction can utilize one or more *resource transactions,* such as an interaction with a database. In the example new_customer transaction, the business transaction visits four application servers, each of which updates a database. The business transaction is visibile to synthetic and real transaction monitoring. The application and resource transaction are visible to logging, appliance, and instrumentation technology.

My highly simplified new_customer business transaction, containing four resource transactions, does not need additional visualization to understand the relationships. But a real-world transaction profile is going to be much more complex. Fortunately, there is a visualization model called a *transaction trace*[12], which is diagrammed in Figure 1-7.

---

[10] Wikipedia, "UNIX process," http://en.wikipedia.org/wiki/Unix_process

[11] Wikipedia, "component-based software engineering," http://en.wikipedia.org/wiki/Component-based_software_engineering

[12] Here are three of examples of transaction trace visualizations: http://blog.codechart.com/ http://www.hpl.hp.com/techreports/2008/HPL-2008-210.pdf http://developer.apple.com/mac/library/documentation/DeveloperTools/Conceptual/InstrumentsUserGuide/ViewingandAnalyzingData/ViewingandAnalyzingData.html

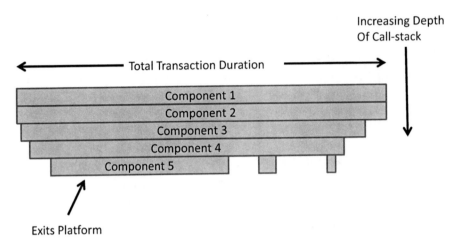

Increasing Depth
Of Call-stack

Total Transaction Duration

Exits Platform

Figure 1-7. Transaction trace visualization

This diagram is simply the various components that contribute to the transaction, presented in the order that they are invoked, which is referred to as a *call stack*[13]. How the call stack varies in depth over the total duration of the transaction is called a *transaction trace*. I will discuss transaction traces in more detail in Chapters 7 and 12.

Reporting Characteristics

The final aspect of your reference architecture is often the first major gap that your organization will need to address: reporting. Making effective and consistent use of the APM information is where you'll experience the greatest organizational resistance. Some pre-APM companies are today working with minimal real-time visibility and getting performance reports the following day. There is nothing wrong with this arrangement—until you make hourly data available, and eventually real-time data. Folks will not know how to use this new level of frequency of information to change their routine, let alone know what might be most useful from the performance data.

Reporting, then, has its own evolution among the following four elements:

- Real-time dashboards
- General reports
- Baseline reports
- HealthCheck reports

---

[13] Wikipedia, "call stack," http://en.wikipedia.org/wiki/Call_stack

The new report will be the *dashboard[14]*. This metaphor, frequently used to summarize multiple data sources in a single spreadsheet, can be expressed through a variety of graphic constructs such as gauges, graphs, and indicator lamps. When you superimpose key performance indicators on top of a solution architecture diagram, it becomes very easy to understand the relationships of the performance metrics with respect to the physical or logical architecture.

General reports is just a catch-all for any reporting that you are doing today that would then be delivered with performance metrics as the source.

Baseline reports are specifically focused on just the critical components for an application when it is under test or in production. A baseline is an arbitrary definition of "normal" which you can then use during triage to confirm when you have an abnormal situation. Baseline practices are discussed in Chapter 12.

HealthCheck reports combine metrics from baselines, platform metrics (CPU, memory), and other metrics that are established to track capacity and performance. They may be focused on a critical period during your operation's daily, weekly, or monthly summaries. They are intended to provide a forum to detect subtle changes in the application prior to a severe performance degradation. They will be immediately familiar to your folks who are responsible for *capacity planning[15]* but they are really intended to foster collaboration around *capacity management[16]*. The difference between the planning and management functions seems subtle. I keep them straight by reflecting that *planning* is for the long-term and *management* is for day-to-day decision making.

The basic reporting, either baselines or healthchecks, is fundamental to effective capacity management of the APM solution. I will pick up this topic in Chapter 10.

The First Meeting

Monitoring of applications and their resources, such as databases and web services, has been provided for since the mid-1960's predominately by the Simple Network Management Protocol (SNMP)[17]. The SNMP protocol, and its attendant technologies, are limited in the number of metrics and the frequency that they may be delivered to a monitoring workstation. It is also difficult to implement an interface between the internals of an application and SNMP for applications that are already developed. APM avoids the complications of adding new interfaces to existing code by either focusing on response times or automatically inserting instrumentation points. That's the short reasoning behind why folks look toward APM technology. It lets them measure things that they did not originally plan for.

---

[14] Dashboard by Example, www.enterprise-dashboard.com/2007/07/23/gis-dashboards-for-an-operations-monitoring-center/

[15] Wikipedia, "capacity planning," http://en.wikipedia.org/wiki/Capacity_planning

[16] Wikipedia, "capacity management," http://en.wikipedia.org/wiki/Capacity_management

[17] http://en.wikipedia.org/wiki/Simple_Network_Management_Protocol

Of course, that is not the whole story. There are a number of concerns and goals for any technology initiative that an IT organization undertakes. These initiatives take money and staff to complete so they are not activities undertaken lightly. In my attempt to create a book that fits all situations I've decided that the best approach is to simply follow what my first interaction with a client would be.

So in this chapter, I will talk about the what's on the agenda for a first meeting, This may be among your peers, management, or even with a vendor representative.

Note In this chapter I will define terms and language as if you have no background in IT. I use these initial presentations to establish a forum as well as open the discussion—to help you understand the APM perspective and requirements and to hopefully stimulate your thinking about your goals and concerns. I cannot share transcripts of the meetings that will serve as examples in this book, so I have tried to capture all of the major themes and situations that lead to exploration, acceptance, and delivery of a monitoring initiative. Please treat these themes *a la carte*—pick and choose what is of interest to you.

My goal in this first meeting is to begin with the end state in mind: an overview all of the activities that lead to the realization of an APM initiative. Then I define the appropriate steps to make it happen. Depending on the overall experience and maturity of the client processess around monitoring, this results in either increased efforts on developing requirements and business justification, a pilot evaluation, a skills and visibility assessment, or an initial solution sizing. Sometimes it will result is the client deciding not to go forward at this time. My role is not only to set expectations but to help clients decide if they are truly prepared to take the next step in monitoring maturity—APM.

There is a broad spectrum of potential responses to a first meeting but the following should give you an idea of what you can achieve with the appropriate level of experience in positioning APM—a tangible, actionable plan of what to do next. You do not need to have many meetings to figure it out if you have the right people in that first meeting.

I will detail all of these actionable activities in the first part of the book, "Planning an APM Initiative." So if the opportunity presents itself, you can move that first meeting forward on your own.

The following are the themes that I choose for that idealized first meeting. Remember that every organization is at a slightly different maturity level and has slightly different priorities and goals. So you need to vett this list to build your agenda for that first meeting.

- What is APM?
- Realities of packaged software solutions.
- How the monitoring game has changed.

- Limitations of Availability Monitoring.
- The impact of APM visibility.
- Addressing the visibility gap.
- Demonstrating value for a monitoring initiative.
- Establishing an APM implementation.

The most important charactistic of this agenda is that it has nothing to do with talking about the product or technologies that may be employed. In my experience, attempting to talk about best practices along with details about a vendor's technology is simply incompatible with the client's goal: assessing the opportunity for a performance monitoring initiative. You need to keep product discussions completely separate from best practice discussions.

> **Note** If there is anything you think I should have covered in this book, or if you have a differing opinion or approach, I invite you to join my blog at realizingapm.blogspot.com (if it would benefit the APM community) or email me at realizingapm@gmail.com. It is hard to identify a scope of topics to satisfy everyone and every situation, but I would be interested to understand what I have missed or what I could do better.

Meeting Themes

The following themes are each stand-alone topics that you may select *a la carte* to put together an agenda for your internal discussions. I have tried to keep them in a relative progression of topics but they are not really intended to flow from one topic to the next.

The reason for this buffet approach is that your company is at a different stage of maturity with respect to APM issues than any other company. Some of these themes will be old news to you while others may be an epiphany. It is just different for everyone.

What is APM?

APM has two related but different meanings. The more common is that it represents Application Performance *Management*. This suggests a life cycle view of an application and the supporting processes to maintain and enhance the quality or performance of that application and the IT resources that it employs.

The second meaning for APM is Application Performance *Monitoring*. This has a much more limited scope and represents a class of software solutions (tools) that contribute to the effective management of software systems.

The difference in language is subtle but it points to a significant gap between the goals of the IT organization (to manage the application life cycle) and the goals of the software vendor (to sell a software tool). Just because you can purchase a tool—for all the right reasons—does not mean you will actually know how to exploit it. This point is what I will explore in the first part of the book, "Planning an APM Initiative."

AP monitoring is the use of software technology to expose the relationships between software components, resources, and user transactions. All of these pieces contribute to the implementation of an application[18] or service[19] so I will use these terms interchangeably. *Software components* are often hosted within an application server and are based on Java or .NET technologies. The *resources*[20] are generally anything else that does not run on an application server, including databases, messaging, transaction processing, authentication and web services, to name a few. Often resources are labeled as *distributed* (or *remote*) and accessed via a network but this term in no way excludes mainframe applications and technologies that are often considered *centralized*. Being able to monitor the progress of a transaction among the contributing components is called *component-level visibility* and is often referred to as *deep-dive* or *call-stack*. User transactions are interactions that are initiated and presented in a browser session. Using a transactional perspective helps avoid the complications of the underlying implementation, distributed or centralized, but ultimately you need to be able to map transactions back to the components or resources that they interact with in order to identify the source of a performance problem.

■ **Note** Transactions are not solely initiated via a browser but may originate from or target some other automated system, rather than being human-mediated. While this is an important distinction, and one I will take up later, I will keep the language around end-user transactions as this is an important focus of contemporary monitoring.

---

[18] *Application* and *Application software* are interchangeable. Wikipedia, "application software," http://en.wikipedia.org/wiki/Application_software

[19] Applications based on components are often called *services*, when object-oriented techniques are employed. Collections of applications operating to fulfill a business function are also considered *services*. For the purposes of this book, a service is something worth monitoring, as much as an application. http://en.wikipedia.org/wiki/Application_components

[20] When an application server architecture is employed, any component of the software solution that is external to an application server instance is considered a *resource*. Some examples include databases, web services, mainframes, batch processes, and even other application servers. An important goal of APM is to uncover which components or resources of the application instance are contributing to the performance problem.

AP *management* is the monitoring of decisions across the application *life cycle*[21] that impact the overall quality or user experience that the application, or the service represented by two or more applications, supports or enables. Ultimately, the user experience directly relates to the performance and stability of an application and this is why you need to expand your perspective to include the application life cycle and issues of software quality. The application *life cycle* includes commissioning, funding, design, modeling, development (build), testing (functional, performance), quality assurance, user acceptance, production deployment, triage of application and user issues, and sun-setting/end-of-life.

Realities of Packaged Software Solutions

Various software vendors provide APM tools. The marketplace has consolidated in the last few years as the startup innovations and strategies matured and standardized. This means that today many of the major players in IT offer solutions for APM. While each vendor solution has appropriate documentation and professional services to support their products, these activities are typically limited to that vendor's solution. Despite over ten years of activity in the APM marketplace, no one has yet addressed the gap between AP *Monitoring* and AP *Management*—until this book.

Why this occurs should be no surprise. Startup ventures have a singular focus and that is solely to establish the value of their offering and achieve as wide a distribution as possible. They simply do not have the resources to highlight the alignment of their technology with the greater IT management goals. Market consolidation provides an opportunity to employ the greater resources of the parent organization (that acquired the startup company) to fill in the details of how to best employ the APM tools.

How the Monitoring Game has Changed

Monitoring IT systems was first realized in the 1960s to address a simple but urgent use case: before a user takes a long walk to the soda machine, is there in fact a soda available? The mechanism to interrogate a device and exchange this status information later became the Simple Network Management Protocol (SNMP)[22]. Today, SNMP is in use world-wide to assess the status of devices attached to the network.

The ubiquity of this SNMP technology gave rise to *Availability Monitoring* (AM), a core responsibility of every modern IT organization. SNMP allows for five operational states: up, down, coming-up, going-down, and user-defined. Changes in these states are communicated via a *trap* or alert delivered to a central

---

[21] There is a related discipline called Application Lifecycle Management (ALM) that looks at the lifecycle from the software engineering perspective. I am extending this concept here to indicate the use of performance monitoring across the application lifecycle, where appropriate. http://en.wikipedia.org/wiki/Application_lifecycle_management

[22] Commercial implementations of SNMP were not available until the late 1980s.

monitoring station. An agent monitors a platform (resource or application) in order to determine what state the resource is in currently. It may also consider information available in a *logfile* and may have other mechanisms to collect data about CPU or disk usage, among other useful platform parameters.

The trap is propagated to a management console and ultimately to a trouble management system where an operator responds to the alert. This involves a restart of the affected system or an initiation of a bridge call to involve additional subject-matter experts (SMEs) to help analyze the incident and create a resolution. The entire process takes about 10 to 30 minutes before a response is ready.

IT organizations are measured in part on their *availability percentages*, up to five-nines (99.999%) of availability[23]. This is calculated by taking the total time an application was down or unavailable, subtracting any scheduled downtime (for maintenance, upgrades, etc.), subtracting that from the time the system could do useful work, and dividing that calculation by the total time the system could do useful work. Improving uptime by reducing downtime is often the primary goal of many IT organizations.

Limitations of Availability Monitoring

In the 1960s and 1970s, batch processing operations were the dominant form of computing activities. Batch processes are scheduled activities; they often have a number of dependencies, frequently other batch processes. Let's consider a simple example: Before the billing process can begin, all regional billing data has to be transferred to a certain file system. Getting notification that the transfers are incomplete or that the billing process did not start or finish is critical to realizing the revenue that the billing cycle should generate. In this use case, SNMP technology is the ideal technology.

Enter Two-Tier Client Server and FCAPS

The next generation of computing architecture was the interactive 2-tier client server. Here, a dedicated client workstation interacted with a database via discrete transactions (read, write, update). This introduced the concept of *user experience* where the response time of the requests and responses affected the productivity of the user. As these systems increased in scale, messaging and transaction middleware were introduced to automatically divide or partition the processing load across multiple resources. SNMP was useful here as well. If the system appeared slow, the number of complaints would rise and the IT organization had to figure out what platform (client or server) was affecting the overall availability of the service.

---

[23] How availability is calculated can be the subject of debate. I prefer to exclude scheduled downtime. It is only important that you understand exactly what comprises your availability goals. Please also consider the following links for additional background:
www.weibull.com/hotwire/issue79/relbasics79.htm
www.availabilitydigest.com./public_articles/0101/calculating_availability.pdf

In parallel with the expanding application of SNMP, standardization bodies began to establish the framework for a systems management system. One of these efforts in the telecommunications industry resulted in FCAPS (fault, configuration, accounting, performance, and security) management. These efforts were intended to establish a more rigorous set of objectives for the various systems, following the conventions of SNMP.

What is interesting from the FCAPS perspective is that it separated performance and fault responsibilities as follows:

- Performance: Software metering and event monitoring
- Fault: Troubleshooting, logging, and backup/restore.

When you consider an alert, it is directly associated with event monitoring. Why is this then separate from troubleshooting? I have always thought that no one should ever consider using alerts as a basis for triage[24]—despite the overwhelming number of client initiatives attempting (unsuccessfully) to do exactly that.

Today there is the Information Technology Infrastructure Library (ITIL)[25] , which was defined by the United Kingdom Computing and Telecommunications Agency as the generally accepted model for IT service management, of which *performance* is a designated discipline[26]. It has a broader scope than the FCAPS initiative but includes the same basic ideas.

As I will explore in this book, if you really want to be *proactive* in reducing the potential number of alerts that you might receive—and thus improve the overall user experience—you really need to achieve this *before* you start receiving alerts. This also suggests that FCAPS is no longer an appropriate model for application management[27]. In fact, it is largely supplanted by the ITIL initiatives for service management. It is essential to understand where your sense of monitoring came from as much as where it is going. APM may be considered a bridge between FCAPS and ITIL, for example. This is part of what makes APM such a challenging and rewarding initiative.

The Need for a New Perspective

With the emergence of the internet, middleware-enhanced client-server computing came under additional pressure. Not only were transaction capacity gains needed, but the pace at which applications were changing (new features and functionality) revealed that highly distributed application architectures were an advantage to larger, more monolithic applications in terms of the expense of software

---

[24] *Triage*, in the IT perspective, is a process to determine the mostly likely contributor to a system outage or performance degradation.

[25] Wikipedia, "ITIL," http://en.wikipedia.org/wiki/ITIL

[26] Specifically Book 2: Service Delivery -> Capacity Management -> Performance Management

[27] FCAPS is now part of the Telecommunications Management Network (TMN) standard but remains an important first example of network management functions. http://en.wikipedia.org/wiki/FCAPS

maintenance and the pace at which these changes were needed. At this point, it became clear that SNMP technology was being pushed into an area for which it was not suited; it could not scale easily and had some critical security shortcomings. In some respects, the success of SNMP had fostered an over-confidence that network and system management issues were all sufficiently understood and well managed.

The problem was the growing complexity of distributed applications.

In the 1970s, computers were limited both in number and pressure for management and networking. Internet standards continued to evolve during this period. In the 1980s, the number of small computers exploded with the acceptance of the Personal Computer (PC) by businesses. As CPU speed increased and the cost of system memory and disk storage decreased, it became possible to distribute applications from the mainframe onto the new generation of mini-, and eventually micro-computers. Simultaneous pressures on software engineering and computing infrastructure operations in the 1980s did not result in equal investment to resolve them. This overconfidence allowed IT organizations to conclude that the monitoring infrastructure was sound and that it was solely the problem of reliable software engineering that was disrupting application availability. They managed to shift the blame, but with that blame went the investment dollars. Software engineering became much more disciplined as a result. Investment in monitoring initiatives leveled off or began to decrease.

The gains from improving software engineering were then extended to other stressed resources, middleware in particular, giving rise in the 1990s to the message brokers, integration middleware, and the application server. Again, this repurposing of mainframe capabilities was possible because of the ongoing increases in CPU performance and reductions in the cost of memory and disk. Application complexity was further accelerated now that the foundation of distributed application engineering was established: the internet, Java/.NET, the open source movement, and web services.

Investment in traditional monitoring tools simply did not keep up. They were not accessible to the growing community of application stakeholders and, more significantly, usually did not have information of value to assist resolving application performance issues. Availability information is simply not enough to identify and resolve the user experience requirements in the internet age of distributed computing. The monitoring organization itself began to wither, relegated to operational overhead and exposed to the unforgiving eye of cost reduction and outsourcing.

The new millennium would usher in the next generation of monitoring tools specifically designed to overcome the limitations of traditional SNMP monitoring and eliminate the additional programming needed to generate more useful performance metrics. In parallel, and somewhat unexpectedly, the IT environment began a significant re-sizing in terms of investment and staff. Suddenly, business was not only looking over the shoulder of IT but actually assuming more direct responsibility for performance issues. This business participation accelerated the focus on transactions and user experience because these are the quantities that have meaning for business.

Emphasizing Transactions in Addition to Resources

The essential difference between APM and availability management (AM) is the visibility into each and every user transaction. The *transactional* context is what makes analysis of a distributed computing problem tractable. Otherwise, you are left with a complex web of software components, resources, and web services to unravel. There is simply no way to approximate this transactional visibility with SNMP-era technologies. You need a different kind of agent or monitoring point. You need:

- Something that can handle thousands of metrics, instead of a dozen or so.

- A mechanism to persist the new metrics so that they may be utilized at different points in the application life cycle and maintained for as much as one year online.

- An architecture that can support updates from the agents at one minute (or less) reporting intervals.

- The ability to dynamically determine instrumentation points and so avoid the software maintenance costs of hard-coding monitoring points into the application.

- The ability to extend the monitoring configuration to accommodate the wide variety of applications encountered.

Some solution vendors have promoted the use of *synthetic transaction* monitoring as a step up from AM and as a bridge to this next generation of monitoring. This is not an ideal solution. While synthetics have an essential and practical utility when there is little or no traffic on a web site, they have little or no diagnostic capability and thus do not add much more visibility than that provided by AM. The limitation is the frequency at which the synthetics may be applied—often 15 to 60 minute intervals. They do provide a very narrow view of the transaction, but it is a little hollow. You will know which synthetic transaction failed but you get no insights into why or who is affected. More subtly, are user transactions also failing or are the transaction definitions out of date?

There are also arguments against the deployment of APM technology for certain environments and applications. There are a large number of legacy applications and technologies that are not addressed by APM technology and remain excellent candidates for AM. Nothing changes for those applications and resources, but it is important to understand what they are and what their impact may be, if any, on the distributed applications on which APM is focused.

In my experience, in order to understand if it is time to move beyond AM, you need to consider just one question: *How do you know that availability monitoring has reached its limit of usefulness?* When the help desk is a more accurate indicator of application availability and performance than the information provided by the monitoring infrastructure, you've reached that limit.

This, of course, does not mean that you will rip-and-replace your AM investment. It is simply the wake-up call that initiates the process of justification, analysis, selection, investment, and implementation. These activities are detailed as this book unfolds.

Moreover, just because you have AP monitoring or plan to employ AP monitoring does not mean that all of your existing applications will directly benefit. APM *technology* exploits characteristics of web-based (Java and .NET) applications that are simply not available in earlier application implementations. However, when you look instead at AP management, there are a number of benefits realized because of process improvements and collaboration, even if the legacy applications are not directly monitored by APM technology. Following APM processes, especially those related to assessments of your environment, will give you the details of exactly what benefit you may derive from an APM initiative. The assessment system is detailed in Part 1 of this book.

The Impact of APM Visibility

At this point, you should be able to acknowledge some of the differences between AM and APM technology and reflect on the confusion that may arise when the technologies are applied to the same problem. Now I'll delve into the confusing points as well as the vast differences.

I will begin with the concept of *visibility* into a performance problem, as illustrated in Figure 1-8.

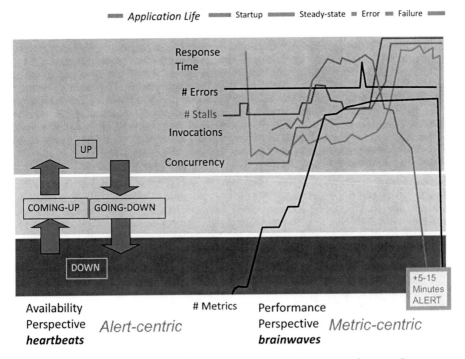

Figure 1-8. What is the practical difference between availability and performance?

This is the essential value proposition for an APM Tool—enhanced visibility into the nature of a performance problem.

Figure 1-8 depicts the startup and eventual failure of an instance of an application as viewed by AM and APM technologies. As discussed, AM provides state information, basically "up" and "down." This is represented on the left side of the figure. The resolution time of this information is on the order of 5 to 15 minutes. This means that any change in state is presented 5 to 15 minutes after the change actually occurs.

APM provides a host of details, many of which would be unfamiliar to an AM team. This information is updated every 15 to 60 seconds. The end result is the same: an alert is generated and is processed by the trouble management system some 5 to 30 minutes after the application has failed.

So why do clients invest in APM technology when the outcome (an alert) is the same? Do your operational capabilities improve if you shorten your alert generation from 15 minutes to 15 seconds? Regrettably, not very likely. So what's the point?

The point is that there is no such thing as Availability++. The AM paradigm simply is not intended to take advantage of this additional visibility. You need not only to add the technology, but you need to change the process through which that technology is employed.

The hard questions here are as follows:

- How would your organization respond if it could avoid the alert and associated downtime altogether? Who has that responsibility?
- How would your organization respond if this incident were encountered during QA testing? Who has that responsibility? What would be the response if the application did not actually crash or fail during testing?
- If the additional visibility were available, who in your organization is prepared to interpret this additional data and make it digestible by your application stakeholders?

This is what I call the *visibility gap*. At first, it appears that the gap is simply a bunch of new metrics. Believe me when I say that every vendor today pretty much gets the same metrics. The resolution might vary but the basic information is essentially the same. The real gap is how your organization will respond once the additional visibility is available. This is process-related—how your organization will exploit the visibility from both a procedural and corporate culture perspective. The APM tool does not provide you the process by which to exploit it. This is what you have to provide. And this is what this book will guide you through—how to address the process gaps in your organization so that you may get the maximum value from your APM investment.

Addressing the Visibility Gap

So how do you address the APM visibility gap that your organization will encounter?

Getting Those New Metrics

The first challenge is getting the technology that will allow you to collect useful metrics without disturbing the system being monitored. The impact is referred to as overhead, and it is the relative increase in the CPU usage and memory that simply putting an agent in place will incur. Due to overhead considerations, some vendors' solutions may be limited to use in development or QA environments only, with a much smaller configuration allowed for production. This does not mean the tool is unusable for production, but you will need to understand exactly what you are giving up in terms of visibility and you'll need to build a process that will let you reproduce problems in the pre-production environments where you can use the additional visibility to identify and resolve incidents.

Let's also be very clear that every monitoring technology has some type of overhead that negatively affects the service performance or capacity. This is what I refer to as "The Laws of Physics." You can't make a measurement without some perturbation of the system under measurement. Our role, as performance engineers, is to find a strategy that balances the overhead with the visibility received. As quickly as I can illustrate how to measure overhead, I can just as quickly realize that the tests are worthless. Some organizations simply lack the apparatus (process and tools) to measure overhead. This is why I continually refer to organizational maturity. How can you expect to measure 1 to 5% overhead when your response time varies itself by 20 to 50%? How do you assess the reproducibility of your load environment?

Many client technology evaluations get bogged down in two major areas—overhead and scope—to the point of doing nothing. That is unacceptable. One of the goals should be to improve *visibility* and there are many choices that will do exactly that. They may not represent the most complete vision but they will let you move forward and begin to experience the benefits of enhanced visibility. Related to the overhead question are the types and variety of metrics collected. It is not the *quantity* of metrics but the *quality* that matters. Can the collected metrics be used to identify problems? Will your organization take advantage of these metrics?

For example, a very popular category of metrics are those generated by JMX or PMI interfaces. These can generate thousands of metrics. But they have very little utility when it comes to identifying and resolving a performance incident. They are normally configuration-related and static (time invariant), and while a few may vary in real-time, they quickly contribute to overhead and can have a significant expense. Measuring overhead and configuration baselines are discussed in the Practitioner's Guide.

The second major concern is scope. If you only have responsibility to select a solution appropriate for one or a few applications, you really do not have to address the utility of that solution for other applications. This is how corporations end up with multiple technologies that overlap in capabilities or simply do the same things. It is not efficient in terms of investment cost, but it does allow you to explore a number of technology and vendor relationships and will put you in a better position to find a model that works best for your organization. APM best practices take this common situation into account; this is one of the reasons why I focus on vendor-neutral processes and techniques.

The other side of scope is when it is too narrow. This is a trait of many initiatives where they focus on the overhead and variety of metrics but to the exclusion of all other considerations. Effectively, their scope stops precisely at this point on the page and off they go. Understanding the metrics, managing them, and using them collaboratively never gets consideration.

Understanding Those New Metrics

What is so hard about these new metrics? That is pretty easy. Availability monitoring is about the computing *platforms:* CPU, disk space, network interfaces, process status, etc. Each of these elements is measured and reveals something about that computing platforms' utilization. It is generic for every computing platform and there will be some obvious differences in the values if the computing platform is a database or a mainframe, for example.

Performance monitoring is about the *application:* the software components and services, and the relationships among the various resources employed. Software systems are very dynamic and subjective with respect to what they may be doing. That is one part of the challenge—correlating and identifying significant events. Software components also come in four major flavors: Java, .NET, web services, and legacy (C and other languages). I don't really worry about monitoring legacy components in detail because they are usually stable and not undergoing additional development. AM is fine for those legacy pieces, and that contribution to the overall picture of application health is valuable. The real opportunities for trouble come from the new components. These new components are not fully mature and often contribute to the majority of root-cause identifications. These new components are the ones that you need visibility into in order to understand the relationships they form because they are simply not part of your current teams' expertise.

Before performance monitoring, your monitoring team had responsibility for monitoring platforms. With APM, the team now has to work on application–specific issues. The response is no longer restarting a server but collaborating with multiple stakeholders to identify and resolve the performance issue. It is a new set of skills. Who is going to be responsible for the collaboration and interpretation of the performance data?

Managing Those New Metrics

Many of your key applications have one or more specialists dedicated to working on issues with those applications. At minimum, they are monitoring the performance and capacity so that they may forecast when additional instances or hardware upgrades are going to be necessary. They may also be supervising bug fixes, maintenance releases, and configuration tuning. The monitoring tool has a similar requirement, just like those other applications, yet many proposals simply do not address the long-term needs of the monitoring environment.

As the monitoring initiative gathers steam and becomes useful to the application teams, the number of users increases sharply. These users will loudly complain when they can no longer get access to their metrics. Someone has to monitor the capacity and performance of the metrics storage, as well as other devices that are capacity limited. Who is going to be responsible for the ongoing capacity and performance management of the monitoring infrastructure?

It is a common trait of first-time monitoring initiatives, where they have an unusually limited scope, that they are committing only to *stand-up* (undertake a simple, initial deployment) the APM technology and make it available to appropriate users. Three or four months down the road, when the monitoring environment is at or beyond capacity, someone realizes that no one is actually responsible for the APM initiative.

Exploiting Those New Metrics across the Application Life Cycle

The last visibility gap is for useful collaboration that insures that goals are achieved and the best possible value for the investment is realized. Very often the use of the APM tool is restricted to the operations team. These folks are generally responsible for monitoring, so any new monitoring tool falls under their purview. As the depth of responsibility for APM is beyond the scope of the typical operations charter—including managing monitoring configurations, interpreting metrics, managing capacity, and performance of the APM environment—the leadership for dividing these responsibilities among the other stakeholders in the application life cycle (development, QA, application owner, etc.) is simply a bridge too far.

Collaboration is what offers the greatest potential to realize all of the benefits that APM has to offer. You know that you will need to collaborate simply because the operations team does not have the mandate to insist on the collaboration, nor the skills to fulfill these responsibilities on their own. However, if you envision the division of responsibilities across these diverse groups, what kind of supervisory model is appropriate? Who undertakes the funding and drives the initiative?

Demonstrating Value

The biggest challenge for many APM initiatives is that they are new. There is just nothing comparable in the collective experience of most IT shops. You may break down the initiative into a number of smaller sub-projects that have familiar activities; this is the essence of the pragmatic approach that I advise. This needs a word of caution. Your sponsors need to look at the value proposition as a whole, keeping the big picture up front and not subjecting the sub-projects to extensive financial or value-based analysis. The projects are just elements that may be efficiently scheduled and executed. The initiative is only realized when all of the underlying projects are complete.

If your sponsors become enamored with the sub-project approach without committing to the full initiative, it will lead to failure. While you may easily track the percentage complete of the initiative, it does not necessarily correspond with the percentage value realized. It is really an all-or-nothing effort.

You should be uncomfortable with this situation. Historically, many IT initiatives followed this deferred-value-realization proposition. Typically, it states that if you stay the course for a few years of investment, a great value will be realized at the end of the effort. Unfortunately, there are few successful examples of this approach.

What you need to do is dramatically shorten the time it takes to realize a demonstrable value without compromising the integrity of the overall initiative. You need to do this incrementally, in order to accrue the targeted value as portions of the initiative are realized. Fortunately, most APM tools today are relatively easy to deploy. So you may be confident that you can demonstrate incremental value. All you need concern yourself with is how to manage the harder elements of the initiative— what to do with it once it is deployed.

Part 1 of this book, "Planning an APM Initiative," will go into more detail on the specific value propositions. Let's move now to what the incremental or phased approach to the APM initiative looks like.

Good-Better-Best

The challenge with a monitoring initiative is not to overstep what you may reliably deliver and not to understate what you would actually achieve. It is a familiar proposition, yet any number of missteps may jump up at you. Like the game of golf, the hole may be only 175 yards away but there are a half-dozen sand traps along your path. How will you improve your chances at getting to the green without encountering trouble?

Your sponsors likely will have embraced the value of the monitoring initiative without a real understanding about those potential traps. They are going to be annoyed if you deliver anything less than the vision they have adopted. This makes for a really delicate negotiation. Despite their ambitions, you need to be pragmatic about how you may realize their vision.

Of course, no executive wants to hear that his vision is too ambitious. Simply stating that the goal is a "bridge too far" is not going to be helpful. You have to devise a plan that will let you deliver what is solidly within your current capabilities and still allow for some time and flexibility to achieve the other activities that are not yet within current capabilities. The spectrum of what you have today and what you may reliably implement later breaks down nicely into skills, processes, and competencies, as you will see later. You will also need another dimension to allow for a finer granularity, which I introduce as the concept of *Good-Better-Best*.

This simple concept is borrowed from the world of museums and fine furniture. While everything that is old may be considered an antique, certain expressions or implementations of those designs and construction are definitely more interesting than others. Thus, examples of a given historical period of furniture are organized as

- **Good**, when they faithfully represent the period.
- **Better**, when they represent a marked improvement in the quality and execution of the style.
- **Best**, when they represent the finest achievement that the period can offer.

The skills, techniques, and level of execution increase markedly with each example of a given furniture style.

I make a hobby out of building and restoring furniture, so I have come to appreciate the differences between good, better, and best. I use it as an analogy for realizing an

APM discipline because it allows the practitioner to demonstrate useful skills with the technology in a very short period and then continue to grow their skills over time in a reliable and predictable fashion. Not surprisingly, I have yet to achieve "best" for my furniture efforts, but—and this is key—I know exactly how much further I need to progress. For my restoration clients, knowing the expense and time associated with a museum-quality repair versus a stable and fully functional repair is an enlightening and clarifying opportunity for reflection. They reassess their ambition, cost, and intended function, and they come back with a more informed decision as to how they want to proceed.

You need to be able to accurately describe the time and expense needed to realize that executive's vision as it relates to an APM monitoring initiative in terms of what you can reliably deliver as good, better, and best. To achieve this, you need to understand what of your current skills, processes, and competencies apply to the initiative. You need to propose what a good, better, and best solution will encompass. You need to know what to ask for in terms of resources, training, and technology to reach each of those levels. All of these questions are answered through an assessment, which will I detail later.

It is also important, as you begin to appreciate what a successful APM initiative looks like, that you understand when you are not the right fit for the project under its present constraints. This is the parable of the "second mouse." No one likes to turn down an opportunity but if you cannot get the appropriate funding, time, and resources to achieve the repair, you will actually be in a better position when you detail why it's not the right situation for you, and then you let another team take the project. If they are successful, the company wins. If they stumble or fail, then you will get the "cheese"—likely on your terms.

Note The more positive use of the "second mouse" parable is simply because you are in a position today to consider an APM initiative and that you actually have a book to study! For many early adopters of this technology, success was not at all assured, despite many commendable efforts. There were no references to study. Those struggles and successes are the foundation of the best practices I present here. So do not begrudge "being first" and missing out on the early success of APM. A lot of those "first mice" did not make it.

The fundamental advantage of the Good-Better-Best approach is that you are following a schedule of incremental skills development, trying and repeating an activity a few times in order to achieve competency before your sponsor gets to the agreed date on the schedule. Where appropriate, you want to repeat an exercise three times in order to achieve competency. This is the real difference between a traditional initiative where the goal is simply to get the technology deployed and the maturity model prescribed by the APM Best Practices: you allow time to demonstrate competency before your sponsor expects you to show value for the initiative.

Establishing an APM Project

My objectives in establishing an APM project are to demonstrate value, do it quickly, and adapt to the client circumstances. I want to balance the long-term goals with short-term deliverables but do not want to compromise usefulness or correctness. The successful strategy is to establish a few reasonable goals, achieve them quickly, and then iterate over the same topics two more times, with each successive iteration expanding the skills and capabilities of the APM team using the Good-Better-Best approach. The expanding capabilities of the team are immortalized as milestones towards achieving a *catalog of services* that you will provide for your application and business sponsors.

The AP *monitoring* marketplace, defined by the various products that the solution vendors provide, focuses on ease of installation, rapid time to usefulness, and overall ease of use. Regrettably, these worthy platitudes do not really address the AP *management* processes that promise that IT will deploy effectively, collaborate on QA test plans, triage accurately, and encourage collaboration across the application life cycle to ultimately lower overall application cost and ensure a quality user experience.

These AP management processes are also fine platitudes but these are more in line with the goals of your application sponsors. Thus, these are the ones for which you need to *show value*.

Figure 1-9 summarizes how to employ Good-Better-Best to evolve an organization and some of the major activities. The themes on the left are captured in the broad themes of this book: planning (assessments, visibility), implementations (deployments), and practitioners guide (triage and other techniques).

	Good	Better	Best
Assessments	Interviews	Transaction Analysis	Application Audit (On-Boarding)
Deployments	QA+prod	QA+DEV+Prod	Match Monitoring Need: High Value Apps Service Level Management
Visibility	Availability	Application Context: Performance Capacity	Transaction Context: User Experience KPIs
Triage Capabilities	Individual Metrics	Baselines	Trending and Forecasting

Figure 1-9. How to evolve an organization

I will introduce a lot more detail for each of the major areas as I go through the process of establishing an APM initiative. This iterative scheme also reappears as a maturity model to help you assess organizational skills and later becomes the catalog of services that an organization presents to the various stakeholders in the application life cycle.

I employ this iterative approach, adapted pragmatically for the realities of your organizational and operational constraints, to realize a future state that your sponsors will find useful, predictable, and manageable—and something that they will want to fund.

What about other strategies to implement service management, like ITIL (Information Technology Infrastructure Library), or other standards already defined by telecommunications standards? I will take up this topic in the planning section of the book. For now, while ITIL is a compatible goal, I am instead focused on a shorter duration and a more pragmatic approach, contrary to the time frames and broad processes on which ITIL is commonly practiced. In other words, ITIL is an important *strategic* goal and I am instead pursuing a *tactical* approach based on very short iterations (on the order of weeks) and specific and timely capabilities.

This book focuses on the first use of these techniques, leading to the realization of an APM initiative, but these same techniques are employed by the resulting APM discipline as an on-going activity. You can expect to have multiple deployment phases because there will be hundreds of applications to consider, and it is simply not possible to improve or normalize their monitoring in a single step. Organizational priorities are likely to change throughout the initiative, so you insure that every activity results in incremental visibility and capability. You can expect to be interrupted—delays and pre-emption are just things that can happen during any significant initiative.

Monitoring is a luxury. The priority is always on doing business. With planning and opportunity, resources can be devoted to improving the IT operation and enhancing application performance and value to the end-user. Monitoring technology gives you the visibility to identify and resolve performance issues and improve software quality. This does not happen overnight nor does it happen on a generous schedule. My experience is that it evolves in bursts and always a little earlier than your schedule anticipates. My goal is to ensure that you know exactly what needs to be done next in order to move consistently towards the realization of an APM initiative.

Let's now look at what each iteration of a phased deployment includes for an APM initiative.

Initial Iteration

The goal in the initial iteration is to get a deployed footprint on a few key applications. You need to focus on a conservative monitoring configuration, as there is often little or no time (or no interest) to do a full validation. In this iteration, there will be an initial form of the *monitoring runbook*, a summary of how to deploy, configure, validate, and employ the monitoring solution. This is for the operations team so that they will have sufficient documentation to meet their production needs, and an obvious first collaboration. A first attempt at solution sizing is introduced to forecast the anticipated footprint of the metrics storage and monitoring capacity (number of agents and applications). A triage presentation and analysis methodology is established. Some key metrics are established in QA/Stress & Performance/UAT, and introduced as a non-binding minimum application quality measure. This is, in essence, a limited second collaboration where the role of QA is simply to generate some additional reporting on their current testing schedule.

The services that are established in this initial iteration are rapid deployment, basic triage and analysis, application survey, and monitoring solution sizing.

Follow-on Iteration

After an operational period of at least two weeks (preferably longer), planning for the next deployment begins. Ideally, there will be a bit more breathing room (less pressure on the deployment team) now that the basic monitoring has been deployed, such that a validation of gold configurations can take place. A *gold configuration* is an extension of the default configuration but optimized for a specific class or type of application. This process validates agents for use in a variety of applications, such as portal, .NET, J2EE, POJO[28], etc. Such validation is done once in order to confirm the ideal configuration for each application type. Then this configuration may be reliably deployed whenever that application type is again encountered.

The breathing room afforded by getting an initial footprint up and monitoring going also allows a bit more attention to be devoted to maintaining and documenting various configurations and packaging requirements. The result is a more efficient deployment model and one that can accommodate a larger number of applications deployed concurrently.

You need to take a little time to finish the deployment artifacts so you can deploy more efficiently and reliably than without them. It is an unfortunate characteristic of an immature organization that they will undertake too broad a deployment and with little performance monitoring experience. It is important to assuage their zeal and still provide an opportunity to do it correctly, simply by limiting the potential damage and number of agents to be reworked by undertaking a small initial deployment.

An important advantage of this incremental approach is that after the initial operational period, there is a wealth of data that can be fed back to QA in order to validate or correct their load profiles and strategies. This is important visibility for QA, simply in understanding the accuracy of their load profiles, and a key value proposition to realizing use of the monitoring technology prior to the production experience. This helps address situations such as being unable to reproduce production issues. Now you will have the visibility to understand exactly why. The additional agent validation will have introduced some process changes in the QA schedule to support the concept of *baselining*, a technique employing a series of 20 minute (minimum) load tests to establish configuration, application, and

---

[28] POJO (Plain Old Java Object): A type of java application that is not deployed in a standard container, such as that provided by an application server.

performance baselines. This information is then fed-forward and used to enrich the triage capabilities and enhance the operational effectiveness of dashboards, reporting, and alerting.

Getting the QA function capable with monitoring information will later establish the ability to realize proactive management practices. This is an important objective but very often not addressed when the organization is under pressure to "show value" for the production monitoring initiative. It will allow the organization to continue to deliver monitoring value and avoid being pigeonholed as a production-only tool set.

An additional parallel collaboration point is with the *application specialists*, those individuals, often from the business, that have domain expertise and supervise the application life cycle for their application set. The primary interaction is via the application audit that identifies the various baselines and key performance points for each application, giving an early view into the performance challenges and opportunities that the application presents. This is of great value to the application specialist because it allows, among other tangible things, a forecast of the capacity *prior* to production deployment. There will also be some initial collaboration with the development arm as some applications may require some more sophisticated configurations to realize optimal visibility. Developer participation is brief at this stage but there will be some interest in using monitoring as part of unit tests and also in understanding how to use the tools during triage.

As the pace of deployment increases, it will be prudent to put some process around the servers that manage the metric data. In a large environment, the number of these servers and the attached users viewing the information can easily make it among the largest and most valued application in your enterprise. This means that the monitoring environment will be subject to the same availability, performance demands, and expectations as your internal and external user community. This is not a concern initially because the deployed footprint lacks the complexity. But as the deployed footprint increases, the number of users accessing the performance information will increase at least proportionally, if not at a significantly greater rate.

The services added in this iteration are the Application Audit, Performance Tuning, and Capacity Forecast. Depending on the organization model of the APM system (centralized or distributed) it is advised (in the distributed team model) to introduce a pre-production review of the monitoring configurations that application teams have prepared in order to align with your emerging standards and systems.

Closing Iteration

At this point you will have achieved the initial traditional goal of getting a successful production monitoring implementation and you will have established a number of collaborative initiatives with development, QA, application specialists, and business owners. The production environment will likely not need any additional consideration so you will instead focus on the collaborative initiatives, making them more systemic in terms of organizational processes, seeking out additional opportunities to demonstrate value, and trying out the artifacts that will train the next generation of APM participants. These tasks are not very hard to accomplish now that you have begun to consider and experience the supporting processes— and nearly impossible to consider without taking a few trial swings at what they should look like and how effectively they are adopted and made part of the corporate DNA.

This is not insignificant. If you were to follow the traditional path and allow the monitoring initiative to proceed without these considerations of phased deployment, you would only end up with the production monitoring footprint. There would be little energy for anything else. This is the typical result of an unenlightened approach to APM; frankly, it results in the initiative being considered a failure. As pointed out earlier, the business and other stakeholders are very much expecting these additional collaborations and value propositions to be fully realized, even if the IT team has not explicitly promised to address them or does not understand what is expected of them.

If all of this is apparent to you already, and you find that much of what you have read is already consistent with your own thoughts and objectives, then you are ready! A successful APM initiative will have many of these attributes, and it is not at all hard to achieve anything more than what common sense would indicate. But you should also realize that this enlightened view is simply not shared by the teams you are working with. If they doubt your approach, at least you have this book to demonstrate that there are in fact a few practitioners for these techniques. It makes a pretty effective argument, considering that all of the techniques and considerations in this book were born of this exact situation.

More likely, you will need some additional ammunition to support your strategy for a monitoring initiative to overcome additional points of resistance or the absence of a well-considered plan of action. In that case, you will find additional details and practices in the sections following. These are broken down by the major themes of planning and evangelizing the initiative, the full details of the implementation, and how to successfully employ monitoring technology for it most common and sophisticated usage. Please feel free to explore the Practitioners Guide.

Summary

So now you have a good overview of the issues around getting an APM initiative underway and what a successful initiative might look like. If you find that your current or proposed activity has missed a few points, then the next part of the book, "Planning an APM Initiative," is where you will find some tactical activities to help address those gaps or to flesh out a comprehensive plan.

If you have already completed the initiative planning and have made a technology selection, then you are ready for managing a deployment. I would expect you to skim over the remaining chapters in this first part and maybe find something you overlooked. Otherwise you should jump ahead to the "Implementation" section to see how your project management lines up with my best practice recommendations.

And if you are already deployed, please start with the "Practitioner's Guide" to see how your existing practices line up with specific APM best practice competencies. These are presented as independent activities, following the mentoring that would occur if you were pursuing a APM service bureau.

Finally, if you are not sure of your current maturity level, consider doing the skills self-assessment to get a sense of where you fit in the APM maturity model. Any gaps identified here are matched with the specific sections and competencies you should understand to improve your mastery of APM activities. This may also be used to help you get the best use of this book by guiding you to specific topics.

Planning

Business Justification

Always do right; this will gratify some people and astonish the rest.

—Mark Twain (1835-1910)

To justify an APM initiative is to establish the motivations and benefits that the initiative will address from the perspective of the business or sponsor. The justification is usually a written document and often focuses on the financial aspects of the proposal: the initial investment and ongoing maintenance. The emphasis on finances is not only historical but also reflects the lack of any prior experience on which to refer to for the "real" costs and impacts of the initiative—the unique circumstances of a new APM initiative. This is the first clue for the client that they are moving into unfamiliar territory. At this point, no one can tell them what the monitoring initiative is really going to cost!

If you happen to be a consultant, the absence of a realistic business justification is readily apparent. If you are spending more time with procurement, rather than with the implementation team, you can pretty much be assured that no one has prepared a realistic business justification. I will address this by presenting the more common justifications that I have encountered. Sometimes I have been tasked to help draft these documents but this is a rare scenario and should always be considered with some suspicion unless you have an existing consultative relationship. As a business manager, you really need be the owner of your justification. If a business justification is something foreign to you, then you should move cautiously.

Justification Is Not ROI

Very often a business justification is confused with a ROI (Return On Investment)—a clear sign that you are in the domain of the procurement folks. ROI analysis is appropriate for well-known, often repeatable initiatives. An APM initiative simply does not have any meaningful history on which to base a ROI. An accurate ROI is very difficult to establish if your organization is not already tracking KPIs (Key Performance Indicators) on software quality, deployment frequency, operational incidents, staffing costs, and the real costs of the different services in your service catalog.

A focus on ROI is also a dangerous avenue to pursue since any meaningful result would likely be based on an earlier experience—and this quickly becomes an effort to force an APM initiative into a mold that reinforces the realities and circumstances of a different technology but glosses over the significant differences that APM presents (as discussed in Chapter 1).

It is possible to develop a ROI after the APM initiative is established, but it is not an easy task and not something which you may hope to boilerplate and use in advance of the APM initiative.

If you find that you simply don't have the data with which to finalize a ROI analysis, please consider again the alternate technique I introduce here, which is to bring forward a small-scale, rapid time-to-value, monitoring initiative—one that neatly sidesteps a larger-scale funding justification.

Simply because completing a ROI analysis is difficult does not mean that the costs are unbounded. You may easily estimate the costs of the initial and successive phases of the monitoring initiative. Quantifying the value received, in monetary terms, is the difficulty when you do not have appropriate KPIs.

Entry Points

In my APM consulting work, I have encountered many different motivations driving organizations to evolve their use of APM. Not all are appropriate for a first APM initiative. I classify these different motivations by the nature of the entry point: at what stage of their APM evolution am I joining their efforts?

If you view the process of implementing an APM initiative as a continuum, then there will be various "entry points" along the way where an APM initiative might currently stand or have progressed. Many initiatives do not start at ground zero. Some have attained a certain status and leveled off, while others await a push to get to the next step. Likewise, all parties involved must account for the relative maturity an organization has demonstrated with APM. The reality is that you cannot approach an APM initiative with a generic program. One size does not fit all. So a consideration of entry points allows you to tailor the planning and delivery aspects of the initiative. You expect all APM practitioners to end up with the same skill set but they will have vastly different starting points and adjustments because of their prior experiences or perceptions with APM.

An *initial entry point* is pretty much a blank slate and you should expect to address many misconceptions in order to ensure a successful APM deployment.

A *growth entry poi*nt is the result of an attempted APM initiative that has either failed or had limited success. If it is limited success, then the upcoming initiative will either need to address the gaps or move to another environment. The issues concerning this entry point—for continuing the initiative—are unique. There will likely be some bad practices to undo and some perception issues to turn around but it requires a different approach than that of the initial entry point.

The *mature entry point* is a condition found with more sophisticated users of APM, those with multiple successful deployments and mature, consistent practices. There may be some gaps in their skills and processes, but their real need is to enhance the collaboration with other stakeholders.

Here are some common business justifications organized by their likely entry point:

- **Initial** : Where there is no prior APM implementation.
  - Availability vs. performance monitoring
  - Improving application software quality
  - A single view of performance (dashboards)

- **Growth:** An APM deployment has been achieved, and it has been employed to some effect (often limited to a single environment).
  - Resolving application incidents and outages
  - Enhancing the value of the monitoring tool investment
  - Trending and analysis
  - A single view of performance (dashboards)

- **Mature:** A largely successful APM system exists but they are looking to improve coordination among stakeholders.
  - Managing service level agreements (SLAs)
  - Proactive monitoring

For each of the items (themes) above, I will have some discussion, as appropriate, and then summarize the technological objectives, optional strategic objectives, benefits, and investments required. The following is an outline of what your justification should cover, but you will still need to work up the dollar costs. The final cost is what you work out among your vendors and their subcontractors. The list above only provides the broad strokes for which your vendor should provide full details in a statement of work. All of these APM services are optional and could be completed by your own staff—that what this book is for!

Initiative Themes

Each of the *justification themes* that follows is intended to be an outline of the technological objectives, strategic objectives, benefits, and investments to support a proposal that results in the funding of an APM initiative. One size does not fit all circumstances, so you should expect to adjust the details to your specific situation.

What is most important to take away from the variety of these themes is that every team believes that they had the same idea as everyone else when it comes to justifying an APM initiative. The motivations for moving to APM are actually quite diverse, but many simply have no idea how unique their requirements are and how that would affect the perception of the initiative by management.

The next sections present nine themes for an APM initiative, in terms of technology objectives, strategic objectives, benefits, and investment. You need to find the theme that best fits your current perception of what you want APM to do for you. And then make sure that you consider each of the detailed points in the context of your proposal. You do not need to implement every detail but knowing what you are not interested in is just as important as your accepted objectives when it comes to communicating the scope and motivation of your APM initiative.

Availability vs. Performance Monitoring

This is the principal justification for moving to APM and an initial entry point. As discussed in Chapter 1, AM (availability monitoring) is focused on the computing platform and physical resources. When the complexity of the environment in terms of the sheer number of devices that need monitoring includes hundreds of devices, it becomes difficult to quickly identify the root cause of an operational incident. It also introduces a dependency on maintaining a highly skilled and experienced staff with knowledge of the varied relationships among the monitored devices, often resulting in specialist roles that will be very difficult to replace or quickly augment if the scale of the environment increases.

The technology objectives here include the following:

- Moving from the monitoring of the physical aspects of the environment (platform monitoring) to a monitoring solution that highlights the business transaction as the mechanism to help automate a relationship mapping of the participating components.
- De-emphasizing availability as the primary indicator of service quality and focusing instead on the quality of the user experience.
- Helping support the organization in moving from a batch-centric mode of service into an interactive mode of service.
- Increasing the variety and resolution of performance metrics that may be gathered from the operational environment.

The strategic objectives, which you may consider optional, include the following:

- Enhancing cooperation between pre-production (stress and performance testing, user acceptance testing) and production (operations).
- More support of new technologies, such as those utilizing Java and .NET
- Introducing a new level of responsibility for performance issues, supported by appropriate technology.
- Reintroducing support of application servers and other infrastructure technologies that were previously outsourced when modifying or terminating a service provider relationship.

- Moving to the next generation of monitoring technologies as a pilot initiative to gather experience and get a better handle on the challenges ahead.

The benefits include the following:

- Enhanced visibility into the behaviors of distributed systems and how to correlate and resolve various incidents.
- Reduction in the time to first alert for a performance incident.
- Performance monitoring capability across HTTP, Java, and .NET technologies (or other protocols, as appropriate).

The investment would include the following:

- Assessment of existing skills and capabilities.
- Pilot of appropriate monitoring technologies.
- Identification of an initial and follow-on set of candidate applications, leading to an initial solution sizing.
- Solution sizing and procurement of appropriate hardware.
- Product licensing and maintenance (annual).
- Vendor product training.
- Solution installation (initial deployment).

For this business justification, I am really not looking beyond the operational capabilities. I have limited the scope to the responsibilities of a conventional monitoring organization, which is to get the technology up and available to application teams. I have set aside a lot of other points that I would like to see in a comprehensive monitoring initiative but what results is a typical set of objectives. I have not included any KPIs as they may be inconvenient to determine. You can increase the overall scope of the justification by adding some of the other justifications but you cannot really trim this business justification any further without ensuring that it would be denied.

Of course, this justification has a number of risks, as I have already discussed. There is nothing to insure that the monitoring solution will be employed successfully. There is no definition of the capabilities that the initiative will support. There are no criteria for or confirmation that the initiative is improving the monitoring situation.

Resolving Application Incidents and Outages

This justification for APM is undertaken by a monitoring team that has achieved an initial deployment of APM technology but Management is not satisfied with the capabilities of the team in employing that technology. This is a growth entry point and may be considered incremental to an "Availability vs. Performance" justification, provided that your plan specifically allows for a significant operational period before moving on to the incident management activities. If the deployed monitoring is itself unproven or otherwise unstable, you will have little chance of success in attempting to use that environment for triage.

The technology objectives include the following:

- Assessments of incidents to identify monitoring gaps.
- Assessments of monitoring technology to insure appropriate tools are employed.
- Managing monitoring configurations to ensure appropriate visibility.
- Managing monitoring technology capacity and performance to insure appropriate visibility and utility.
- Defining operational baselines and reporting, which result in performance and capacity thresholds.
- Integration of alerts with trouble-management.
- Deployment of additional agents or integrations to bring disparate performance information into a single display.
- Definition of the roles and responsibilities for a triage activity.

The strategic objectives include the following:

- Enhancing cooperation among operations, helpdesk, triage, and application teams.
- Decreasing the number of participants on bridge calls by being able to go directly to resource owners with well-defined issues.
- The use of an on-boarding process to bring applications into the operations environment with a short round of pre-production monitoring and reporting.
- Enhancing incident reporting to separate availability (loss of platform) from performance and capacity incidents (degradation of service).
- Establishing a separate notification (degradation) to the app team and triage, separate from operations alerting from platform monitoring
- Integrating APM alerting to trouble-management, with notification to operations and responsibility assigned to the application and triage teams.
- Establishing a capacity management and planning practice for the monitoring tools.

The benefits include the following:

- Enhanced utility from the monitoring investment.
- Establishment of small group dedicated to triage skills and process development.
- Establishment of a group responsible for tracking and resolving performance issues.
- Decreased reliance on the bridge call for initial triage and the assignment of the incidents.
- Definition of monitoring activities pre-production, setting the stage for more proactive management.
- Separate responses for availability and degradation incidents.

- More effective use of performance information by application teams in parallel with additional participation by operations.
- More effective use of the monitoring tool infrastructure through active capacity reporting and planning.

The investment would include the following:

- Assessment of existing skills and capabilities.
- Run a HealthCheck of the existing environment to ensure consistency with best practices for monitoring configuration and capacity management of the monitoring technology.
- Validation of the monitoring configurations for appropriate visibility.
- Incident analysis to document separation of alert /response streams.
- Services for alert integration and integration of legacy scripts and other sources of performance instrumentation, as needed.
- Services for mentoring of appropriate techniques, as needed.
- Services for definition of performance views for operations usage and training.
- Definition of triage activities to establish and refine triage techniques.
- Assigning personnel to participate in mentoring activities and minimize the need for additional services.

As discussed in the introduction, this level of capability is what the business expected with the initial deployment. There is often a complete miss for this expectation because the team deploying the APM technology is treating it just like any other monitoring technology and assuming that interested parties will employ the tools as needed. They did not have to do anything additional when they rolled out the availability monitoring so they are unprepared to do anything different with APM. They simply get the tool deployed and functional.

So this follow-on effort is to fix the process gaps and establish a consistent discipline to employ the technology. The simple goal is to demonstrate triage of the significant problems you need to take care of to ensure you are getting involved with appropriate problems and that you allow a few iterations to practice the new skills. If you are to maintain this capability, you also have to address the integration issues between stakeholders and establish a framework for sharing performance information. This includes consistent and timely notification of the monitoring of any availability of performance information discovered by other means.

Improving Application Software Quality

The prior APM justification hinted at moving APM monitoring pre-production by focusing on the on-boarding of an application into the operational environment. Now you make a meaningful commitment and move from an optional activity to one that is embedded in the QA and testing processes. This justification is largely an initial entry point, even if there is an existing production APM system. There is simply not much that will be reused from the initial deployment. Also, the use of APM pre-production is quite a bit different than the operational use of APM.

When you start employing APM as part of an on-boarding exercise, you are exercising the application under load in order to confirm the suitability of the monitoring configuration to provide visibility and help identify the root-cause of a problem in the production environment. For problematic applications that have never before been evaluated under APM visibility, details of potential operational performance incidents will already be evident. There may be simply no process to stop the deployment and no confidence that APM is even correct. Effectively, no matter the outcome of the earlier QA testing, you are retesting the application with enhanced visibility as part of the on-boarding process. While the on-boarding test result will not initially affect the application deployment schedule or head straight into an operational incident, someone will advance the following proposition: if we could already see this problem prior to production, why didn't we do something about it?

I will discuss in detail how this situation—identifying problems but having no will or process to abate the deployment—becomes embedded in many organizations in Chapter 8 when I look at pre-production processes with APM. For now, you need only appreciate that moving APM visibility earlier in the application lifecycle does not happen automatically. You need to justify this objective as a separate initiative because traditionally monitoring is one objective and testing is another. An APM initiative is different because you expect to monitor throughout the application lifecycle. You do not limit monitoring to production only.

There is also a distinction between improving application quality and true proactive management. You cannot expect to be proactive until you have addressed software quality, but you need to have a consistent infrastructure in terms of process and integration before you have sufficient KPIs to document the benefit of proactive business practices. Focusing instead on software quality lets you set aside the process and integration issues in favor of getting a better result out of your existing test infrastructure.

The technology objectives include the following:

- Getting visibility into performance problems prior to production deployment.
- Forecasting application capacity and performance.
- Rightsizing the application platform (virtualization).
- Improving the accuracy of load simulation by comparing QA testing results with the production experience.

The strategic objectives include the following:

- Increasing the efficiency of new application delivery.
- Consolidating applications (functionality, platforms).
- Improving manageability of deliverables from off-shore partners (audit).
- Reducing pressure on the operations team by detecting problems earlier in the application lifecycle.
- Establishing performance KPIs that are shared among application stakeholders.

The benefits include the following:

- Decreased overall cost of the new application life cycle (testing, deployment, incident management).

- Decrease overall time-to-market for getting new software systems operational.
- Confirmed accuracy and utility of load testing.
- Increased collaboration across the application life cycle.
- Detected and resolved problems earlier in the application life cycle.
- Improved the production experience with more stable applications and a consistent set of KPIs.
- Formalized the exchange of application status and testing results (HealthChecks).

The investment would include the following:

- Assessment of existing skills and processes.
- Additional product licensing to support the pre-production environment.
- Product training (if this is a stand-alone initiative).
- Services for deployment and runbook documentation (Chapter 8), as needed.
- Services for mentoring of testing and reporting strategies, as needed.
- Organization changes to accommodate the definition of minimally acceptable performance characteristics (see Chapter 13) and remediation of applications that miss these emerging minimally acceptable performance standards.

Again, the software quality improvement initiative is often formed independently from the initiative to use APM monitoring in the production environment. Both initiatives can benefit if they can be coordinated—both in justification and in showing progress. Software quality will benefit from having APM visibility to help resolve performance concerns. APM will benefit from having a presence pre-production to validate monitoring configurations and accelerate triage.

This is not unusual. I often find organizations who are uninterested (or unwilling) to considered APM for use in production but are quite interested in using it preproduction. For them, the benefit is to advance software quality. This justification may also be used stand-alone and can be the first use of APM in an organization, so this is why there is some allowance in the investment for product training. When there is existing APM, the pre-production use can actually advance easily through peer mentoring. The pre-production environment simply doesn't need careful monitoring configuration. Pre-production stakeholders are relatively insensitive to overhead concerns because they are usually operating at a fraction of the production capacity and have a limited number of application instances to manage.

This brings up another significant issue, however: what happens when the monitoring configurations are then promoted to production? No one has any idea how they should be tuned, and whether there are gaps in deployment planning and capacity management of the APM technology. While the vendor education will have covered all of these topics, there is little or no opportunity to exercise those skills while in pre-production. Having a successful pre-production practice has limited bearing on success in production. This leaves a gap which is neatly handled by the next justification.

Pre-production Readiness and Deployment

This justification is meant to bridge the successful use of APM during QA testing and address the gaps in preparing a go-to-production use of APM. This is a growth entry point as it depends on the existing QA artifacts as a starting point. Typically, a client has employed APM as the QA environment for a single application initiative. Even if there have been prior efforts, they all co-exist independently and with little sharing of process or experience. The ongoing efforts have not yet achieved enough inertia to make it into production.

The technology objectives include the following:

- Deployment planning.
- Metrics storage capacity management and planning.
- Agent and metrics storage packaging.
- Acceptance testing and criteria.
- Validating the agent configuration and transaction definition.
- Defining the application runbook with monitoring details.

The benefits include the following:

- Validation of low overhead of agent and transaction definitions.
- Model for phased deployment and acceptance.
- Growth forecast for metrics storage.
- Definition of the monitoring dashboards and reporting.

The investment would include the following:

- Assessment of skills and capabilities.
- Services and mentoring for pre-production review of candidate applications, as needed.
- Services and mentoring for deployment sizing and planning, as needed.
- Additional product licensing to cover the deployment footprint for initial and follow-on phases.
- Product education to support production and QA use of APM.

Managing Service Level Agreements

This is a mature entry point and requires a successful QA and production APM discipline. Here, APM is in effective but isolated use. so you are really not doing additional technology deployments. Rather, you're focused on process and organization of the APM initiative. Service management is governed by a SLA (service level agreement). Unfortunately, and because much of monitoring is availability-centric, the IT community has made this interchangeable with service-level *availability*, which is not really the same thing.

With mature availability monitoring, every resource and service of interest is being monitored. As the number of devices under management increases, it becomes apparent that availability monitoring cannot present a view of the business service in terms of the resources that constitute it. They want to monitor the availability of the service, they have every resource under management, and yet they cannot achieve their goal. They will then look into new technologies like CMDB (Configuration Management Database), and others to organize all of these monitoring end points into a consistent view of the service.

While technology like CMDB is very interesting, your problem is still just one of visibility. There is another path that might be helpful; it is an optional path. Constructing a view of the service and its underlying resources may be achieved by considering the application-context and the transaction-context. These additional contexts, which APM directly supports, allows you to prioritize business transactions of interest and directly track what resources are contributing to the performance of those business transactions. You may then uncover additional details when those transactions involve application servers, which are the modern model for wrapping legacy services with a web-enabled interface. This is a much more efficient process than "boiling the ocean" and trying to map every bit of technology to one or more applications that utilize it. Instead, you get a cup of water and pop it into the APM microwave. As you will experience, identifying transactions and uncovering the underlying resources is an activity on the order of hours and days. And you have to keep repeating that activity until you understand all of your priority transactions. Mapping the enterprise will take years and a significant portion of those resources will probably disappear with the next technology refresh.

There are few technology points to this initiative and these will most likely be additional integration points among metrics sources that already function well rather than new deployments of technology. The real jobs in this initiative are education, requirements, and assessments. All of the metrics data is there, but no one has had a broad enough plan to employ it for service management.

The technology objectives include the following:

- Retiring silos in favor of horizontal shared services.
- Evolving from availability-based to performance-based SLAs.

The strategic objectives include the following:

- Establishing and maintaining realistic SLAs.

The benefits include the following:

- Enhanced relationships with business owners.
- High value transactions that are defined and focused.
- Accurate and rapid performance and capacity forecasting.

The investments include the following:

- Services for skills assessment, as appropriate.
- Services to establish (mentor) a monitoring team, supporting all monitoring efforts including APM, as appropriate. This would further detail the process changes for monitoring integration and capacity management of the monitoring environment.

Enhancing the Value of the Monitoring Tool Investment

This justification is intended for organizations that have had at least one reasonably successful deployment of monitoring technology, and it is a growth entry point. Your real concerns are to achieve a much better capability than the prior effort. This is largely accomplished through a definition of the service catalog and establishing a schedule consistent with the skills and resources of the current organization. It is not necessary to define the entire service catalog at this point. Frequently, you find that an organization will focus on a single portion of the application life cycle, such as a QA, deployment, triage, or operations. This is done for budgetary constraints but this frequently is due to an overly narrow scope for the monitoring initiative, which means that broad support for the APM value proposition is still not yet achieved.

The technology objectives include the following:

- Enhancing the pace of deployments.
- Consistent and reproducible triaging of operational events.
- Establishing a monitoring Service Bureau or Center of Excellence.

The strategic objectives include the following:

- Centralizing and amplifying the definitions of standards and usage of monitoring technology.
- Reducing the time to realize program goals.

The benefits include the following:

- Decreased time-to-market schedule.
- Financial right-sizing (cost containment, cost reduction).
- Optimal use of existing and proposed monitoring technology.
- Evolved skill sets and competencies of technical staff

The investments include the following:

- Services for skills assessment, as appropriate.
- Services to establish (mentor) a monitoring team, supporting all monitoring efforts including APM, as appropriate. This would further detail the process changes for QA, deployment and triage technologist practices.
- Additional technology and/or licenses to support monitoring of the future environment.

Proactive Monitoring

This justification is generally a larger-scale undertaking and requires ongoing executive support to help mitigate the cross-silo politics. APM monitoring will have undergone a number of deployments and is used to good effect. The challenge is to get more applications and groups on board. What is impeding broader usage is the relative isolation of monitoring efforts in QA and production, and likely the use of different tools by other lines of business. Each group has its own processes and techniques for the tools and very little of those experiences is reused for new efforts. This results in a duplication of efforts in deploying and using APM monitoring.

Your goal is to accomplish the following:

- Get some groups to share monitoring services and thus reduce the duplication of staff.
- Establish consistent processes through which each of the different tools are employed.
- Encourage cooperation between QA, production, and other stakeholders in the application lifecycle to share monitoring information.
- Establish consistent standards for what metrics and thresholds a "ready for production" application will demonstrate.

Why are these points important? Not only are they addressing the gaps in the current technology practices but they are also the necessary characteristics of proactive management practices.

I define proactive monitoring as prevention: reducing the number of operational incidents by *preventing* problematic or unstable apps from reaching the production environment. You become proactive because you simply do not let badly behaving apps into production. This seems a very obvious proposition, but much of the application life cycle today is simply getting apps to production *on schedule*, regardless of their actual quality or stability. Sure, this is insane! But it's the result of a long tradition of little or no visibility into application performance and the desire to keep the schedule at all costs.

This is what I call dysfunctional IT: everyone suspects problems exist but no one can single-handedly "stop the train" without all manner of pain being directed at them. All the participants in the application life cycle—the individual silos—are practicing their own brand of dysfunction. The result, in my opinion, is a persistent level of general distrust and an absence of cooperation among individual silos, extending even within individual lines of business.

A *proactive monitoring* initiative is going to take on the not-quite-cooperating silos and business units by establishing an umbrella organization with connections into all silos and lines of business and with the public objective of establishing quality standards for the promotion of applications into production. This will occur, of course, in an incremental fashion, but it begins with the establishment of a *gold environment*, which will have a higher SLA than the current production environment. Entry into this environment is only after an *application audit*. This audit accomplishes two things. First, it prepares the operational monitoring. Second, it assesses the stability of the application before it ever gets to the production environment. Only well-behaving apps go forward.

The success measure is obtained by closely tracking the operational incidents prior to, during, and after the initiative has been established. As you move stable apps, including those which can be remediated during the app audit, into the gold environment, you not only demonstrate a more successful operational experience (fewer severity incidents), but you actually exacerbate the proportion of incidents in the original production environment, having removed a number of stable apps from that environment. While this is appears undesirable, as the gold environment demonstrates greater stability, it brings to light the reasons why the prior environment was problematic. And this will result in much greater attention to addressing those problematic applications.

Why, then, the potential for such "interesting times?" Two points: measurements and accountability. A proactive monitoring justification is very near a true ROI analysis because it is targeting a portion of the major incidents, proposing to reduce their number, and tracking the progress of the initiative based on the most complete reporting capability most organizations have available: incident tracking. Add to this a direct comparison between legacy and the new gold operational environment, and you are in a position to directly track the savings of each incident avoided versus the investment in the new tools, processes, and environments.

From the engineering perspective, it is a clear and obvious path to follow— when the numbers make sense. Who would not want to reduce the overall number of high severity incidents[1]? But from the political perspective, it is almost a total gamble that the initiative will be funded, no matter if the economics make sense or not. Some organizations are unusually resistant to change and require broad strategic initiatives to force the politics to the background. While the political challenges may dwarf the technology in determining if the initiative will go forward, executing on the proactive initiative is unremarkably predictable along its timetable.

Technology objectives include the following:

- Integration of availability and performance information to the operations center.
- Performance monitoring in QA environments.
- End-to-end monitoring of the application infrastructure.

The strategic objectives, which you may consider optional, include the following:

- Unifying support groups under a single set of standards.
- Centralizing all runbooks and other application documentation in a single facility (Share site, knowledgebase, wiki, etc.).
- Defining minimum performance criteria in order to enter production.
- A single view of change control and incident management.

The benefits include the following:

- Achieve proactive management by catching performance problems during QA and UAT (User Acceptance Test).
- Create uniform standards for application documentation: support, administration, deployment, and triage.
- Create uniform processes for change and incident management.

---

[1] Incidents will vary according to an arbitrary determination of severity. Severity-1 is the most severe and needs an immediate response. Severity-4 is minor and a response may be deferred up to 24 hours.

- Establish a high-performance subset of the production environment.
- Enhance triage of performance problems.
- Enhance overall software quality from the operations perspective.

The investment includes the following:

- Services for enterprise visibility assessments, as appropriate.
- Services for integration of disparate monitoring points with the NOC (Network Operations Center), as needed.
- Additional technology and/or licenses to support monitoring of the QA environment.
- Services to establish (mentor) a monitoring team, supporting all monitoring efforts including APM, as appropriate. This would further detail the process changes for QA practices, deployment practices, and triage practices.
- Technology and implementation for the runbook repository and management.
- Technology and implementation for the knowledge base repository and management.

Trending and Analysis

This is a somewhat narrow justification but appropriate when an APM initiative is already established and capable with traditional availability monitoring and basic triage. This is a growth entry point. In this scenario, for whatever reasons, the initiative has not been extended to exploit the historical monitoring data for analysis and longer-term trends. This appears to be a side effect of only focusing on deployment of APM technology. In this case, the stakeholders have figured out how to use it for monitoring but are otherwise missing some of the more evolved capabilities.

Technology objectives include the following:

- Integrating historical metrics with existing analysis tools.
- Services for a HealthCheck of the monitoring environment to confirm appropriate configuration and capacity to support the initiative, as appropriate.
- Services and mentoring for techniques and processes to support trending and analysis with APM metrics, as appropriate.

The strategic objectives, which you may consider optional, include the following:

- Performance monitoring in QA environments to add capacity forecasting.
- Triage focused on using baselines collected during QA testing, in addition to the trend analysis.

The benefits include the following:

- Increased use of the monitoring environment.
- Establish comprehensive capacity management planning practices.
- Establish more capable triage technical practices.

The investment includes the following:

- Services for a HealthCheck of the existing environment, as appropriate.
- Services for integration of historical data with existing tools, as appropriate.
- Services to establish (via mentoring) a capacity management team, as appropriate.
- Services to enhance (via mentoring) the capabilities of a triage team, as appropriate.

Single-View of Service Performance (Dashboards)

This is also known as End-to-End (E2E) Service Monitoring and may be an initial or growth entry point. This is a much larger-scale and strategic initiative (multiple years) than any of the prior business justifications, though the portion for APM will still be a well-defined initiative (concise, rapid stages). You simply end up with more potential integration points, multiple technologies (as-is and future), and a strong need to establish a process infrastructure on which to pin elements of the service catalog as the strategic initiatives progress. You may also incur any number of delays as parallel activities vie for resources and shifting priorities. So being able to advance the monitoring initiative in rapid, well-defined stages when opportunities present or as priorities change is an important advantage for an APM initiative. As much as I might put monitoring at the center of the IT universe, we are entirely subordinate to the needs of the business. Monitoring is important but ultimately secondary.

For this type of justification you really have to rely on broad assessment activities to gather the planning and justification information and to help establish a plan to evolve the organization to the desired end state. Typically, you need to foster a sense of collaboration by example, working among the various stakeholders to demonstrate that decisions are not being made in a vacuum and that the ensuing recommendations are not arbitrary.

Technology objectives include the following:

- Visibility into network, security, mainframe, transaction and message integration, distributed resources, legacy processes (batch and interactive), application and web servers (legacy, .NET, Java), web services from the perspective of link, batch, synthetic, and real transactions.
- Alert/Event integration into trouble-management.
- A consolidated or single view into monitoring information for the NOC.

The strategic objectives, which you may consider optional, include the following:

- Enhancing software quality.
- Enhancing QA, stress, and performance accuracy.
- A reduction in severity of incidents related to application quality and stability.
- Proactive management of performance problems prior to operations.

The benefits include the following:

- Eliminated duplication of monitoring tools, long-term.
- Real-time view of business service performance.
- Visibility into application component interactions.
- Visibility into the end-user experience.

The investment includes the following:

- Services for enterprise visibility assessments, as appropriate.
- One or more pilot exercises.
- Multi-year, multi-stage technology and process implementation plan.
- Multi-year monitoring tool platform provisioning and deployment.
- Multi-year, multi-product licensing and maintenance.
- Multiple vendor product training.
- Internal project management staffing.
- Staffing the monitoring service bureau.
- Services budget for monitoring tool integrations, as appropriate.
- Costs associated with sun-setting, duplicate, or outdated technologies and applications.

Summary

Justifying an APM investment appears complicated because of the wide variety of motivations and entry points. You can easily break it down into a concise justification by understanding what the objective is, the current status of the APM initiative, who is currently employing the technology, and who hopes to employ APM technology.

Attempting a justification solely based on economic goals is very hard to do without detailed KPIs for the historical state, an analysis of the operational incidents, and a forecast of the reduction in incidents. It is highly unlikely that at an initial entry point you will have any of this information. It is more likely that at a growth or mature entry point you will have the data, simply because that is the primary benefit of performance management: real measurement in real time. Thereafter, there is nothing special about doing a ROI analysis, other than doing the work.

Any of the justifications here should be preceded with an assessment of skills, processes, and competency, which I introduce in the next chapter. This is the first measurement among many that you can look forward to. Assessments are something that all elements of IT should be proficient in because they provide a way to take measurements in the absence of historical information, support a business proposition, and track its progress. The better you understand your current state, the more robust a proposal you may put forward to management.

Assessments

To measure is to know. Anything else is just a guess.

This chapter introduces the most useful APM activity—assessments. These are not just for APM practitioners, they are for all the other folks, too. Assessments are simply measurements and observations about your current business practices. I will focus on monitoring, but the technique is fundamental to documenting the state of any variety of systems. Essentially, to figure out where you are going and how to get there, you need to first assess what you are already doing.

To figure out the path to an efficient APM initiative, it's is very prudent to assess the utility of the staff and tools, as well as the overall scope and motivation that the initiative hopes to satisfy. The more you know about what you are getting into, the better prepared you can be to employ your experience and skills to avoid any of the distracting issues that can confound the monitoring initiative. An *assessment* is completed prior to the finalization of the implementation plan and may also be used periodically, as the monitoring initiative unfolds, to document progress (or gaps).

The four types or *dimensions* of assessments (and the pertinent questions they answer) are as follows:

- **Application** assessments are used for prioritization of monitoring efforts and solution sizing.

    - What are the variety of applications, base technologies, number of instances, and current monitoring configurations experienced across the app life cycle?

- **Skills** assessments are used to develop roadmaps and proposals for remediation or re-organization.

    - How does a group or organization compare against the skills, processes, and competencies that are critical for effective use of monitoring technologies?

- **Visibility** assessments are used to develop proposals for remediation and tools acquisition.

  - Does your organization have the metrics necessary to achieve their operational goals?
  - What management model is possible?
  - What technologies generate your metrics?

- **Performance** assessments audit an application during stress and performance and/or review the production experience. Generally referred to as an app audit, this assessment is covered in detail in Chapter 13.

  - What are the configuration, application and performance baselines for an application?
  - What metrics should constitute the operational dashboards and reporting?
  - What are the performance, stability and scalability issues observed under synthetic (or real) load?
  - What is the potential scalability of the application or service?

Of these four, the *applications assessment* (or *app survey*) is the most crucial as it helps you to establish the overall implementation scope and to size the initial and successive deployments. The other dimensions help quantify the training and process engineering budget (skills), balance the role of APM in the context of the other available tools (visibility), and confirm the capacity sizing and suitability of both the application and monitoring solution (performance). Assessment findings will also document good practices as well as unsuccessful practices called *anti-patterns*[1]. APM anti-patterns prevent broad use and acceptance of the APM technology or otherwise diminish the potential of the APM initiative. I discuss anti-patterns in more detail in Chapter 4.

For a small initiative (1-5 applications) you could probably skip the skills, visibility, and performance assessments if a detailed justification is not called for. However, if you fail to do the app survey, you are flying blind and at risk to keep scope creep out of you efforts.

I have included all the details of the assessment processes in this chapter because it does not require a skilled APM practitioner or availability of APM technology in order to get a useful result.

You do anticipate the arrival of APM technology with the pilot evaluation and the application audit. Both of these activities can occur in parallel with the assessment activities and may precede or follow the assessment. It is necessary to keep assessments separate from pilots and audit so that the assessments findings remain unbiased. Otherwise, you will find that assessment findings only support the pilot evaluation and do not consider the enterprise realities. The pilot is introduced in Chapter 6, along with details on how to conduct that activity. The application audit is introduced in Chapter 13. The difference between the two is that the pilot is more focused on exploring the monitoring technology when you have little or no

---

[1] Wikipedia, "anti-patterns," http://en.wikipedia.org/wiki/Anti-patterns

experience with the technology. The app audit is documenting the performance and manageability characteristics of the application; it requires a skilled APM practitioner to conduct it.

Considering a pilot exercise suggests that the overall assessment is completed and you are beginning to plan the implementation—or you have decided to defer the APM initiative. I really see a decision to go ahead or a decision to defer as equivalent results of a successful assessment. Be the second mouse! You should only pursue a monitoring initiative when you can show that you have a plan (and sponsorship) to bridge the gaps between your current state and a successful APM implementation.

Assessment activities need time and cooperation more than money. Most of the assessment activities are interviews and paper-based (research) activities, including spreadsheets and other document types. However, you may apply the Good-Better-Best principle to assessments and generate a spectrum of simple-to-highly-detailed information about the potential scope and benefit of the monitoring initiative. Proper guidance as a result of the assessment should be the overall goal of the deployment, in terms of the number of unique applications that are coming under management. The larger the scale of the initiative, the more likely you will avail yourself of the a full assessment activities. This is because the larger the initiative, the more you will need solid evidence of needs and gaps as these issues form the basis for your recommendations.

I will start with an overview discussion and then move into the details of the various assessment dimensions: what to collect, what it means, and how to assemble your findings into a summary and recommendations.

■ **Note** Examples of the assessment tools and reports (*artifacts*) are available in the "Source Code" section of this book's web page on apress.com. Each assessment activity has a detailed *cookbook* (a sequential list of instructions) to help you reuse the artifacts.

■ **Note** The greatest challenge in delivering assessments is keeping perspective. You are being engaged to conduct conversations that document current and desired practices that the sponsors themselves may be unable to accomplish. You have to be neutral and thorough for the activity to be meaningful. For much of what you will learn, the remediation will be painfully and frustratingly obvious. For the sponsor, they may simply not be in a position to bring all of the pieces together, and so they cannot yet appreciate what may already be obvious to you.

Overview

The parable for this chapter is a derivative work, with a twist, from Lord Kelvin (1824-1907) who stated that when you could measure a thing, you could then expect to know quite a bit about it. The twist is: what do you do when you do not have a measurement available? You guess. I want to take the guesswork out of the APM initiative as much as possible—and so the motivation for a robust assessment.

Assessments are considered by some folks to be a luxury. But spending hundreds of thousands of dollars on monitoring technology with little more than a personal assurance is out of character in a modern IT organization. My presumption is that you are under heavy financial scrutiny with your proposal for an APM initiative. If that is not the case, then you are one of the fortunate few and you may advance directly to the "Implementation" section beginning with Chapter 7.

Pressure remains for assessment activities; due to limitations of time or staff, you may not have an opportunity to do a full and thorough job. You will apply the principles of Good-Better-Best and identify the minimum, improved, and optimal sets of activities to pursue. The advantage of being the second mouse is that when your management will not even allow you to pursue a minimum assessment, you really have the evidence that it is not your time to pursue this monitoring initiative.

Here is an outline of your assessment choices:

- **Good**
    - Interview/survey critical apps.
    - Assess the monitoring benefit.
    - Understand the metrics already available.
    - Review current operational[2] incidents.

- **Better**
    - Good PLUS…
        - Survey the critical transactions (this could also be collected during a pilot).
        - Monitor high-value transactions in production with transaction filtering.
        - Confirm or redirect[3] where additional monitoring is needed.

- **Best**
    - Better PLUS…
        - Application audit.
        - Rapid deployment of APM technology, as would result during a pilot evaluation.

---

[2] Operational, as coming from the current operation of the production environment.

[3] The outcome of a pilot exercise may be to conclude that the wrong application was monitored or that some other resource would be a better candidate for monitoring.

- Evaluation under load simulation.
- Identify which metrics best capture availability, performance, and capacity (APC).

The real difference among Good-Better-Best is being able to commit staff to undertake some sort of **pilot evaluation**. There is nothing more significant in predicting the success of a monitoring initiative than trying out the technology with your own processes and environment. However, a pilot evaluation is not the only assessment activity you should consider. What one group may be able to realize in a pilot may not hold for other groups within your enterprise. You also need to consider that the pilot delivery will be with vendor assistance, further masking any gaps in your own processes to exploit the technology. The vendor has all the experience; you should not assume that your organization's staff already possesses the necessary experience or could successfully absorb all of that experience over the one to two week period of the pilot. You also need to consider your success criteria for the pilot evaluation.

If you have completed a proper assessment of your organizational DNA in terms of skills, processes and competencies, then a pilot exercise will validate your findings. If you have not completed a meaningful assessment, a successful pilot may establish a false confidence that your organization will actually realize the value of an APM initiative. If the pilot is unsuccessful, you have wasted organizational resources—and that stain that will be hard to wash away. Remember, your goal in the assessment is to confirm that your organization is ready and willing to commit the resources that insure the initiative will be a success. Why anyone would do anything else—it just stuns! Ours is not to reason why. Ours is but to assess—and be the second mouse[4].

If you need to justify even undertaking a Good assessment, here are descriptions of the deliverables:

- Confirm a list of applications that need monitoring.
- Confirm how much additional visibility is needed.
- Confirm which stakeholders would benefit from additional visibility.
- Document what visibility exists already.
- Document what effect visibility gaps have on overall service management.
- Document how much and what should be deployed.
- Document staff capabilities to support deployment and use of the tools.

Assessments are a crucial ongoing activity for a monitoring system. You don't hope to get lucky with your monitoring deployments and process improvements. You want to plan and control your success. Assessments are how you get that information so that you can manage the expectations about what the organization may reasonably achieve, given the current energy (time, resources, politics, whatever) available.

---

[4] A complete hack of Lord Tennyson's epic poem:

Wikipedia, "The Charge of the Light Brigade," http://en.wikipedia.org/wiki/The_Charge_of_the_Light_Brigade_poem

If you find that the assessment process is undervalued by management, you should bring up the reality that assessments are an ongoing activity of a mature IT organization, and that the absence of this process is a clear indication of low organizational maturity. It's worth a try!

Visibility

Visibility is perhaps the most charged term in the conversation. Many organizations have lulled themselves into believing that they are doing a full and commendable job of application management. They may be doing so for availability monitoring but for little else. If a third-party service provider[5] is involved, they may not be doing very much at all to communicate or share visibility into their activities. This is called *reactive-negotiated*: when you have to request status information, rather than that status being communicated automatically. You emphasize AP*Management* because you know that while an organization may outsource the administration and operation of the platforms supporting their services, it does not mean that they abdicate their rights to the performance information.

When you help an organization evolve from availability monitoring towards end-to-end monitoring and performance management, what you are really doing is moving that organization from a daily reporting schedule to receiving that same information (and more) in a matter of minutes and as the status changes. Identifying any barriers, culturally or process-related, to achieving this more frequent reporting and establishing the new process to review and respond in similar timeframes is what will actually dictate the progress of the APM initiative. Deploying APM technology is not a difficult undertaking. Getting the organization in a position to employ this additional visibility is the challenge. The assessment activities serve as a mechanism to help communicate what will be possible as the initiative unfolds.

Of course, not all daily reporting activities benefit from increasing the frequency of reporting to minutes. You need to be selective and focus on the reporting impediments that create *visibility gaps*. You will find more discussion of this topic in the Chapter 3 artifacts on apress.com.

Another simple method to highlight gaps in business service visibility is to look at the types of monitoring technologies employed. Although I have not yet defined some of these technologies, here is a quick spectrum of monitoring technologies, ordered from deepest to shallowest visibility:

- Instrumentation technologies
- Real transactions
- JMX/PMI
- Synthetic technologies
  - Transactions to test response time

---

[5] Wikipedia, "service provider," http://en.wikipedia.org/wiki/Service_provider

- Robot platforms or clients
  - Remote control
  - Remote deployment targets

- Home grown or purpose-built systems

  - Internal status reporting
  - Interrogation or status scripts

- Platform alerting technologies
- Logging technologies
- Network technologies
- Service providers

This list only focuses on technology commonly employed in a production environment, so I have left out profiler technologies often exclusively used by developers. These deep visibility tools are still useful. But because they have very high overhead, they are dangerous to use in production. They also require a high level of experience to use effectively. Even though they are useful, they are a lower priority for the monitoring initiative where you want to increase the number of variety of stakeholders who may access metrics plus enhance visibility. Specialist tools simply do not address the needs of a broader audience (the rest of IT as well as the business).

Following the goal of increasing access to performance metrics also means that you may allow for dedicated monitoring tools, such as database, router and firewall management, without specifically mandating their use. Depending on your outsourcing model, these tools may be limited to the service provider and are not especially helpful to understanding business transactions anyway. They are significant in terms of assessing monitoring maturity, so make sure to account for their use. The advantage of APM is to identify performance problems quickly. The final resolution may still require specialists and their use of dedicated tools.

Another interesting opportunity to enhance visibility is the review of any purpose-built monitoring scripts or extra devices that support remote interactions. Both of these offer some great integration potential and can often be very economical to begin with. If you have thick-client software, you might allow for an extra, unused workstation. You can use it to practice deployment; when it is operating, you may use it to run transactions and confirm the availability of network links and back-end resources. You will need to architect these capabilities into that thick-client software but if you have made that investment, then you only need to account for integrating that stream of metrics within the NOC. When you develop a plan for an APM initiative, you need to consider all sources of metrics initially and let operational experience (in trying to employ those metrics to address incidents) sort out what metrics contribute consistently to the understanding of a performance incident.

I also include JMX and PMI metrics, which are readily available in production configurations, despite their many limitations. The significant point is that many of these metrics have more to do with management of configuration settings for the application than they do in helping to identify performance problems. They are very hard to interpret consistently, can have devastating overhead, and while you can get a lot of them, they are not especially helpful, in my opinion. They are really intended for developers and systems administrators to tune application server configurations. They are not especially helpful for all the other stakeholders in the application life cycle. I certainly do not need them to assist in my firefight activities, although some of my peers still prefer to look at them. I have not been able to identify a consistent set of practices around them, outside of the initial configuration of an app server, when they are immensely helpful. You really need a lot of experience with the JVM (or CLR) and application server tunables to exploit the JMX and PMI metrics, which goes against the stated objective of making performance metrics available to regular folks.

Regardless, if a stakeholder mentions that they are making use of JMX and PMI metrics as part of their monitoring system, you should get the details and make sure that those metrics remain available. A number of tools make JMX information readily accessible, in addition to platform monitoring, so it is a still a step forward in the evolution of a monitoring solution.

I will close my overview discussion on the motivation for assessments and dig into the details and artifacts employed.

Assessment Dimensions

There are a number of assessment dimensions (variables). They break down into two major areas: *interview-based* and *reporting-based*.

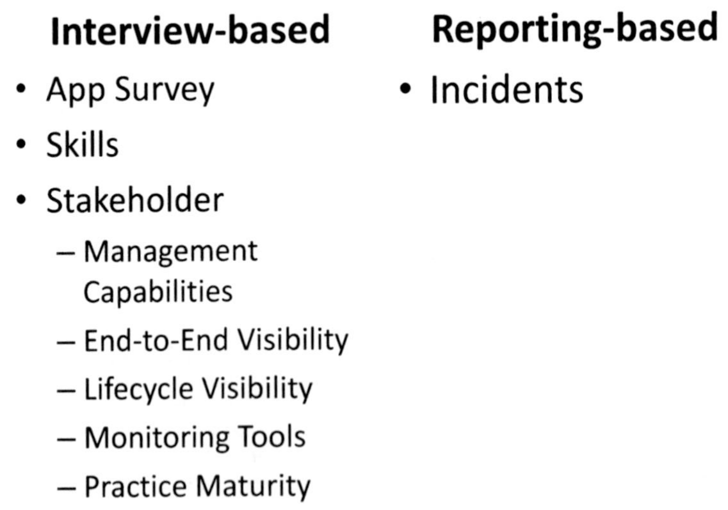

Interview-based

- App Survey
- Skills
- Stakeholder
    - Management Capabilities
    - End-to-End Visibility
    - Lifecycle Visibility
    - Monitoring Tools
    - Practice Maturity

Reporting-based

- Incidents

Figure 3-1. Assessment activities

As suggested earlier, you need to keep the pilot evaluation and application audit as separate activities because assessment activities can influence the definition of the pilot, and vice versa. You don't want to perturb the process through which the product evaluations are conducted because they, too, are a measure of how successful the greater organization will be in adopting the technology. You definitely want to include their findings in your recommendations. It is a semantic point because transaction or application audits are a valuable contribution to an assessment activity. The difference between pilots and audits is your experience with the technology. If you are new to APM, you can't realistically expect to deliver an audit service. You do not yet have the experience and the process, and the technology simply will not do it for you. However, for an experienced APM practitioner, the interview-based activities fall away in favor of the audit activities. For a project involving an established APM implementation, the focus is more on confirming the deployment impact, whereas the novice is more likely concerned with justifying the monitoring initiative. Regardless, you will keep all the assessment activities in play because organizations grow through merger and acquisition, so you can expect to assess these new environments as they turn up.

For the novice team, with respect to an APM initiative, you look at the pilot to *confirm* the assessment findings and recommendations. Sometimes you will find that the assessment activities are progressing concurrently with the pilot exercise. That does not present an issue, provided that the pilot and assessment teams are separate. Otherwise, you will find that the assessment may be tainted and the scope of stakeholder interviews too narrow to be representative of the IT organization as a whole. Similarly, you have to be careful in how you select the initial set of applications so that they are representative of the spectrum of applications that are present operationally. The resulting *candidate application list* does not have to be proportional, such as 50% batch, 30% appliance, or 10% Java. The other dimensions of the assessment will take care of that proportion, especially the Incident analysis. The candidate applications do need to cover the variety of significant technologies, with at least one high value representative application in each category. Figure a minimum of three and a maximum of twenty candidate applications, with six to ten applications as ideal.

As you finalize your list of candidate applications, you should also ensure that at least one of them is suitable to pilot with one or more APM technologies. While you want those pilots to be independent activities from the assessment activities, you also want to measure them. This will help maximize the accuracy of the sizing dimension, which you will first estimate and then confirm with the pilot findings. Ideally, you should pilot a single application against multiple APM vendors so that the results are directly comparable. If that is not possible, then at least evaluate the same application server version across multiple applications with a single vendor for each. This compromises your ability to make direct comparison but it also dramatically reduces the time needed to evaluate the candidate vendors. If neither of these approaches is possible, and unrelated applications are piloted with different technologies, you will still have a good sizing result but you will be more dependent on a broad and successful assessment to ensure that you have a solid path to an APM implementation.

The next sections will show how to conduct the different assessments and how to employ the relevant artifacts, along with an outline to summarize the findings. Details for defining, conducting, and reviewing a pilot evaluation are found in Chapter 6.

Application Survey

There are two goals for the App Survey. The first is to get details about the proposed application (monitoring candidate) so that you can appreciate its role, stability, the technology employed, and its complexity. These will each have an impact on the work effort and monitoring tool capacity and will confirm the suitability of the monitoring tool. The most important quantity to identify is the number of instances of each application or resource to monitor. Often this is a count of the number of JVMs (Java Virtual Machines) or CLRs (Common Language Runtime - .NET) but it can also include other types of agents. For real and synthetic transactions, having an accurate count of the candidate applications will be sufficient for the initial sizing. You may safely assume 5-10 transactions for each application to start; be sure to note if the stakeholder believes that more transactions might be appropriate. After the application survey is completed, a more detailed sizing is conducted. Your goal at this point is to survey. Don't get bogged down gathering details that may be unnecessary depending on the monitoring strategy employed.

The second goal is to prioritize the monitoring candidates so that critical apps have their monitoring deployed first and less-critical apps are deferred to the second or third round. A subtle goal of this approach is to identify stable candidates to be included in the first deployment phase. If you only focus on problematic applications and then find that the monitoring does not seem to be working well, how can you be sure if it is your deployment process or the difficulties of the candidate app? Ideally, your first deployment should only involve stable applications but sometimes this conflicts with the traditional goals of the monitoring initiative (get visibility into a real problem).

Many legacy[6] applications, especially those having established platform, process, log, or robotic forms of monitoring, do not require the level of detail that the App Survey may provide. This is not a problem because these legacy apps are likely inappropriate for APM. Sometimes these legacy apps are included in order to document their current state, setting the stage for sun-setting and replacement by a modern application architecture largely based on .NET or Java[7]. Legacy apps are important contributions as they are usually supported by very robust processes for change control and problem management that will be modeled for the APM initiative.

Figure 3-2 shows an example of a map of application priorities.

---

[6] Wikipedia, "legacy application," http://en.wikipedia.org/wiki/Legacy_application

[7] DevTopics, "Most Popular Programming Languages," www.devtopics.com/most-popular-programming-languages/

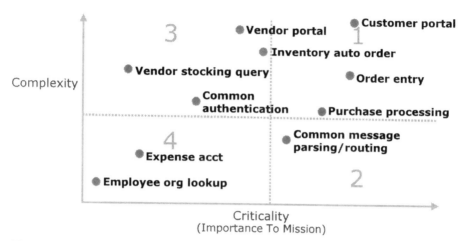

Figure 3-2. Application prioritization

The business realities for each of these quadrants are as follows:

- First quadrant: Highest priority, urgent need for management.
- Second quadrant: High priority, potential business impact.
- Third quadrant: Lower priority, may drain IT productivity.
- Fourth quadrant: Lowest priority, manage these last.

In Chapter 7, I discuss details of the *phased deployment model*, which breaks up a large-scale deployment into three distinct phases of deploy-operate-review. Focusing on the high-value, high-priority applications is an easy mechanism to achieve success in the first deployment phase, provided they are amenable to APM technologies. Once you have achieved that success, you'll be under much less pressure to complete a monitoring deployment of the remaining applications.

If the APM initiative is biased toward process improvement rather than deployment of monitoring technology, this incremental implementation (called *phased deployment)* is still appropriate for realizing the initiative.

Once you have the list of candidate applications, you are ready to conduct the App Survey.

Survey Dimensions

You want the survey to answer three questions. First, you want to validate that the candidate application is suitable for monitoring via instrumentation or if another technology is indicated. Second, you want to understand if this application has an ongoing development life cycle that might allow some visibility into the QA and UAT environments, or if is it a stable or packaged application that is limited to the operational environment only. Third, you want to forecast what the impact of this application will be on the monitoring solution storage infrastructure.

There are four recommended dimensions to the survey: Business, Environment, Resources, and Software Architecture. An optional fifth dimension, Monitoring Technology, can further automate the collection of information that would normally come during an interview. I consider it optional because it should be limited to a reasonably mature application team with respect to monitoring. You need to be the judge if it will work for your situation.

You can use a simple spreadsheet with lots of drop-down lists (see Figure 3-3) to make it easy to fill out this form and maintain consistency among the types of responses you expect.

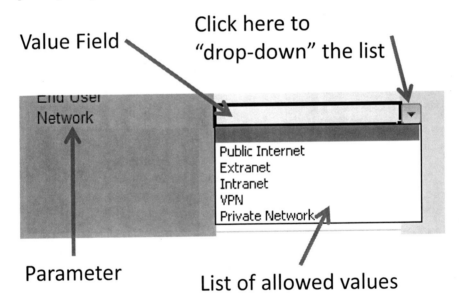

Figure 3-3. How a drop-down list works

For a small-scale assessment, drop-down lists can be a distraction. What you are trying to establish is a model that will scale to hundreds of applications. For a durable APM implementation, you need to ascertain what kind of monitoring technology is most appropriate for each application. Not all applications will benefit from APM; you need to identify when this is the case.

Business

The first dimension, illustrated in Figure 3-4, collects details of the business or application sponsor. I often find some confusion as to how an application owner is defined within the corporation. When you send out these survey forms you do not really get a lot of choice as to who fills them out. You may have a solid contact or you may have someone who believes they can forward it on to an appropriate individual to be identified. I define the *application owner* as the business entity that funds the development and maintenance of the application. Often, however, a technical lead, business analyst, or third party contractor is assumed to be the owner. You will have identified this candidate application because it meets your criteria for the APM initaitive, which may be very different than how the application sponsor actually views and values their role. Whatever is the more consistent role is what you want to identify. You can use the notes field to detail the variety of responses you may receive. As part of the final report you will communicate any trends about how the stakeholders interpret their role, back to management, to improve that alignment for the future.

It is very important for the business sponsor to list the stakeholders that they are working with. You will use this to correct the list of candidates being considering for *stakeholder interviews.*

Questions	Response	Notes
	Business	
Business Sponsor (group/division)		
Type of Application		
Criticality		
Business Domain/Function		
Who are your main stakeholders? (list in notes)		

Figure 3-4. App Survey - Business

The free form fields are useful to start organizing which applications are associated with different business units and what function they perform. This is not essential for sizing, but while you have the attention of the stakeholder, dig for a little extra data to help IT understand the business. This will be an on-going effort.

The other important fields are Type of Application and Criticality. Both of these are predefined lists. For details, please look at the file Ch 03 - Assessments - Application_Survey on apress.com

The Type of Application field will eventually dictate the number of unique agent configurations or transaction definitions you may have to validate and maintain. Assigning applications to a consistent description gets complicated quickly. I start with twenty different types but there are always a few unique applications that just do not fit and require a new name. All of these details are in the definitions tab of the survey spreadsheet, and I have included the Type of Application list in the Chapter 3 artifacts (on apress.com) to give you a flavor of what is needed.

The Criticality field also will effectively give you an insight into how much this application will add to your stress levels. You want to have an initial deployment with at least three stable applications. For a new monitoring system, you need to build confidence that the monitoring technologies are deployed correctly, even if the less stable applications are going to be more interesting. If you do not make this effort to get experience with a few well-behaved applications, than you are at risk for getting kicked out of production in short order.

Environment

Here you confirm if you have appropriate support for the targeted operating environment to estimate the level of effort, assign the type of monitoring, and validate the monitoring configuration.

For the Environment category, there are three sections of concern, shown in Figure 3-5.

- Section 1: General platform and operating system information.
- Section 2: These fields are direct inputs to the upcoming APM sizing (Chapter 10), including synthetics, real transactions, and instrumentation.
- Section 3: Details about what is available for pre-production testing and the potential to uncover performance problems pre-production, conduct application audits, and validate agent configurations.

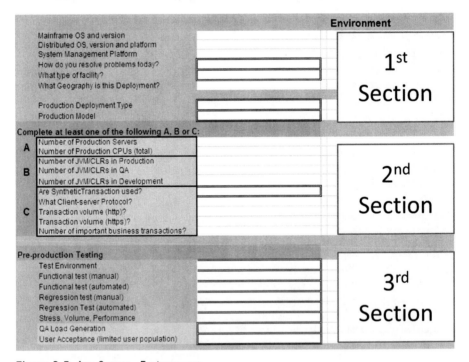

Figure 3-5. App Survey - Environment

Many vendors employ CPU count as the basis for technology licensing, and you can support a future audit by getting the client perspective and then following that up with a direct measurement from the APM tool. However, the CPU count does not give any insight into the number of agents used by the application. For agent technology, you need the number of JVMs or CLRs utilized by the application. Each JVM/CLR will have its own agent and corresponding stream of metrics.

The emphasis on pre-production testing is critical for a successful APM initiative. Before you get to move your monitoring to production, you have to prove it is safe in pre-production. Testing capability is a very strong predictor of APM success. When load generation is not adequate, you will need to confirm an agent configuration while in production. This will increase the time to complete the monitoring deployment, due to limitations of doing changes in production. What takes a few hours in QA may take a few weeks in a live environment. You will also need to be more conservative and cautious while making changes in production. This does not mean that you cannot deploy quickly; it just means that any tuning of the configuration will be undertaken slowly. These considerations are critical for the implementation planning that you will start in Chapter 7.

Resources

With this dimension, there are two goals. The first is to confirm the software architecture. The second is to confirm that you have sufficient technology to monitor the various resources. All of these resource questions are answered via a dropdown list for Yes-No-DoNotKnow.

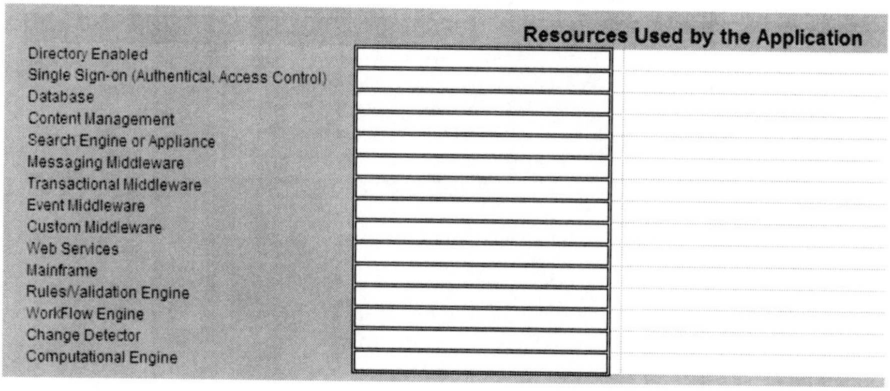

Figure 3-6. App Survey - Resources

The resources being used by the application, summarized in Figure 3-6, give you a goal for the overall visibility you may hope to achieve for a given application. For everything indicated "yes," you need to insure that you have at least one transaction, synthetic or real, that reliably exercises that resource. I cover these load generation concerns in Chapter 11.

Software Architecture

Where you have a compatible application component technology, you may get visibility into the component relationships themselves. Actual coverage here will vary considerably for each vendor solution, so it is important to know what you have to support. Figure 3-7 illustrates the components to look for.

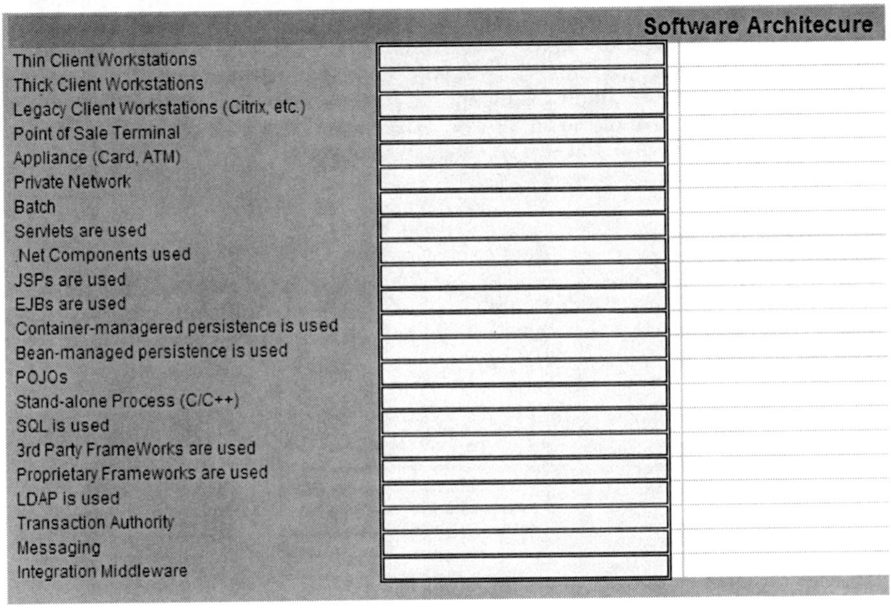

Figure 3-7. App Survey – Software Architecture

An instrumentation agent will have a number of configuration settings to target particular components. Other APM technologies will not have any significant visibility into components. However, collecting this information now will let you be more agile in the future, should other APM technologies become available.

Existing Monitoring (Optional)

This final dimension is to capture details about the monitoring already in place. This is optional because many candidates for APM are not actually utilizing any significant monitoring. You might get better information from the stake-holder interview than from allowing them to summarize what they have in place for monitoring.

In Figure 3-8, the Production Visibility column presents a list of monitoring technologies with just a bit more detail then presented initially in Chapter 1. The list is ordered from lowest to highest *monitoring utility*. This is not a reflection on the individual technical capabilities but more about the ease that various stakeholders can access and interpret the results. I also find that as an organization matures in its monitoring capabilities, it will have experience with each level of monitoring utility; these experiences will help them to appreciate the benefits and limitations of each technology.

Production Visibility	Is it in Use?	Existing Monitoring	QA Visibility
		Who Get the Data	
Network Availability	None	Not Monitored	None
Platform Availability	Light	Monitored but not in use	Light
Network Protocol Monitoring	Average	Service Provider	Average
Platform Monitoring	Heavy	Application Team	Heavy
Logging	Extensive	Operations	Extensive
Custom Metrics or API	Do not know	Resource Specialist	Do not know
Configuration Metrics (JMX/PMI)		Support/HelpDesk	
Synthetic Transactions		Capacity Planning	
Real Transactions		Trouble Management System	Do not know
Instrumentation		Multiple consumers - please	Do not know

Figure 3-8. App survey – Existing Monitoring

You will see this pattern of increasing monitoring utility, as in the Production Visibility column of Figure 3-8, used in a variety of ways throughout this chapter. Everybody is doing monitoring. Some will even talk about how they have visibility into transactions and performance. That is their perception. Having them detail exactly what monitoring technology is being employed and who gets the data often results in a very different picture.

When the App Survey is completed, you need to set aside a few minutes to review it. Make sure they have really made an effort to fill the key details. You should actually validate the App Survey during the stakeholder interviews. For now, a completed survey is a treasure-trove of useful information to guide your monitoring initiative.

Avoiding Scope-Creep During Deployment Planning

If your initiative is well supported, you will find yourself under significant pressure to increase the pace or number of applications that are to be deployed. Everyone wants to be part of a successful initiative. However, each additional application exposes you to additional risk. So how do you push back without offending that stakeholder?

You need to expose the risk in a collaborative fashion. The assessment is the mechanism that will either get you the necessary information to help lower your risk or help the stakeholder to realize that perhaps they are not a good fit for the initial deployment. Usually the App Survey alone is enough for clients to stop applying pressure. The less they know about their own application, the more likely that the App Survey will take a bit of time to complete.

For more complex applications, actual measurements of performance and stability (either in terms of specific transactions or a full pilot with instrumentation) is better. This will provide everything you need to understand the monitoring configuration and the potential impact on the overall environment's stability when additional applications are added.

The business will dictate the first applications to be deployed. In parallel, you can use the Better and Best assessments to encourage the client to develop a more complete picture of what you are getting into. Yes, it is more work for them but the end result (if an app audit is completed) is a fully validated monitoring configuration which will have minimal impact on your deployment schedule. Even if you get just a passing grade on your initial deployment, your second deployment will be a home run. The third deployment, when all the attention has moved elsewhere, is where you can satisfy all of the exceptions or lesser-vetted applications. These will need more work on your part but the business goals will already have been satisfied and you can settle in to the realities of ongoing management of performance monitoring.

Skills and Processes

In order to assess skills and processes, you need a maturity model for comparison. Chapter 1 included an APM maturity model to support this type of assessment.

Developing maturity models is an important topic and outside the scope of this book. And while I have never submitted this APM maturity model to an independent organization or standards body for review and validation, I offer it here simply as an example of how to employ one as part of the assessment process. The details of the maturity model are embedded in the Skills Assessment Interview spreadsheet (at apress.com) but the tenets are as follows:

- Monitoring is an activity across the application life cycle, not restricted to a production or operational environment.
- Efficient triage is the essential value of any monitoring effort.
- Proactive management is only possible when you have monitoring processes prior to production/operations.
- Deployment is the basic goal of any monitoring effort.
- Collaboration is possible when stakeholders have ready access to monitoring data.
- Capacity management and planning is the longer-term value of monitoring.
- *Skills* are specific activities to support and employ the monitoring technology.
- *Processes* are the activities by which you leverage the organization in concert with the monitoring information.
- *Competencies* are the activities, collected in the Service Catalog[8], which you may reliably deliver to your internal clients as part of an APM initiative.

I identify five dimensions of monitoring maturity in typical organizations, as follows:

---

[8] Wikipedia, "service catalog," http://en.wikipedia.org/wiki/Service_Catalog

1. QA practices
2. Pre-production practices
3. Production/operations practices
4. Organizational practices
5. The monitoring self-service portal

Dimension 5, the *monitoring self-service portal*[9], is really a goal set far off on the horizon. When I first thought about what different companies needed to help their establish their monitoring system, I imagined how I would interact with a monitoring portal to request guidance, review test results, and look at my current application status. And as I thought about that imaginary interaction, I started listing out all of the artifacts (documents, spreadsheets, displays, and reports) that I would need to provide real functionality for the monitoring portal—a classic top-down design[10] and bottom-up implementation. The dimension 4, *organizational practices*, are what I focus on, as these lead directly to self-sustaining monitoring teams. This book is a foundation for those activities.

In practice, I never find an organization that is entirely dimension 1 or dimension 3, but I do find organizations that largely do monitoring in QA with limited production rollout, as well as organizations that do it exclusively in production (no pre-production activities). Regardless of where your monitoring focus is, you can use the maturity model to assess and confirm what you do well, along with identifying how to address your current gaps.

Incidents

The most valuable chunk of data, and sometimes the most difficult to obtain, is a list of severity-1[11] incidents. It is valuable because if every significant failure is documented with the appropriate analysis, you can determine which systems would benefit from the APM initiative, and thus you can easily quantify the potential benefit of going ahead with the initiative. Therefore, you will spend a bit of time understanding how to perform this analysis and interpret the results.

The difficulty is that this information is highly confidential and often very closely guarded. You may not be able to get access to it. This is a great loss but there is really

---

[9] There are a variety of portal solution architectures. Self-service is one such model. Extending this concept to allow monitoring self-service is a strategy to help keep personnel costs low, for the monitoring initiative. More definitions of portal may be found at www.steptwo.com.au/papers/cmb_portaldefinitions/index.html

[10] Wikipedia, "top-down and bottom-up design," http://en.wikipedia.org/wiki/Top-down_and_bottom-up_design

[11] When there is a severe problem in a production environment, these are recoded as an incident and assigned a severity number, usually 1, 2 or 3. A severity-1 incident usually results is a significant loss of revenue and has the highest priority in assigning resources to effect a resolution. For more information about incidents, see www.itlibrary.org/index.php?page=Incident_Management

nothing you can do if it can't be shared. There are still other paths to justify a monitoring initiative—just none as useful as incidents.

If you have never seen incident reporting (it's actually pretty boring), I will go through a scrubbed analysis so you can appreciate how it may be used. It is a little work to do the analysis and you need some skills with a spreadsheet, but it provides a solid justification for a monitoring initiative.

Fortunately, most folks can generate an incident report list in spreadsheet form from the incident management system. Otherwise, you need to go through the summary document (as in a monthly report) and build your own spreadsheet. You will want one to three months of incidents for any meaningful analysis (maybe three dozen incidents at a minimum) and in order to have some confidence in any conclusion. One point does not make for a trend!

With a spreadsheet in hand, you are going to add a few more columns and basically re-interpret the original incidents and assign them according to the follow dimensions:

- **Environment**: Service Provider, Network/Facilities, Security, Third Party App, Change Control, Platform, Process, Transaction, Business Logic, End-user, Alert Response, Monitoring Procedures, Help-Desk
- **Technology**: Network, Facilities/Infrastructure, Appliance, Backup Management, Batch, ETL, B2B/EDI, Database, Transaction Processing, Message Queue, Integration Middleware, Event Middleware, Process (C/C++), Process (Mainframe), Process(Java/.NET), Directory, Antivirus/Firewall/VPN, Access Control/Authorization, Workflow, Web Server, Web Client, Thick Client, Monitoring Integration, Application Server, Portal, Web Service
- **Outage Duration**: Service defect, Short <20 min, Medium <1 hr, Long < 4 hrs, Rollback version
- **Visibility (APM vs. other monitoring tools)**: Parallel, likely, unlikely, exclusive
- **Would APM Help:** Yes, probably, unlikely, no

These values are encoded as lists (for input validation) in the example spreadsheet Ch 03 - Assessments - Incident_Analysis (on apress.com). Typically, these additional values are not highlighted because the real role for incident reporting is to track the progress of the incident towards resolution, not to help justify an APM initiative. You need to enrich the more narrow view of the incident to serve your purposes. It is fun for about the first 10 incidents and then it becomes a chore. So what do you get for all of this work?

Figure 3-9 shows the Environment results for a few hundred incidents.

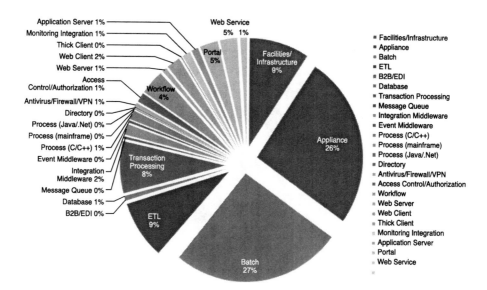

Figure 3-9. Incident technology

What does it mean? It means that the bulk of the incidents occurring are related to infrastructure. I use "appliance" to represent any embedded type of device where a full operating system is not available, which can include point-of-sale (POS) and green screen terminals, network switches, firewalls, etc. The next chunk of incidents is around batch activities, so it is easy to conclude that this environment is composed of largely legacy-based applications around a mainframe.

The remaining significant chart segments are related to extract-transform-load (ETL), integration middleware, and facilities. Therefore, you may also conclude that you are in an availability monitoring-focused organization.

Of course, that this is a mainframe transactional environment would be obvious in just a few questions, but what this analysis helps expose is what they are not seeing from their current monitoring capability. You really do not see a significant proportion of incidents related to those involving application servers or other types of web-based applications. You look first to web-enabled applications because the interactive nature of these apps means that any performance degradation is likely going to be logged as an incident. Interactive users are very sensitive to the overall response time of the system and they will be the first to complain.

Does the absence of incidents imply there are few web-based applications having problems? Or does this imply that the web-based application issues are simply not visible to the current monitoring solution? When you can answer these questions accurately you are well on your way to justifying the monitoring initiative.

By looking at the environment that the incident is occurring in, you get a better sense of what *process* problems contribute to the incident. Again, this information is usually present in the standard incident reporting. All you have done in this incident analysis is create a separate dimension to further categorize and understand the incidents (illustrated in Figure 3-10).

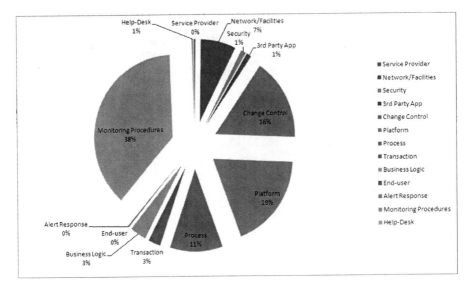

Figure 3-10. Incident environment

This Environment view of the incidents gives you some insight into the underlying organizational maturity in dealing with performance issues. Again, you cannot yet be sure that the lower proportion of transaction and business logic incidents, for example, is due to lack of visibility or lack of complex, web-based applications. You can clearly see that the organization has significant problems with monitoring procedures and change control, in addition to incidents with platform and process monitoring.

The last dimension you consider is "Would APM Help?" If APM technology were available for the incidents, where would it have had a significant impact? Figure 3-11 illustrates the findings.

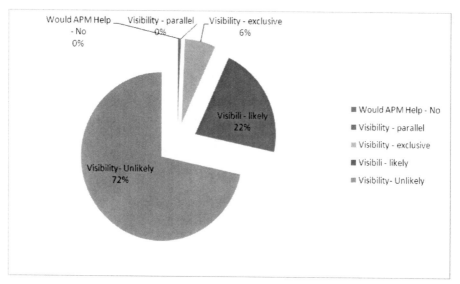

Figure 3-11. Incident impact of APM

No surprise here as you find that the bulk of incidents would not be impacted by APM technology. With a high proportion of appliance, network and batch technology, there is little opportunity for APM technology to participate. You do have a significant portion of incidents (22% +6%) that would likely benefit and you would argue for the move from reactive to proactive management capabilities.

What is significant is that 6% of the incidents would have *exclusive visibility*. In other words, you only have visibility into these incidents with APM technology. For example, if your infrastructure monitoring indicates there is no problem but your helpdesk is getting hundreds of calls, then APM is the only technology that is going to get you visibility into that problem. This establishes a unique benefit of APM versus availability monitoring. When you add this benefit to the benefits of increasing the visibility pre-production, you have a solid foundation for some strong messaging around the advantages of employing APM visibility to improve the overall situation in production.

There are, of course, more benefits to enumerate and a full discussion of how to define the goals of the monitoring initiative is available in the previous chapter. You don't expect that an incident analysis alone is going to complete the justification of the monitoring initiative. You should be confident that it will capture the current state accurately and may offer some interesting findings. In the best situation, you want to prove the motivations for the initiative from multiple angles or dimensions, even if one of these assessment techniques seems convincing enough on its own.

■ **Note** Please be careful about reusing these example results to justify your own particular situation, no matter how similar you think your situation is. These results apply to a specific client environment. They are not validated as a trend for the industry. The incident assessment process is only appropriate when repeated on incidents from your target environment.

With these charts in hand, your discussion about the incidents needs to cover the following points:

- How were the incidents gathered?
- What operational period do they reflect?
- What incidents, if any, were omitted from the analysis?
- What is the general interpretation of each of the chart findings?
- How reliably does the organization deploy changes?
- How well does the organization test prospective changes?
- What proportion of incidents are hardware failures versus process failures?
- What proportion of incidents are unresolved (no root cause)?
- What proportion of restarts were undertaken without a specific alert being generated (no visibility)?
- What opportunities do the unique visibility of APM offer the organization?

Cookbook

How to conduct an Incident Analysis Assessment:

1. Get the incidents into spreadsheet form. A scrubbed version of the spreadsheet that supported the example analysis is available for reference as Ch 03 - Assessments - Incident_Analysis at apress.com.
2. Create a Definitions tab to contain the definition lists for the new dimensions.
3. Insert the columns for the additional dimensions.
4. Evaluate each incident and evaluate each dimension via the Validate List feature of the spreadsheet.
   a. Duplicate the incident if it does not fit easily into a single category.
   b. Always use the List Validation feature. Any typo at this point will cause problems later.
5. Copy the completed outage analysis into additional worksheets, one for each new dimension.

6. Copy each value from the corresponding dimension to the top of each column. Create a formula that evaluates if an incident matches that header value. Sum the counts for each dimension value (column).

7. Insert a few blank rows at the top of the worksheet and create a pie chart with the sum values and column header labels.

8. Summarize the incident analysis methodology and findings by considering the outline of questions listed just before this cookbook.

Stakeholder Interviews

You can't expect to get all of the data for a business justification of the monitoring initiative from incidents alone. You have to interview the various stakeholders across the application life cycle to confirm your suspicions about the overall management capabilities, collect some testimony about their experiences and objectives, and gather their insights on what would make their activities more effective. This is a validation activity to follow up on the incident analysis.

Allow an hour for each stakeholder interview. This time, along with the identification of appropriate resources and scheduling of the interviews, is what takes the major portion of the overall assessment schedule. You need a good project manager to get this all set up. Simply identifying the correct candidates is likely to be difficult, so you need to allow for about a 20% "wrong candidate" rework. What kind of questions will you pursue to account for these sixty minutes of conversation? Whom do you select?

You want to target stakeholders for the applications identified through the App Survey. For these applications, you can expect to have the most knowledge but whatever the path to get this IT-centric information, you also want to have an independent path to validate the accuracy of the information as well as an opportunity to collect unexpected information about the application environment and processes surrounding it.

Organizations tend to take on the characteristics that are supported by their ongoing reporting processes, in much the same fashion as pet owners seem to take on characteristics of their chosen breed of animal. An organization that is very good with availability monitoring finds that performance monitoring is not very useful. Performance monitoring really does not improve on availability monitoring. It is a completely different paradigm and one that is complementary, if not wholly benign. This doesn't mean that AM teams are incapable of having different goals for monitoring; they just don't recognize its benefits. Interviewing for observations that are outside the current reporting is very useful to get the overall assessment.

So, while you have a couple of questions that establish the structure of the interview, you are really expecting to overload this interview activity so that you can draw out other information that may be useful in planning the initiative (also known as *extra findings*).

For example, in an architecture that is largely managed by service providers, getting alerts in a timely fashion can be difficult, especially when the practice is to generate incident and status reporting once per day. Usually there are not many opportunities to change, in terms of getting the alerts and status updates on a more frequent basis. When you move your focus to user experience—a typical APM goal—having timely information is critical to understanding how to respond to user performance issues. For this gap, I recommend that you negotiate with the service provider to share the alert, when it occurs, or at least update the Trouble Management database at hourly intervals. This results in some improvement with alerting notification. You get to the point you would normally expect to be, and with some understanding of the realities of service provider-centric alerting limitations, but you are not quite done with this example

During the course of stakeholder interviews for this same service provider-managed architecture, you learn that an appliance present in each customer-facing location is actually generating a real-time status of the communication link, and that this status is monitored by the business. This link also carries web application traffic for which no monitoring is currently available. The link status is almost immediately (1 to 3 minutes delay), communicated by the client to the network service provider who then investigates, confirms, and begins to restore service. The incident and status is reported by the service provider the next day to the IT teams, as usual. Instead of proposing to undertake negotiations with the service provider, as you would attempt at the close of the prior paragraph, you can simply suggest that the application owner simultaneously notify the Network Operations Center (NOC) when they advise the service provider. The NOC can then use this status to correlate with any end user service degradations—and performance monitoring begins in earnest!

These *extra findings*, those findings above and beyond what I expect for a typical stakeholder interview, occur in about 20-30% of the interviews that I have undertaken. This is consistent over a couple of dozen distinct assessments in the last four years, and something that I find very interesting. I am unaware of what to call this activity in any physiological or sociological sense but I think it is a form of social engineering.

Social engineering is today associated with the use of non-technology techniques to get people to reveal security information as part of a concerted attempt to break into computer systems and networks. There is nothing in your assessment system that is trying to do something bad, but the innocuous activity of asking questions about skills, processes, reporting, and training manages to reliably uncover all manner of information that is helpful in improving the accuracy of the current-state assessment as well as enhancing the goals for the monitoring initiative overall.

Summarizing the interviews into a consistent set of findings is challenging as the number of stakeholders increase. This is why you want to control the scope of the assessment in terms of number of applications and potential stakeholders. For an intermediate or mature monitoring organization, you will find a more narrow scope, so getting the findings digested is not difficult. For an immature monitoring organization, you will need to organize a detailed list of the findings and recommendations. This suggests that you present it as an alternate analysis process.

APM Roles

During the interview process, you have another agenda. In addition to information of the current skills, processes, reporting, and training, you also want to watch out for individuals who would serve as example candidates for some of the APM roles necessary to support the monitoring initiative. When you think you have such a candidate, take the opportunity to describe some of the activities for that APM role. Ask how they think their organization would respond to that assignment or if another group would be more appropriate.

If time permits, treat this like an informal interview. This does not mean that your candidate will have this APM role in the future, but you do want to get a sense of how well the current organization will respond to the demands of APM. You will need to advise the APM initiative sponsors if the appropriate skills and capabilities are available in the current staffing. You should not assume appropriate staff are available. You need names of real people.

Figure 3-12 is a quick summary of what the APM roles are. I will go into compete details of staffing and responsibilities for an APM initiative in the next chapter.

APM Role	Activity
APM Administrator	Agent installs, transaction recording, metrics storage administration
APM Project manager	Coordinate tactical service engagements, assessment activities, deployment planning, upgrades, vendor management
Application Specialist	Design of Application –specific dashboards and reporting, Alert integration strategy, Guidance for triage activities, Establish acceptance criteria, Supervision of efforts to extend agent visibility
Monitoring Architect	Monitoring tool identification and implementation, Monitoring Solution Planning and Sizing, Definition of QA testing procedures and reporting with APM, Definition of Acceptable QA performance characteristics, Definition of Key metrics, Dashboards and Reporting, Strategy to enhance visibility, Alert integration strategy
APM Specialist	Advance installation and configuration of APM, Triage activities, Advance integration and customization

Figure 3-12. APM roles and responsibilities

You should also make use of these roles to tailor an interview for each stakeholder. I put this in the filename, along with the application name and interview candidate, resulting in the following filename convention:

```
interview_APMrole_appName_candidate
```

This allows you to easily revisit the notes by application or by role to build up your impression. I have followed this convention in the artifacts available at apress.com so that you have a collection of interview templates to employ. I have tried periodically to tailor the questions to a particular role but have never been satisfied with that result. I have preserved the roles by incorporating them in the name of the interview document so that maybe you can take it a bit further. The broad topics, discussed next, have remained consistent. I depend on them to keep the interview on track.

Topics by Stakeholder

Figure 3-13 summarizes which topics you should lead with for specific stakeholder interviews. While larger organization will likely have someone for every role, smaller organizations may combine a few roles under a single individual. At a minimum, you need at least one application owner and one IT- related role for each application identified during the App Survey.

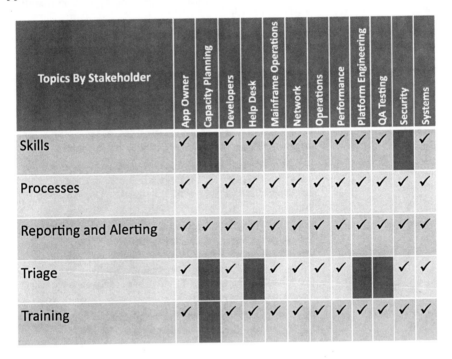

Topics By Stakeholder	App Owner	Capacity Planning	Developers	Help Desk	Mainframe Operations	Network	Operations	Performance	Platform Engineering	QA Testing	Security	Systems
Skills	✓		✓	✓	✓	✓	✓	✓	✓	✓		✓
Processes	✓	✓	✓	✓	✓	✓	✓	✓	✓	✓	✓	✓
Reporting and Alerting	✓	✓	✓	✓	✓	✓	✓	✓	✓	✓	✓	✓
Triage	✓		✓		✓	✓	✓	✓			✓	✓
Training	✓		✓	✓	✓	✓	✓	✓	✓	✓	✓	✓

Figure 3-13. Interview topics by stakeholder role

I have tried a few times to really align the interview with the stakeholder responsibilities, but I have not achieved anything more insightfull than simply leading with the current list of topics. Figure 3-13 confirms that the same list of questions is appropriate for every interview role, with just a few exceptions. You need only keep this idea in mind—not every topic is appropriate for every interview.

Reporting Dimensions

Reducing the raw interview data is a mostly mechanical process, provided you spoke with the right folks and were able to get them to open up about their activities and experiences. My preferred technique is to go back through the interviews after a day or two and highlight points of interest with red for bad and green for good. This allows me to later revisit the interviews by application or by stakeholder role.

If their background is appropriate, you should also indicate which APM role best aligns with their current capabilities and future interests. You want to be able to show management what kind of background is appropriate and if there are any folks who would be a model for the APM role. This is not an invitation to poach that employee but more to reassure management that the appropriate skill sets exist within the organization today. Of course, not finding anyone appropriate for any role is also an important measurement. Review *Figure 3-12. APM Roles and Responsibilities* for a refresh. Note that the next chapter is devoted to staffing and roles if you need more background.

As mentioned, I later go through the interview notes and use colors to indicate good, problematic, and questionable activities. To be honest, this is tedium, at best, but it makes it easy to revisit the interviews and quickly go through the notes for a particular application (all stakeholders) or a particular stakeholder role (all applications). This allows you to quickly get a grasp of what each view contributes to management maturity.

I then open up a presentation and record each of the significant findings along the following dimensions:

- Monitoring System
- Gaps and All-stars
- QA System
- Integration Opportunities
- Monitoring Team Responsibilities
- Support/HelpDesk System
- Change Control
- Training System
- Short-term Recommendations
- Medium-term Recommendations
- Long-term Recommendations

Cookbook

How to conduct and review the Stakeholder interviews:

1. Prepare a short message around the motivation and goals of the stakeholder interview and its contribution to the monitoring initiative.

2. Identify the stakeholders you will pursue for each application identified via the App Survey. A single stakeholder role for multiple applications is very desirable but not necessary.

3. Schedule each stakeholder for a one-hour meeting.

4. Record your notes directly into the interview worksheet. Save each worksheet with the stakeholder role, application, and name of the candidate. You can easily end up with 10 to 30 such interviews.

5. For each meeting, review the short message and confirm if the candidate has appropriate knowledge. If they disqualify themselves, they will often be able to identify a more suitable candidate for the interview. This will happen about in 10 to 20% of your interviews.

    a. Even if a candidate disqualifies himself or herself, get a better understanding of their role. Focus on they how they interact with change management or incident reporting. Sometimes you get candidates who are more aligned with governance than application monitoring, but it is useful to understand how they measure and control applications.

6. If the candidate is qualified, follow the appropriate topics and get some details about what their role is for the application(s), and what their experience is for incident management and the application lifecycle as a whole. The more the candidate is talking, the better information you will glean. Your job is to get the conversation rolling, keep it on track, and listen as much as possible. Take notes on any significant tools and processes employed.

7. Reflect on the APM roles. If the candidate is well informed regarding performance monitoring benefits, take the opportunity to introduce appropriate APM activities and ask how their organization (stakeholder role) would support them.

8. Review each interview and score it for management maturity and capabilities (process), monitoring and life cycle visibility, monitoring tools employed, and internal training processes.

Management Capabilities

For organizations that demonstrate a variety of management capabilities, it is useful to divide them among the major points of the application life cycle. This highlights gaps or inconsistencies in terms of achieving the full potential of APM.

A trap many organizations fall into is to limit APM technology to a single area of the overall application lifecycle. Typically this is the operation team's use of the technology. The operations team delivers monitoring for the enterprise. They see

APM as an excellent monitoring technology and develop very robust practices around it. Yet they are left wondering why that cannot become proactive in their management capabilities and actually affect the incident frequency that their organization experiences.

It should be obvious that using APM technology earlier in the application life cycle will help them to become proactive. The stakeholder does not see it as they focus on their own portion of the life cycle. The culture reinforces this rigid partitioning. You need to help expand their perspective. Figure 1-1, which was introduced as part of the reference architecture in Chapter 1, presents these gaps simply.

I use a modified version of the Management Capability chart (see Figure 1-1) to highlight the gaps in management capability along with desired capabilities. This is to address the reality, for some organizations, that even the concept of the application life cycle is foreign to them. In these cases, it helps to go back to the resource or application tier point of view, as illustrated in Figure 3-14.

	Gap	Reactive - Negotiated	Reactive - Alerting	Directed	Proactive
End User	I				
Network Infrastructure		I	D		
Web Tier			I		
Portal/App Server Tier			A		D
Resources		A	D		

I Incomplete Capability   D Desired Capability
A Acceptable Capability   S Satisfied

Figure 3-14. Summarizing management capabilities

This results in an operations-centric view of the application, but still lets you highlight obvious monitoring gaps and the absence of visibility preproduction. As you defined in the reference architecture, directed and proactive management require monitoring at pre-production. If you do not have any capabilities indicated by the Directed and Proactive columns, this implies there is no monitoring pre-production. This client is also limited in that the service provider is not making alert information readily available. This is what I call *reactive-negotiated:* there is alerting but you have to ask for it—you do not receive it automatically. I have yet to meet a stakeholder who is satisfied with this situation.

Cookbook

How to conduct and summarize an assessment of management capability during the stakeholder interview:

1. During the stakeholder interview, ask what alerting is available and what their process is to exploit that information.
2. Ensure that you interview stakeholders throughout the application life cycle.
3. Discuss what they would like to achieve with alerting and what they would use performance information for.
4. Discuss any technology that they believe would improve their situation.
5. Discuss any processes they believe would improve their situation.

End-to-End Visibility

Another summation exercise is to get details around the types of equipment that are deployed, end-to-end, that support the applications you have in your focus group. Often, one or more stakeholders can sketch out the technologies that are involved or they will have an architecture diagram that captures the details. Your goal is simply to condense this information down to a single slide, as shown in Figure 3-15.

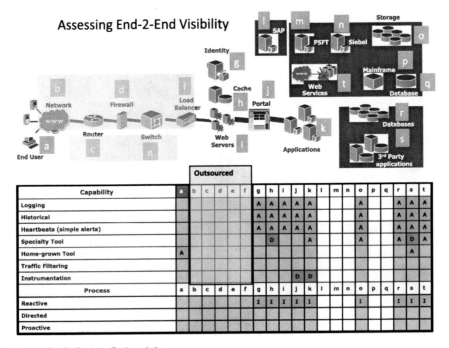

Capability	a	b	c	d	e	f	g	h	i	j	k	l	m	n	o	p	q	r	s	t
		Outsourced																		
Logging							A	A	A	A	A				A			A	A	A
Historical							A	A	A	A	A				A			A	A	A
Heartbeats (simple alerts)							A	A	A	A	A				A			A	A	A
Specialty Tool								D			A				A			A	D	A
Home-grown Tool	A																		A	
Traffic Filtering																				
Instrumentation									D	D										
Process	a	b	c	d	e	f	g	h	i	j	k	l	m	n	o	p	q	r	s	t
Reactive							I	I	I	I	I				I			I	I	I
Directed																				
Proactive																				

Figure 3-15. End-to-End visibility

What this does is allow you to easily summarize what visibility you have, where it is, and how effective it is in terms of the management capabilities.

As helpful as this graphic is, it is difficult to maintain from one assessment to another. I also use a spreadsheet-based model (see Figure 3-16), which is easier to update but lacks the graphical impact of the earlier model.

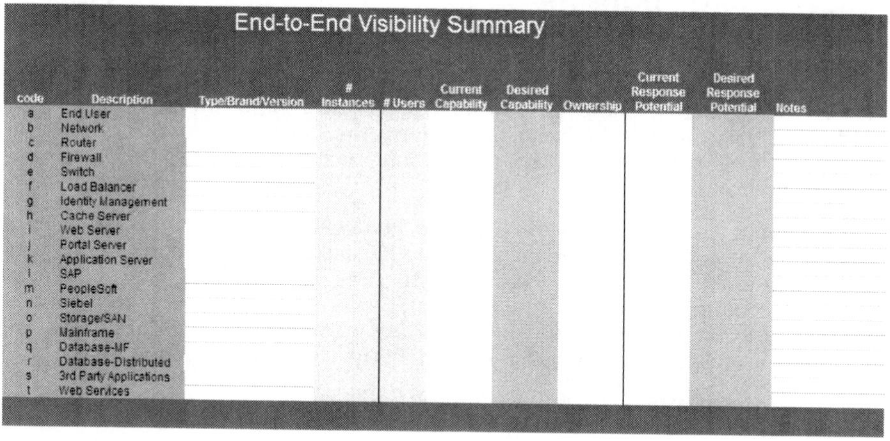

Figure 3-16. End-to-End visibility summary

In either case, you are trying to document what is available for monitoring and present it in such a way as to make the visibility gaps obvious and readily understood. This second form lets you capture detailed information and is more appropriate when you have an expectation of needing to refer to that information later. This is useful when the infrastructure is shared among multiple application teams so that everyone benefits from the effort.

Cookbook

How to conduct and summarize the End-to-End visibility during the stakeholder interview:

1. Interview appropriate stakeholders and identify what technology is in place, end-to-end.
2. Note what type of monitoring technology is employed, the management capability they are using, and what they would prefer in terms of tools or capabilities. You should also note who owns the resource so that you know who to negotiate with when monitoring is deployed for that component.
3. Summarize the visibility gaps of the current monitoring and contrast them with the visibility benefits of a future state.

4. (Optional) Repeat this visibility assessment for the QA environment, if that environment is attempting to match production. In your summary, report on the gaps and differences in the QA versus production environments.

Life Cycle Visibility

If you look at the assessment artifacts—and the visibility worksheet in particular—you will see that there are a number of drop-down lists. One of those is for the monitoring capability. However, you only present that end-to-end detail for the production environment. Sometimes you have the QA environment assessed for visibility as well. It becomes difficult to present such a volume of information for multiple environments.

To get visibility into the application life cycle, you need only summarize the types of monitoring capabilities that each stakeholder has available. You do not really need the full end-to-end details for each environment, as in Figure 3-16, simply because outside of production (and QA if appropriate), everyone is dealing with a smaller footprint of technology anyway. Understanding who has what tools allows you to hunt down useful practices as well as document the visibility gaps.

Figure 3-17 summarizes how to present these findings.

Visibility	Proto	Dev	QA-Func	QA-Perf	UAT	Prod
Generation or Simulation			A	A		
Platform				A	A	A
Synthetics					A	A
Metrics (APC)		A	A	A		
Transactions			D	D		D
Baselines						
Service Level						

APC : Availability, Performance, Capacity

Figure 3-17. Assessing lifecycle visibility

The color-coding legend for Figure 3-17 is the same as Figure 3-14. Notice that you have reduced all of the equipment details in favor of a summary of the technology employed (left-most column) for each environment (column headings) across the application lifecycle.

The technology levels are summarized as follows:

- **Generation or simulation**
  - Is load generation technology employed?
  - Manual load is not sufficient

- **Platform**
  - Are platform metrics collected?
  - Basic availability and capacity information: Is the platform up? Is there sufficient disk space?

- **Synthetics**
  - Are synthetic transactions employed?
  - Often used to confirm resource availability prior to a test.

- **Metrics (APC)**
  - Are availability, capacity and performance metrics available via any form of instrumentation (logs through BCI)?

- **Transactions**
  - Are specific transaction monitored?

- **Baselines**
  - Are baselines collected and maintained?
  - See Chapter 13 for details

- **Service Level**
  - Are SLAs confirmed and validated?

Cookbook

How to conduct and summarize lifecycle visibility during the stakeholder interview:

1. Interview appropriate stakeholders and identify what technology is in place for the environment that the stakeholder is responsible for.
2. Note what type of visibility is achieved and the names of the tools that yield this visibility.
3. Summarize the visibility gaps of the current monitoring system and contrast that with the visibility benefits of a future state. This is done by generating a chart for both current and future states.

Monitoring Tools

During the stakeholder interviews, ask about the types of monitoring tools employed. Many organizations are concerned with redundant tools and with overlapping capabilities, so a survey of tools and their effectiveness is useful. The real goal is to identify specialty tools and visibility gaps. Specialty tools are important because they already justify the usefulness of visibility beyond the traditional availability monitoring. They are often scripting-based solutions that are readily integrated with the trouble-management system but may also be stand-alone monitors with SMS and e-mail alerting.

Even load generation tools offer some performance monitoring capability, so you are interested in how testing teams use this information. You're also interested in any specialty tools that perform a HealthCheck of the test environment prior to the execution of a test plan. Anything that is repeatable has the potential for automation. Anything that you may automate is a good candidate for integration into the monitoring initiative.

Mgmt Capability \ LifeCycle Stage	Design Dev	QA-Func QA-Perf	UAT	Prod
Deep Dive	Profilers	Vendor-1 Vendor-2		
Reactive		Load Tools Systems Mgmt Specialty Tools	Systems Mgmt Specialty Tools	Systems Mgmt Specialty Tools
Directed				
Proactive				
Service-driven				

Monitoring Gaps across the Application Lifecycle

Figure 3-18. Assessing monitoring tools employed

Organize the findings in a spreadsheet, as illustrated in Figure 3-18. I have this one set up with a value list to help insure consistency in the tool description. I have generalized the values here but you can restore this list to include the specific vendor names, as appropriate.

As before, you can easily find out the current tools in use but you use the interview to confirm how useful they are and to learn about the overall state of affairs for the stakeholder.

Executive Summary

So far, you have seen a number of techniques to expose and organize details about the current monitoring capabilities. When you are ready to make your recommendations, you really need to distill this down to the essence. This means a diagram that summarizes the current state, along with some type of evolution to a future state.

Figure 1-8, back in Chapter 1, shows a streamlined overview with a summary but without the details of specific tools. I find it is crucial to present recommendations with as few slides as possible. Graphics are something that executives can lock onto and easily promote as the funding dicussions move up the management chain.

In order to show an evolution of capabilities along with the current state, simply shade each type of visibility that can be obtained, regardless of what technology is used for each stage of the initiative. Figure 3-19 is an eye-chart that summarizes what this can look like for a current state, followed by the benefits of each Good-Better-Best stage of monitoring improvement. (Normally, I would not put these all on one slide. It's done here only to save pages!)

Visibility	Current State			Visibility	Good	Better	Best
Transaction	Y Log	Y Synthetic	Real	Transaction	Log	Synthetic	Real
Application	Y Log	JMX/PMI	Instrumentation	Application	Log	JMX/PMI	Instrumentation
Platform	Y Availability Monitoring	JMX/PMI	Instrumentation	Platform	Availability Monitoring	JMX/PMI	Instrumentation
Network	Availability Monitoring	Y ppliance/Ho megrown	Packet Tracing	Network	Availability Monitoring	Appliance/Home grown	Packet Tracing
Visibility	Good	Better	Best	Visibility	Good	Better	Best
Transaction	Log	Synthetic	Real	Transaction	Log	Synthetic	Real
Application	Log	JMX/PMI	Instrumentation	Application	Log	JMX/PMI	Instrumentation
Platform	Availability Monitoring	JMX/PMI	Instrumentation	Platform	Availability Monitoring	JMX/PMI	Instrumentation
Network	Availability Monitoring	Appliance/Hom egrown	Packet Tracing	Network	Availability Monitoring	Appliance/Home grown	Packet Tracing

Sufficient	Gaps	Missing

Figure 3-19. Visibility summary for the monitoring initiative

The upper left quadrant is the current state with the gaps indicated with a "Y" in the box. You define a gap as minimum but insufficient capability. No additional shading means the technology is not used.

As the monitoring initiative unfolds, you get to score more visibility as shaded. You can use lighter shades to represent initial or limited use of a given technology. When you cannot use color, just add in a single letter. I find that most executive presentations use many colors. Of course, it's up to you to define the tasks and investments that will help evolve this initiative.

Cookbook

How to prepare an executive summary of the Monitoring Tool visibility:

1. Select the appropriate worksheet. Use Monitoring Tools if you have a large number of technologies. Use Visibility Summary if monitoring tool use is low.

2. During the stakeholder interviews, note the tools employed. Be sure to cover all aspects of the application lifecycle where metrics and other visibility are generated, even if tools are not currently used.

3. Also note what tools and technologies have been attempted but were not successfully employed and what the impediments where at that time.

4. Where tools or technology are employed to good effect, try to get samples of the reporting or analysis that they support. Ask how many people can use the tool/technology and how much effort was required to get it deployed and useful.

Detailed Findings (Alternate Technique)

Much of the prior assessment results are more appropriate for an executive summary. This will be the case for a small-scale assessment or for assessments within intermediate and mature monitoring implementations. There is simply less background and justification necessary to support the findings and recommendations. Everyone has the same vocabulary and level of understanding.

Sometimes you will need to provide more detail so that specific task lists and sub-initiatives can be derived. This is necessary because extensive process and organization changes are required in order to support the monitoring initiative. You're not just talking about empowering the monitoring team; you're talking about enhancing business practices across monitoring, support, testing, development, and operations. And you will probably be moving from a service provider-centric or out-source-monitoring role to an in-house model with either dedicated staffing or tactical consulting services. This means you have a lot to document and you need to introduce a kind of requirements tracibility into your monitoring strategy. You need to make sure that everyone understands your language and terminology, and exactly where every recommendation comes from and how it contributes to the overall initiative.

Instead of focusing on tools and technology—and their evolution, you get a finer level of detail by noting the capabilities and gaps with a number of dimensions, as summarized in Figure 3-20 .

Detailed Finding Dimension	Evolutionary Plateau
Alerting	Lifecycle Availability, Platform Metrics, LifeCycle Performance
Technology	Availability, Metrics (Platform, Log, Custom, Configuration), Synthetics, Real Transactions, Instrumentation
Reporting	Availability (Daily, Hourly), Synthetics (Hourly, 15 min), Real Transactions (15 min, 5 min), Instrumentation (5 min, 1 min)
Testing	Compliance, Functional, Automated Regression, SVP (Batch, Use case), Dedicated Testing Environment, Acceptance Criteria (Optional, Mandatory)
Support/Training	Best Effort, Run Book, Wiki, Shared Repository, Document Standards, Knowledge Base, Training Repository, Self-training and Certification
Change Control	Compliance, Requirements Tracking, Synthetics (Operations Validation, Environment HealthCheck), Performance Validation (QA, Operations),

Figure 3-20. Detailed findings dimensions

This is not intended to be a comprehensive list. This is simply what I have found useful in the last four years. I expect that other dimensions are possible.

Each of these dimensions has a corresponding set of capabilities that evolve as the supporting organization evolves. I have summaried these as *evolutionary plateaus,* as an organization may stay at one of these levels for a long time. It is not necessary that an organization follow this evolution strictly. This evolution is ideal. Real organizations tend to have competencies at various plateaus, which could be the result of merger and reorganization. I am not really interested in understanding how they got to their current state; I just need to document that state and then craft a set of recommendations that help them to fill in the gaps and increase the overall capabilities.

I have captured these dimensions in the assessment worksheet Ch 03 – Organization Maturity Worksheet (on apress.com). Please refer to it for the full details. I use the spreadsheet to document each input, referencing the application or stakeholder who mentioned it. This allows me to construct a graphic that summarizes the current state and the improvements, Good-Better-Best, that would apply as the recommendations are implemented. Figure 3-21 shows an example.

Alerting Evolution

	Service Provider Availability	Application Availability	Operations Availability	QA Availability	Platform Metrics	Operations Performance	QA Performance	Application Performance
Current	G G G	Y R R	R R R	R R R	R R R	R R R	G R R	R R R
Good	G G G	G G G	G	G	G			
Better	G G G	G G G	G G G	G G G	G G G	G G G	G	G
Best	G G G	G G G	G G G	G G G	G G G	G G G	G G	G

Note		Reference
1	Some apps have availability metrics in use by the App Owner, not shared with the NOC	App1, App2, App3
2	Sharing of Application Alerts, along with Service Provider Alerts, in the first integration point with the NOC. Trouble Management is the proposed tool.	recommendation
3	Acceptable alerting includes, phone/email, alert propogation, threshold (defined by NOC)	recommendation
4	A number of Perl scripts run every 30 minutes confirming resources.	App1, App2, App3
5	Synthetics with App1 limited to login/logout	App1

Figure 3-21. Interview summary alerting evolution

It is arbitrary how you assign the overal status. I use one to three cells along with red-yellow-green (here indicated as R-Y-G) to summarize the quality of a particular attribute. In fact, this is a similar approach to what was done with the skills assessment. You need only assign numbers corresponding to the cells and colors, and you end up with a numerical summary. I just have not had much reason to do this.

Nothing that you summarize here in the detailed findings is really any different from the conclusion you may reach from the earlier assessment artifacts. You just provide a lot more detail for the folks that pick up the assessment recommendations and have to implement them. A separate cookbook is not appropriate. Simply complete the stakeholder interviews, mark up those findings, and then go through each of the significant findings and assign them to the appropriate dimension. Make sure you have plenty of caffine available in whatever form suits you!

You will also notice that this layout is a little different that what was presented in Figure 1-4 in Chapter 1. The only difference is that the table of attributes has been rotated. This is to accommodate the detailed notes that are extracted from the stakeholder interviews.

The benefit in all of this analysis is that you get solid, referenceable findings upon which to weave your goals and recommendations. This is especially helpful if you divide up the interviews among a couple of analysts. You can collaborate and keep egos and opinions in check. Instead of saying "I believe that...", you can say "I found that..." It makes a big difference.

Solution Sizing

Solution sizing is a necessity with an APM initiative that is not a significant concern for the existing availability management. As discussed in the introduction, this is a major gap, and it limits the overall success and scope of your use of APM technology. This is an area where each vendor implementation introduces a number of vendor-specific parameters. These affect the number of appliances, servers, and workstations that comprise the APM solution. You cannot account for these directly (without compromising vendor neutrality) so you should focus on sizing for three general technologies: synthetic transactions, real transactions and byte-code instrumentation. All of the sizing worksheets are in the file Ch 03 - Assessments - Solution_Sizing.

The principles of sizing are straightforward: count the number of transactions or agents, account for the metrics or other attributes that they generate, and choose an appropriate configuration. You will provide some estimates but the Best way to get these details is with a pilot deployment. Not everyone will be in a position to pilot, so you will go with Good-Better, and rely on the App Survey to collect the basic info you need.

You will need to perform a slightly different sizing, depending on the varieties of APM technology that you are using. Please refer to the "APM Architecture" section of Chapter 1 for the major measurement points that you should consider here.

Synthetic Transactions

Each application has one or more transactions of interest, depending on the complexity of the resources attached to the application. Initially, you would focus on a login transaction, which would confirm availability of the application, firewall, and authentication management. For something better, you want at least one transaction for each resource that the application uses. Try to pick transactions that represent stable use-cases. Otherwise, you will need a definitions update process to follow the release change control, should an application change break the transaction definition. You should also be looking for reversible transactions or make provisions to link the activities to a synthetic user ID. The best measure is where there is an actual update/query to the resource. Otherwise, you are not getting true resource availability.

Yes, that is an annoying set of caveats but synthetics are an important capability of an APM system. They can measure availability more realistically than platform monitoring alone, and they are the perfect solution when there is little or no traffic on the environment. For health checks off-hours, such as confirming you are ready for business or confirming that all of the components are ready prior to starting a load test, synthetics have a solid job to do. Even if you know that real transaction monitoring is in your future, there is always a job for synthetics, even with their challenges.

■ **Note** An important goal in an initial deployment is to first go broad in terms of application coverage, and then follow up with a separate, deeper visibility in a successive deployment. More visibility means more metrics and greater initial capacity. How do you ensure you have adequate metrics capacity when your sizing skills are just being established? Sizing is an activity best performed incrementally so that the sizing forecast is validated by the actual deployment (or corrected, if there is disagreement). You can decrease the overall number of metrics by first implement availability alerting across many applications, limiting the performance and capacity monitoring onto the most critical applications. This builds in a buffer of metrics capacity by allowing a reserve of metrics storage in case of a sizing error. But you also get to validate the number of metrics that are needed to support performance and capacity alerting. You also need to validate the thresholds on those metrics, which takes some practice. Determining thresholds for availability is easy. Establishing performance and capacity thresholds takes a lot more work. Do not try to do it all in one shot. Please see the "Implementation" section for more details.

Often an application will be load balanced across multiple instances of web servers and application servers. Usually you can overlook that circumstance because you are testing for availability of the service, not each component of the underlying application infrastructure.

In addition to the availability metric, you will also get a response time metric. Both may generate an alert. In setting the threshold, you can begin with an arbitrary value, which is then tuned based on the operational experience.

The final parameter is the generator frequency, the interval at which synthetic transactions are generated for the synthetic transactions. If you are using synthetics to evaluate the application availability prior to the operational day, this will be a batch activity run once. If you are using it throughout the day, then plan to start with 30-minute intervals for medium to large environments, down to 5-minute intervals for small environments.

Synthetic Transaction Sizing

Application Name	# Transactions	# Instances	Interval s (min)	Availability Alert	Performance Alert	Total Synthetics Per Hour	Total Alerts
Portal	5	1	10	yes	yes	30	10
						Summary	30	10

Figure 3-22. Synthetic transaction sizing

Figure 3-22 summarizes the sizing data. Once the total transactions per hour and total alerts are calculated, you then need the details of your vendor's sizing constraints in order to figure out the number of servers (robots) required. The overall number and capacity of the servers is simply a function of how many synthetics need to be generated at each scheduled time. The technology will spread these out a bit, but when you are unable to get all the transactions generated for a given period, then you either need to increase the system speed or divide the activity over another server.

Real Transactions

Solution sizing for real transactions is a bit simpler. You do not have to worry about individual instances of the application, but you do need a good estimate of the potential transaction volume in terms of expected http requests per hour, for example. You also do not have to worry about the interval between transactions because you are going to see each and every one. It is important to appreciate that while you see all of the transaction traffic, you are only interested in a subset of that traffic. You have to insure that the subset of traffic is going to be an appropriate load on the vendor's technology.

As before, you want to first identify a few key transactions that indicate application availability and then go on to use cases that involve specific resources. Because of the larger number of transactions to measure, you can expect strong statistical information about the performance of the transactions, which will be mathematically built up over a short time (days to weeks). This eliminates the need to assign response time thresholds, as most solutions will create an alert when there is a significant deviation from normal. You will still need to assign priorities and alerting based on the application and the significance of the transaction with respect to the business goals.

Real Transaction Sizing

Transaction Volume (http requests per sec) 125
Transaction Volume (https requests per sec) 75

Business Domain	Total # of Business Transactions Enabled	# Business Transactions observed per hour	# User Groups per Hour	# Logins per Hour	# Unique Users in Database	# Expected Defects per Hour	Availability Alert	Performance Alert
Public Internet	600	150	5	1200	150000	0	yes	yes
Private Banking	100	50	1	75	10000	0		

Figure 3-23. Real transaction sizing

I do not show any sizing summary information here as the variety of vendor solutions have their own specifics for configuration and sizing needs. Figure 3-23, however, represents an example of the sizing parameters that are needed.

The upper constraint for real transactions sizing is an estimate of the size of the subset that will contribute to the monitoring. You may quickly exclude non-matching transactions and then have a bit more time to process the individual transactions that you're interested in. The precise capacity, in terms of the maximum percentage of transactions that can contribute to monitoring, will vary from vendor to vendor but it will never be anything close to 100% of the traffic.

Performance monitoring is a balancing act between visibility and overhead. The more visibility you strive for, the more realistic your performance measurements can be, but the less overhead you can tolerate (or you compromise the realism). Being selective about what you look at in terms of business or component transactions is the key to keeping the balance in your favor—and maintaining a real-time visibility with minimal overhead.

> **Note** If you are planning to add real transaction monitoring to your overall capabilities, do not get distracted by the larger amount of transactions that you can easily monitor. You primary goal is always to validate your monitoring—before you put the information in the hands of other users. Focus first on the transactions for which you have already defined synthetics so that you can directly compare with the real transaction visibility. This will demonstrate why your organization will still benefit from synthetics, help correct any problems with your thresholds, uncover any problems with your synthetics generating architecture, and even point out additional transactions that would benefit from having synthetics directed at them. Many applications you encounter in your monitoring efforts will not benefit from real transaction monitoring. A successful monitoring solution has to have a strong competency with synthetics.

Instrumentation

Instrumentation[12], getting measurements about a system, encompasses a variety of techniques that may be divided along two major approaches. *Invasive* techniques, such as logging, JMX, and ARM[13], require changes to the application code. Alternatively, *late-binding* techniques add instrumentation code at run-time but don't require any changes to the application code as is done with byte-code instrumentation and real transaction monitoring.

[12] Wikipedia, "wiki instrumentation," http://en.wikipedia.org/wiki/Instrumentation

[13] Wikipedia, "Application Response Measurement API," http://en.wikipedia.org/wiki/Application_Response_Measurement

Sizing for instrumentation, with the exception of logging, requires that you allow enough storage capacity to support all of the metrics that you expect to collect. I will present a technique to estimate the metrics impact that takes into account the different application types and the typical number of metrics they generate. For logging instrumentation, you really only need to confirm sufficient disk space to contain the logs. Logging itself can introduce significant overhead when it is used excessively because all of that disk activity can degrade overall I/O performance. If that is your situation, then please take additional steps to size the logging impact.

Bytecode Instrumentation (BCI) offers the deepest potential visibility and thus the greater consideration for sizing the total metrics capacity. It allows you to fill in all the details of the real transactions that you are monitoring when the application technology supports BCI. Currently, this is limited to applications built with Java Fortunately, a great deal of resource information is obtained simply by getting deep visibility into the components hosted on the application server and understanding their relationships with each other as well as the resources that they mediate.

What this means for the sizing effort is that you can generate an enormous spectrum of metric quantities from the instrumentation agent—potentially millions of metrics for a large-scale environment. Unlike platform monitoring, where every platform agent generates the same dozen metrics no matter what its role, each instrumentation agent can generate a completely different quantity of metrics depending on the complexity of software architecture and the resources employed by the each application.

To complete the instrumentation sizing, you need to account for each type of application you will encounter. You will get these details from the App Survey, including enough information to estimate the complexity of the application, along with a count of the number of instances that constitute the overall service.

I use a drop-down list and a lookup table of application types and metric quantities. An overview of the worksheet for a single environment is in Figure 3-24. Vendor implementations will vary a bit so please do not hesitate to modify my experiences with your own in terms of the number of metrics you see for different application complexities. As you will see later in the "Implementation" section, these application types will correspond with a number of gold configurations. These are agent configurations which extend the vendor default configuration in order to better align with the client application environment. It also gives you a very reliable deployment model once the gold configurations are establish and validated. You may easily select the agent configuration simply based on the details of the App Survey.

Environment/Domain	1 Prod						
Application Name	Complexity	Base Metrics	PMI/JMX	Web Service Complexity (this app)	#JVMs or app instances or # CLRs	Total	
Change Control	1 Servlet/JSP	200	300		2	1000	
Customer Portal	7 Portal	6000	300		8	50400	
Empty	1 Servlet/JSP	200	300		0		
Empty	1 Servlet/JSP	200	300		0		
Empty	1 Servlet/JSP	200	300		0		
Empty	1 Servlet/JSP	200	200		0		
Empty	1 Servlet/JSP	200	200		0		
Empty	1 Servlet/JSP	200	200		0		
Empty	1 Servlet/JSP	200	200		0		
Empty	1 Servlet/JSP	200	200		0		
					10		
						51,400	

Figure 3-24. Instrumentation sizing

You will notice in the example sizing that you make a separate allowance for PMI/JMX metrics as well as web service complexity. These metrics add another layer of variability in terms of the total metrics that may be experienced, which are actually determined largely by the software developer. Both JMX and PMI provide configuration information about the application server environment and may also be used by the developer to send additional information about the application. You will enable JMX or PMI metrics as part of the agent configuration but you will not really be sure of how many metrics they will generate until you exercise that agent. Technology such as PMI[14] is separately controlled via the Application Server Administration Console, such that you can control multiple levels of metric details. The result is that using this additional information can add a few hundred to many thousands of additional metrics.

You need to be methodical in your estimate of the number of metrics because you have to allocate sufficient storage and presentation capacity to support both historical and real-time views into the data. As before, each vendor will have different strategies for partitioning this metrics load but all of them will start from the total metrics and total agents that are expected.

Cookbook

How to conduct and forecast a solution sizing for APM:

1. Collect the basic sizing information via the CH03 - Assessments - App_Survey for each application. All spreadsheets are available at apress.com.

---

[14] The PMI interface is being deprecated in favor of JMX. IBM, "PMI client interface (deprecated)," http://publib.boulder.ibm.com/infocenter/wasinfo/v7r0/index.jsp?topic=/com.ibm.websphere.express.doc/info/exp/ae/rprf_implementpmiclient.html

2. Make an entry for each application in the sizing spreadsheet for the technology you are employing, via CH03 - Assessments - Solution_Sizing
3. Verify the overall sizing quantities.
4. Divide the overall quantities by the vendor guidelines for each technology.
5. If appropriate, extrapolate the sizing over three years to account for deployment growth using multiples of the initial sizing. If exact application counts are not available, assume deployments of 10%, 30%, and 60% (corresponding to each year), with a total of 100% at the end of year three.

Summarizing Your Findings and Recommendations

Whatever selection of assessment activities you pursue, you will need to get all of this in a form for presentation and review by the sponsoring parties. In my experience, you will never have all the time you would like to analyze and prepare. So begin with the end in mind and use a presentation format, starting with the overall plan. Use this to collect your summary findings and recommendations as they become available. No matter where you are in the assessment execution, you should always be ready to present something to communicate what you are finding. After all, an assessment is simply a structured form of communication. Be ready to communicate.

If your sponsors desire a written report, simply add notes to all of the slides. I prefer a presentation format because it ensures that you break topics down appropriately for your stakeholders. If you can not fit it on the page and still be able to read it, then you know that you have not concisely addressed the topic.

Cookbook

How to prepare a summary report of the assessment activities, findings, and recommendations:

1. Open a fresh presentation and resolve to do nothing that cannot be in electronic form! ;-)
2. Determine the candidate applications. These are key applications that will likely benefit from APM technology but may also include core applications that are well managed and thus are opportunities to uncover and document successful practices—even if APM will not be a direct benefit.
3. Determine the overall objective for the monitoring initiative. Please refer to Chapter 2 if you need to review the common initiative themes.
4. Request one to three months of operational incidents. These should be high-severity server incidents (SEV-1, SEV-2). Analyze these incidents following the Incident Analysis cookbook in this chapter.

5. Identify stakeholders across the application lifecycle for each of the candidate applications. If there is shared infrastructure, then it is not necessary to interview multiple stakeholders for that role. Schedule a one hour interview with each stakeholder. Try to get these face-to-face until you have polished you interview technique. Thereafter, you can use a conference call. If you have a number of remote stakeholders, then do all of the face-to-face interviews first.

6. Update your presentation with the schedule of stakeholder interviews and projected availability of the incident analysis. If you are achieving 10 to 15 interviews per week, that is an excellent pace. But it is also very ambitious. Make sure you communicate a realistic schedule.

7. Follow the Stakeholder Interview cookbook in this chapter. Expect some cancellations and reschedules along with some no-shows.

8. In parallel with the stakeholder interviews, post-process the interview artifacts to highlight the useful findings and comments.

9. In parallel with the stakeholder interviews and depending on the number of target applications and unique stakeholders, select an appropriate summary format to capture the assessment findings for management capability, end-to-end visibility, and lifecycle visibility.

10. In parallel with the stakeholder interviews, review the post-processed artifacts and summarize your findings and recommendations in the presentation.

11. In parallel with the stakeholder interviews, and as your findings and recommendations evolve, try to get some feedback on these plans during the interviews.

12. Schedule a meeting with your sponsors when you are in the last week of your stakeholder interview schedule. This puts a bit of pressure on you to bring everything together. I find that a little pressure helps to keep me ahead of schedule. You want to allow for an iteration or two during the findings, just in case you hit a nerve and need to soften a recommendation. You have to constrain your recommendations along the original goals for the initiative if you are to have any support from your sponsors. This does not mean you have to agree with them. Just do not stray from the original scope of the assessment.

13. Assemble all of the assessment artifacts into a compressed archive and back them up!

14. Summarize the assessment as a presentation and cover the following agenda:

   a. State the goals for the assessment.
   b. Describe the assessment process and schedule.
   c. Describe how the candidate applications were selected.
   d. Discuss any advantages or liabilities in that selection.
   e. Review the incident analysis findings.
   f. Present your findings for the current state of the monitoring organization/initiative. What are the significant skills, processes, and competencies available to support the monitoring initiative?
      i. Review overall management capabilities.
      ii. Review end-to-end visibility.
      iii. Review lifecycle visibility.
      iv. Review tools and technology available.
      v. For the detailed finding dimensions, comment on processes that should be emulated and processes that should be avoided.

   g. Present your recommendations as to how they may achieve the monitoring initiative goals, following the precepts of Good-Better-Best. Use appropriate graphics to describe the capability evolution gained as the different recommendations are implemented.
   h. Summarize your overall recommendations in terms of major funding initiatives.
   i. Identify and review the next steps to keep the initiative on track.

15. Review your presentation for consistency of delivery and try it out on your peers. Tune as necessary.

16. Whatever length presentation you produce in the previous steps, find a way to shrink it down to under 30 slides. If you can get one hour with the executive sponsors, this will allow for 45 minutes of delivery and 15 minutes of discussion. The shorter, the better.

17. If the assessment recommendations are well accepted, you will then have an opportunity to present the findings to senior management. You will need to further shrink the presentation down to 10 to 15 slides, as you will only have 30 minutes. Getting down to five slides is not unreasonable for an existing monitoring system, as most senior executives will only allow 15 minutes for the presentation and 15 minutes (or less) for discussion. If it is a recommendation that will affect multiple groups, you are justified in pushing for 20-25 minutes of presentation. Otherwise, get it down to five slides. Assessments are lonely, hard work. Your first instinct will be to show all that you accomplished. Instead, you have to really get to the essence of what the organization needs to do in order to realize their goals. This is just the first gate. You still have a lot to do.

Conclusion

To measure is to know. Assessments are how you document the terrain and articulate a plan that will get you reliably to the goal. A well-executed assessment is a snapshot of the current state and the rationale on how to move forward. It is very hard to ignore or set aside because it is a measure of the timeliness of an opportunity—and nobody wants to be a signpost of how to miss an opportunity or to make an attempt prematurely.

The measure of intelligence in man is the ability to keep two (or more) competing ideas in mind at one time[15]. For an APM initiative, the choice is to go forward or to defer. If you can keep these two conclusions in mind right up to the final recommendation, then you can be confident of having done a thorough assessment. You do not simply assess enough to support a desire to go forward with an initiative. You assess until you can support and defend your recommendation without reservation.

The App Survey is a Good tool to gather basic information and set the stage for sizing and validation. The stakeholder interview is Better as it allows consistent communication about the goals of the monitoring initiative, and it lets you build consensus about what APM needs to achieve to be meaningful for the organization. As time and energy allow, you can continue to push for better and more detailed information, documenting component relationships, and making the first measurements about the kinds of visibility APM can bring to the organization.

You want to do enough validation through assessments as is necessary to go confidently forward. You cannot dwell here, constantly checking the map and your orientation. You need to get back on the road and continue the journey.

---

[15] "The test of a first-rate intelligence is the ability to hold two opposed ideas in mind at the same time and still retain the ability to function." —F. Scott Fitzgerald

Staffing and Responsibilities

Always two there are. A master . . . and an apprentice.

—Frank Oz (as Yoda)

Monitoring of the IT infrastructure has been a familiar capability ever since the 1960s, when that first programmer sought to see if the soda machine was empty without having to take that long walk down the hall. Any measurement results in a metric indicating some quantity. In this case, the number of a particular soda remaining. An agent makes the measurement and uses a communication protocol to transfer the metric (count of soda remaining) so that someone may evaluate and make a decision. Hence, the Simple Network Management Protocol (SNMP) was born. Now 50 years later, the basic idea remains the same. In order to support business decisions in APM you need to get metrics about capacity and performance. You need to deploy an agent[1].

The problem with this simple model (deploy agent, get metrics) is that initially, the number of metrics were few and the variety of measurements limited to availability (up, down) and other slow-changing platform characteristics (CPU, disk space, temperature). Application and transaction monitoring changed the game, and offer thousands of metrics where only a dozen were available before, and have the potential to present these metrics every minute, instead of at the 15- to 20-minute reporting intervals that SNMP is capable of. This increase in the quantity and frequency of metrics allows monitoring to extend its reach into all aspects of the application life cycle—not just infrastructure monitoring. It isn't simple monitoring any more—it's visibility into the relationships of individual components and transactions comprising the application. It is brain waves, not just heartbeats.

---

[1] An agent today can mean any variety of processes and technologies that undertake measurements and deliver metrics. See http://en.wikipedia.org/wiki/Software_agent for more examples.

When you have a handful of applications, all this capability is almost transparent. You can use it, or you can ignore it and just treat it as if it were SNMP-like. It doesn't matter, because your handful of applications fits neatly within the capacity of a single metrics storage server. You don't have to worry about tuning the number of metrics that your agents generate. You don't even have to think about running out of capacity because your view of the future of your applications is pretty much static.

If instead you had dozens of applications, you would find that you were throwing around millions of metrics every 60 seconds, with half a dozen metrics storage servers—big iron[2] for sure!

How do you evolve from a single metrics storage server to millions of metrics? How do you account for the costs of that big iron? How did these other applications end up on your APM storage manager anyway? How do you manage this eventuality? Who will take care of this new monitoring infrastructure? Who will use APM information to solve performance problems?

These questions need skilled staff to evaluate and address. Where do these people come from? How many do you need? Don't you already have these skill sets today? What kinds of new skill sets will you need?

The Staffing Question

Staffing is a difficult topic; for an APM initiative, it's just tough to get around. Either you have no concept of a staffing gap or you are overly concerned that significant staffing will be required—or somewhere in between. The assessment results are your guide to reality, in terms of what your team can absorb and deliver independently. From those recommendations, we are left with four approaches to consider:

- The full-time equivalent (FTE) approach
- The staff evolution approach
- The staff augmentation approach
- The turnkey approach

The turnkey[3] approach is simply to bring a third party in to complete all of the deployment and operate the resulting APM solution on your behalf. This is a perfectly valid business model but one that has yet to emerge in the industry in support of APM. Nothing more can be said except that you will be the first adopter, if this is your strategy.

Irrespective of what you are considering for the realization of the APM initiative, someone has to be responsible for the various APM-related roles, which I will define shortly. This is the trap that many organizations step into, in that they do not address the new roles, and thus end up with a fully functional deployment that no one knows how to use or maintain. It is directly related to the availability monitoring (AM) experience, which does not have these staffing/role considerations, and so results in a poor scope for the APM initiative.

---

[2] http://en.wikipedia.org/wiki/Big_iron

[3] http://en.wikipedia.org/wiki/Turnkey

The level of monitoring maturity also is a significant factor in properly staffing an APM initiative. The less mature a monitoring system, the more work needed to bring the environment under effective management. This can result in a staffing surge, involving combinations of the staffing models that will need to be reduced about one to two years later.

The single challenge for all of the staffing models presented is that monitoring a single application or a small group of applications is not a full-time job. While there are monitoring activities resulting from the management processes, across the application life cycle, they have a very short workload compared with the activities that they support. For example, reviewing data and generating an audit report takes about four hours. Conducting the load tests that generate that data will take one to two weeks.

These short-duration APM activities make small monitoring efforts difficult to staff consistently because the personnel with appropriate skills are off on other projects. Eventually, when the APM initiative reaches about a dozen applications under management, pressure on staffing will lead naturally to a shared monitoring service. For small efforts, without the benefit of a shared service, it becomes necessary to combine the various monitoring roles, which are always needed, into a role for a single individual, in order to make effective use of that staff assignment. But this is a very dangerous scenario. With all of the monitoring experience focused on a single individual, the initiative can easily fail with any variety of staff turnover. And so the inspiration to pinch a quote from Master Yoda, to crystallize the theme for this chapter: you really need to have two individuals sharing the APM role, even for a small APM initiative.

Staffing is a surprisingly sophisticated topic, depending on your corporate culture. This makes it easy to overlook; failure to address it successfully will cripple a large number of APM initiatives. It also highlights the major theme of this book: that technology alone cannot address the organizational processes that have to evolve in order to get the best possible value from the APM initiative. Developing a rapid-response, demand-driven APM staffing model that is incremental and self-sustaining is a broad objective. It is absolutely achievable. I will show you exactly how. I will also show you how to do it with traditional planning.

Who Has Responsibility for Monitoring?

Depending on how your organization is beginning with APM, your answers to this question will reflect your immediate scope and motivation—why are you trying to employ APM? If your scope is only a single application, you will have a set of objectives that are very specific to your team and likely not shared across your enterprise. These immediate goals most likely will not involve a lot of different processes or standards, and you will probably be completely responsible for your own staffing and education issues. In this case, you have a *project focus*.

If your goals are shared across the enterprise, the scope of the undertaking may be very different because there may be a number of existing processes and standards to navigate. Multiple application teams may be participating with very specific sets of roles and responsibilities. This results in a *program focus*.

Your situation may in fact be somewhere in between these two extremes. Figure 4-1 summarizes some of the typical entry points and the situation existing at each point.

You can see that the motivations—what is driving you to undertake an APM initiative—will actually be quite different, depending on the entry point.

Stakeholder	Motivation	Existing Skills	Existing Process	Monitoring Maturity
Developer-centric	•Deep visibility •Profiler-like	•Profilers •Complex configuration mgmt	•Private •Single application focus	•More problem analysis than monitoring •No formal monitoring
Platform Engineering	•Tools upgrade •Standards	•Packaging and distribution Tech savvy	•Revision mgmt •Deployment •Tech analysis	•More specification and standards than actual monitoring
Operations	•Need more than Availability monitoring	•Manage dozens of different technologies •Alert mgmt	•Trouble-ticket •Bridge-call •Release Mgmt	•Solid Availability mgmt and traditional capacity planning
Line of Business	•Reduce severity incidents •Improve performance	•Performance trends and forecast •Early tech adopter	•Application design •Requirements definition •Performance analysis	•Manage KPIs and have limited visibility into platform performance
Stress & Performance	•Need more than functional test •Pre-prod triage	•Rapid monitoring assessment •End to end savvy	•Release control •Regression test •Complex problem resolution	•Multiple tools employed but with limited historical responsibility

Figure 4-1. Monitoring Initiative Entry Points—Stakeholders

Where in the process you enter into a monitoring initiative is not as important as understanding what the APM technology will serve to improve. Your goal is to both meet those expectations and manage users toward a consistent use of APM tools that experience shows to be successful. Otherwise, the initiative will be limited to the goals of the stakeholder who acquires the technology, even if other stakeholders had planned to take advantage of it.

APM technology and instrumentation in particular, can provide a very sophisticated tool for its users. However, while easy to use once implemented, it can be difficult to employ successfully without appropriate processes and an understanding of how the tool will be employed by different stakeholders across the application life cycle. Figure 4-1 summarizes how these motivations and skill sets are different for each category of stakeholder.

If we look to the executive management instead of the stakeholders for leading a monitoring initiative, we obtain a quite different set of expectations and personnel capabilities, as summarized in Figure 4-2.

Business Need	Motivation	Existing Skills	Existing Process	Monitoring Maturity
Competitive Upgrade or Replace	•Need better visibility and lower overhead •Not successful with earlier tool	•Anything from Bad to Great – depending on the experience with the incumbent tool	•From Bad to Good but may also not have been able to scale usage of the incumbent tool	•From Bad to Great, depending on success with other tools
Strategic Initiative	•Service-mgmt initiative •Quality evolution initiative	•One or more successful, or on-going solution rollouts	•Well-defined processes	•Well-established •Reactive Management – ready for more

Figure 4-2. Monitoring Initiative Entry Points—Business Needs

The APM Expert

In today's modern IT organization, there is simply no one person who has direct responsibility for maintaining and coordinating APM. Individual groups may undertake to employ the technology, but there is no one responsible to implement, operate, and assist the various stakeholders in employing the APM information consistently. This monitoring role is instead fragmented across multiple stakeholders in the application life cycle, with little or no coordination, and certainly no single person or organizational entity responsible for "performance monitoring." This is due in part to our thesis, "monitoring is not a full-time job," as well as the organizational reality that there is no traditional job title for "monitoring expert," as there is for database administrator or capacity planner. Figure 4-3 summarizes who might be considered the "monitoring expert" at different points of the typical application life cycle.

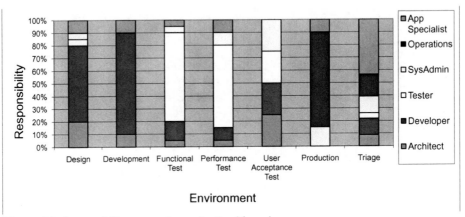

Figure 4-3. Responsibility across the application life cycle

Thus, we find that our "monitoring expert" is a developer/QA tester/operations/ application specialist. We know that no single individual, in a traditional organization of size, can undertake all of those responsibilities, so you might be inclined to conclude that a new role is needed—the "monitoring specialist"—but that would be premature.

The problem in defining such a monitoring expert role is that most IT organizations cannot accommodate an individual that spans all of these environments across the application life cycle. At minimum, development, testing, and operations are all separate from one another—they're very often silos of activity with their own goals, cost centers, and so on. This organizational impediment, maintaining and enforcing multiple silos of expertise, is what we later attack via collaboration across the application life cycle.

More significantly, the actual instrumentation activities that the APM tool is employed for, or configured as, will vary across the application life cycle as well. We not only need to account for the organizational resistance to a shared role, we have to account for the widely different perceptions of what that role should entail. Figure 4-4 shows the primary activities for APM technology and the proportion of time each is emphasized at each environment of the application life cycle.

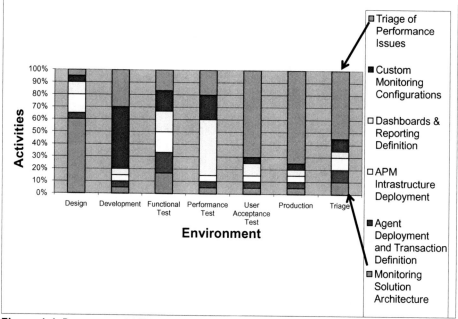

Figure 4-4. Percentage of APM activities in the application life cycle

The order of activities, established in the legend on the right-hand side in Figure 4-4, is the same for each environment. All activities are present at each environment. Only the percentage of each activity varies among the different environments. So, in the design environment, monitoring solution architecture is the dominant activity. Outside of the design environment, triage takes on a greater percentage of activities in the remaining environments, as the APM solution has increasing utility as the monitored application becomes functional. I define *triage* as using the APM technology and processes to get visibility into urgent or apparent strategy, performance, and stability problems. I also treat triage as a separate environment and characteristic of an application. You have to establish a number of tools, processes, and capabilities to undertake triage in any environment. So it only makes sense to establish an environment for triage and to manage and evolve the capabilities in that environment.

Some level of triage is needed in all environments of the application life cycle—it is a tenet of general problem solving: do you have visibility into the problem? That question is what triage answers after indentifying (or excluding) suspect components.

At QA/functional test, all of the activities are needed in approximately equal proportions. QA/functional test is really the first point where the entire application, packaging requirements, and deployment processes come together. It is the first validation of the design and the first clue that things are going well, or poorly, for the release schedule.

At this point you might be considering adding a responsibility for triage or hiring a person for this role. While that idea appears reasonable, the problem you will encounter is in having enough work for this triage specialist to remain active. You already know that problems will not appear on your schedule. They happen in their own time, and you will very often go for weeks or months without significant problems. What is that specialist supposed to do with their time?

The strategy I employ is to designate a shared pool of APM resources who are used for their functional role as needed, and then returned to the pool when that task is completed. This model is a significant departure from conventional IT project staffing where a team is assembled to deploy a new application and then remains with that application for years to follow.

When we get to Chapter 5 we will look at the services this APM practice is providing, when we examine the service catalog for APM, and how we evolve the capabilities and offerings of this catalog in an incremental fashion. For now, let's move on to definitions of the various roles that support an APM initiative.

Roles and Responsibilities

In this section we present details about how to partition the responsibilities and activities necessary to support APM into meaningful APM roles and also a key consumer of APM: the application specialist. It is not uncommon, especially for smaller organizations, for all of these roles to be condensed onto a single individual. This is not a resilient or scalable model, but it is completely realizable for an individual with the right background and temperament. But it is an economic choice and risk to concentrate all of the APM expertise onto a single individual. Inasmuch as performance monitoring is a great advantage to the business overall, a small company can lose its APM system overnight and remain in business the next day.

A larger company has a bit more at stake simply because the performance and availability of their software-based services are likely critical to the profitability of the enterprise. The company may have negotiated specific performance agreements and guarantees that, if performance suffers, exceptional penalties will result. Or it may have begun to realize that software quality is really what keeps the business growing, and performance monitoring helps it to better manage that critical application life cycle. Whatever the motivation, larger enterprises need to ensure that a return on APM investment is achieved. Whether this is license costs, training costs, personnel costs, or opportunity costs, the IT organization has a responsibility to ensure that the same investments are not made twice. Proper staffing is how a large organization maintains continuity of operations, expertise, and management of the costs of the APM initiative.

Much of what we are trying to illustrate with these roles is the division of responsibility that *most* organizations will identify as desirable end states for the APM initiative.

Once you have an appreciation for how to divide the responsibility for an APM initiative, and while making some allowances for overlap and redundancy, you will be in a better position to appreciate how to evolve those roles from your existing staff, as I will detail later in this chapter.

APM Administrator

This role deploys and configures the APM technology for each of the monitored applications. This includes agent configuration and defining transactions for both real and synthetic APM transaction monitoring components. For agents, a small modification in the startup script for the application server, which is hosting the application, is necessary to complete the APM configuration. Usually a systems administrator or web administrator can accomplish this task with minimal additional training. The transaction definition will usually be accomplished via a GUI, but an understanding of the business domain is helpful to improve communication with the business analyst while deciding which transaction is to be monitored.

The APM administrator may have a second function, or a separate role altogether, and would be focused on administration of the metrics storage, or other APM infrastructure components, such as the servers hosting the synthetics or appliances doing the real transaction monitoring. Many companies divide administrator roles between applications and platforms. Anything that is administered as a physical computing platform is handled via platform engineering. This includes the hardware platform and the operating system. Anything application-related is handled by web engineering. This includes installing and configuring databases, application servers, and other resources, as well as deploying the application code. An APM administrator can easily accomplish both responsibilities, so we only make this distinction to accommodate the existing organizational structure.

As the APM administrator role is closely aligned with the existing skills sets of your traditional systems administrators (sysadmins), repurposing these sysadmins is the first step to avoiding the unnecessary addition of staff. All you need to achieve this is a "cookbook" of instructions for how to define transactions and install agents, with a review of typical error messages and remedies. Figure 4-5 summarizes their responsibilities.

ACTIVITY	Tasks
Server configuration and operation	•Everything necessary to get a computing platform installed and provisioned.
Software deployment and configuration	•Installation of the application server •Deployment of the application code
Updates and upgrades	•Follow change control practices •Perform updates to the APM infrastructure
Other responsibilities	•Deploy APM monitoring (define transactions, configure agent) •Deploy APM infrastructure components and APM workstations.

Full details of the tasks are in the Chapter 4 artifacts on apress.com

Figure 4-5. APM Administrator Activities

The gap that will trip you up is assuming the sysadmins will simply read the APM product documentation and decide what should be in these APM cookbooks. Somebody needs to establish that document and validate that other sysadmins can reliably employ it. Someone needs to own the APM strategy, schedule, and goals—and it is not the system administrator. I will introduce some candidates for this responsibility shortly.

You should also notice that we do not expect to have this APM administrator doing triage or supervising load testing. Of course, I have seen many clients who immediately overload this administrator role with those of triage, deployment planning, report design, and so on. It is not that the individuals lack talent or skills—it is often the case that the client organization adds these new APM responsibilities on top of their existing responsibilities. This invariably results in the familiar tasks having a higher priority than the APM tasks—and the initiative stalls.

This is easily solved. An immediate benefit of APM is that it installs very quickly and is easy to use, once you know what to do (once you have the cookbooks). With appropriate processes, you can make the extra APM tasks very efficient and predictable. So what remains is to do a little priority inversion and make the APM tasks the highest priority, so that they are never deferred or overlooked. This simply means that any APM activity is immediately addressed, while the current task moves to the background. APM is job number one. APM activities are often of very short duration, and the interruption to the traditional tasks is therefore minimal. Since we accept that APM monitoring is not a full-time job (for a single application), there will be infrequent but acceptably short delays of the traditional tasks in order to keep the APM initiative moving forward. The end result is that by avoiding any delays in configuration or interpreting APM, stakeholders get the benefits without frustration and delay—and the APM initiative moves forward. Otherwise, trivial APM activities get delayed for days and weeks, and as frustration grows, interest dissipates and the initiative stalls.

APM Project Manager

This role is often completely overlooked, and this can be a terrible gap for a large organization in its use of APM. This is evident when you need to coordinate with third-party-services delivery, which often requires a project manager (PM) role. And if you are feeling frustrated that any additional APM roles are actually needed, then this is the one role that will ensure you longer-term success. If you already know that additional staff, or even repurposing of staff, is going to be unacceptable, then at minimum you need to have someone in a position to coordinate the APM activities. Figure 4-6 summarizes the activities that an APM PM will coordinate.

ACTIVITY	Tasks
Coordinate of tactical services engagements	•Work with 3rd parties to complete specific APM tasks, when they are needed.
Deployment planning	•Plan, schedule and track he APM infrastructure deployment, QA testing and validation, production deployment of APM monitoring configurations and review of operational experiences.
Maintain the plan of record	•Document the requirements, exceptions, outstanding deliverables, incidents and remediation
Review incidents related to APM tools	•Document incidents by application, environment (prod, QA, etc.) and resolution
Other responsibilities	•Manage any skills and visibility assessments (Chapter 3) •Coordinate QA testing, dashboard and report design, and alert definition. •Coordinate resolution of critical performance incidents

Full details of the tasks are in the Chapter 4 artifacts on apress.com

Figure 4-6. APM Project Manager Activities

When you are unable to address the APM staffing question confidently by directly supporting the various roles, the APM PM role is really the best way for you to ensure that you get the benefits of APM while still having direct control over the pace and scope of deployment. Any PM can do these tasks. You simply have to get them trained on what they need to do to properly support an APM initiative. Part 2 of this book, begins with what the PM needs to understand. I'm not sure that this book alone will get the PM capable, but with one to two weeks of education and mentoring, the PM can be a powerful ally in getting APM moving.

Many folks have narrowly focused on deployment as their sole goal for APM, and have not availed themselves of the PM resources that are at the ready to help them do exactly that. Managing projects is what they are skilled at, and thus they will be much more attentive than many other IT professionals that might be available. Again, it is the relative ease with which APM may be deployed that can cause a stakeholder to think that the PM is unnecessary, especially when they do not have an appropriate scope for the APM initiative.

Application Specialist

This role is really where we want strong triage and interpretative skills—with the folks who absolutely know the most about the application. We have to balance that with the fact that they already have multiple responsibilities, and one more might be too much. So this role is not so much APM-specific as it is completely dependent on the other APM roles in order to be effective in exploiting the APM visibility. The application specialist wants to use the APM visibility to manage their application. They need the APM roles to set up and maintain the APM environment, and provide some expert guidance as needed. Figure 4-7 summarizes what we expect them to do.

ACTIVITY	Tasks
Software development lifecycle	•Interface with each stakeholders in the application lifecycle.
Business and IT metrics	•Definition of KPIs and metrics assignment among available monitoring technologies, review Platform metrics.
Time-to-market strategies	•Prepare contingency process for remediation of performance incidents, pre- and post-production
Other responsibilities	•Design of application–specific dashboards and reporting •Design alert integration strategy •Supervision of efforts to extend APM visibility.

Full details of the tasks are in the Chapter 4 artifacts on apress.com

Figure 4-7. Application Specialist Activities

You should notice that a person in this role is not undertaking an actual deployment or configuration of APM technology. The application specialist also does not need to worry about sizing the metrics storage or other monitoring capacity responsibilities. They do have the responsibility of defining the dashboards and reporting, though. This is not difficult, and the specialist is the best person to know what those dashboards and reports need to show, to be useful for the business, even if someone else completes the implementation.

These tasks, listed in Figure 4-7, are a reasonable addition to a traditional specialist role. The application specialist does not have responsibility for the APM initiative. The only expectation is that they exploit APM technology as part of their existing role. You will need to do some mentoring to get them up to speed with APM technology and capabilities. However, this shouldn't be a problem since you will already have the APM administrator and PM to get the necessary monitoring configurations deployed and to establish appropriate processes.

For most situations, we now have enough of APM covered to be successful. Everything is deployed and we have a number of individuals that know how to use the tools correctly. The last gap is in identifying to whom the application specialist turns for help with standards, advanced integrations, and exceptionally hairy performance problems: the APM architect.

APM Architect

Part of the guidance the app specialist needs will come from an APM architect. This is an architect who really understands the use of APM across the life cycle, and is also prepared to deal with different integration needs, as well as overall organizational standards. We will also merge in a bit of the capacity planning role to ensure that the APM infrastructure is well positioned for growth.

We could leverage an existing capacity planning role, but this decision will be highly dependent on the organizational culture, if they will embrace the new responsibilities. Take a look at the responsibilities in Figure 4-8 and see who among your current staff would be most appropriate.

Activity	Tasks
Estimating app complexity	•Assessing client-server solution architectures , application design strategies
Determining appropriate monitoring technology	•Assessing application value, visibility and overhead, monitoring tools and strategies
Assessing end-to-end environment	•Define solution quality acceptance criteria, risk analysis in deploying unstable or untested releases ,contingency for remediation of performance incidents, pre- and post-production
Alert integration and goals	•Defining which alerts are propagated, ensuring there is an appropriate response to the alert
Forecasting APM performance and capacity utilization	•Review performance and capacity reports, review utility and suitability of upgrade opportunities, Schedule hardware and software upgrades
Solution sizing	•Choosing hardware to support the metrics storage and other APM components

Full details of the tasks are in the Chapter 4 artifacts on apress.com

Figure 4-8. APM Architect Activities

Even as I have suggested that the application specialist can go to the APM architect for help with difficult performance problems, this is only a temporary solution. When an APM architect role is staffed, you can have an expectation that they will understand many of the complexities of APM and how to exploit that visibility. However, while they will know how to get the triage role empowered with APM, they are never going to be a dedicated triage resource. The primary goal of the APM architect is to define many of the processes needed to employ the APM technology effectively, across the application life cycle. Someone needs to oversee the process definitions to ensure consistency with corporate standards. An architect is usually already well versed in moving across the various organizational silos in order to build consensus for the APM processes.

APM Specialist (Triage/Firefighter)

This role is one that takes a bit of experience and work. You should not expect to start immediately staffing this role, as it expects experience in all of the former roles, plus a number of unique responsibilities. It is hard to find people to operate in this role. Realistically, you need to build them.

This situation—needing to grow your own APM specialists fully versed in your environment, procedures, and culture—is what the APM best practices were designed to support. You just have to set your expectations to allow time for this skill set to evolve. And it will evolve, from any of the prior roles, if the right conditions are present.

Notice that I also associate the APM specialist with both triage and firefighting capabilities. Triage is a problem documentation technique that employs all manner of instrumentation to get visibility into a performance problem—you just focus on the metrics available. Firefighting is a service capability combining rapid deployment of APM technology with problem documentation (triage), and will require significant experience and skills. Firefighting brings new visibility to the application problems, at an urgent pace. More details on triage and firefighting are found in Chapters 14 through 17.

Stakeholders will expect an APM specialist to walk on water with respect to using APM. This is not realistic for a new initiative, because you simply cannot accomplish triage or firefighting *reproducibly* without significant experience. So this is the challenge: how do you account for an APM specialist role when they will not be functional for 6 to 18 months? What can you do today, tomorrow, and next month to ensure that you are on track for filling this role? What conditions and environment can you establish to grow these roles?

What those conditions are and how they evolve follows the principle of good-better-best. See Figure 4-9 for a summary of the tasks for this role. In a large organization, we want to start a lot of people at basic skills, and then select the ones who thrive, enhance the skills of that subset, and select again. After a couple of iterations, you will arrive with at least two APM specialists. Where an application specialist knows everything about their assigned application, the APM specialist knows everything about employing APM and managing its infrastructure.

Activity	Tasks
Managing expectations	•Communicate the relationships between accurate load testing profiles, baselines and triage •Communicate the correct use and limitations of APM
Communicating remediation	•Presenting monitoring findings in a non-inflammatory manner, while retaining integrity and conviction
Other responsibilities	•Scope and level of effort and sizing of the APM solution •Coordination of initial load testing in QA, validation of agent configuration •Outline of production deployment procedures, pre-production review •Define baseline processes and interpretation •Prioritizing opportunities to correct defects

* Full details of the tasks are in the Chapter 4 artifacts on apress.com

Figure 4-9. APM Specialist (Triage/Firefighter) Activities

We will revisit this point later in this chapter, in full detail.

APM Evangelist

This last role is a characteristic of every successful APM initiative I have seen to date. It is more of a personality type than a defined title appearing in an organization chart. It is often a manager or executive that believes passionately that APM is something needed for their organization to mature and directly address software quality. The APM evangelist understands APM technology, where it is successful, and who is doing well with it, and will readily communicate APM progress at every opportunity. They bring together the APM practitioners with the application teams that need help. They help guide stakeholders to available technology and define pilot exercises. They find ways to shake out funding to help APM initiatives get started.

Staffing Strategies

There are a number of approaches to addressing the questions of how to get appropriate staffing for an APM initiative. Here are the strategies to consider:

• Adding new personnel
• Product training
• Repurposing existing personnel

- Best practice mentoring
- Staff augmentation

I will discuss what each of these activities entails and then explore how to respond to the staffing demands of the APM initiative.

Adding New Personnel

This is the most direct, but in the modern funding climate, it's not a very likely scenario. Additional personnel require a consistent workload for economic justification. This is not the reality in a first initiative. In fact, there can be little for the APM team to do in the absence of a deployable application. Most clients will use a short services engagement to establish the monitoring environment for two to five applications. In this situation, an APM project manager, with a 12- to 18-month period of responsibility, is appropriate to oversee the activities. The PM is really a placeholder for the successive deployments and a repository for the accumulated experiences and strategy.

If you are asking, "If I'm only deploying two to five apps, why do I need a PM for 18 months?" That's exactly the thinking that dooms the nascent initiative. A first deployment is exactly that. There will be follow-on deployments of the same size or larger. Using a PM up front at least ensures there will be continuity from one set of applications to the next. And it ensures that there will be someone to coordinate all of the prep activities—a really simple idea that few folks realize spontaneously.

As the deployments continue and some value is derived, there will be an opportunity to add personnel. What role will give the biggest return for the investment? The application specialist would be a key role to help grow relationships and increase the number of apps under management. That would be the strategic choice. The APM specialist (triage/firefighter) would be the tactical choice, if there were a greater emphasis on performance problem analysis. All we are doing here is looking for opportunities to flesh out the APM system. The difference is between making your staffing decision in isolation and involving your stakeholders in the decision. By offering strategic staffing choices you are exposing and managing the expectations of your sponsors. If they want more triage capabilities, they have to invest. If they want more deployments, you show them the schedule. You are moving from a model where individual deployment efforts, with little coordination, are effectively isolated from one another, to one where you have a continuing presence, keeping requirements and relationships intact, and getting more efficient with each deployment increment. And you are bringing your stakeholders into the process, which will improve the success of the initiative overall.

Product Training

Using the software correctly is important, but this does not provide a thorough background into the strategies, processes, and techniques for APM. Product training is often narrowly focused on how the technology is used, with respect to the installation, user interface, and key product features. The documentation for the technology and the training materials are designed to support each other. But they do not cover how to establish and operate a performance management system. It is assumed that this foundation is already established, or is to be provided by others.

If your organization is not sufficiently mature with regard to the processes for planning, maintaining, and employing performance information, you will have a lot of work remaining to establish these processes after you complete the product training. Without them you cannot hope for rapid adoption and proliferation of the APM tools, nor can you hope to realize the full value that you invested.

The easiest way to appreciate this situation is to do the following exercise. Follow the ITIL system of defining a catalog of services that your APM system will provide and propose this to your target business sponsors (the folks who will benefit from your investment). If you have a hard time defining this list and/or your target sponsors are not enthusiastic, your initiative is going to be at risk.

This should not be taken as a suggestion that you should start looking for personnel with ITIL certification, but it does strongly suggest that you should partner with another organization that understands the service management area, so you can develop a viable plan—ultimately defined as a catalog of services for performance management.

Repurposing Existing Personnel

If your current staff are to be repurposed for the APM initiative, this should be tempered by the reality of needing to allow some time for them to become proficient. Product training is a useful initial investment, but it needs to be proximal to the actual deployment in order to reinforce that education. You want to stage your deployments so that the skills are reinforced. You want to avoid deploying everything in a single deployment effort. You want to be practiced and efficient with your deployments, which can only come through repetition. Three small deployments over six months will be much more effective than one deployment every six months. When the timing is too difficult in terms of training schedules or staffing, a mentoring approach is indicated.

Mentoring is learning by doing, by working side by side with a consulting architect. It is never a substitute for product training. Putting someone with minimal experience with APM technology alongside a consulting architect is just a waste of the mentoring opportunity. Everything that candidate sees will be new, and there simply will not be anything significant retained. Retention requires some repetition, even for the brightest candidates. You want to leverage mentoring to reinforce and advance the APM initiative by first completing all of the core education and initial activities and later using the mentoring opportunity to get introduced to more sophisticated issues and techniques than a novice practitioner would expect to encounter at their own pace, but under the guidance of a more experienced practitioner. Also, if you are confident in the direction and funding of the APM initiative, specific best practice mentoring will help you to establish the appropriate processes and demonstrate the necessary competencies. This approach is usually indicated when you expect to undertake significant future deployments with your own staff.

Best Practice Mentoring

If your monitoring organization is established, you've made some progress in realizing a service catalog, and you are looking to quickly fill some gaps in your APM activities, a longer-term mentoring relationship is indicated. This is a sequence of service engagements where your APM team will be guided through a variety of activities to achieve competency on specific aspects of the APM system. I use the following themes:

- Preproduction program
- Deployment program
- Triage program
- Service bureau program

Each program focuses on a small set of applications so that the participants get sufficient practice with the APM activities.

The duration typically will be four to eight weeks over three to nine months, depending on the availability of applications or other scheduling constraints. Each week consists of lectures, design and planning sessions, and specific implementation activities led by an APM specialist in a mentoring role. In the intervening weeks, the team members follow through on various activities, as well as attending to their other roles. This is intensive knowledge transfer, and all participants will have already completed their product education and have had significant experience with the tools prior to undertaking any of these APM programs.

The key elements of these APM programs are presented in Parts 2 and 3 of this book. You will also find more details on the skills, processes, and competencies that comprise the APM best practices, in Chapter 5.

Staff Augmentation

In the absence of candidate personnel that may be repurposed, or a shared initiative to establish an APM system, some folks must pursue a staff augmentation engagement in order to realize their target scope of performance monitoring. You will receive a fully functional monitoring environment, but you will not necessarily establish any internal expertise. Your augmented staff is there to do the deployments that you do not have the resources to support.

At the very least, you must assign a PM to oversee the activities. This is for coordination of the initial deployment, of course, but also your point of continuity for future APM activities. You should plan to invest in the PM by having them work closely with the consulting architect, in a mentoring relationship, to understand the deployment planning, installation, and incident management that an APM initiative will involve. This mentoring activity will occur over a one- to two-week period and can be realized in parallel with an ongoing services engagement, if that's where your APM specialist is coming from.

Staffing an APM Initiative

The question of staffing is frequently dismissed for an APM initiative. As discussed in the introduction, this is because many organizations see APM as the next step in product evolution from availability monitoring, which they are already familiar and largely successful with. What these organizations overlook is the variety of roles that are needed to maintain and interpret the enhanced visibility into the applications that APM provides. Along with these new roles is the reality that they will operate across multiple areas of IT expertise and also within the business units whose applications are supported by IT. Monitoring is no longer the sole responsibility of the IT operations team. This results in two unforeseen challenges for the APM initiative: operating across traditional organization boundaries (across silos) and operating collaboratively, instead of at arm's length. This is not going to be a typical, limited deployment of an IT monitoring tool—APM will benefit nearly every interaction along the application life cycle—provided there is someone available to show all of these new stakeholders how it gets done.

This is why executive sponsorship of the APM initiative is so important. IT organizations are not really empowered to operate across business units. Someone else, usually higher in the corporation, needs to take the IT requirements, along with the principles presented in this book, and negotiate support for the initiative among the business units that will essentially fund the activity. Simply put, funding is how you help an organization to change.

This does not mean that you cannot get APM started without such sponsorship. It does mean that you have to be practical in what you may realistically achieve without such sponsorship. Our goal is to make every APM initiative successful, no matter what scope is proposed. An ambitious scope is not a recipe for success, unless you have a plan for the appropriate level of sponsorship to support it.

What Staffing Is Appropriate for APM Success?

So far we have considered the various APM roles and looked at a variety of strategies to empower candidates to become APM practitioners. If that is your reality, then you already have everything you need to go forward with the APM initiative. That is actually an infrequent outcome, however. The reality presents a much bigger obstacle. The challenge is simple: how do we get staffing for an initiative that is has limited adoption and unproven value, and needs significant investment? Well, you don't! Everybody knows that management is not going to invest in a project that has not demonstrated value. And this is where many IT teams pull up and stop. They don't really commit to solving this staffing problem for the enterprise. If they can get it working for themselves—well, that's all they wanted anyway.

And this is the loop within which many organizations find themselves trapped. They don't have a clear mandate to provide APM for the enterprise, so no one is in a position to address the *eventual* need for dedicated staff. So how can we keep things going forward without adding staff prematurely? How can we add staff "just in time"?

One important attribute is *commitment*. Someone has to take responsibility for the APM rollout in such a way as to make that experience reusable for the successive rollouts. That is a tall order, but one that is typically available in abundance—a PM. This role is designed to intercede on behalf of the initiative, get folks lined up, identify problems, and work off of a schedule.

The PM role is one that interfaces with all of the silos supporting the application life cycle and is in the dedicated position of coordinating resources (very often consultants) to realize the APM initiative. But the PM is not hands-on, and will not directly undertake the details of completing the deployment of APM components, for example. But they can be readily trained in understanding what needs to be deployed and when, in order to support the monitoring initiative and make sure someone is getting it done properly. It is really just like any other application deployment—maybe even a little easier.

The PM will direct resources, usually system administrators, to complete the detailed tasks. Initially, these systems administrators are selected based on who is available to work on a task, rather than who may be the best candidate. You may not be using any of these resources on a consistent basis and at some point, rather than working with different folks each time an APM component is deployed, you might assign resources for specific tasks. An assignment may not necessarily be a full-time head count (permanent staffing) for APM, but instead someone who has a *first priority* for monitoring tool deployment or issues. The actual utilization for APM tasks alone may only account for 10 to 20 percent of the resource's time, but it is critical that this role is of top priority—for the reasons discussed earlier. Adding this responsibility as an additional, optional role simply doesn't work.

At some point, when the pace of deployments is sufficient, this individual will become the APM component administrator. The urgent goal at this point is to quickly get a second person in this role—before the first one leaves or gets burned out. And then, without too much fanfare, you have the core of an APM monitoring team.

As the pace of deployments or triage events increases, it will be appropriate to establish the remaining roles: application specialist, monitoring architect, and triage specialist. Again, this begins by making APM a priority, dedicating a portion of utilization from available staff, increasing that portion as APM activity warrants, and finally, designating dedicated staff when appropriate.

Let's look in detail at the overall staffing strategies, as each situation will be a bit different. To achieve a broad, enterprise usage of APM, we look to staff the following roles, as we introduced earlier:

- **APM administrator**
  - APM agent administrator
  - APM metrics storage administrator

- Application specialist
- **APM triage specialist**
- APM project manager
- APM monitoring architect
- APM monitoring evangelist

The two roles in boldface are the most readily accepted and are easily achieved through product training and operational experience. However, the APM administrator role is usually the only one that will actually be "funded," in terms of training. The triage specialist is often expected to sprout spontaneously by simply having APM monitoring tools available. This is a common assumption and is the result of many years of tool purchases with little demonstration of value. Regrettably, some organizations will acquire APM technology with no more ambition than to placate a key contributor.

By understanding these biases, we can use the planning phase of an APM initiative to educate personnel or avoid those biases as much as possible, in order to generate support for the APM initiative. Of course, "avoidance" is not a comfortable strategy when corporate traditions speak to "cooperation" and "teamwork," but this is a reality we all face. You have to pick your battles, and the easiest way to avoid confrontation is to have a deep understanding of the issues, and thus be able to control the time and place of the discussion. The first battle you have to prepare for is on the question of staffing. The ongoing availability monitoring initiative requires few dedicated staff. Why will the APM initiative be any different? How many will you need? What will they do? This chapter and your understanding of your corporate environment are the tools with which you will keep control of the discussion.

When your stakeholders bring up the staffing question, it is also a bit of a gambit, so be careful not to reply with an integer number. Head count is a very unattractive topic, and probably under severe constraints. So how do you engage this discussion and drive the value proposition for the APM initiative?

There are two approaches to address this topic: the FTE approach, and the reprioritization of existing staff. I will discuss the reprioritization in the next section. The FTE approach is the traditional approach to understanding the staffing requirements for an initiative. This analysis makes perfect sense when sponsorship is high and the scope of APM is going to be broad. If you are going to implement APM across 10 to 50 applications each year, the FTE analysis is going to give you a good estimate.

Unfortunately, most APM initiatives start with just a few applications (or one) and you end up with some odd fractional needs for staffing. And if the overall scope is limited, there will be little opportunity to repeat the planning and deployment activities that need repetition to become reliable procedures. So even if the FTE recommendation is followed, what results is not a sustainable, reliable system.

Very often, organizations have no problems assigning additional roles to an individual contributor. And that is what often happens when a fractional FTE is determined. What becomes a problem is that no one establishes the real priorities for competing tasks, and the individual contributor is left to their own sense of what is a key activity and what may be preempted by an APM-related task. Naturally, the priority tasks often become the ones that the staff member is most familiar with. This leaves the less familiar tasks, like those necessary to support the APM initiative, unlikely to get any real attention.

The FTE Approach

To complete the FTE analysis, you need to identify all of the APM tasks and roles. That is a bit of work, so you might also consider the following spreadsheet, called the Full-Time-Equivalent Calculator: CH 04 - Staffing - FTE Calculator.xls (available on the Apress web site, www.apress.com).

Figure 4-10 summarizes the workload for each of the roles, across all of the instrumented environments, and then sums this to reveal how many folks you need if you cannot get anyone else to participate. The inputs are across the top. This example if for a large initiative: 1,300 JVMs, 25 APM storage servers, and 70 applications, indicated on the upper right. On the upper left, the working days, with adjustments for weekends and the hours per day available for tasks, are defined. These parameters define the scope of the deployment that will constitute the APM initiative, and results in 5.64 FTEs, or 20 percent utilization of 28 existing staff. This range is just a suggestion and you would interpolate between those two values to reflect the amount of staff you are contributing or change the formula to reflect your reality. The spreadsheet has additional tabs, not illustrated here, that detail the workload and time required on a frequency-based model, meaning that new applications/configurations are always arriving. This is an important characteristic of an APM initiative—that it is rarely a one-shot initiative (if successful). It has a number of recurring activities.

				Hours per Year							
Days per month	20							1300	# JVMs (all environments)		
Hours per day	6							25	# MS (all environments, standalone, fail-over, etc.)		
								10	# distinct platforms (WAS, WLS, POJO, etc.)		
								24	# APM Workstations		
								70	# distinct Applications (unique lifecycle)		
		Dev	QA-Func	QA-Perf	UAT	Production	Triage	% FTE			
Roles											
Agent Administrator				326	321.5	324		67%			
Metrics Storage Administrator				893.5	319.5	331.5		107%			
Application Specialist				233	227	227		48%			
Triage Specialist				984	1264	476		189%			
Monitoring Architect				1016	320	852		152%			
								564%	28.1771	20% availability	
									9.39236	60% availability	

USAGE
1. Update the Platforms with the appropriate info
2. Update this sheet, YELLOW FIELD ONLY, for #JVMs, distinct platforms and distinct applications

COMMENTS
Triage is blank because problems are identified earlier in the lifecycle. If you ommit QA and UAT, then please put double the time in the TRIAGE Column.
DEV and QA-Func are filled in with your best guess. if you want to account for those environments. DEV is capable to do it all themselves. QA-Func is not helpful.
%FTE assume 20 days per month and 35hrs per week. Feel free to adjust to your own reality.
You may discard DOMAINS but you may not eliminate ROLES.

Figure 4-10. Workload summary for each role

If we consider a smaller initiative—five JVMs, one metrics server component, and one application—we get 1.23 FTE, or 20 percent utilization spread across six persons (or 60 percent of two persons).

Let's look at an example of the underlying calculation. Figure 4-11 shows a sample activity (task list) and task frequency for the agent admin role.

Scenarios

Activity	Duration	Per Platform	Per Application	Per Release	Weekly	Monthly	Quarterly	Annual	QA Perf	UAT	Prod
APM Administrator Training	3							1			
Agent Install First Time	2	1	1								
Deploy incremental agent config	0.5			1	1				1	1	1
Preserve/Transfer Logs	1					1			1	1	1
Upgrade Agents	1							1			
Upgrade JVM (pre-1.5)	0.5	1						1			
JVM Config	0.5	1									
Agent Extention Install/Upgrade	0.5	3.5	3.5	3.5					1	1	1
Workstation Install	0.5							1			1
		0	0	0	0	0	0	3	3	0	0
		4	2	0	0	0	0	0	0	0	0
		0	0	0.5	26	0	0	0	26.5	26.5	26.5
		0	0	0	0	12	0	0	12	12	12
		0	0	0	0	0	0	1	1	0	0
		1	0	0	0	0	0	0.5	0.5	0	0
		1	0	0	0	0	0	0	0	0	0
		3.5	1.75	1.75	0	0	0	0	7	7	7
								2.5			2.5
		9.5	3.75	2.25	26	12	0	7	50	45.5	48

Figure 4-11. Sample activity and frequency for the agent admin role

You might have some other tasks to add or a different perception of the duration and frequency that a task may involve, but you can use this spreadsheet as a starting point. When I'm in the assessment phase of an APM initiative and I've got enough data to complete the FTE analysis, I'll share these findings. No matter what the result, I always come up against the same recurring theme: show us how to do APM with no increase in staff. So what is the point?

The point is that your sponsors want confidence that you have exhausted every angle is completing your justification for the APM initiative. If you don't have the knowledge to undertake the FTE analysis, you don't get the funding. If you don't understand all of the APM roles and tasks that contribute to the FTE analysis, you don't get the funding. And it doesn't matter if you come back with 1.3 FTE or 5.8 FTE—you are not getting any more staff, even if it results in an excessive workload for you current staff.

Realistically, when you need to add staff, most paths lead to "not funded." So you need another option: the staff evolution model.

Evolving Your Organization's Use of APM

Individual contributors in the APM initiative will be identified by interest, aptitude, and circumstance. This is a profound reality for most organizations simply because performance management is an emerging discipline—it is not a traditional function within many IT organizations. So we do not need to follow traditional patterns of tool adoption. We may instead employ modern strategies following how timely and efficient organizations are assembled today: highly distributed and just-in-time. This allows us to address the impossible constraint of building an APM capability without adding any extra staff.

The core principle in leveraging these modern strategies is *prioritization*. We all realize that we may assign any number of responsibilities to an individual contributor. But what are they actually going to be doing in any given circumstance? If you correctly establish what their priorities will be, there will not be any surprises.

Many organizations embrace principles of distributed teams and just-in-time but simply fail to adjust the priorities. They add new responsibilities, but unless explicitly stated, this will not cause a reshuffling of priorities. In fact, if management does not make clear that the priority for all activities is to be on the emerging responsibility (that being the APM initiative), the team will simply shrug off the incremental responsibility in favor of what was a priority yesterday.

Building a Scalable Monitoring Organization

The single greatest risk to an APM initiative is to have all of the monitoring expertise within a single individual. Inasmuch as we might be predisposed to assigning a single individual the responsibilities for establishing, maintaining, and employing monitoring results, we must instead spread the load over as many individuals as practical and rely on process to establish our "APM expert." The APM processes involve specific documentation of the procedures and techniques to deploy and employ the monitoring technology, such that any competent IT professional can undertake a given task with a high confidence of success.

The challenge in establishing the APM processes is to not only identify who, what, where, and when the activities should take place, but to ensure that the generalized processes are tailored to the specific realities of your IT and corporate culture. The challenge is to adapt those processes quickly and effectively to your reality.

From the staffing perspective, Figure 4-12 reflects the essence of this strategy.

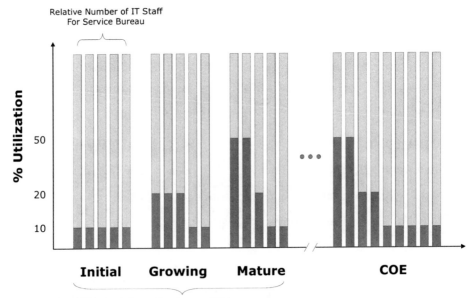

Figure 4-12. APM specialist utilization as APM usage matures

We begin with a group of individuals equipped with basic skills and training (agent deployment, initial triage) who should otherwise be interchangeable. Everyone is a casual user of APM at this point, spending about 10 percent of their time (available utilization) doing APM tasks. As the organization matures, moving from "initial" to "growing" to "mature," you begin to develop some individuals a bit more, but all of your staff retains the core set of skills and understandings. It is most valuable to move each of the participants into the higher level of responsibility for some period of time (3-6 months), first based on aptitude and later on a strict rotation. This encourages sharing of results and techniques and eliminates any single point of failure. It also ensures that your process documentation is accessible by all skill levels. So just because one individual has tremendous aptitude does not mean you isolate all the others onto the less demanding activities. Everyone needs to be able to fill any role, if only for a couple of days or weeks. In a mature organization, this results in at least two individuals, each operating at 50 percent utilization, in order to sustain the APM initiative. You do not attempt a higher utilization simply because your staff will fail to scale, in much the same fashion as you cannot expect to fail-over a physical server onto another and exceed 100 percent utilization.

As the APM initiative matures, in terms of staffing and capabilities, other organization forms may be appropriate. The highest organization is called a *center of excellence (COE)*, and is designed to span multiple business units. There will also be two individuals at 50 percent utilization and the remaining staff at lesser utilization levels. The goal at this point is to rotate candidates into the APM COE for three to six months, moving up to that 50 percent utilization level, and then rotate them back to their respective business units after they have achieved the requisite APM competencies. This ensures a growing pool of APM practitioners who have deep appreciation of the APM COE processes and standards.

Now, this utilization target of 10 percent to 50 percent does not suggest that the individuals sit idle until APM tasks appear. It suggests that the priority is to do whatever is needed for the APM initiative, as it is required, up to that utilization target. Thus, they need to have a workload that they can defer (without prejudice) in order to focus up to 50 percent of their available utilization on monitoring tasks. In the event that one of the pair becomes unavailable, the remaining contributor would then be able to devote 100 percent of their time, until that staffing situation was corrected.

Looking further ahead, if the mature organization were to evolve into a COE structure, where these two monitoring specialists were leveraged across the enterprise, you would find that you would scale to about 25 to 75 applications under management, across the application life cycle, with a complete set of APM capabilities.

The motivation to move to a COE is that the traditional evolution (from initial to growing to mature) can be initiated multiple times, independently by other business units or application teams. Each of these other teams will be creating (and potentially maintaining) the core pair of APM specialists—resulting in significant duplication of effort and likely without any coordination among business units. The COE and service bureau organizational models are strategies designed to harness these independent efforts into a consistent set of activities and process, reduce the duplication of effort, and ultimately reduce the costs in education and staff augmentation.

For organizations that do not follow this approach, you instead find that they will continue *deploying* APM successfully but will not progress to the more advanced capabilities without first making some commitment to building and sustaining an APM specialist role.

There are, regrettably, a number of anti-patterns[4] (Figure 4-13) for APM- deployment, related to staffing, that result is significant underutilization of the technology and poor realization of the potential value of the investment. If the circumstances of your deployment appear to be reinforcing one of these anti-patterns, please do not hesitate to hit them over the head with this book.[5]

Anti-Pattern	Technique	Goal	Motivation	Result
Monitoring Aspect	Deploy everywhere with monitoring disabled	•App teams enabled as needed •Consume ELA	No additional personnel will be needed	•Rarely used •No concept of APM capacity •No process evolution
Fire Alarm	Deploy only when there are problems, and then remove after use	•Deep dive when needed •Limit license consumption •Save disk space	No allowance for utilization of existing staff	•Triage is very difficult without a reference baseline as they are never collected or established •Multiple tools maintained
Highlander	Single individual manages all use of the tool for 100's of apps	•Consistency •Full employment	Let's try it with one person first and see where that gets us	•Value limited •No processes established •Single point of failure
Geek Pack	Single vertical Employs monitoring, usually Operations	•Monitoring excellence •Full employment	Our farm runs great – now get off our land!	•No lifecycle management •No improvement in app quality

Figure 4-13. Monitoring Anti-patterns

An APM best practice skills assessment (a two- to four-hour activity or service engagement) will document the details of any anti-patterns that may exist in your organization and prescribe appropriate corrective applications. You will find complete details in Chapter 3 to help you expose and document these anti-patterns.

Real-World Staffing Evolution Scenarios?

Many of the challenges for the IT organization are a result of time-to-market constraints. As much as management may craft thoughtful and inspired plans for enhancing its operations and capabilities, the business has all of the trump cards. The previous sections have established a new understanding of staffing for an APM

---

[4] http://en.wikipedia.org/wiki/Anti-pattern

[5] This is a metaphor for an urgent but corporate-appropriate and respectful invitation for constructive dialog on the merits of a well-considered APM initiative. Please do not actually hit anyone with this book.

initiative. Now let's put it to use. The following scenarios attempt to capture some of those realities wherein you may fully realize what you *need* to do, but you are *compelled* to operate according to certain circumstances.

First APM, Accepted but Constrained Budget

A first APM project usually exposes the unintentional bias toward availability monitoring in that the long-term management of the APM tool is entirely unconsidered. For a single project, with only a few applications and no extensive mandate to support additional monitoring deployments, it is easy to assign the initial responsibilities to a single practitioner. The profound risk is the total loss of all accumulated expertise when that solo practitioner moves on.

This is easy to address—simply have two practitioners at all times and you will have the continuity to maintain the monitoring solution. As you are not growing the environment (you have accepted the use of the tool but your company is not actively committed), there is no justification for additional best practices, provided that the monitoring solution is meeting your objectives. If you are not realizing your goals, it is easy enough to assess and recommend training/mentoring to fill the gaps. In a larger organization there are often multiple independent monitoring initiatives following this same rationale. Each is evaluating these same considerations and possibly scheduling training and services. Some are better than others. Some perhaps are struggling.

So, it is not uncommon in these larger organizations for there to be 6 to 12 of these isolated efforts ongoing. For each of the teams, the monitoring solution meets their needs, but for the corporation there is significant duplication of effort and thus an opportunity to enhance the efficiency of the investment and further promote the advantages of performance monitoring.

This is what the APM best practices are building toward: organizational models to enhance the efficiency and utility of the investment. For example, if 1 to 2 of those 6 to 12 individual monitoring efforts have really strong success, then there would be an advantage if the other groups could share those resources and practices. Promoting one of those groups as the service bureau for the remaining groups is the mechanism to realize the benefits of collaboration: sharing resources and techniques. Alternatively, if performance monitoring is recognized as strategic advantage, the corporation may implement a COE. This provides the same benefits as the service bureau but adds a mandate to further deploy the approach as well as establish formal standards and training.

Significant APM, Committed but Has Gaps with Current Practice

In this scenario, a single group has established the performance monitoring initiative and demonstrated ongoing success in adoption of the tools. The pace of deployments begins to take off and the solution appears to be scaling poorly. Application owners are having difficulty accessing the tools, some agent configurations have dangerous and destabilizing side effects on the monitored applications, and the metrics storage infrastructure has numerous performance incidents and outages. Last year everything was going along smoothly. Now frustrations are high. What is going on here?

Whereas the earlier *new-to-APM* scenario suffers from lack of commitment and vision, in this scenario there is clear vision of the future state and a commitment to broader use of the technology. However, this effort is directly related to that earlier scenario, with the sole distinction that their early success in employing the monitoring tool prevented other groups from establishing their own separate systems. Unfortunately, the staffing strategy that supported the earlier progress is not likely to scale for the larger deployments.

While it remains absolutely true that modern monitoring technology is easy to configure and use, as you scale the solution you will encounter issues that are simply not present in the earlier stages of the monitoring system. Very often, the ease of use and richness of data revealed creates a false sense of confidence. You don't know what you don't know. Upon reflection, most clients realize that they were much more dependent on services than they thought they were.

The single largest problem is the management of the metrics archive. It simply was not an issue in the new-to-APM scenario because the environment was not in growth mode. So no one paid any real attention to that storage infrastructure. No one realized how significant a gap was created when no one was assigned the *responsibility* of administering the infrastructure of APM—metrics storage and sharing.

Without any metrics storage admin, there was no one in a position to baseline, realize, and document the creeping performance degradation that was responsible for the increasing number of incidents and outages. Without standards for agent deployment, or for reporting or dashboard design guidelines, monitoring capacity is wasted and the resulting solution terribly inefficient. The team watches in horror that just as adoption begins to peak, the whole monitoring infrastructure falls over. As quickly as they see their goals being achieved, the whole initiative comes crumbling down.

The fix for this scenario is to simply assign the APM administrator role. This is often divided between the agent admin and metrics storage admin, as many clients assign the metrics storage admin role to platform engineering/support, and the agent admin to the web tier or application teams. As most organizations do not look to administrators to establish standards and other guidelines, it is also prudent to assign an APM architect (part time) or an APM project manager. Successful deployment is really about careful planning and standard practices. A PM role is ideal to keep this focused, but an architect role would accomplish the same and also lend more weight to establishing standards and procedures.

The APM maturity model presents the best practices as stepping stones to realizing broad, consistent, and stable use of performance monitoring technology. It replaces the blind confidence of "don't know" with the sober realization that success requires preparation. It isn't necessary that you have a complete plan from pilot to COE, but it does require that you take some responsibility for understanding the impact that staffing gaps will have on your eventual success.

Significant Existing APM, Recommitted but Constrained Budget

This next scenario is regrettably very common. The stakeholder may have used competing technology (a comparable offering but from a different vendor) and was not entirely successful. Usually this will follow one of the earlier scenarios. They have significant APM experiences but some bad habits may be entrenched. They will invest in a better tool, but management will not commit until value/benefit is realized—the bar is much higher than it was for the initial undertaking.

What was the lower bar set at? Often the success criteria for an APM initiative are for rapid deployment and minimal impact on the monitored applications. These are pretty easy criteria to achieve. The expectations are often something different: to identify performance problems, improve software quality, and reduce production incidents. The gap between expectations and success criteria is what caused the last effort to stall, or the last vendor to get tossed out.

The visibility offered by APM technology is really nothing that most IT organizations have had significant experience with. Your IT organization simply does not know how to employ that APM visibility in order to solve problems and address the expectations of the user community. Very often this is simply because the primary responsibility of IT, with regard to a monitoring solution, is to get it deployed efficiently. They didn't really sign up to be the practitioners of the tool. This leaves a pretty significant gap.

So, did the monitoring team fail in the last initiative? We don't think so. They did exactly what they normally do. They set up the tool, made it available to the application owners, and moved on. In fact, there was no monitoring team. The application owners *assumed* it would be easy to use, just like all the other monitoring tools—those non-performance/APM monitoring tools—that they have had prior experience with. They were woefully unprepared for the new visibility and simply did not have suitable processes in place to exploit it.

In this scenario, the APM admin role needs to be reestablished within IT and management needs to recommit to supporting an APM role. Recommitted, by way of analogy, suggests that the APM office will now be in a trailer (heat, air-conditioning, water cooler, etc.), not just a tent on the lawn, and that there is a plan to establish a permanent building—once the new success criteria have been met. IT has already demonstrated that they can deploy the tool successfully. The real gap is with the application owners and other necessary sponsors, in committing appropriate resources to the APM initiative.

The appropriate role to test the level of recommitment is the application specialist. A candidate from the application team is mentored to understand how to employ APM technology across the application life cycle—how to monitor in QA and production, what to look for, how to build dashboards and reports, how to successfully triage performance incidents. And this isn't simply a check box for mentoring—the candidate will demonstrate competency in delivering an *application audit*. This activity confirms the efficacy of their skills and is a management milestone in realizing the new success criteria. The other portion of new criteria is typically a successful identification for a production incident.

The application specialist interacts with the APM administrator. This keeps the monitoring infrastructure firmly in the hands of the IT organization (platform engineering, system administrators) while simultaneously holding the stakeholders accountable for demonstrating value. The application audit competency is the demonstration of value.

If the number of applications is growing or already large, it will also be prudent to establish the triage/firefight role. As much as the application specialist role can assist in root-cause analysis of their host application, it will probably be politically difficult to share this resource with other application groups. The triage role avoids that complication and has the additional benefit of quickly accruing significant experience by gaining exposure to multiple applications.

If neither of these roles seems suitable, it is likely that you will pursue an outsourcing strategy and bring in solution architects to take care of setting up the monitoring infrastructure, monitoring the application life cycle, and triage assistance. In this case, the APM project manager is the suitable role to ensure successful use of the APM technology.

Significant Existing APM, Recommitted and Budgeted for APM Practice

Where an APM initiative is already thriving, usually with multiple teams, it is likely that the APM administrator and application specialist roles are already realized. Management may have observed the duplication of support and is interested to preserving the successes while making the organization more efficient. This is not to achieve a wholesale reduction in head count, but to reapportion the responsibilities in order to enhance the collective experience and industrialize the system.

The organizational model for the APM system (service bureau, COE) will drive the ultimate reallocation of resources, but it will be prudent to have staffing for the APM monitoring architect role in order to provide oversight and alignment with corporate standards. Often, clients in this scenario may be overbalanced toward production monitoring and are not realizing the benefits of performance monitoring prior to reaching production. They might instead be more focused on the on-boarding of applications rather than management of software quality across the life cycle, for example.

This presents a couple of distinct paths. If the desire is to maintain the existing on-boarding system and industrialize the processes and techniques, then a skills assessment and appropriate mentoring will be sufficient. There will likely be no necessity to add or contract the exiting roles.

If the goal is instead to broaden the use of performance monitoring into QA/preproduction, then the initiative will consist of two steps. First, the app audit competency will be established as part of the on-boarding. This will bring a portion of the QA environment—or stress and performance environment—under control of the production/operations team. This team will establish the QA systems while simultaneously establishing this capability for their service catalog. This allows the most experienced users to establish and refine the QA processes. This would be shortly transferred to the QA teams, and they would operate that system independently going forward. It is also important to provide a solid alternative for those application teams who are unable to recertify their applications under the new QA system. The newly minted service bureau, if allowed to retain the intermediate testing environment, establishes the alternative testing path.

Significant Existing APM, Retrenching, Maintain Existing Footprint Only

When a client is unable to maintain their commitment to APM technology but is otherwise reluctant to pull the monitoring out, the APM project manager role is a necessity. As the monitoring initiative winds down, staffing will be pulled. There are no anticipated deployments, which should limit opportunities to unbalance the monitoring environment. It is prudent to schedule an APM infrastructure health check and tuning to ensure that the metrics storage is optimal and that availability to the users will be high. Except for application performance incidents and outages, and assuming no new software functionality is being deployed (for the existing application set), the triage activities may also be outsourced. Any upgrade of the monitoring software, if support is maintained, is easily outsourced, but will require PM coordination across a production environment.

In the event the APM investment is restored, the APM PM will be the seed of the new monitoring organization and allow for an efficient reestablishment of a robust monitoring system.

Summary

The staffing gap is what often prevents an APM initiative from achieving broader use across the enterprise. Skills are too easily isolated as many corporations silo each stakeholder, throughout the application life cycle, from one another. When insufficient staffing occurs, the initial apparent success of the initiative gives way to failure, with the departure of a single "key" staff member. Overstaffing an initiative simply does not happen because most organizations are very reluctant to incur additional head count.

The challenge in staffing an APM initiative is that APM-specific activities are sprinkled throughout the application life cycle. Most APM technologies today have very brief deployment and configuration activities. This does not present a problem, provided that personnel are encouraged to keep APM activities a priority. For a single application, there is rarely enough work to justify a full-time resource. You need a plan to share resources, while deployments are ongoing, in order to accumulate multiple applications, and thus enough activities to keep staff busy in their APM roles.

Understanding the APM roles and the gaps with your current organization in filling these roles presents another staffing challenge. We cannot expect to simply go out and find the correct experience on a jobs web site. You really need to grow your own team. How do you grow staff for these APM roles and manage initiative progress while correctly leveraging the application life cycle for the training opportunities? This is discussed in the next Chapter 5 and also in Part 2 of the book.

APM Patterns

A lot of times, people don't know what they want until you show it to them.

—Steve Jobs

The preceeding chapters have covered the traditional topics in the planning of an APM initiative: architecture, terminology, assessments, roles, and staffing—hopefully, what you expected. This chapter covers the primary gap that may cause your APM initiative to fall short: the absence of processes through which the stakeholders can exploit APM. I have been hinting that something is missing from many efforts to employ APM. Now I can expose this consistent gap, characteristic of unsuccessful APM efforts: processes. To help you understand what these processes are, I introduce a simple but powerful concept to both define and organize your APM processes, and also monitor the progress of the initiative and demonstrate your increasing management maturity: the service catalog.

The *service catalog*[1] is a mechanism used to define, measure, and fulfill services that the IT organization provides. The definition of a service originates with the business stakeholders, so the service catalog can be considered a contract among the business, consumers of the service (both internal and external), and the IT organization. But when you extend the service definition to APM, you find that very few folks know what to put in an APM service catalog.

Part of the difficulty is because the *service catalog* is a generic concept and can contain just about anything. If you look to the standards bodies, you can find a great number of processes[2] defined. This only complicates the problem and results in extensive planning and implementation—none of which is appropriate for an APM initiative. It is not that planning is a luxury; it's just that an APM initiative needs to be achieved rapidly and with demonstratable value—all within months and with a competent but otherwise unprepared team. If you pare down your service catalog to the realities that

---

[1] Wikipedia, "service catalog," http://en.wikipedia.org/wiki/Service_Catalog

[2] "Applying ITIL to Performance Management" www.networkworld.com/community/node/26064

an APM initiative faces, you can start with a core use case and context for the processes that you'll need.

To provide a context for your APM service catalog, you'll follow the single most anticipated APM process: deployment. The ubiquity of this process should be of no surprise: You can't do anything until the technology is deployed! And this is what often distracts the teams who are tasked with getting APM going. If they could only get APM deployed correctly, then they might get the time to figure out how to employ APM and what to put in the service catalog. Unfortunately, that just never seems to happen with the traditional approach that IT follows for implementing software systems, which effectively amounts to "deploy it and let someone else figure out how to use and manage it."

Along the way, I will also discuss application management maturity, which will be employed to keep track of the progress of the APM initiative. This was introduced in Chapter 3 as part of the assessment activities but with a simple technology focus. Here, I will expand your understanding by introducing the process requirements that demonstrate the different maturity levels. These maturity levels align with specific APM patterns. Establishing a service catalog, demonstrating value, and tracking management maturity—these all contribute to the successful realization of APM.

Of course, you simply can't put all of your APM processes in to an APM service catalog without some entity to take care of it, and this is the motivation to introduce organization models for APM. These are the real "patterns" for APM—how support for APM is organized. In particular, I will look to a *service bureau model* as an example, and follow how it would establish and refine an APM service catalog as the owner of the onboarding process. *Onboarding*[3] is the process of bringing a new application or hardware platform into the operational environment, which is exactly what you are doing when you introduce APM. So if you consider what APM processes you need in order to support onboarding applications with APM technology, you will end up with a solid foundation for your APM service catalog.

The last topic for this chapter is to determine if the processes in an APM service catalog are the real deal or just fluff. For this, I introduce a bit of process called a *competency*: a demonstration that you have mastered all of the necessary elements to support a particular APM activity. The cookbooks you have been encountering are your foundation for the competency exercises, and they are what I use to assess if an APM practitioner is ready for primetime. Ultimately, "you can't manage what you can't measure."[4] Competencies are how you will measure the effectiveness of your processes so that you can manage the APM initiative.

If you are feeling that this scope of discussion is drifting a little wide of planning and getting a little too close to the concerns of an APM practitioner, you're right. But the planning phase of your APM initiative is where you need to raise these concerns for process definitions because by the time that your stakeholders realize they are missing

[3] Onboarding is conventionally associated with getting new employees functional through a consistent process. It is used frequently in IT operations as "Onboarding Operations Lead." What is most interesting is that this role is doing a lot of APM-like activities, as evidenced in this recent job description: www.gm-jobs.com/job/Detroit-SysOps-Onboarding-Operations-Lead-Job-MI-48201/933282/?utm_source=Juju&utm_campaign=J2W_Juju.

[4] Attributed to David Packard, co-founder of Hewett-Packard.

something, it will likely be too late to save the APM initiative from a long spell of broad disappointment.

Processes, Skills, and Competencies for APM

There are very specific activities that your organization needs to establish in order to support an initial and potentially enterprise-wide roll-out of APM. Let's presume that this is not your responsibility today. And let's also presume that you only need to establish a consistent process framework and not "boil the ocean" to attempt to define every possible process. What tasks may you reasonably assume ownership for in the initial stages of your APM initiative without diluting your immediate goals or burning too much budget? How can you divide the long term objectives into something may be achieved iteratively?

The APM best practices, which are a collection of the activities that a successful APM discipline will use, are the foundation for your service catalog. APM activities include the skills, processes, competencies, and services that an organization will utilize and maintain as the organization establishes an APM system and matures with APM. Figure 5-1 summarizes the basic service catalog. As your maturity with APM evolves from Initial to Growing to Mature, each of these service descriptions is added to the service catalog.

Service Catalog		
Initial	**Growing**	**Mature**
Monitoring needs survey	App audit	Capacity management
APM deployment	Dashboard design and implementation	Performance tuning
On-boarding	Reporting design and implementation	Service-level management
Triage	Alert integration	Gap and visibility assessments

Figure 5-1. Evolution of the APM service catalog

The goal for the APM initiative is to implement each of these basic services according to the schedule and budget established by your sponsor. Additional services are possible, depending on the organization model that you are targeting; I will cover that a little later in this chapter.

The service catalog is how the business (consisting of stakeholders and application owners) interacts with IT to start getting value from the APM initiative. IT has to establish a foundation of expertise in order to become a successful APM practitioner. The business needs to know that IT is on schedule and that the needs of the business—managing the business-to-client interactions—is going to be on schedule and robust. Service-level management is the one popular strategic goal but this could also be cloud-computing or other innovative software service strategy as they become established. Whatever shows up in the service catalog needs some kind of measurement in order to manage it. The job for IT is to implement and operate an appropriate framework of measurements. Those underlying services are what IT gets to define with a set of skills and processes.

For APM, these skills (already encountered in Chapter 3 via the skills assessment) are summarized in Figure 5-2. These skills are what your IT staff needs to master in order to contribute to the APM initiative. The skills indicated in boldface are covered in the book, each with their own chapter. The remaining skills are too vendor-specific, in their implementation, to present any detail at this time.

Skills		
Initial	**Growing**	**Mature**
Critical app assessment Ch 3	APM capacity management	**Triage with baselines Ch 15**
APM solution sizing Ch 10	**Thresholds and alerting Ch 13**	**Triage with trends Ch 16**
Rapid deployment	Reporting	Advanced APM configurations
Triage with single metrics Ch 14	Dashboards	

Figure 5-2. Evolution of the APM skills

Once the skills are established, they are then used to support the basic APM processes, summarized in Figure 5-3. Again, those indicated in boldface are covered in this book, mostly in Chapter 8. Baselines are covered in Chapter 12.

Processes		
Initial	**Growing**	**Mature**
QA acceptance Ch 8	**Agent promotion Ch 8**	Capacity management and planning
	Agent configuration and customization	Proactive management
	Agent validation Ch 8	
	Alert review and escalation	
	Quality review and escalation	
	Baselines CH 12	

Figure 5-3. Evolution of the APM processes

The benefit of processes is that they can be reduced to a cookbook so that any capable contributor can utilize them effectively. Establishing and maintaining these cookbooks is a critical responsibility of some part of your IT organization. In this case, you will assume that Operations, as part of their on-boarding service catalog, will be the caretaker. With these APM cookbooks, everybody benefits and multiple APM initiatives can be achieved. Without them, everybody has to re-invent the wheel, which rarely happens effectively—and thus everybody suffers!

The final element of your APM service catalog are the competencies that confirm if your current skills, processes, and experiences will result in something useful, summarized in Figure 5-4. If you are going to promote that your organization can fullfill the services defined in your service catalog, you need to show your stakeholders exactly what you will do.

For example, if you assert that you are competent for Rapid Deployment, you need to discuss how you will plan, configure, install and validate an APM component. You will show what platforms are supported by your cookbook, how long it takes, how you detect problems with the activity, how you fix them, and what kind of problems your have encountered. It is usually a short presentation—if you are competent. If you're not, you're going to have a miserable time because there is an *expectation* that you will summarize your competency and establish your credentials to deliver on the service catalog. Your stakeholders will know exactly what to expect from the service catalog because they also have this book!

Competencies		
Initial	Growing	Mature
Rapid deployment	**Application audit Ch 13**	Performance optimization
		Gap and enterprise visibility assessments CH 3

Figure 5-4. Evolution of the APM competencies

This is, perhaps, the dark side of building a collaborative solution for APM. Everyone knows everyone else's business, with respect to APM. You do not have to achieve all of these skills, processes, and competencies in the first weeks that you have APM technology. You simply want to be prepared to exploit opportunities within your application life cycle to establish these tasks and competencies when they arise and use this roadmap of capabilities to make sure that you continue to progress. That's the real goal of this book: to get you to establish a roadmap, accelerate your progress as opportunities present, act as an advisor, assess your progress, and ensure you have the skills to be successful in achieving the goals of your monitoring initiative. There is much more to achieving this roadmap of capabilities which I will detail later in the implementation section (Chapters 7-9). Implementation (the initial deployment and configuration of APM technology) is the ideal opportunity to start introducing and validating APM processes.

Demonstrating Value

An APM initiative very often involves acquiring some APM tools. After a tools acquisition, management wants to see results. They want evidence of the value of their decision to invest. You need to show value and you need to do this quickly and periodically over the duration of the monitoring initiative.

The easiest way to show value is to achieve some well-defined success criteria. Your management has an expectation that if they invest, you will deliver. As long as the invest-deliver exchange is relatively short (less than a quarter), it has potential to be a loving and supportive relationship.

Your challenge is to set expectations with management that you can reasonably achieve and that management ultimately perceives as making progress towards demonstrating value.

Figures 5-5 and 5-6 summarize the value that each of the initial skills, processes, and competencies will demonstrate. This example is leading to the Application Audit competency.

Goal/Task	Value	Investment	Type
Basic Triage	Diagnose and interpret performance problems using individual metrics. Leverage performance visibility throughout the application lifecycle and be able to identify the "smoking gun" in some hairy outage.	•Education •Mentoring	Skills
Rapid Deployment	Be able to quickly support a new platform or deploy additional agents as needed and build a foundation for eventual self-service (where someone else completes the deployment). A key process when access to your environment is outsourced and you want to ensure correctness.	•Education •Mentoring •Services	Skills
Metrics Storage Sizing	Understand the relationship between application complexity, agent configuration, and the fundamental capacity of metrics storage. Be able to manage the cost associated with additional metrics storage platforms.	•Mentoring •Services	Skills
Agent Customization	Understand how to manage multiple configurations and when they would be employed. This helps to provide an appropriate level of visibility and also to tune the number of metrics that the APM solution has to support.	•Education •Mentoring •Services	Skills

Figure 5-5. Skills and competencies for APM MM - Initial – Part I

Goal/Task	Value	Investment	Type
Quality Review and Escalation	Establish a process where monitoring is used earlier in the app lifecycle in order to catch performance problems before they get to production. The first (of three) installment of this is QA Acceptance.	•Operational •Services	Process
QA Acceptance	The initial phase is to understand and define what the minimum acceptable performance and the escalation process when the minimum is not met. This is done with minimal impact on the existing testing schedule.	•Operational •Mentoring •Services	Process
Baselines	There are three baselines: Configuration, Application, and Performance. These are the foundation of the HealthCheck report that provides a summary of application performance designed to be trended over time. The report summarizes the appropriate agent configurations, transaction visibility, and the components best representing the availability, performance and capacity for the application.	•Operational •Mentoring •Services	Process
Application Audit	This is the primary service in on-boarding an application (preparing for production). It collects the baselines, assembles the report, identifies the thresholds and alerts, and prepares the dashboards for operations, app specialist, and the business sponsor.	•Operational •Mentoring •Services	Competency

Figure 5-6. Skills and competencies for APM MM -1 – Part 2

Regarding the Investment column, the following sources generally apply:

- *Education* – Available from your vendor educational services
- *Mentoring* – Acquired by working with a consulting architect
- *Operational* – Acquired by using the tool in real world situations
- *Services* – Staff augmentation

What you are proposing to management with your service catalog is to develop the skills (Figure 5-5), generate appropriate artifacts (cookbooks), and then demonstrate the application audit competency (Figure 5-6). You can pick the schedule but your service catalog is what you negotiate with your management and stakeholders. Instead of simply deploying a technology and hoping folks will make use of it, you commit to achieving these skills. You might retort that this is what the stakeholders wanted implicitly so there is nothing new here. And that is absolutely right. What is different is that you are committing to demonstrate these capabilities according to a schedule. All parties get exactly what they negotiate, which is captured in the service catalog.

If your stakeholders want even more capabilities, even beyond what you thought reasonable, you need to define how to get those capabilities. At least now you know precisely what needs to be done, what the supporting processes look like, the staffing needs, etc. You are in a better position to negotiate.

Management Maturity

In Chapter 3 I introduced a framework for assessing monitoring and APM management capabilities (summarized in Figure 3-14), including reactive-negotiation, reactive-alerting, and directed and proactive management levels. While these are generally applicable in assessing organizations making their first move to APM, you need to add two more levels to accommodate the complexity of organizations that have already established APM and are moving to the service-bureau or COE patterns. These maturity levels are *service-driven* and *value-driven*.

A *service-driven* management goal directly aligns with the service bureau pattern. Here all of the responsibilities for provisioning, deployment, operating, monitoring, and problem management are collected under a single entity called a managed service provider[5], or simply a service provider. This is an effort to streamline activities by moving the focus from individual applications and resources to the aggregate of these components as a distinct service in order to make management of the service more efficient and accountable. This is an important transition where the IT role moves from "operating" to a more direct responsibility and accountability for the underlying components.

For organizations that are pursuing service management ideals, implementing an APM service bureau will allow them to apply the same principles of service consolidation and efficiency to the APM initiatives in terms of consistent and repeatable best practices in employing APM. It will also put more emphasis on the integration of various sources of performance information, of which APM will be the target or a contributing source. You will see these points in detail when you get to Chapter 16: "Triage with Trends."

A *value-driven* management goal is where the contributions by IT have a direct impact on the profitability of the enterprise. You are no longer an operator, nor are you a lean and efficient practitioner—you are how the business makes money. This is the model for the most innovative internet-based services today; they are completely dependent on the success of their software life cycles to maintain and grow revenue. This is not the same kind of pressure for more established lines of business where they are marching forward bringing with them long-established systems and practices, just as their competitors are also moving forward. This balance of power exists until someone can restructure their operations, innovate or experience some regulatory pertubation, and then the remaining competitors scramble to maintain parity. As the trading interfaces between businesses and among consumers become more fluid, major shifts in business paridigms become more frequent.

You simply do not move to a value-based IT resource and application management model overnight. It takes collaboration—but before that you need to have something to collaborate on. APM is rally point for IT and the business to begin to collaborate in ernest. To get to this point, you need to crawl, walk, and run through the earlier management maturity levels and establish the infrastructure for managing value; skills, processes, and modes of collaboration.

As the organization enhances its abilities to measure application performance, governance, development efficiencies, and operational capabilities, it's now in a

---

[5] Wikipedia, "managed service provider," http://en.wikipedia.org/wiki/Managed_service_provider

position to start taking *service-level agreements* (SLAs) that will allow it to differentiate its services from its competitors in the marketplace. In many cases, competitors have the same technology and business capabilities but differ in the efficiency of the delivery of their software-based services. The definition of your efficiency will be expressed in your pricing strategies and service levels; your marketplace will choose the more capable and cost effective service offering.

The addition of these two maturity levels completes the management capabilities evolution, summarized in Figure 5-7. I've also added some *sound bites*[6] that represent the overall organizational capabilities.

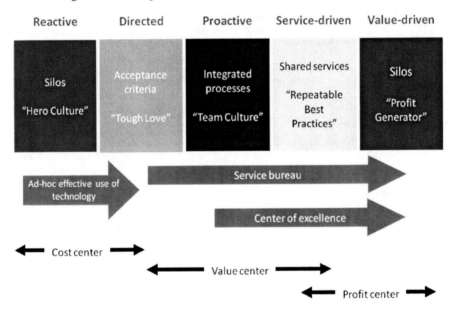

Figure 5-7. Application management maturity

- "**Hero Culture**" In the absence of process or tools, rare individuals continue to solve incredible problems with raw power of presence and extraordinary workloads.

- "**Tough Love**" Simple and brutally efficient acceptance criteria governs the promotion of applications into production as the value of direct measurement of performance is established.

- "**Team Culture**" Collaboration through shared data, reporting, and processes refactor the organization, and silos begin to crumble in favor of shared goals.

- "**Repeatable Best Practices**" Everyone employs the same processes and objectives, and anyone can contribute at the same basic competency level.

---

[6] Wikipedia, "sound bite," http://en.wikipedia.org/wiki/Sound_bite

- **"Profit Generator"** IT as revenue enhancement, not overhead of doing business.

Figure 5-7 also suggests that either a service bureau or COE pattern is effective at enhancing the overall organization's capabilities with APM. It is often just a matter of the starting point and circumstances as to which pattern is selected. It seems logical that a service bureau would lead to a COE but I simply haven't seen enough of those opportunities to say so conclusively.

Deployment Scenarios and Priorities

At this point, you have exposed enough of the realities of working with APM technology to know if you're on a successful path of skills acquisition and appropriate staffing or not. And maybe you have deferred dwelling on the staffing requirements (as with the FTE) question by instead focusing on the value desired and shifting the focus to the priorities for the APM initiative, as summarized here as patterns for APM:

- **Ad-hoc**
  - **Initial**
    - Deploy monitoring, show value
      - Production only
      - QA only
    - Deployment only
  - **Growing**
    - Use metrics storage resources effectively
    - Get processes established
    - Establish acceptance criteria and app audit capability
    - Division of labor
  - **Mature**
    - Deep visibility and integration
    - Mature processes
    - Catalog of services and specialties

- **Service Bureau**

  - Take charge of the onboarding process
  - Build towards service-level management

- **Center of Excellence**

  - Establish education and self-service
  - Leverage existing staff and technologies
  - Establish and share triage specialists across the enterprise

There are three major organizational patterns: ad-hoc, service bureau, and center-of-excellence. Ad-hoc is exactly that: no real plan, coupled with some dedicated practitioners and, over time, you can get some very capable APM systems. Very often, these ad-hoc initiatives are limited to very narrow definitions of success, which seems reasonable but actually makes it difficult to continue to grow the scope of the initiative. The motivation and support to undertake an APM initiative, for example, is completely different if you are in a QA or production environment. The three ad-hoc sub-patterns are production-only, QA-only, and deployment-only, reflecting the different motivations.

Each of these three sub-patterns is a completely bonafide use of APM. It is just challenging to extend from one sub-pattern to another, which gives rise to the various starting points for APM initiatives that I introduced in Chapter 2. The executive support, goals, and techniques that made you successful in one sub-pattern are not directly transferrable to another sub-pattern. As the organization matures in its use of APM it will naturally attempt and refine the remaining sub-patterns, eventually ending up with an implied or explicit service bureau for APM. This is what the skills assessment (see Chapter 3) is documenting and how you can identify the gaps in your organization's use of APM.

The advantage of the explicit service bureau pattern is that you can achieve in 6-12 months what would have taken you 3-6 years following the ad-hoc pattern and sub-patterns. You also have the opportunity to staff much more efficiently and, with the center of excellence pattern, establish training mechanisms to ensure that standard practices are established and followed in order to amplify the collaboration that APM supports, to benefit the enterprise.

Thus, if the management goal is simply show victory in a few critical situations, it will be hard to get additional training and assistance—unless you get lucky and someone has some spare budget dollars at the end of the year that could be used for training. Likewise, planning to be faster at resolving outages (reducing the mean time to identify and resolve issues) is not the same as using APM visibility to keep problems from getting to Operations in the first place. Understanding management goals and translating them into a service catalog—with a schedule and a summary of the value achieved at each point—is what will ensure the success of your APM initiative.

Even if you define and schedule your service catalog for realizing APM, the question of staffing will again be the foremost concern for your stakeholders. Focusing on skills, processes, and competencies is fine: How many people do we need to hire or repurpose? However, given the variable staff loads as the initiative unfolds, it's not something you can answer with a specific number. The effort to do the initial deployment is distinct from future incremental deployments as well as the staffing to simply operate (no ongoing deployments). So let's look at a couple of deployment scenarios and see what kind of impact there is on staffing, as well as appreciate some of the drawbacks of insufficient scope.

Small Deployment Footprint Scenario

With a small deployment, you have an opportunity to manage across the life cycle and work with the system prior to production deployment. You will consider a small deployment when you are not yet convinced that APM can be successful, so you reduce your cost and time exposure. The initial management goal, which is typically to show some victory in a few critical situations, still allows for appropriate processes but leaves up to circumstance what would actually be achieved. To improve this situation, you have to demonstrate that any new processes will have minimal affect on the existing pre-production activities but will provide meaningful insights into performance. You are not asking for big changes in the QA model. You are simply stating that using APM pre-production is as important as making the initial APM deployment in production.

Thus the management goal is to start getting experience with APM pre-production. These successful processes, baselines along with rapid deployment and basic triage skills, will be attractive propositions for other application teams. Someone has to go out and start working these processes to prove to the other teams that it can be done and that it offers value.

There is still a gap in managing the APM infrastructure for capacity management and planning of the metrics storage component. With a small deployment, you are unlikely to need this skill set up front. It is too much of a hurdle when there is only a single APM server worth of metrics. Any emphasis on capacity management will not be picked up by successive teams. They will very likely end up with their own APM metrics storage component as this also avoids the difficulties in solving how APM resources should be shared and licensed.

From the staffing perspective, you need two people to ensure continuity of APM expertise. They will take care of deployment, testing, and triage over the 2-6 months before APM is established, working fractionally with APM over that time. It will be a challenge to keep the skills fresh for that small team, depending on the pace of testing and deployment along with the frequency for triage of operational incidents. There will be little or no reuse of their efforts by a separate group or follow-on initiative.

To get a better benefit from this small deployment scenario, you need to insure that you start with more than a pair of practitioners and allow them to migrate as additional projects come online. This allows you to move the most skilled forward and onto the next initiative, leaving behind the lesser skilled to continue developing but at a more relaxed pace. Thus the follow-on initiatives gain from starting with an experienced team, increasing the pace as well as the scope of the incremental deployment. You need to ensure that the experienced pair works with a novice pair, handing off the APM responsibility while moving on to the next deployment. This can continue for quite a while and is how the ad-hoc pattern can achieve as effective a result as the service bureau pattern—even if that was not the initial goal. This staff evolution is illustrated in Figure 4-12 in Chapter 4.

The other necessities are that the most experienced pair maintains a dotted line management of the novice pairs to insure consistency of APM service delivery and provide mentoring. It's also important to bring the novice teams into advanced situations to further extend their skills. Because you are allowing two people to move from project to project, you are effectively adding two FTEs to the staffing answer. The other roles are virtualized and their participation will average out as 2-4 hours per week, exclusive of training.

Multiple Independent Initiatives Scenario

Without the benefit of migrating APM specialists, once the small deployment has shown value and other teams begin adopting the processes across the life cycle and using APM for their own applications, you are at some risk of ending up in a poor state of affairs due to poor communication among the participating teams.

On the staffing front, you will have some combination of redundant staff or sharing violations to contend with. IT and application teams naturally form somewhat impenetrable silos of specialty with minimal sharing of staffing resources. As each team starts up with APM, they are naturally going to borrow expertise, if possible, from the existing deployments. Otherwise, it effectively becomes multiple independent small deployments. Hopefully, they will then establish their own pair of APM practitioners, especially if the sharing becomes too frequent.

In the absence of planned coordination of these multiple deployments, the major risk to the APM initiative is the collapse of the APM infrastructure. As discussed in Chapter 2, stakeholders tend to treat APM as a traditional monitoring technology and do not make any allowance for capacity management of the APM infrastructure. It may be that each deployment stands up its own servers and avoids the capacity management issue by each having excess capacity. If the APM infrastructure resources are consolidated, someone has to establish guidelines and actively manage the capacity on behalf of the participants.

Solving the cross-business-unit problem is the real measure of organizational success. If you can find a path to sharing resources and infrastructure as appropriate, you can eliminate the staffing redundancy and also establish a capacity management system for the APM infrastructure. Once you have achieved these additional processes, you can continue in this deployment model for years, achieving up to 5-15 independent deployments of APM before someone starts a re-examination of the value delivered by the APM initiative.

Unless you are exceptionally lucky, each of these 5-15 groups will really be independent from each other. They may all share the same emphasis for using APM across the application life cycle, but they will probably not share much of anything else. Few common processes, few common acceptance criteria, significant APM staff redundancy, multiple vendors, and overlapping functionality—the list goes on. The state of these affairs really demands a standardization of processes and techniques if you are to continue maturing the monitoring organization. This is going to be difficult to change because it means some groups will have to give up close control of their APM activities.

When you know that you will have multiple deployments ongoing among independent teams, you have to start with the appropriate APM pattern in order to avoid these issues. You can still implement it as needed, provided that you have a roadmap of how all the pieces are going to come together. It is rare that the enterprise will arrive at a functional discipline for APM behavior without some centralized planning and guidance.

Of course, you will not always know when APM will be limited to one or two independent teams, or that these teams are in fact the vanguard of an enterprise deployment. It can be years before there is sufficient interest to expand the scope of APM implementations and the teams that started will not likely be in the same roles when the reassessment occurs. But how many independent initiatives are too many? Three? Five? Ten? There is no concrete threshold except that the more initiatives you have, the greater effort it will take to rein them all back in to a consistent APM pattern.

Because the initiatives are essentially independent, no single initiative owns the big picture; everyone experiences the same strain to establish and maintain APM expertise, and no one can really achieve the full value for their investment. There is simply no one to coordinate the initiative. Ignorance (of the other initiatives) is bliss—until someone adds up the costs, inefficiencies, and missed value. As the APM marketplace has matured, this is the dominant scenario, and it's something to avoid recreating now that its inefficiencies are evident. It is completely solvable with a bit of work and raises some interesting questions. Who has the best processes? Who are the lead practitioners? Which of the independent initiatives becomes the service bureau or center of excellence?

Service Bureau for a Line of Business Scenario

The service bureau deployment model avoids the limited efficiency of the multiple deployments model by simply starting with a shared APM resource. The challenge is to plan a reasonable path to introduce and grow the service offerings that comprise the service bureau. Implementing the processes is easy. Getting the right integration points and leveraging existing processes and standards is more challenging. Here you try to get multiple groups interested in using APM but not really interested in taking on all of the deployment and higher level skills and responsibilities. You first establish that you have effective rapid deployment and triage skills—things that the various groups may already lack interest in supporting themselves. Any experience with APM that you have, beyond the stakeholders, is going to be attractive. You will be in a position to guide and augment their growing use of the APM information. You help them to understand what the app specialist role will look like with APM, which is really all they want to be responsible for. If you are in a position to share your initiative and service catalog planning, you even have an opportunity to show what additional APM capabilities will come online as the number of deployments increases.

At minimum, using a service bureau for ongoing deployment of multiple applications is going to be more successful than incremental ad-hoc deployments of the prior model. Evolving the services that the APM team provides will take longer to demonstrate value. You will need to complete a few cycles of identify-fix-test-retest-deploy so that you have enough success stories to bring more application teams to your APM initiative.

When I'm working to establish APM best practices with stakeholder teams, I find about half of my service bureau initiatives are taking existing APM deployments and consolidating or refactoring their existing practices. The remaining portion includes new APM initiatives and is split between stakeholders who are leveraging the efficiency of the initial deployment (following the phased deployment model) and clients who are moving directly to a service bureau for all APM activities. It remains a challenge to have stakeholders break the habits of traditional monitoring, to look beyond the initial deployment and appreciate how APM will actually be employed by all stakeholders and not simply those in Operations.

Center of Excellence for a Corporation Scenario

To date, I have only delivered COE initiatives for stakeholders that had multiple APM deployments. No IT organization has yet decided to go from zero APM usage and capabilities to an APM COE in a single step. I do not think this will ever be a practical choice as there is simply too much that needs to be decided and real experience is the best guide. However, it follows that moving from a service bureau pattern to the COE is going to be more efficient than moving from multiple independent APM initiatives to a COE.

For stakeholders that pursued a COE program, almost all will have been using multiple tools (different vendors), so the primary emphasis is on achieving unified processes and standards and enhancing the value they receive from monitoring. There is sometimes a reduction in the number of tools employed but that is not the primary goal of an APM initiative. Somebody else gets to make that decision. You should focus only ensuring that you have appropriate visibility with whatever tools are left—avoid the politics of choosing which vendor is employed.

Typically, COE initiatives more fully embrace using APM across the application life cycle at minimum with both QA and production; otherwise, you really end up with a service bureau pattern. The initial teams involve 10-20 individuals, which generally reduce down to 3-6 people after about two years, depending on the deployment pace. The reduction in headcount occurs as most staff transition to application specialists with distinct lines of business. A smaller number of staff may move on to other opportunities. I don't know if there is continuing growth among application specialists being APM capable, other than those that participated in the COE initiative. I simply do not have any mechanism to track those statistics. My primary measure of the success of an APM initiative is the growing footprint of applications using APM. Typically, the growth year-to-year (or six month intervals) for a significant application looks like: 9, 25, 50, and 75. For smaller applications, you can easily grow into the hundreds and thousands. This growth is not expected to continue forever as APM is usually targeted at high value applications and these should be a finite quantity in a corporation. However, the pace of APM adoption among multiple business units can take a few years to develop inertia.

What differentiates a COE pattern from the service bureau pattern is the emphasis on uniform processes, education, and initiation of appropriate standards for the corporation. It is a consensus on how APM will be employed. Gaining consensus takes time and that's where the service bureau pattern allows for variations, from which a COE can select or meld the successful strategies. You can avoid politics by equipping each line of business with the same service catalog schedule and seeing who makes the best progress.

Defining Your Services Catalog

It's time to lay out the details of the service catalog so that you can establish your own. The service catalog is actually an ITIL concept; other than mentioning this lineage, I do not really focus on ITIL definitions and processes because they simply do not meet my criteria for a rapid and incremental establishment of an APM system. I have found that organizations that are pursuing an APM initiative simply don't have the KPIs established on which to deliver service-level management. And this is the real goal of ITIL-focused organization.

You will need to guide the nascent APM organization move correctly and predictably to a metrics-based culture and the correct foundation for service-level management. If you follow the APM strategy in this book, what results is compatible with the ITIL architecture and this is all you need at this point. You'll need to make sure that every activity achieved has a place in the future ITIL service management model, despite the fact you are making no effort to ensure every ITIL service is accounted for. My concern is to help you articulate and define what is really necessary to *establish* an APM system so that you may manage the expectations of your sponsors and deliver value for the APM investment.

To be successful with your APM imitative, you need to show your sponsors exactly what they are going to get, when those capabilities will be available, and what resources and support you need to get it done.

Why is a Services Catalog Such a Valuable Strategy?

The challenge for many APM initiatives is that both management and the implementation team may lack the experience to confidently govern the initiative. This may be due to experience with an earlier, unsuccessful initiative or an appreciation of exactly how much they do not yet understand about APM. Even as you may now grasp how these considerations come about, you still need to provide a framework on which the progress of the initiative may be confidently tracked.

There is nothing wrong with caution except when inaction results. You can be cautious and pragmatic provided that you establish meaningful goals along a timeline of incremental, short duration activities that establish the monitoring initiative in a predictable and managible fashion. I call this framework of actions a catalog of services or *service catalog*. Through the service catalog, you define exactly what you are going to do for the business by defining the services that the business may expect you to competently deliver for APM. ITIL folks put it most succently:

> "A set of specialized organizational capabilities for providing value to customers in the form of services".[7]

The big value for this service catalog approach is that it provides for rapid implementation and realization of capabilities—and it also has a number of objectives that may be easily tracked by management.

Assessing Role Competency

The payoff for a well-considered service catalog is getting to build the APM system. The payback for this opportunity is giving your sponsors a big stick with which to beat you should the schedule slip for the target skills and services. The most significant deliverable of the service catalog approach is that it provides a natural management point for tracking the progress of the initiative. You have a detailed list of service objectives. Now you only need to add a measure of when those objectives have been achieved. The mechanism for this is the *competency*—a verifiable activity that demonstrates mastery of a number of interrelated skills and processes. As you build the service catalog, you conduct competency evaluations to confirm that the proposed service is now realized and ready for ongoing delivery.

For this planning phase of the service catalog, you need to indicate in your proposed schedule when you expect the competencies to be achieved and what they will cover. The details can wait until the next part of this book— Implementation.

For the APM roles identified (see Chapter 4: "Planning – Staffing"), you now summarize the detailed skills, processes, and competencies that document progress in the evolution of an APM implementation. These details constitute the basic set of capabilities and are arranged as Good-Better-Best. Any of these details may be achieved via self-study or mentoring engagements. The competencies represent the core function of each APM practitioner and these are indicated in boldface in Figures 5-8 and 5-9.

---

[7] ITIL, Service Design, page 11.

Role	Good	Better	Best
Agent Administrator	•**Rapid deployment**	•Agent promotion •Agent customization •Agent validation	•Custom and advanced instrumentation
Metrics Storage Administrator	•Metrics storage (MS) sizing •Basic triage (MS)	•Metrics storage (MS) capacity management •Baselines (MS) •Thresholds & alerting •Reporting •Dashboards	•Capacity management & planning •Triage with baselines (MS)
Application Specialist	•Critical app Assessment •QA acceptance	•MS capacity management •Quality review and escalation •Baselines •**Application audit** •Threshold/alerting •Reporting •Dashboards •Alert review and escalation	•APM practice management •Capacity management and planning •Triage with baselines •**Performance optimization**

Figure 5-8. Role competency – Part 1

Role	Good	Better	Best
APM Project Manager	•Critical app assessment •Metrics storage (MS) sizing •Deployment planning	•Agent promotion •Quality review & escalation •Agent validation •Alert review & escalation	•MS capacity management •Gap & enterprise assessments •Basic triage •Staffing strategies
Monitoring Architect	•Metrics storage sizing •Basic triage •Critical app assessment •Solution certification •Deployment planning •Agent validation	•Metrics storage (MS) capacity management •Quality review and Escalation •**Application audit** •Alert integration •Backup/failover	•Capacity management & planning •Proactive management •**Performance optimization** •**Gap and enterprise assessments**
Triage/Fire Fighter	•**Rapid deployment** •Basic triage •Metrics storage sizing •Critical app assessment •Agent validation	•Metrics storage (MS) capacity management •Agent customization •Agent promotion •Baselines •**Application audit**	•Triage with baselines •**Performance optimization** •**Gap and enterprise assessments** •Advanced triage •Custom and advanced instrumentation

Figure 5-9. Role competency – Part 2

Some of these, like rapid deployment or gap assessments, are stand-alone activities with no other skills required. The others require a number of skills before the competency should be attempted, including app audit and performance optimization. In general, you cannot expect to be successful with a competency in the second and third columns until you have completed all the activities preceeding it.

The Last APM Pattern

I've set this topic apart because this last pattern has not yet been realized. It was the original design goal for my APM best practices and in addressing it, I derived all of the other skills, processes, and competencies. This last pattern is the *self-service portal for APM*. I have had a number of conversations about what an ideal APM solution would be and the consensus is that it would should require minimal training; be simple to use; that it should present and manage various workflows; it should manage all of the data and reports; and expert help should always be available. Different from an APM monitoring technology, it should implement the processes and integrations that you need to realize APM. A portal architecture best fits these ideas. It needs to be more than a single application. It needs to scale to hundreds of users. It needs to be a familiar interface so that users can interact with it after a minimum of training.

There is nothing unusual about this idea—except that I tried to build it. I tried to identify the major workflows and use cases. I tried to identify the forms that would be used, the interviews, technology selection, approvals, and so on. I imagined generating tickets to cause agents to be deployed and transactions to be defined or captured. I imagined uploading baselines and automatically comparing them with prior baselines. I imagined selecting a trouble ticket and seeing the key metrics automatically identified for the hour prior to the incidents, potential root causes listed with probabilities, and statistics summarizing the frequency where the potential root causes were confirmed. Everything was feasible but nothing was in the scope of what I could undertake single-handedly.

What I could do was define the use cases, processes, artifacts, and roles to prepare for some future state when the portal would become available. At least I would have content. And that is the state of things today.

I mention this last pattern because I don't accept that APM requires continuous development and effort to achieve a complete and useful capability. I expect that the final state for APM is to fade into a portal that oversees the application life cycle, including governance, design, development, testing, deployment, and operations. It requires additional effort today in order to establish these processes and artifacts, and to train stakeholders to expect and utilize the data and analysis of APM—much the same as the introduction of the telephone, television, word processor, or the Internet required time for adoption. It will take time for APM to become ubiquitous and then it will fade into the fabric of technology-based business practices.

Cookbook

To define your service catalog, you need to first determine what management capability and organizational model your initiative will establish. This will make it easier to identify the target service offerings. You then want to consider what roles will be targeted and from this will follow the timing of the competency activities.

1. Define your target management capability (reactive, directed, proactive, service-driven, value-driven).
2. Define your target organizational model (APM pattern) for the initiative.
3. Determine what options you will have to account for the cost of your initiative—cost recovery. These might be chargeback[8], activity, or shared resource models.
4. Identify what other stakeholders will support your initiative by providing funding and resources to participants in the chargeback or other cost recovery model.
5. Identify the resources you will need for the initiative and the training and mentoring schedules. Refer to Chapter 4: "Planning – Staffing" for additional guidance. Select the roles and competencies that your initiative will pursue.
6. Identify which applications will benefit from the initiative and a suggested schedule of when these applications will be under the APM system. Refer to Chapter 3: "Planning – Assessments" for techniques to manage a number of candidate applications.
7. Identify the services provided, the competencies that will confirm that the service capability is established, and a schedule of when they will be available.
8. Put all of the prior findings in a presentation, not to exceed ten slides.
9. Begin socializing your proposal with your immediate stakeholders and practice delivering and defending the presentation. Initiate contact with other parties that may be supportive and try to bring them into the program.
10. Work with an executive sponsor to tune the proposal and get on the funding calendar. This need not be the last step but do not involve your sponsor until you have a reasonable plan and you are able to defend it.

Summary

APM has patterns of successful use in contrast to the unsuccessful or anti-patterns that were introduced in Chapter 4 (Table 4-8). These successful patterns show you what the future state of the initiative should look like. That future state can be expressed as a service catalog for APM, which also gives you a mechanism to plan, schedule, and assess the success of the APM initiative.

---

[8] Wikipedia, "virtual chargeback," http://en.wikipedia.org/wiki/Virtual_chargeback

You focus on deployment of APM technology as the opportunity to sketch out the processes of a successful APM system, and then refine them over the few deployment iterations. I will discuss this in detail in Chapter 7.

The capabilities of an organization are summarized in terms of what they do today and what they are willing to do tomorrow in order to make progress toward successful use of APM. Assessing the current and future management capability was introduced in Chapter 3. However, there are three more levels to consider that lead you from the traditional perception of the role of monitoring and into the more capable arena of application performance management: service bureau, COE, and self-service portal. These patterns are the horizon you will be working toward.

The Pilot Evaluation

Try it before you buy it.

The penultimate assessment of the utility of a monitoring initiative is to try out the tools in your own environment. I believe that everyone appreciates this simple concept. My concern is that it is very easy to define a pilot evaluation that completely fails to address the potential for the organization to correctly adopt the technology being considered. When this potential is zero, it can be a tremendous barrier to success in both applying the technology and in helping the organization mature its monitoring capabilities.

What compromises the usefulness of a pilot evaluation is that they are more often focused on features than the actual utility of the technology. As introduced in Chapter 1, many organizations are blindsided by the increased responsibility and collaboration across the application life cycle that APM introduces. So you should not be surprised that you need to move the definition of the pilot from the narrow focus of the sponsoring end-users of the technology to a broader set of roles and activities. Simply put, most evaluation teams only have their own concerns as priorities and do not have sufficient perspective to assess the utility of the technology across multiple stakeholders. You need to ensure to that the proper perspective is explored.

These considerations will *not* make the pilot evaluation more complex. They will make it more realistic and, ultimately, more collaborative. Otherwise, you end up with multiple tool sets overlapping in capabilities and reserved for a chosen few practitioners. Thus, it's no surprise that management continues to invest in APM tools, yet has nothing to show for the investment in terms of more effective triage, fewer incidents, or better software quality. It's often a problem of poor pilot scope.

In this chapter, I will introduce the elements of a broader APM pilot scope to be completed within a five day period. You will evaluate a sample application under load and make a first attempt at delivering an audit of the application. An application audit, which is detailed in Chapter 14, fully exercises use cases for QA, pre-production, and production. You will want to coordinate with those stakeholders for the wrap-up meeting. You'll also want to give them an opportunity to drive the tools, in their chosen roles, for the scenarios in which APM will be employed.

Participation

There should be at least two people participating during the pilot, exclusive of the vendor staffing. They should be available at least 50% of the time and both should be present for critical activities. As much as possible, you should be doing the "work" under the direction of the vendor. Just like team programming, you drive while the vendor helps you navigate. You may make adjustments in what activities you participate in but the more you do, the more information you get out of the pilot evaluation.

As you already know that different roles are leveraged by APM across the application life cycle, you should involve the appropriate stakeholders. Developers will appreciate the customization and integration details. Testing folks will appreciate the reporting and dashboards. Operations and support folks will appreciate navigating among the metrics, reporting topics, and alert integration.

And if you had an existing monitoring team doing the evaluation, it would be perfect! That's just not very often the case. I find that pilot sponsors are evenly divided as application owners or operations. It is rare that I actually work with an established monitoring team during a pilot evaluation.

Finally, take screen shots of everything you are doing. You only have the technology in place temporarily. Make sure you visually document everything of interest. This will make it a lot easier to compare how different tools approach different activities. It is also a way to demo your pilot experience to other interested parties later on, when you don't have the whole environment set up.

Goals

The typical pilot goal—and biggest mistake—is to get the software installed in your environment and confirm that it "works." This is why many folks refer to this activity as a POC (Proof of Concept). The APM marketplace is over 10 years old, so I find the use of the term POC a bit of an embarrassment. You are not working with a startup and assessing if they have an installable product; you are working with a mature technology. I redefine and elevate these activities to "pilot" and really focus on how to use the technology in your environment, not simply see if it is compatible.

I prefer to write a goal that establishes if the technology will actually help you do something meaningful and if your organization can leverage the tool and achieve the value proposition of APM. You should, too. This does not mean that you put installation issues aside. It means that you put them in their correct perspective.

You assign goals in three different categories:

- Installation
    - Can you install it?
    - Is it compatible with the firewall rules?
    - Is it stable?

- Visibility
    - Can you configure transactions/agents of interest?
    - Can you identify metrics of interest easily?

- Organizational Impact
    - Can you deploy additional instances on your own?
    - Is the reporting/alerting compatible with existing tools?
    - Do you understand who will be using the tools?
    - Will you know how to employ the new information?

If your pilot addresses these points, there will be no surprises when it comes time to implement and realize the value of APM.

Some of you reading this may see these goals as too difficult or too distracting. If so, you need to be pragmatic and reconsider if you are in the best position to undertake the pilot. A *POC* is simply "kicking the tires" with little or no commitment to doing anything meaningful with the technology. A *pilot* is a validation that the technology will be compatible with not only your technical environment but with your processes and corporate culture as well.

Another challenge is that your vendor sales team will use the POC as a mechanism to keep your team engaged and thinking about their product offerings. Their definition of the POC may not satisfy the needs of a pilot and you may end up with a false positive: you have a successful POC but you still do not know if you can actually exploit the technology.

Engaging the vendor sales team to define the pilot exercise is still mutually beneficial. You get to learn more about how to use the technology and the sales team gets to keep the conversation going. If you then take the time to complete the Skills Assessments from Chapter 3 and discuss with your vendor how they are going to help you address any gaps or how their technology would support those activities, you are going to get a lot of value from that pilot interaction. It is simply a much more meaningful exchange to pilot and get a thorough review of how the technology will benefit your organization, rather than a one-size-fits-all POC.

Connectivity

The first key test of a candidate APM technology is the ease in which it may be integrated with your environment. If you can't have appropriate communications among the various APM components (appliances, agents, metrics storage, and workstations), you really have nothing to pilot. The critical components are the firewalls that comprise your security architecture. They have to be configured to allow the monitoring traffic. You will need to share a diagram of your solution architecture with each of the technologies employed and activities or functions identified. This may also include Network Address Translation (NAT), authentication, and load balancing. The type of network link and available bandwidth is also important if the APM components are going to be geographically distant from one another. Even if you are limiting your pilot to a pre-production or testing environment, connectivity issues can arise unexpectedly. Ultimately, you need to understand both pre-production and production environmental constraints in order to complete a solution sizing.

A secondary consideration is any additional security that allows you to remotely administer the applications. Often, you'll have the applications on a different network than your staff workstations. This may introduce an additional layer of security that restricts which workstations may access the application network. There is no reason to wait until the vendor is onsite to uncover these issues. You need to have these details for your scope call in order to get guidance from the vendor as to what you need to configure or what the work-around will be.

Platform Suitability

For the APM workstation, transaction generators, and metrics storage components, you will need to supply appropriate hardware to host them. This need not be the same capacity you would use for the production environment; it does, however, need to be of sufficient capacity to support the pilot. Usually any modern platform will be sufficient. By modern, I mean at least as capable as your child's laptop; today this means 2-4 cores, 2GB RAM, 100GB disk. It should be dedicated to the pilot as you will evaluate multiple vendors and you may need to thoroughly scrub the system between vendor installations, as some products may not cleanly uninstall.

You should only evaluate hardware and operating systems that will actually be supported operationally. You may be anticipating a platform change and wish to accommodate that future state, but insure that a supported platform is available, even if you don't test it directly. It is not necessary to test multiple platforms as part of the pilot. Just use the one that covers the most scenarios with those matching operational realities as preferred.

Application Suitability

The single most important characteristics of the pilot application is that it works! I cannot relate to you how many times I have been involved in pilot evaluations that were little more than an excuse to get some technology in to help triage a problematic application. Of course you want to employ the technology in a realistic situation, but are you testing your ability to use the tools or are you testing the ability of the vendor to identify your problem? If you want urgent help that may or may not result in a sale, then avail yourself of a firefight service package. This way you get an experienced triage consultant who is only focused on your issues, and your team is free to do other things.

Otherwise, when you try to leverage a pilot as a firefight, you will most likely end up with neither activity being satisfactory. You will not complete a valid pilot. You will not get your operational problem identified. You will burn two to three weeks in the effort.

When you are genuinely interested in exploring your organization's ability to use the technology, consider defining the goals of the pilot to match the objectives of the application audit, discussed in Chapter 14. This will let you collaborate among developer, testing, and operations, and at least insure that everyone knows how the technology will be applied initially. This might also bring up concerns for existing tools and capabilities that the pilot might overlap. Rather than shut down the pilot opportunity, engage these stakeholders to detail what they need so that everyone can evaluate the suitability of the technology.

Pilot evaluations often come with a high expectation from the vendor that if they can meet your requirements, you will buy something. That is completely fair, provided that they appreciate that the pilot must be designed to indicate if the client is *not ready* to take proper advantage of the technology. Simply having a successful installation of the technology is not enough. You have to show the value of using the tool amongst your current processes and environment.

Pre-Production Visibility

Having the ability to detect performance problems pre-production and working collaboratively to resolve them is how I define proactive management[1]. I prefer this more generic definition (from business management) because it emphasizes process and collaboration as well as being pre-emptive. If that is your goal, you need only establish or leverage the existing testing capabilities and you have an opportunity to catch problems proactively.

There are other definitions for proactive management that are less stringent and somewhat narrow. They may be alert- or helpdesk-focused (noticing problems before users start complaining) but are really just a recasting of reactive management. As you learned in Chapter 3, a great many production problems may be avoided with appropriate processes pre-production. It is not enough to simply respond more quickly; you need to eliminate the problem from your operational experience if you are going to improve software quality.

Often, true proactive management is not your goal and this presents a challenge. You can still use APM technology to improve your visibility in production. It is just harder to be truly proactive and this puts the initiative at risk, unless expectations are set appropriately. You may not have a testing environment to use. You may not even have a practice of load testing the application prior to deployment. In these cases, make sure that "proactive" doesn't appear in the pilot scope or wrap-up. It will be difficult to meet this expectation in the future without the required investment in load testing or similar activities pre-production.

---

[1] Vietz, Osmond. "What Is Proactive Management?," www.ehow.com/facts_5701467_proactive-management_.html

At minimum, you want to configure the APM technology outside of the production environment and do a manual exercise of the application. This will confirm that the initial configuration is correct and will increase your probability of a successful production deployment. It also helps you establish that the technology is compatible with your pre-production environment. Pre-production environments usually have very different capabilities from production, so this is a latent concern to diffuse. There is not a lot you will see with this manual load, but you will get some evidence of the potential to see problems prior to production. You need this small example to help management understand the benefits of supporting a testing system, as well as the greater benefits of a full APM capability.

If you have an established testing system, you will want to complete the bulk of the pilot in this enviroment. Automated load generation is the preferred process but you can still get good results with batch activities. Manual exercises can be helpful but this will also introduce a lot of variation into the results depending on how the users are exercising the application. A reproducible load is the foundation for management of application performance.

You will want to evaluate a variety of configuration options, depending on the type of application and the type of APM component, including at least one low overhead and one optimal visibility configuration. The testing environment can withstand higher overhead, and thus a more detailed visibility configuration, because the application does not support actual users trying to do business. For production use, you want to minimize the overhead so that all remaining processing power is available for the user activities. You want the pilot to show you exactly how this is achieved and what the trade-offs are in terms of visibility and configuration.

If you have automated and reproducible load testing available, then you also want to collect information to establish three types of baselines. The first is the *configuration baseline* and it summarizes the different configurations tested, what impacts on memory footprint and response time were observed, and what issues (if any) occurred in obtaining those configurations.

The second is the *application baseline* and it summarizes which business transactions were exercised and what signatures were observed that uniquely identify each transaction. You also want to summarize the range of response times experienced and the overall count or proportion that each transaction contributed to the load evolution or test plan. This is useful in order to confirm the consistency of the load generation and also to confirm the proportions of use cases covered—QA testing versus the production experience. You will usually have a use case associated with one or more transactions and you should have a list of the use cases you want to get visibility into that will be shared during the scope call.

The third baseline is for *performance*. Here you identify the components with the highest response times and those components with the largest number of invocations during the load testing. These will be used, at minimum, to set up dashboards, reporting, and alerting You also use this information to assess and diagnose the performance of the application. Navigating to find this performance information, as well as the mechanics of dashboards, reports, and alerts, are the essential exercises to assess the usability of the overall solution.

All of these activities lead you to an audit of the application. If you can complete the various baselines and identify the critical transactions and performance characteristics, you may then increase the load or try alternate use cases and document how the application responds. If you can load the application to failure, you can then verify target capacity, scalability characteristics and, most importantly, validate that your alert thresholds will be giving you accurate guidance.

Completing an application audit is about 80% load automation and 20% visibility. It takes about five days to schedule and complete all of the load generation. You will have 10-20 load tests of 20-30 minutes duration, dependent on the variety of APM configurations evaluated. A load to failure test takes 2-8 hours, depending on the test plan. The application audit is a core service, and also a key competency that you look for when you evaluate the maturity of a monitoring organization. The full details of conducting the audit are found in Chapter 14.

Production Visibility

Most pilot activity is focused on a testing environment because there is minimal risk to the business if a configuration or test becomes problematic. Also, the automated testing is usually reproducible—the same test always generates the same response time. This makes it easy to compare different APM configurations (agents and transactions). Not all pilot evaluations will have a testing environment available, so you need to allow for another path. Often this may be a pre-production or User Aceptance Test (UAT) environment. This is a portion or sub-set of production to allow for limited use of a new release without exposing the entire user population to the updated functionality. It is really more risk mitigation than a testing technique. There will be no automated load, which limits your potential to regression test[2]. It's really an functional test of the release candidate.

You may still collect your baselines. You just have to allow a week or two to aggregate consistency among the findings, when only 1-3 days would be needed in a test environment. This is because the pre-production environment is not necessarially reproducible, from one hour (or day) to the next. Where you have more control of your test plan while in QA pre-production, absolutely anything can occur during a UAT day, so you need to aggregate many days to confirm if are the audit results are consistent. One benefit is if you have any installation or configuration difficulties, they will only impact the subset of the user population, so you are still at low risk to negatively impact the normal business operations.

The same situation holds for a pilot in a production environment, with the exception that the potential risk to interfere with normal business is significant. It is not just the APM components configuration (robots or agents). It is actually the potential firewall changes that will be the most devastating. You really need to exercise your change process pre-production to reduce the risk. This is the challenge with an immature organization—there are so many potential negative outcomes for the pilot that you should really consider other activities to help establish a business justification for moving to APM.

---

[2] Wikipedia, "regression test," http://en.wikipedia.org/wiki/Regression_test

The other route is to do a production audit (Chapter 14), firefight (Chapter 18), or visibility assessment (Chapter 3). This is not a repudiation of pre-sales technical expertise but if you need to deploy directly to production in order to accomplish a pilot evaluation of APM technology, you simply want to use consultants who do this all the time. The challenge is the cost of the consulting engagement.

A good *production* audit, a variation of the application audit in QA, is going to take 2-3 weeks to collect consistent data to support the various baselines. If you have an urgent problem, a *firefight* service is the correct route; this is a poor substitute for a pilot, however, because you are not really evaluating the APM solution, you are leveraging the ability of the vendor to get visibility into a production problem. None of your staff is really going to be involved in actually using the APM technology, so you do not really get a correct assessment of your ability to be successful with the technology. This leaves the visibility assessment, which will analyze your incidents and look at the effectiveness of your current monitoring technology—which is not really a pilot at all, but will help you to build a case for APM.

The visibility assessment, detailed in Chapter 3, allows you to understand and document the current state of the organization and its ability to exploit APM technology. This can take from 4 hours to 10 weeks, depending on the scope of the assessment, and is even more expensive than the production audit or firefight because of the time commitment. The value is that you get a fully documented and validated plan on how to successfully employ APM technology. If you can use your own staff to deliver the visibility assessment, you may eliminate the outside consulting cost, but you still need to allow sufficient time to complete the assessment and recommendations.

Criteria

I have included a sample pilot scope document that summarizes how I like to approach a pilot. What follows here is a bit more dicussion of the details and some issues I have encountered so that you can tune the document to more closely align with your environment and goals.

Compatible with your Environment

You should not have to do much to get the APM solution up and running. Depending on the APM technology under evaluation, you may need to provide a computer platform for one or more components, the specifications of which will be shared by the vendor. One exception is when you are working in a "hardened" environment where your available computing platforms have had some functionality removed. You may then be required to add packages to restore the operating system configuration back to "typical." Hardening[3] is performed to remove potentially dangerous services from the operating system so that the resulting platform meets security guidelines. Sometimes this is done with a heavy hand and ends up punching some holes in unexpected places.

---

[3] Wikipedia, "hardening," http://en.wikipedia.org/wiki/Hardening

Of course, any security requirements would have been raised during the pilot scope call. Platform hardening is often unknown to casual users of the client environment, so any late adjustments to this should be accommodated and noted for the wrap-up meeting.

Some APM technology is appliance-based and only has requirements for physical connections—network and power. Again, this would have been discussed during the scope call. No other hardware options are supported or necessary.

Some APM technology will have a limited set of platform configurations (brand/vendor, operating system) that are supported. This is also not a problem, provided the client guidelines allow the configurations. This is also apparent from the scope call.

Ease of Initial Installation

This is often very subjective. I have a simple strategy to assess if the installation is easy: no one goes for lunch until it is working! This way you will get a "gut feel" even if you are not in the habit of trusting your instincts. Realistically, please share your goal for the installation with your vendor so that they can prepare. Sometimes, pre-sales folks are new and need to deliver a couple of pilot evaluations before they hone their skills. They should be mentored through this process, so do not be alarmed if you find two people doing the install. In the best situation, you should actually be doing the install, guided by the vendor. You should be the one getting the mentoring.

Installation should break down into two distinct phases. The first phase is to establish the APM platform, which you typically do only once. This would include any APM component that is physically independent of your application, typically the appliance, transaction generator, or metrics storage system. The second phase is what you will do repeatedly—every time you add a new application or transaction. Make sure you actually complete a couple of agent deployments or transaction definitions from transferring the files, completing the configuration, and confirming correct operation. This is what you will be doing to support ongoing deployments of the APM technology.

At some point, you will consume the initial APM platform capacity and need to deploy additional instances. You should get a good idea of when that is likely going to happen for your environment and deployment plans. Capacity planning can be difficult for an inexperienced team. You really need to leverage the vendor and have them forecast your consumption and deployment frequency to get a complete picture of what you are in for.

Flexibility of Technology Configuration

Another on-going activity is the ease with which changes to the monitoring configuration, agent, or transaction are accomplished. Many products have a variety of configuration options to optimize their visibility into specific technologies, like a database or a portal platform. Make sure you evaluate how each of your deployment scenarios is supported.

If you identify three different types of applications, this will give you a realistic impression for the ease of configuration. In the Java environment, I like to choose candidates for POJO, J2EE, and portal. POJO stands for "plain old java object" and is the simplest application you can have in Java. J2EE means that a container, and likely an application server, is being employed. This results in a medium complexity application. Portal is a variety of pre-packaged services on top of the application server, resulting in a complex application. Each of these varying levels of application complexity results in a different configuration of the agent or the transactions, depending on the type of APM technology you are evaluating.

Assessing Overhead

This is a complex topic that almost everyone has an opinion on. You will find a sample test plan in Chapter 13 that sets up a reliable process for comparison.

What you need to decide is if you will pursue this as an objective for your pilot. Any APM technology has some overhead considerations. In general, they are small and thus very difficult to measure accurately. Unless you have a very mature QA system with automated and reproducible load, you really do not have the tools to measure overhead. You just do not have the ability to discriminate among small performance impacts.

Sometimes overhead is huge—and those are situations that you want to capture during a pilot, without the complications of precise load reproducibility. The challenge here is to have some technology available that lets you assess transaction timings. Often this can be in the form of log messages about each successful transaction, usually specifying the timing. Even if the logging is known to be expensive, this is a simple way to get overhead information—providing the same log levels are used for each configuration—with and without APM technology in place. CPU measurement is generally not useful. It is both too coarse and not representative of the impact on the business transaction and the user experience.

If you believe that overhead measurement should be part of your pilot, first evaluate your ability to reproduce load before you commit to the pilot. Understand what you testing team may deliver. Otherwise, you are evaluating your testing organization and not the APM technology. If you plan to conduct overhead testing, please notify your testing organization so that they will be prepared to support the pilot requirements.

Assessing Deployability and Scalability

While the pilot install is going forward, you need to be capturing enough details so that you will be able to reproduce a functioning environment. Questions of capacity need to be answered in terms of product capabilities as well as monitoring points that tell you when capacity limits are being exceeded. The number of metrics that the pilot configuration can support, in contrast with the number of metrics you actually generate, should be readily accessible. The first agent installation and configuration may take 1-4 hours but the second and third should take 10 to 30 minutes. Make an effort to deploy agents on your own so you can directly appreciate the ease or difficulty in encountering and resolving errors.

Your vendor will have a wealth of information to help you size and plan your initiative. You need to be honest about your intentions and how you expect that your organization will adopt the technology in order to get the most useful information from your vendors' experience in similar situations. You want to do everything appropriate to ensure success for a particular vendor in order to correctly compare each vendor's offerings and find the best solution for your current circumstances.

Solution Certification

Another goal for a pilot exercise is to specifically confirm compatibility of the APM solution with target environment in order to certify that the proposed technology solution is compatible. This usually means that an internal standards body has intervened in the proposed deployment of a technology and wants to insure that packaging, security, and deployment characteristics are compatible with their existing standards and procedures. This group is not an actual user of the technology. They are only interested in the tool and general standards around tools.

Hopefully, the end users of the APM technology will have already completed their pilot and made a formal selection of the vendor prior to the certification effort. The *solution certification* is a separate internal process where you confirm that a monitoring solution is compatible with your application or target devices. Sometimes this certification will occur prior to monitoring user acceptance—this is not a desirable approach. Certification may select technologies without the rigor of actually evaluating effectiveness or process compatibility. What results is a mandated use of the "certified" technology, which often leads to conflict with the application owners. The problem is that the team completing the certification is not likely to use criteria that is meaningful for the application owners. You end up with a solid anti-pattern for APM—deployment only, with no consideration for how the APM technology will be employed.

Certification efforts may also be defined differently than simply compatability with your environment. Sometimes it is part of the RFI (Request For Information) process, which is looking to understand the attributes of various candidate APM solutions.

It may also mean a *limited operational deployment*, where scripts, processes, and integration are finalized and operational experience is gained before being released to the general population. While this parallels the phased deployment strategy of Chapter 7 (a good thing), it has so far been a prelude to ubiqutous deployment: making the APM technology part of every standard build, usually with the APM disabled. This is a bad thing and the number one anti-pattern for APM. The idea is that the application team will activate it when they need additional visibility, making APM more of a production debugger. More often, it becomes a completely stealth deployment and the application teams don't even know about it. And without any centralized guidance on how to correctly employ APM, these teams have little chance of success.

Typical success criteria for a solution certification include the following:

- Repeatable, automated installation.
- Confirm connectivity: APM workstation or browser.
- Confirm connectivity: APM agents, robots, transaction monitors.
- Confirm compatability with existing processes and installed components.
- Acceptable quality and quantity of metrics.
- Confirm that application functionality is not impared.
- Confirm that application performance is not degraded significantly.

In general, certification is unnecessary for all but the most serious financial applications. This is because monitoring is *out-of-band*[4] with APM components, which means that the monitoring activities are independent and do not participate in the same transaction as the business logic. This is, of course, potentially more significant with agentless or appliance technology than for agents because they intercept the transaction, though this may be accomplished on a copy of the network traffic. Certification thus becomes a validation of the security issues. Is private information exposed? Will the technology impact the security in any way? These considerations will be less time-consuming than having to re-certify all of the business transactions.

If the production environment is very different from QA and pre-production in terms of connectivity, including firewalls, authentication technology or other identify management technologies, certification is probably going to be required and useful. Just don't confuse compatibility with the environment as a demonstration of acceptable APM technology. Of course your APM solution must be compatible in order to operate in the producton environment. However, a compatible solution is not necessarily useful if it does not have appropriate APM capabilities or the the organization is uninterested in exploiting those capabilities.

---

[4] *Out-of-band* is a telecommunications concept where the monitoring runs on a different channel (out-of-band) than the actual system that it is monitoring. If you extend this concept to a business service, all of the transactions that comprise the service are *in-band* and thus subject to security certification. The monitoring of those transactions is *out-of-band* and thus subject to a relaxed level of certification.

Cookbook

There are four phases of a pilot exercise: Planning, Scope Document, Implementation, and Review.

Planning Phase

1. Research the need for product certification. Cover requirements that make sense but allow for a formal certification after you have made a vendor selection.
2. Research what load testing capability is available and if a QA or pre-production environment is available.
3. Research what firewall changes may be needed. Make sure you understand the process to request changes and the time required for the changes to be implemented.
4. Research the process to get equipment into your facilities if you are expecting to pilot transaction filtering technology. Understand what kind of lead time and information they will need to get the equipment set up.
5. Select one or more candidate applications that have appropriate complexity, load generation, and value to the business.
6. Source equipment to support the workstation and metrics collection.
7. Identify who will participate in the pilot evaluation.
8. Develop evaluation criteria as critical, useful, and optional.
9. Prepare the pilot scope document (see the Scope Document in next phase).
10. Contact appropriate vendors and negotiate a mutually accepted scope.
11. Develop a rough schedule of activities, day to day.
12. Schedule the pilot evaluation.

Scope Document

1. Installation Requirements
    a. Supported platforms and operating systems
        i. Appliance Requirements (form factor, power, network)
        ii. APM metrics storage platform
        iii. APM agent—supported app servers, containers (J2EE, .Net)
    b. Security and identity configuration
        i. Firewall settings required
        ii. Encryption key activities

    c.   Ease of initial installation (duration, level of effort)

        i.   Appliance installation
        ii. Metrics storage installation
        iii. Workstation installation
        iv. Any browser requirements

    d.   Ease of incremental installation (duration, level of effort)

        i.   Transaction definition, promotion
        ii. Agent deployment and configuration

2. Ease of Use
    a.   Ability to login for various users
    b.   Navigation among various screens, dashboards, and reports
    c.   Confirmation of correct functioning of the monitoring solution

3. Basic Operations
    a.   Defining transactions
    b.   Identifying long transactions
    c.   Identifying long response time components
    d.   Identifying high invocation components
    e.   Defining alert thresholds
    f.   Defining dashboards
    g.   Defining reports

4. Evaluation with load generation
    a.   Are updates and navigation responsive?

5. Pilot Summary and Wrap-up
    a.   What was installed successfully?
    b.   What was deferred or skipped?
    c.   What problems were encountered and how were they resolved?
    d.   Were pilot objectives satisfied?
    e.   How did the sample applications present themselves?

Implementation

Allow a full week for a pilot exercise. Start Day One with a kick-off meeting to review the environment solution architecture, application details, and pilot objectives. The base installation and testing should be complete on the first day, ideally before lunch. The first round of load testing should be complete that afternoon, resulting in confirming a fully functional installation.

On Day Two you should focus on the more critical use cases for APM. I like to get the proof points addressed and out of the way early as you never know when something will go wrong or if you will encounter something unexected. Then I will go back and cover the easier proof points. I always prefer to iterate over the use case and objectives so that I can avoid any hiccups in the environment.

For a simple pilot, I am usually done on Day Two. This is why I favor following an application audit as the model for a pilot. It has more structure and many more findings to review. An app audit will involve 2-3 days of load testing. While this is unfolding, you can spend time building dashboards and reports, and hosting discussions with other stakeholders.

It is important to get screen shots of all your significant activities and findings. This is very useful to review findings with the stakeholders as you do not need to be on the APM workstation. I prefer to present findings or to demonstrate the APM workstation via a projector because you can really only fit two people around a laptop display.

On the final day, Day Five, I devote the morning to preparation of the wrap-up presentation, and maybe one or two other details that slipped from the prior days. The afternoon wrap-up meeting reviews everything that was done during the week, discusses the interesting findings, and makes a few recommendations for performance tuning or other considerations for future use of the technology. Ideally, you should have the wrap-up presentation delivered to you before the pre-sales folks leave. They can always do more and send it to you in the following week, but you want to have your artifacts in hand. You may very well be evaluating another vendor the next week so you should try to avoid having your pilot team extend over into the next evaluation waiting for findings—things will get confused and you will diminish the value of the pilot exercise.

Review

After many weeks of evaluation, you will have a fair amount of material that is readily distilled, via spreadsheet, into a simple score card. I prefer to arrange the Scope Document outline in one column, with each vendor in their own column. Allow a scoring of 1-5 for each objective in the scope document. This will yield a simple numerical evaluation of the vendors.

When you get down to two vendors, assign one of your participants to a vendor and have them present the vendor wrap-up. You can cut this down to 3-4 major points, unless there are significant (and useful) features about particular vendors that you want to highlight. You want your team to be behind both products, in a friendly competition. This will help expose your own understanding, or gaps, about the technologies. Any questions from that meeting can be directed to each vendor if additional clarification is desired.

Alternatively, after the pilots evalutions are complete and you have selected your top two candidates, you can bring those vendors back in to present their pilot results, one in the morning and one in the afternoon. My preference is where you undertake the friendly competition internally because this gives you some feedback on your teams abilities to absorb the technologies.

Summary

Understanding your motivations for a pilot exercise are as important as conducting the pilot evaluation successfully. A pilot exercise is convenient for both the technical team and the vendor for keeping a technology discussion going forward. It is up to you to define the pilot goals in a way that confirms the utility of the technology and your organizations capability to exploit it.

If you can define a single pilot scope document and use it for each of your vendor evaluations, you have really taken a solid step toward understanding how APM activities are going to affect your existing and future processes. A single scope document is a challenge because there may be unique functionality that you want to evaluate. Plan to look at those functionalities but realize that you have to compare all vendors on the most common denominator first, and leave the evaluation of unique advantages second. You have to compare apples to apples.

If you can leverage a pilot as an app audit, or if you set up an audit independently, this is the best way to evaluate the utility of a vendor solution to see exactly what you have to do to get that technology into production.

Implementation

Deployment Strategies

The secret of getting ahead is getting started. The secret of getting started is breaking your complex overwhelming tasks into small, manageable tasks, and then starting on the first one.

—Mark Twain

Part 2 of the book focuses on the implementation of your APM initiative. Part 1 discussed all of the planning concerns and ended with a pilot exercise. Depending on the result of the pilot, you may have deferred the APM initiative or moved ahead and selected an APM technology. If you made a selection, then the next step is to get it deployed, which is what we will discuss in this chapter.

Chapter 8 discusses the necessary APM processes; Chapter 9 discusses the growth toward specific service capabilities. As introduced in Chapter 5, the service catalog is useful to keep an initiative on track, even if you are not moving to an APM service bureau to organize your initiative. It also helps your stakeholders to understand exactly what capabilities the APM initiative can support, at any phase of its realization.

First, a word of caution. *Implementation* is often used interchangeably with *deployment*. Deployment of software does not include getting the software to do what you want. This is the largest point of confusion and dissatisfaction with performance monitoring software—IT thought its responsibility was to deploy the monitoring solution while the business expected an implementation that would help them identify performance problems. Part of this confusion has to do with who "owns" the software. IT deploys lots of applications on behalf of the application owners; why is APM different? APM is not an end-user application. It is part of the IT infrastructure, and use of the tool will be divided over many stakeholders. Often, an initial APM deployment is limited to a single stakeholder, and the reality of APM being more of an infrastructure choice is lost. Here, I mean *implementation* to cover the initial physical deployment, developing essential processes for employing the tool and how these processes are assembled into service capabilities.

The ideal audience for this second part is the project manager (PM) responsible for completing the deployment. However, many organizations simply merge this responsibility into existing staff. You need to understand what the deployment looks like and how to spot a deployment that has too narrow a scope to match the stakeholder expectations. Once a decision to deploy has been made, there is often very little time to correct the project scope and to reset expectations for what the deployment will deliver—"ready, fire, aim." You need to ask the questions that will compel more attention to what the "aims" of the initiative should be. To understand those questions—especially for large initiatives with multiple and recurring monitoring deployments—you should consider moving to an APM-specific PM, along the lines of what was outlined in Chapter 4.

As part of the initiative planning, we will assume that you have undertaken the initial solution sizing (this is covered in detail in Chapter 10). Often, the deployment team will focus on a very small set of applications. This effectively defers the sizing question to a successive deployment, which, regrettably, will assume that the sizing was correct for the initial deployment.

Depending on the forecast of the number of applications to be managed, in the first deployment, you will fall into one of two categories: a stand-alone (single instance) or a *phased* deployment. The actual number of applications that may be supported will vary with the vendor technology and the number of metrics that their solution will support. For discussion purposes, let us assume that this limit will be 350,000 metrics for a stand-alone configuration. Anything bigger would follow a phased deployment model.

Fail-over considerations, which may double the amount of supporting hardware, and other high-availability schemes, are discussed in the later section "Deployment Necessities." Fail-over becomes a concern in large solution configurations and is often discounted in small solution configurations. But the real focus should be on the overall scope of monitoring, and this is best captured simply by considering the number of metrics that will be created with the deployment. Fail-over may require additional hardware, but it does not affect the overall number of applications that will be monitored.

If you have any expectation of successful follow-on deployments, you really need to preserve the steps you undertook to achieve the first deployment, especially if another group is going to be doing the work. The primary document to achieve this is the production runbook (see Chapter 8), and this may be supplemented with details of the preproduction and operations procedures as they pertain to the activities within your enterprise. These processes are essential because avoiding reinvention of the wheel is the easiest way to control the overall cost of successive APM deployments.

Stand-Alone

For monitoring configurations of 350,000 metrics and less, a stand-alone configuration is indicated. A stand-alone deployment means a single instance of the APM metrics management server supporting some number of APM components and APM workstations. The actual number of APM components (agents, appliances, transactions, and workstations) supported will vary according to the vendor technology implementation. The number of applications monitored is only a rough guide, as the applications may each have multiple instances. Agents are deployed against each instance of the application, and the quantity of agents will often be a more accurate indicator of the overall level of effort. Each agent will generate a different number of metrics, depending on the nature of the application and its resources; the number of metrics is still the best measure of the overall scale of the deployment.

When there are multiple groups, or lines of business, that are interested in employing APM but are otherwise working independently of one another, multiple stand-alone configurations are appropriate. Combining different lines of business onto a single instance can be problematic politically. There may be competing agendas and unequal usage among the business units that make a shared-resource model unworkable. It is sometimes simply more effective to allow each business unit to manage its own server, even if it results in duplication of responsibility and resources.

When the corporation does not have a unified APM strategy and is instead allowing the individual groups to justify, pilot, select, and deploy an APM solution, this will often result in multiple vendor solutions being deployed—all stand-alone instances. Regrettably, there is little opportunity to share experiences when groups work in isolation this way, as they are more focused on realizing their objective than exposing their plans. Any additional review only slows down their schedule.

Of course, non-agent-based APM technologies (using synthetic and real transactions) depend on traffic flow and number of transactions for sizing, rather than the number of metrics and agents. We focus first on the instrumentation technology since it has the potential for greater resource needs and potential complexity.

An example of an initial architecture is shown in Figure 7-1.

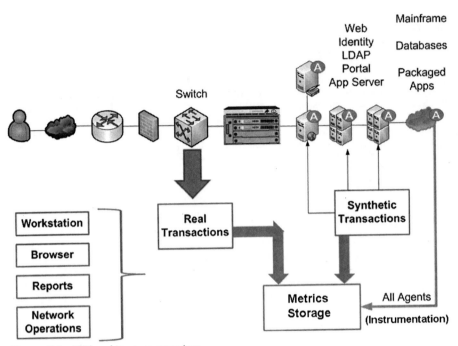

Figure 7-1. APM architecture overview

I say "initial" here because we have yet to layer on the fail-over requirements, if any. Ideally, you would always undertake a stand-alone deployment prior to considering a fail-over configuration. This allows you to gain some operational experience with a simplified configuration that may enhance your initial experiences with a fail-over or clustered configuration. At the very least, you will be able to differentiate between metric storage problems and fail-over problems. Otherwise, you may experience difficulties simply because you have insufficient experience in managing the combination of agents, Metrics Storage and fail-over.

In the solution architecture, the generic APM components are represented by the three largest boxes: Real Transactions, Synthetic Transactions, and Metrics Storage. Each of these will usually require a separate platform to be deployed, apart from the infrastructure supporting the applications. Agents can also be considered APM components, and in Figure 7-1 they are indicated by the letter *A*. Agents share the platform with the application, so no additional hardware is required to host the agent.

The Real Transactions component will take a copy of the network traffic data, called a *tap*, and filter out the transactions of interest. The Synthetic Transactions component will periodically direct transactions against specific application components (web server, app server, etc.) via one or more transactions to exercise those components. The instrumentation agents report their information to the Metrics Storage (MS) component. For display and reporting purposes, each of the transaction components may be integrated with the MS component, or each will have its own display—all of which will be managed into a single view. A single view of all of your different APM components is often a requirement of your network operations group. These folks have to consolidate all of the different monitoring information streams in order to supervise and direct efforts to resolve performance problems (operational incidents). The NOC (network operations center) is often a key collaboration point for the APM initiative. Integration of alerting, along with alignment of various processes from the NOC, is a strong statement of support for your APM stakeholders.

The overall sequence of activities for the APM initiative follows. Suitable hardware for the Metrics Storage server is identified and made available on the network. This is to allow for an instance in QA or preproduction (which may be temporary) and a production instance. IP addresses and ports are fixed. Any firewall considerations are indentified and appropriate ports and traffic are opened.

1. At least one workstation is deployed and configured to communicate with the Metrics Storage server.

2. The Metrics Storage server software is installed, configured, and started. Startup logs are examined for anomalies.

3. Communication between the workstation and Metrics Storage server is tested and any issues resolved.

4. An agent is deployed against the target application. This involves the transfer of software to the target machine and configuration of the startup script in order to activate the agent.

5. The application instance is "bounced," and the agent begins reporting. Agent logs should be examined for any anomalies.

6. Communication between the agent and the Metrics Storage server is confirmed and any issues are resolved. Metrics should be observed from the APM workstation.

7. QA testing should now progress to capture baselines for the target application and validate the agent and monitoring configurations. Please see Chapters 11 and 12 for details on load generation profiles and baselines. The agent is now ready for production. If you cannot test the agent configuration, then use the default configuration until you have more time for testing. It may not have the best visibility, but you will avoid any production issues.

The production Metrics Storage server is stood up (installed) and tested, as before. This is usually a separate piece of hardware. Otherwise, and depending on the vendor solution capabilities, multiple instances may be installed on a single box.

Even if you combine the QA and production agents in a single instance of the Metrics Storage platform, you really want to take advantage of this simple opportunity to practice the installation and configuration before you get to the production environment. It is perfectly reasonable to make a few mistakes on your first time out with the technology. No one is perfect. However, no one wants you to use production for practice! Do not attempt production before you have validated your ability to install reliably. This means "at least twice." And since good engineering practice would state that "two points do not make a trend"—you should really make three successful attempts before going to production.

This Metrics Storage platform install can happen in parallel with the agent validation, as that validation may take a day or two to complete. Often, QA testing requires some scheduling, which usually means some wait time, so there may be an opportunity to get the production Metrics Storage server operational. This is a necessity in order to confirm correct installation of the agent later on, even if that occurs days or weeks later.

Another important benefit of standing up the production metrics collection server early is to avoid the common phenomenon of "last installed—first blamed." For organizations that are new to APM, there is a lot of emotion building up. This may be due to inexperience or justified concern, but if anything goes wrong in production, the APM solution will be suspect. The easiest way to avoid this is to use a little "social engineering": Install the metrics collection server with great fanfare but don't deploy any agents. After a week or two, start quietly deploying agents. Anything that happens in the first week is easily deflected—no agents! By the second week, folks will have lost interest. The other approach is to undertake the initial deployment with minimal or no notice, which is a little sneaky, and hope that there are no significant incidents for at least a couple of days. This is what we often do for a firefight, when we cannot get access to a QA or user acceptance testing (UAT) environment. When someone finds out and directs blame toward the monitoring solution, you will have a few days of "good" data to point to. But the best approach, whenever possible, is to get all of your experience and testing done while you are in a QA/UAT environment. It will only add a few hours to the schedule but will really keep inexperience from causing problems with a first production deployment.

You can now transfer the agent files and schedule the configuration changes. Having all of these steps documented in what is called a runbook is a tremendous advantage, especially if you have another group responsible for doing the configuration changes in production. Restarting the application will usually be deferred until off-hours.

Steps 1 through 6 should take no more than 2 hours, exclusive of software download time; 30 minutes is typical for an experienced practitioner. Steps 4 through 6 should take no more than one hour; 10 minutes is typical for an experienced practitioner. Step 7 needs about 2 hours for three 20-minute load tests. Very often the load generation tool is a shared license, so it is prudent to allow a full day (or two) for the testing to be achieved. Knowing that you have the optimal agent configuration is fully dependent on the quality of your load testing. It does not need to be a heavy load—just a reproducible exercise of the application.

Getting the QA team to be responsive can be challenging. Many organizations have really squeezed the QA process down to little more than a functional test. Getting a quick load test may not be possible if the application team has not already prepared suitable scripts or lacks appropriate experience with automated load generation technology. Without proper visibility, companies have put this pressure on QA because no one saw the value of doing testing in preproduction. APM enables a lot of visibility preproduction, so it is an opportunity to get a better QA experience.

Folks do not often realize that they are simply missing visibility and they may voice their lack of confidence in the QA environment because it does not reproduce the production environment, or there is too much difficulty simulating database or message queue access, or simply not enough licenses to generate a suitable load. Using APM technology in QA is an opportunity to restore an important contribution to the application life cycle—realistic testing—but you will need to be mindful of your individual situation. I will go into more detail on the topic of QA testing strategies, which take into account the spectrum of robust to anemic testing capabilities, in Chapter 11.

There are, of course, the other considerations: fail-over, alert integration, review of your deployment plan, solution certification, and so on. These will increase the overall duration of the stand-alone deployment to one to two weeks, typically. This duration can be expected to decrease with successive deployments, provided some attention is devoted to preserving the details of the various steps.

Phased Deployments

The phased deployment model allows us to more accurately schedule and coordinate the resources and activities to support greater than 350,000 metrics. A medium-sized deployment will consist of 500,000 to 2,000,000 metrics when all APM components are in use. We will assume that this is an initial implementation, with no reusable artifacts available and no prior experience with APM and with multiple environments (development, QA, and production) permanently achieved. Sometimes a team, following an overly narrow scope, will actually deploy initially to all environments and then remove it once the production deployment is validated. They deliberately prevent any other team from leveraging their work. This is contrary to the collaborative goals of APM. We want to preserve the artifacts of the implementation so that successive deployments will be achieved in cookbook fashion. We want to make it easier for successive teams to employ APM, not ensure that everyone gets to reinvent the wheel.

It is always a challenge to develop a comprehensive plan and schedule when the client has no prior experience with APM. Basically, we have to allow for some significant changes as part of the implementation. As the stakeholder gains experience with the deployed APM solution, they will invariably change some of their initial assumptions in favor of ones that take better advantage of the technology. To accommodate this inevitability we allow for three distinct increments to deployment and operation: good, better, and best. Each increment needs to demonstrate the full range of deployment scope, functionality, and usability. And this needs to be balanced with the initial lack of experience and growing understanding as the different increments are realized. Good-better-best is an excellent strategy to properly set expectations.

Figure 7-2 summarizes the various phases of the phased deployment model, from which we derive the fundamental practices of solution sizing, preproduction, and operations.

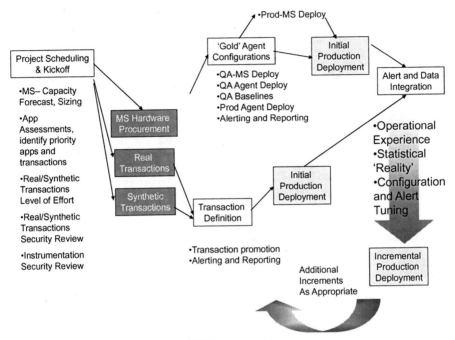

Figure 7-2. Phased deployment for APM implementation

This diagram progresses from left to right. We begin with the project kickoff, which should be more of a checklist activity than an assignment of tasks. We kick off the project having completed the solution sizing, security assessments, survey of the target applications, and estimate of the level of effort for defining business transactions (real and synthetic). There is great variability in how clients actually order and install hardware, which I've highlighted as the next phase after the kickoff. This is a potential risk, but something that the phased deployment model accommodates nicely, as we do not expect to have all the hardware in place in order to start the deployment phases. This accommodation has its limits, usually two to four weeks.

From the application survey and level of effort estimates for the definition of business transactions, we will have all the information we need to identify the general classes of applications for which we will prepare and validate the gold configurations. The test cycles for each application include deploying and tuning of the agent, so we will get plenty of practice prior to the production rollout. After the preproduction review confirms that we have the first phase in order, then we schedule the production deployment. All of the agents may be moved to the target application servers during business hours, the configuration gets completed, and then the agents become active after the overnight recycle—which is typical for many clients.

If we have done our job in QA, the production deployment is usually uneventful, and we move on to the operational phase. This will usually be equally uneventful, as we should have selected well-behaved applications. These operational periods are critical for a number of reasons. The primary reason is to allow any late requirements to pop up, decide if they are important, and then accommodate them in the next phase. Normally, project management is necessarily rigid about accepting late changes. I find that you have to be a little more flexible with APM because most folks simply do not know what they want until they see it! No matter how many scenarios I describe and illustrate, prior to the kickoff, and during the first phase, there is always something that remained unmentioned until the initiative became operational. It is an opportunity to demonstrate the flexibility of APM and accommodate these late requirements.

All we really need to accomplish in the first deployment phase is to avoid any outage or difficulty attributed to the APM initiative. What remains is that the initial deployment was operational after two to four weeks, there were no outages due to monitoring, we were able to accommodate a few late requirements, and we are ready to go on to the successive phases. Usually there is some concern about the time the first phase took and the amount of time left in the schedule. What most folks do not realize is that the significant work is already done for the successive phases, and now the deployment really begins to accelerate. We may have one or two additional applications for testing when we encounter a new gold configuration, but the bulk of the applications will be using the established configurations. There will be some exception adjustments in order to enhance visibility, but these too will be limited. You will actually spend more time in pre- and postproduction reviews than you will in actually deploying the software.

Figure 7-2 is great for the kickoff meeting, but suffers a little from too much compression. The next few figures will fill out the story, in four parts, for phased deployments for a smaller initiative (five to ten applications), and expand what that box for "gold configurations" means, as well as the rationale for the various actions in each part. The difference between a "smaller" and a "bigger" deployment is that the bigger deployment has a lot of supporters and everyone wants to see it achieved. The smaller deployment simply may not have broad support and will often find itself defending the justification to go forward. Folks are often holding the deployment to a very high standard and looking for any excuse to scuttle the effort. That will likely not be your specific circumstances, but this phased deployment model gets it done every time.

The key strategy is to get all of the APM Metrics Storage components, or MS servers, out into their various environments. This serves two purposes. The first is that deploying agents without the MS servers in place deprives you of any knowledge about the success of that agent deployment, so the MS servers always go out first. Second, we want to move MS servers into production, with a little fanfare, so that we can take advantage the classic production gambit: "Last change, first blamed." We make sure everybody knows that we are deploying APM and that we are entering production. No agents are deployed, and we simply start the servers, confirm connectivity with the workstation, and wait for some complaints.

Except for power consumption, there is really no way that the MS servers can interfere with another application. They are completely stand-alone—which makes for some interesting discussions—and after a few days, folks will move on to more productive targets. The ideal situation is where the MS servers in production are up and otherwise fully functional for a week or two.

As Figure 7-3 shows, while the production footprint is cheerily deflecting accusations, we begin promoting (moving) a base agent configuration through each of the different environments. This base configuration represents the minimum settings that will give us decent—or "good"—visibility and that have the smallest chance of introducing a problem. This is important because unless you have some experience setting up the agents, it is very likely you will make some small mistake and then sit there wondering how to resolve it. By moving through the environments repeatedly, you get enough experience to understand how to do it correctly for your environment, and if you happen to make a mistake in production, you can be confident that you will resolve it quickly.

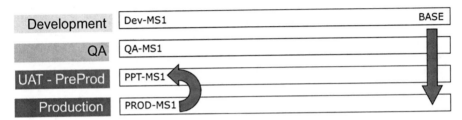

Figure 7-3. Phased deployment strategy, part I

We focus on a base or minimum configuration because we are not allowing for any testing. Ideally, we want to get a couple of agents into production—fully functional against live applications—and just have them sit there without any concerns or needs to triage. We want to select robust, well-behaved apps for this role. Our goal is to simply monitor them in production without any incident being attributed to the new arrival—APM technology. The only way this can be achieved is with a couple of weeks of utterly uneventful monitoring.

Another scenario that gets unusually lavish attention is when you propose to bring a fail-over architecture into production. The operations folks know you need to prove it. And you do not yet know that it will actually work. Kind of a chicken-and-egg problem—which comes first? What I try to do is take advantage of the fact that the MS server is UAT and exercise my fail-over between this pair. All I need to demonstrate is that the few APM agents in production can be configured to fail-over in UAT, and the reverse. For documentation of this event, all you'll need are some screenshots that show where the agents ended up and what fail-over time was observed.

Typically, a fail-over exercise involves whole data centers, firing up generators, and lots of hand-wringing—and all on your kid's birthday weekend. All we need to do to test fail-over is to pop out the network connection, wait 5 minutes, and then put it back in.

For Part 2 of the phased deployment (shown in Figure 7-4), while the production MS servers are being exonerated from dimming the lights or causing the milk to go sour, and we practice our fail-over, we begin in earnest to test the agent configurations that will give us visibility into specific applications. Instru-mentation results, in terms of the number of metrics, will vary significantly, from one application to the next. Validation of configuration is the prudent path, but if you have a few dozen applications, rerunning load testing is going to take a very long time. Instead, we select a representative application for each major category of application. Generally, I start with J2EE, .NET, and portal applications, determine the optimal configuration for each, and then immortalize them as gold configurations. Thereafter, whenever I encounter one of these application types, I simply deploy the gold config and we can be confident that it will work well.

The test plan could not be easier. Simply exercise the application, note the high activity components, and keep them under 20,000 invocations per minute. Full details are found in Chapter 11 and Chapter 12.

If you consider Figure 7-4, you will see a number of gold configurations being promoted from development into QA. This is the major reason for checking overhead early. While we all may agree that production overhead should never be more than 3 to 5 percent of CPU utilization, in preproduction environments we don't really care. They don't need efficient resource utilization. They do need efficient test coverage and deep visibility. In fact, many developers will easily tolerate 40 to 50 percent overhead in preproduction. This is what they get from their profiler technology and, conversely, why no one can ever successfully use profilers in production. What often happens is that developers will configure an agent for maximum visibility, and this results in high overhead. The QA team may not notice this overhead, and the next thing you know, a poorly configured agent hits production—and bad things happen.

The promotion process is how we catch poorly tuned configurations. Whenever we move between environments, we always want to confirm if we are incurring excessive overhead for that environment (details in Chapter 12). The closer we get to production, the less overhead we can expect will be tolerated.

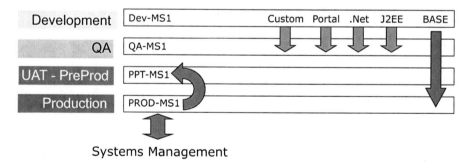

Figure 7-4. Phased deployment strategy, part 2

The other important activity in Figure 7-4 is to start a simple integration with the existing systems management or trouble management system. I really try to keep this simple—one or two actual alerts, and one way (APM sends alerts). Later on, the receiving group may want to grab other information from the APM environment, either via log files or perhaps via an SNMP-Get, if the vendor solution accommodates that. These later integrations will be more difficult; for instance, to establish communications identifiers and understand which messages to collect. All alerting will go via a separate channel anyway for the initial deployments. We are not deactivating any existing system or platform monitoring. We are adding performance and capacity management, which will initially be the responsibilities of the APM team and application owners.

In Figure 7-5, the third part of the phased deployment strategy, we begin promoting the more advanced agent configurations through the various environments, using simple test cycles to validate and tune (as needed). Before we promote these new configurations to production, we want to first establish production fail-over capabilities. We will already have a data set for demonstration purposes, from the prior second part of the phased deployment, so this should be another uneventful activity.

There may be an opportunity to do more with the integration of alerts with systems management or network operations, especially for notification when an APM monitoring fail-over event occurs. This is a great opportunity to discuss who will be managing the APM infrastructure, from the capability-and-performance perspective.

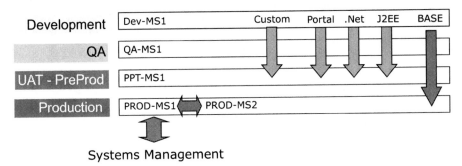

Figure 7-5. Phased deployment strategy, part 3

In the final part of the phased deployment model (Figure 7-6), all of the agent configurations, gold and custom versions, have been deployed to production. There will have been a few iterations over the dashboard and reporting implementations, but these are among the easiest to change and redeploy. Many of the activities around APM simply do not meet the same rick proposition as a new software release, so configurations changes to the APM environment occur as needed. This does not extend to any updates to the environments, which should be going through an appropriate change mechanism. This is, however, focused more on the agents than the metrics collection technology, which is much more independent of the applications that are being monitored.

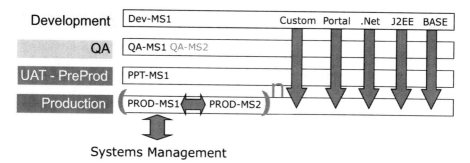

Figure 7-6. Phased deployment strategy, part 4

Depending on the capabilities of the vendor technology, there may be a cluster configuration option. There is no need to wait until you run out of capacity to try out the cluster configuration. At this point, we may have only had a few weeks experience with the stand-alone configuration, so it may be useful to delay the cluster configuration until three to four months later. Someday, you will run out of capacity, either due to growth or a configuration error. When that happens, you want to have experience with how the cluster responds normally, so that the change to clustering during a crisis can allow you to understand how the environment will recover and what might be evidence of a cluster configuration error. We want to avoid, whenever possible, trying something for the first time in a live environment. This does not mean that you will never be capable. It just means that your measure of a successful APM initiative is simply that nothing went wrong that you did not already know how to deal with. As you get more experience, you will of course be able to cut a few corners in order to make things happen quickly in a future deployment. When you have zero experience, this is the wrong time to be heroic.

Preproduction

As already introduced, many organizations will mistakenly focus on the initial deployment as the goal for the APM initiative. We have instead offered a model for an APM implementation and converted the solitary deployment into a rapid deployment process. We now continue with the implementation by focusing on a preproduction process and put a little more depth into understanding exactly what we should consider for successive production monitoring deployments.

The initial deployment, with a goal of "good," employed a best guess, hopefully based on some accurate load testing, of what the ideal monitoring configuration would be. This includes the agent configuration, as well as the dashboards and reports. The phased deployment model expects that the initial deployment will be operated for at least two weeks. This allows operational data to be collected that can be used to confirm both the sizing of the Metrics Storage and the visibility of the monitoring configuration. So, what we need is a process to review the postproduction experience and make recommendations for any changes, and then a preproduction review process to confirm that the changes are implemented, as well as any additional functionality that is part of the second (targeting "better") deployment phase.

Preproduction Review

The duration of the review is a function of the number of applications, or the number of unique monitoring configurations that have been deployed. I prefer to focus on whatever approach results in a smaller amount of effort. With a phased deployment, the emphasis is on the type of applications being monitored—typically J2EE, .NET, and portal—not the overall number of applications, so this results in a natural reduction in the level of effort.

We also want to adopt a philosophy of exception management—we want focus on the configurations that did not operate as expected. If we expected to get 1,000 metrics for an agent configuration and we got 3,000, then this is something we want to investigate, as it is 200 percent above expectations. If we only completed 10 percent of the target applications, we are in no danger of being out of metrics capacity, but we need to understand what changed between our forecast and reality before we deploy the next 30 percent.

The reason for the two-week minimum operational period is to allow a consistent confirmation of the operational characteristics of the APM solution. One point does not make for a trend. I like to see three. For example, if there is a surge in alerts in response to a performance degradation—I would want to see that surge occur two more times before I disabled the alerting.

The more general considerations are as follows:

- Is the agent configuration safe?

  - How many metrics are being generated? Are any of them excessive invocations? Are there any unusual memory profiles?

- Are operational dashboards present?

  - Is there an overview dashboard to summarize what is going on for operations, and does it allow them to drill down for more information?

- What is the target number of agents to be deployed?

  - What is the current Metrics Storage capacity? How many of each gold configuration will be deployed?

- What is the target metrics capacity increment expected?

  - How much capacity will the deployment consume?

- What new alerts are being introduced?

  - Start with availability alerts if going to trouble management. Otherwise, put the performance and capacity alerts on an e-mail alias for distribution. It isn't necessary to alert on everything. We only want to confirm that the alerting mechanism is working as planned.

- What are the characteristics of the application experienced during QA/UAT?

- Do we have stable apps? Which apps are likely to cause problems? Have we prepared baseline reports to help with triage should things go poorly?

I believe that the only successful outcome for the production environment is that nothing went wrong with the monitoring deployment. All of your mistakes and learning should be exercised while in preproduction. It is certainly possible that your APM team will master the deployment of APM without any extra work—but the odds are against you. And if you have problems, you will damage the reputation of the technology in the future.

If this continuous defensive posturing seems a bit relentless, it is because you are coming up against human nature. Folks just do not like change, and APM changes everything. Unfortunately, the politics and emotions are set to hair-trigger, and you have to do everything possible to keep them contained. And nothing defuses a situation like plain and boring success (and the passage of time, to let the tensions evaporate).

Operations

If a monitoring team has been established, or if the app teams are taking responsibility for performance alerts, there is really not much impact for the operations team. They may be seeing some additional alerts for the APM tools, but these should be in parallel with the availability alerting they were already receiving. Very often, the performance alerts will arrive 5 to 20 minutes before the incumbent alerting. Our concern is only that each APM alert is matched by the corresponding incumbent alert so that the overall alerting is validated.

There will also be performance alerts over response time and capacity. These are not usually part of the initial 10 percent deployment, but will be enabled in the successive deployment phases. However, these performance alerts are not typically the responsibility of the operations team. They will not have a response for a performance incident that does not result in a loss of platform availability. Instead, these performance alerts will be delivered, usually via a separate but parallel channel, to the monitoring and application teams. These folks are the ones who will oversee the remediation of the application.

The other significant role for operations is in integrating all of the available monitoring into a single view. This may actually involve multiple screens, so maybe a single room is more appropriate—but it is important that operations benefits from the additional visibility that APM provides. This is not in the depth of monitoring but rather the breath—very often APM has a number of metrics integration strategies that can bring previously invisible apps into the operations center.

Operations is in a unique position to correlate among multiple monitoring technologies, in addition to the availability alerting and trouble management capabilities that it provides. This helps the operations team to triage performance anomalies in the legacy environment, even when APM is not directly providing information.

The intended APM-influenced evolution of operations is to move from being the focus of all alerting to management of a single view of the corporate environment;

hosting repositories for runbooks and knowledge bases that streamline access to information by the support or help desk organization.

Realizing QA and Triage

As suggested earlier, many organizations will unfortunately take a very nearsighted view of "get it deployed" as the goal for an APM initiative. This view focuses on how operations will use of the monitoring technology, the traditional users of all monitoring technology, in the form of alerts. However, any other use of the APM technology in the application life cycle is simply not the responsibility of operations. Also, the management of application performance is simply not the goal of operations. Its primary role is simply to manage and respond to availability alerts. When operations is the initial owner of the APM initiative, this can lead directly to failure of the initiative, with respect to broad use and acceptance of APM. No one is in a position to get any benefit from the APM technology because the tool is restricted to the operations team, at the tail end of the application life cycle.

Some organizations will realize this fate, and even as operations owns the tool, they will select an application team and expect them to employ the APM technology. This is typically for the triage role—and that is a good start. But this group is under a severe challenge: there is always an expectation that they will be proficient in using the APM tools to solve real production problems, as operations often does not consider that part of its responsibility. Where does the application team get this experience? How many times will they have a chance to show what they can do before everyone gives up on the idea?

To give this application team a realistic chance at success, we have to allow them time to get familiar with the APM tools and practice problem-solving scenarios. The phased deployment model allows for this reality by setting aside an operational period for operating the solution and confirming that the information gathered is as expected, before denoting that portion of the deployment as complete. So, on a small, manageable portion of the environment, the APM team can start to use the tools in a live environment. This initial operational use of the tool is called *triage with single metrics*, and the goal for the APM team during the operational period is to identify production baselines and start to appreciate the characteristics of the applications when they are running correctly. Quietly, we also hope that, after a few days of operation, at least one of the applications will experience an incident so that the APM team can attempt to triage it.

This brings up an important point: the bulk of the applications you deploy in the first deployment phase need to be *stable*. This is often counterintuitive. Folks have decided to invest in APM technology because they have urgent problems with some critical application and lack the visibility to resolve them. Naturally, they want to deploy the tool on this critical app and figure out what is wrong and get it resolved. And it is not just inexperience with the APM tools that will cripple the initiative; it is the richness of the metrics and the absence of any reference on how to interpret those metrics that will put the APM team at a profound disadvantage. Sprinkle in a healthy dose of executive interest and pressure to inspect if the APM investment is yielding dividends, and you have a recipe for failure of the initiative.

The motivation for having a greater proportion of stable apps as part of the initial deployment phase is to have evidence that while app 3 is crashing every hour, apps 1 and 2 are operating without incident. Recall our earlier anecdote: "Last changed, first blamed." If you only have an unstable application, are the frequent crashes because you misconfigured the APM tools, or are they because of a characteristic of the application? How can you be sure? Until you successfully deploy monitoring for a few applications, you simply cannot have confidence that you know what you are doing. You need to have stable applications as part of the first deployment phase. And you need to have at least one unstable application to start building the triage experience.

Now, at this point, you should be feeling a little uncomfortable at the proposition of trying to establish triage by drafting behind an initial production deployment, and hoping that you will be able to learn enough in those two weeks of initial operation to not be a complete embarrassment when a major incident occurs. Some stakeholders will have talented staff to help them bridge this gap, but for most clients, this is simply an unfair proposition. Certainly, we can employ professional services to help us ensure that the initial deployment phase is successful no matter what stability the candidate list of applications demonstrates, but all this does is postpone the problem. At some point, you will need to do it for yourselves, and the pressure will actually be more severe after many weeks or months of successful deployments via consultants. That proposition simply does not scale.

So how do you facilitate the necessary experience to ensure a future successful production deployment? You do it in the QA or UAT environment first.

Now you will notice that I often lump QA and UAT into the same environment. What I am really saying is, "Any place other than production!" Production has lots of rules and guidelines, and literally dozens of folks whose primary role is to keep out anyone who does not know what they are doing. Production is "the business." When someone fouls up here, it causes a lot of tension, as major systems may be affected. Simply stated, production is *not* where you practice your deployment!

This does not mean you cannot accomplish a direct-to-production deployment. There are many business scenarios as to why this is a necessity and, frankly, we experienced practitioners do this fairly frequently.

But we have the distinct advantage—we know how to do it! Our advice for you is simple: don't do it until you know how. But often this is not practical for an initial deployment because you, the implementation practitioner, are likely inheriting a whole string of ill-advised decisions and have little choice other than to go forward immediately. So how do you tip the scales in your favor without drawing too much attention?

If you undertake the deployment sequentially, across at least two environments and with a small subset of the target deployment, you will have the confidence to know that if a problem occurs, it would be a remote possibility that it was due to the APM tools. You will make some small mistakes, which gives you an opportunity to establish that you can distinguish a deployment problem from an application or infrastructure-related problem.

If you repeat this at each deployment phase, you will have actually completed at least six individual deployments. The movement of a monitoring configuration, from one environment to the next, we call a *promotion*. When we promote a validated QA configuration to production, we have essentially eliminated almost all of the risk in getting to the production environment. We still have the possibility of a typo or other manual error, but these are scenarios that we can easily document because we will have learned what the characteristics of a correct deployment look like.

If we could start in development and get the initial setup understood, then promote to QA and do some load testing, then promote to UAT and get some live user experience, and then promote to production—we would be getting that six-sigma feeling of control and predictability. Often, that is not practical for an initial deployment either—but we can dream!

Anything we can do in preproduction will be a tremendous benefit to enhancing the success of the production deployment. So why is it that we treat this scenario as the exception, and not the rule? Why would a client *increase* their risk by not undertaking a preproduction deployment?

Understanding Preproduction

The preproduction environments consist of QA/functional testing, integration, stress and performance testing, and UAT. Sometimes they have different names, but we will focus on the following definitions and leave it to you to decide what you call them. For example, some folks use "model" as the name for the preproduction environment. Let us take a look at the activities of the various environments and then discuss some of the problems with preproduction.

Functional testing is where an application is manually exercised to confirm that the specified functionality is present and operating correctly. Most software development is driven by detailed requirements, and someone needs to confirm that all of the requirements have been met. This may be the size of data entry fields, the correctness of calculated values, or the interface with other established systems. We like to monitor functional tests because it gives us a first peek at stability—but memory management issues are a first priority. The disadvantage with functional testing is that load is not significant, and reproducing a particular problem is hard. Sometimes a batch process will be used to achieve a functional test. Here, a file of transactions will be replayed against each release of the software to confirm that it is working correctly.

For some business scenarios, batch testing is always appropriate. For example, many financial/banking applications are really batch operations running either periodically throughout the day or once at the end of a business day. While these make for excellent functional tests, they do not provide any real insights into the actual performance or capacity of the application to support any performance tuning. Performance and capacity considerations are combined into a single acceptance criterion: did the process complete successfully in the batch window allowed? The great advantage with batch testing is that it is very reproducible. A single file of transactions will always give the same result, or something is wrong.

Integration is where packaging concerns are addressed and limited testing of integration interfaces is done. Very often, a *deployment package* is prepared, using a standard technology like pkgadd(), rpm(), or Windows Installer, which combine the application code and resources with the APM agent resources and configuration.

This facilitates automation of the deployment increment and helps avoid any manual errors. The interface testing here is usually done with the authentication technology—setting up passwords, access control, and validating that functionality. Integration is really a specialization of functional testing, with the end result being that the application functions exactly the same as preintegration.

Stress and performance testing, or *load testing*, is where a consistent exercise of the application is undertaken. This will often involve a load generation tool that simulates user interactions in a predictable manner. Load simulation is a sophisticated topic and takes many forms, including "none." The ability to simulate user activity is an easy measure of organizational maturity because a realistic load requires quite a bit of planning and use case capture. Very often, an organization will get hung up on its ability to reproduce the exact load and physical environment of production. This is a throwback to the availability monitoring mindset—if you don't have all the same moving parts, then you cannot have a chance to reproduce the outage. We find that you do not need to reproduce the production load to identify many performance problems. However, the more accurate the load simulation, the more accurate will be the capacity forecast. See Chapter 11 for more details. We also find that many production incidents are easily identified in preproduction, no matter which load simulation capability you have. Most of our preproduction processes need only a modest load of 10 to 100 users to be effective. Monitoring via APM technology in this environment is essential. The challenge for many organizations is simply having some kind of response when APM indicates a problem.

UAT is where a limited subset of the user population, often the more experienced users, utilizes the new application as part of their daily workload. They will also be expected to report on possible bugs or other inconveniences. This may also be called a limited production rollout and will often be an isolated subset of production. This environment is otherwise full production, in terms of databases and other resources. Monitoring here is beneficial because the user interactions may be more complex or more realistic than was possible during load simulation, especially for any use cases that were missed during load simulation. A great advantage of APM technology is being able to compare what was tested with what was actually experienced. This is an important feedback loop to improve the quality of the preproduction experience.

If you are using a UAT environment, this will more accurately represent the production experience in terms of use cases, but it will not be accurate in terms of load. It can't be—UAT is only a subset of the user population. The biggest shortfall is reproducibility—getting the users to do exactly the same things that initiated an incident.

The Problem with Preproduction

If there are such a variety of benefits from undertaking monitoring while in preproduction, why don't the majority of stakeholders take advantage of this opportunity? A number of factors contribute to a poor experience in preproduction: scope, reproducibility, and access to load generation tools. Simply providing load generation is not enough on its own—all three points have to be addressed.

For scope, we mean the variety of deviations from the expected result: what kinds of problems do you expect to identify and are you prepared to resolve? In an availability-monitoring-centric organization, performance is simply indicated by survivability—did it crash or did it stay up? Ultimately, this is all the organization is being measured on so this is the obvious characteristic to confirm before moving to production. If an application *survives* the load test (manual or automated) without any major incident, it is pronounced worthy for production use. Any assessment of measurable performance is limited to some timing data that may appear in log files and inferred capacity via the volume that the testing experienced. This results in a "smoke test"—if it didn't blow up (or catch fire), then it is good. There is nothing else to indicate the contrary. This is truly the definition of pass/fail. Such a test strategy is of limited *scope* because only a single mode of failure may be observed— that of availability. To be successful in preproduction, we need to increase the number of failure modes that may be observed.

The common excuse for why additional testing is not undertaken to supplement the availability or smoke testing is that the environment does not faithfully represent the production environment. This will be due to either missing use cases or, more likely, that the hardware and resources available in production are not available in preproduction. This is a significant challenge. Many organizations simply do not have the resources to build a testing environment that matches production: they cannot match the larger number of server instances nor the dataset size, nor the database performance, for example. And when the testing environment does not accurately reflect what may be available in production, folks pretty much lose all confidence in the findings during preproduction.

Load generation technology has long been associated with helping organizations address these first two points. It provides a convenient interface to generate appropriate use cases and automate the execution of the load profile. The load profile may be ramped to increase the number and variety of use cases, through a simulated or virtual user session, to accurately reflect the load profiles that are expected. It doesn't do much to address the hardware profile and capacity, and introduces some other difficult considerations. For example, where do these use cases come from? How do you know that they are representative of the user experience?

As suggested earlier, adding a load generation/simulation system is a great step forward in managing application quality. But it is only the first step, not the end of the issue. Employing load tools effectively requires another three considerations: getting the load to be reproducible, getting the load to be faithful to reality, and realizing that even with accurate load generation the results are only a good approximation of what is really going on behind the scenes.

So what do we really need to reproduce in order to do a better job in preproduction? The obvious metric is the number of times a component is invoked for a given test. Every time the test is run you should get exactly the same number of invocations for that test plan. Often the test plan has a number of random values in an attempt to simulate a more realistic user activity, so sometimes the number of invocations will vary. The difference between simulation runs should always be a small number— less that 1 percent is a good start. Another metric is the average response time for the key components of the application. This presumes that you know what the key components are, which is easy enough to figure out with APM. For the test interval, we want the average response time to be less than 1 percent different among three runs.

If 1 percent seems a little severe, bear in mind that we are often trying to resolve confirm differences in the range of 1 to 5 percent, as well as configuration tuning in the range of 5 to 10 percent. If your load reproducibility is on the order of 15 percent, you just do not have any chance at resolving those gains. Chapter 11 will present the details of how to design the load profiles and interpret the results.

Repurposing QA Equipment for Production

There is one special antipattern I have encountered that is absolutely contrary to a sustainable QA system: repurposing equipment. I believe the motivation is economic, but it also has a touch of invulnerability. Essentially, you order your production equipment well before it is needed, and when it comes, you use it to test the application. This has the obvious advantage that what you test on will be exactly what you will have in production. And it also allows you to practice your deployment in preproduction. But it also assumes that you will never need to retest the application or that there will only ever be a single release.

This is like building a house and using a ladder to get to the second floor. Then you reach down and pull up the lower rungs so that you can keep building higher. You get to the top but you do not get to go back. I see this situation fairly often, and I guess it is due to a strong project focus for the development team. But to assume that you are never going to need a testing environment is pretty bold, in my opinion.

I used to think that this situation was a variant of the "too expensive to replicate production" antipattern. But the footprint rarely turned out to be that expensive. I just do not have enough insight to understand what the real motivations are here. So I am stumped as how to influence this situation toward a dedicated QA system. I am sure that somewhere, someone must be successful with this test and deployment pattern. I simply have yet to see a commendable system of this form.

Anyway, the phased deployment model is perfectly suited for this situation. We can get a fair amount of testing done, so we are prepared for production. We do not get a stable QA environment on which we can layer our growing APM system. If this is your model, there is not much else I can do for you. You have all of the practice you can utilize in the phased deployment model. Feel free to move to Chapter 8.

What if you could keep your QA environment? What if you could reuse the experiences and learning from each project that passed through? If that is interesting, please read on.

Evolving QA and Triage

Now we are at an interesting crossroads. Let's say that you have been commissioned to move an APM initiative forward, from zero to production. Your company maintains a QA presence, and you are going to leverage it to test your monitoring configurations and also gather information, in the form of baselines, and so accelerate your teams' capabilities for triage. Just exactly how do we schedule these activities when the QA team has never before used APM, let alone the app owners (or monitoring team) who have never performance-tested an application before?

Fortunately, with the phased deployment model, we will have three iterations to get the QA system with APM established. The first point to realize is that the stress and performance testing, along with the APM configuration validations, are a shared exercise. No single participant "owns" the activity completely. Your role is to provide this missing coordination so that there is one voice.

The typical situation is that the monitoring team will deploy agents on the QA servers that host the application under test. A number of agent configurations will be explored, much the same as during the pilot exercise, to find and validate the optimal monitoring configuration. The evidence that APM technology does not affect the application needs to be shared with the QA team, as well as how the final configuration was decided. The team needs to have confidence that its testing will not be compromised. It also needs to be confident that all of this can occur with minimal disturbance to typical workloads.

As the monitoring team moves on to the stress and capacity testing, the baseline reports will be generated. Again, these reports will be shared with the QA team so that it can understand the relationship between its test plans and the information that the monitoring team can then generate. Frequently, the monitoring team will uncover one or more issues with the applications. And, as is the case with many organizations today, there will be no adjustment to the deployment schedule to deal with these issues. Just because APM indicates a concern does not mean that anyone else will accept it. This is the shared pain of QA, the APM team, and even the application owners—the schedule is the priority, even if there is indication that more investigation is warranted.

The applications then go on to the production phase, deployment is completed, and an operational phase is started—typically two weeks. The situation we are looking for is a performance incident with one or more of the deployed applications. Again, it is very important that the initial deployment phase consist of mostly stable applications. This will help the troublemakers stand out, and at the same time deflect concerns that the APM team does not know what it is doing. In particular, we want these failures to be pretty much the same issues that were found during QA testing. We cannot actually control that, but we can hope for the worst, as unsupportive as that might sound.

What this does is highlight the fact that we can detect issues in preproduction, and the fact that there are no minimum acceptance criteria. Every application was advanced along the life cycle in the past because there were no iron-clad acceptance criteria. There was nothing other than a functional test to pass. This is also an opportunity to introduce a remediation process that might allow some extra time to correct the problem, before moving to production.

Acceptance Criteria

For the second deployment phase, we may be able to evolve the QA system a little with the introduction of acceptance criteria. Having demonstrated in the first phase, with the undesirable experience of a production incident, that we had detected the issue in preproduction, someone is likely going to insist that we do not repeat that experience again. If you find a problem, let the appropriate folks get involved immediately, and avoid deploying that application with a known problem.

As we already have a project plan and schedule, and do not want to impact it unnecessarily, we simply have to add a formal preproduction review. Much the same as sharing the testing results with the QA team, we will now share the testing results with the other stakeholders that are showing a growing interest in the APM visibility. To this review of the baseline reports we want to add some suggested criteria. The details as to what these criteria will look like and how they may evolve are found in Chapter 8.

From the PM perspective, the schedule is intact, the stakeholders are interacting at a more beneficial level, and some criteria are being established, likely as an option requirement for the app teams—all dividends of a well-run project. At the conclusion of the operational period, there will be a postproduction review. This review will deal with any changes to the APM configuration that may have been uncovered, including adjusting agent visibility, changing dashboards and alert thresholds, and reviewing the APM capacity consumed and remaining. As hard as we try for an accurate forecast of APM capacity, deployment scope and configuration are dynamic and need to be accounted for. There is still headroom for correct operation, but if the trends indicate that capacity will be ultimately exceeded, then adjustments have to be made. For some cases, the phased deployments will continue until the whole deployment target is achieved without further incident. At least the acceptance criteria are established for the next project to refer to.

More likely, especially given that the next deployment phase is a 200 percent increase from the first phase, we are going to encounter another problematic application during QA testing. During the preproduction review, the data is presented, and there is much rumination about what to do. Sure, the minimum acceptance criteria are there, and the app does not meet the criteria. There is an opportunity to fix the app but that means a big delay for the schedule. Management decides that it must go through with the deployment, for all but the most grievous performance problems. After all, what are the chances that QA testing identified a real problem anyway? It is not like we have a long tradition of using this APM information. Let's go ahead and promote the app to production.

As the second operational period unfolds, the potential for pandemonium is high. Remember, the second deployment phase is 30 percent of the deployment target for the initiative and a 200 percent increase over the initial deployment. If we had one to two incidents in the first deployment, we can expect two to four incidents during the second operational period. It can actually be much worse, because we purposely chose stable apps to predominate the deployment footprint for the first phase. In this second phase, we do not need to follow that same restriction. We have proven that we can deploy safely and reliably. No matter what happens next, no one can take that achievement away.

Depending on the overall software quality, the second operation period can be a firestorm of activity—lots of triage events, leading to recommendations for remediation and fixes, and lots of apps being retested once those fixes are in place. The really good thing is that folks will start to pay attention to the acceptance criteria. Maybe one to two apps that fail the criteria will remain off the train to production. That is the perfect situation that APM is meant to mediate, with the end result of a more stable production experience. From the PM perspective, however, the schedule will be broken.

A broken schedule can be corrected by simply peeling off these unstable apps to a separate project management team, and getting the remaining apps back on track for the third deployment phase. The more apps that fail in the second operational period, the more likely that the acceptance criteria will be fully observed and a number of apps should simply fall off the schedule for the third deployment—60 percent of the total deployment scope. This means that the remaining apps will continue, and we will get to the second preproduction review (with a few empty slots) and into the third and final operational period. Then we're on to the third and final postproduction review.

An important characteristic of the final postproduction review is to collect and review the various artifacts that the APM team produced during the phased deployment. The team needs to review in detail to ensure it preserves what worked and discards anything else. The minimum will be the runbooks for the various APM tools and monitoring configurations. The baseline reports and data archives from the various incident encounters are all important artifacts to help the next APM team to be even more effective, and also to train new APM practitioners to provide ongoing support for the APM initiative. You do not have to wait for a live deployment to practice. Pretty much everything may be reused if you take the time to bring those artifacts together and put them in a place when the next PM can find them.

Triage

With everything going on in QA and issues of acceptance criteria, triage capabilities will be growing in parallel with the gains in the QA system. The most significant of these is the baseline system. A baseline is a signature of the application under simulated load. The full details are found in Chapter 12.

There are three triage techniques. The first is looking at single metrics (Chapter 14). Then we evolve to baselines identifying key components, transactions, and relationships (Chapter 15). Finally, we move on to trends among the different releases (Chapter 16), as the historical foundation is established. While it is possible to collect initial baselines directly from production instead of QA, the variability of the production experience requires a longer period to confirm that the baselines are consistent. The QA environment offers the potential for a more consistent baseline. This requires that the load generation (Chapter 11) be consistent and reproducible, and also gives us the added benefit of being able to feed back differences discovered in production to help enhance and improve the test plan for an application.

Baselines (Chapter 12) actually come in multiple flavors (see Figure 13-10), but the more significant one for triage is the characterization baseline. This is an ordered list of the active components, for both response time and invocations (responses per interval). SQL statements, if available, would also be listed, as these have a direct relationship to the various use cases experienced.

The HealthCheck baseline, which includes the characterization baselines, is something that the triage team will assist in preparing. This presents the acceptance criteria, along with the major components and behaviors, as a summary report for the QA activities, or later the production experience. The HealthCheck is shared among the various stakeholders and becomes a template for the QA teams to use whenever testing a particular application. Setting up this report template is a valuable triage experience as you decide what is significant for the report. Thereafter it is just a tool to help the stakeholders appreciate the performance characteristics of the application, but is not otherwise especially effective for triage.

Once the practice of collecting and maintaining baselines for both QA and production is established, triage may then evolve onto the third stage—triage with trends. Having months of baselines collected for both normal and incident situations establishes a foundation for the higher-level analysis and planning activities. This is normally associated with the capacity planning team, which performs ongoing extraction and analysis of performance and capacity data. An APM system needs only to establish a repository to hold the baseline results in order to fully participate in this planning activity. Typically this means that the baseline reports are generated initially in an easily accessible format (CSV, HTML) so that they may be uploaded to an appropriate database. Very often this will be the HealthCheck baseline rather than the extensive details of the characterization baseline.

We will look in detail at the role for triage with trends in Chapter 16.

Evolving Management Capabilities

The capabilities of an organization to manage its application infrastructure and life cycle, and how it evolves over time, are not really a concern for the implementation team. But it is useful to have some of the terminology in hand to help keep stakeholders' expectations in line. I discussed management capabilities in detail in Chapter 5, so here I will present the criteria that allow a precise and consistent usage of the terminology.

Reactive Management

Reactive management is the collection of alerts and coordination of appropriate responses to those alerts. Operations will have two choices: to restart the affected system, or to open a bridge call and then restart the affected system. The delay between the generation of the alert and the response by operations will range between 5 and 30 minutes. Alerts are consumed by the service provider or by a subset of operations, and are generally not shared with the application teams or other stakeholders. Reporting on the alerts and status of open incidents occurs the next day.

Reactive Alerting

Reactive alerting differs from reactive management in that the alerts are generally shared among the stakeholders. Everyone receives notice that a particular system or service is down, even as a specialist team will be assigned to resolve the problem.

This is important to establish collaboration among stakeholders and to help reduce the delay between the alert event and the notification to something on the order of 5 to 15 minutes. As APM technology is deployed, a separate alert stream for performance incidents, separate from availability incidents, is established. Both alert streams end up in the trouble management system, but responsibility for the alert is divided between operations (availability) and application teams (performance).

Predictive/Directed Management

Predictive (or directed) management places more emphasis on the gathering of performance signatures during QA and preproduction, in order to help improve the timeliness and accuracy of the triage of production performance incidents. All triage begins by first confirming the nature of the incident by direct comparison with the baseline (normal operation). It is important to demonstrate that operational problems may be detected in preproduction, as this will be used to justify acceptance criteria in the future. Most triage activities are still being initiated in the operations environment. The triage team has the responsibility to work with other stakeholders in the application life cycle to confirm and remediate the performance problem.

Proactive Management

Proactive management[1] is where performance problems are largely identified and addressed in preproduction. Sometimes *proactive* management is confused with *predictive* management (detecting a problem based on a threshold before application users are aware of any problem).[2] The operations environment still has responsibility for availability incidents, but these are no longer confused with performance problems. The overall number of operational incidents will decrease significantly while the number of applications delayed from entering production increases proportionately. APM is now fully realized and issues of software quality and stability are largely confined to the QA and preproduction environments. This does not mean that all future operational incidents are eliminated, it just suggests that the obvious performance issues have been revealed and there is an opportunity to do something about it. Management may still elect to deploy problematic applications, but this only continues to confirm the nature of the performance problems. Staff time spent on bridge calls is dramatically reduced, as the proactive management leads to better understanding of the nature of the performance problem and absolute reliance on management-by-restart for those applications that cannot be remediated. When you can't fix it, at least you can be confident as to what actions you have remaining.

---

[1] http://articles.techrepublic.com.com/5100-10878_11-5054790.html

[2] http://management.about.com/od/managementskills/a/predictive_mgt6.htm

Deployment Necessities

This section presents the key activities and considerations that any APM initiative needs to consider, from the perspective of the PM.

Kickoff Meeting

At least one month prior to the start of a phased deployment APM initiative, you will conduct a coordination meeting among the delivery team and the participating stakeholders for the initiative. At minimum, this will include the APM team (or services representative), QA, operations, and the key application owners. The purpose is to review the overall solution architecture, confirm the availability of hardware, access procedures to install appliances, security considerations such as firewall configurations, and the schedule for the three deployment phases.

Other considerations, including alert integration, alert thresholds, dashboard design, and reports, will also be reviewed in general. The specific review will be deferred until the first operational review (postproduction), when a detailed consideration of these points may be made and any adjustments planned for the second deployment phase. These areas are often the most contentious because the folks making the specifications are really too far removed from the details of their implementation. Sometimes folks do not know what they want until they see it. I find it easiest to simply accommodate this eventuality via the phased deployment model.

Table 7-1 best conveys the overall plan, but this is subordinate to the detailed schedule that you will have built, including the work calendar and other constraints. If you are using professional services for the initial APM implementation, either as a staff augmentation or mentoring role, you will develop the schedule with input from the services PM. I've included a generic Microsoft project plan for a phased deployment to help you get started. It is in the Chapter 7 artifacts as Phased_Deployment.mpp on the Apress web site (www.apress.com).

Table 7-1. Enterprise Phased Deployment

Prior to COB	Kickoff	Training	Phase 1	Phase 2	Phase 3
Metrics Storage Sizing	Initial HW order	(2) Persons advanced Remainder – general	10% deployment Initial Gold configurations	30% deployment	60% deployment Final Gold configurations
Gap and Skills Assessments	Finalize training plan		Initial Integrations	Integration Acceptance	
Application Assessments	Identify first 3-10 apps		Limited operational phase (2 wks)	Operational phase (2-4 wks)	Operational phase (2-4 wks)
Solution Architecture	Monitoring architecture accepted		Operational review, resizing, dashboards	Operational review, resizing, capacity forecast	Operational review, resizing, capacity forecast
Pilot			Operational Model adjustment Final HW order	Operational Model acceptance	Acceptance

Notice that product training is targeted to occur prior to the start of deployment activities. The final list of training candidates should be known at the kickoff meeting. All training needs to be completed prior to deployment because there is nothing more pointless than trying to mentor to, or interact with personnel, who have never before used the technology. When training is not considered critical, it is often due to a complete lack of understanding about the responsibilities for the technology—in such cases it is being treated as if it were an availability monitoring technology, which requires little or no training.

Some advanced topics for the kickoff meeting involve packaging, high availability, and backup strategy. These should have already been resolved.

Phased Deployment Schedule

This is core project management, so we will not spend any addition time here. I just included this as part of the primary responsibilities of the PM. Please refer to the sample schedule in MS project.

Preproduction Review

This is the most critical review activity, as it provides a control point to assess process documentation, runbook organization, and report organization. It is also an important sanity check for the monitoring configuration. Testing should have confirmed the suitability, in terms of potential overhead, of the monitoring configuration, and this result should be documented in the runbook. We simply exercise the application under load and review the invocations metrics. Anything over 10,000 to 40,000 invocations per minute (depending on vendor) will likely contribute to measurable overhead and should not be promoted to production. Chapter 8 discusses all of the details for the preproduction activities.

The preproduction review is also an opportunity to confirm that any changes proposed during the prior postproduction review are addressed in this deployment phase. This is, of course, only pertinent to the second and third deployment phases. Each review session should ratchet up the agenda. We want to ensure that everyone has an opportunity to raise issues and have the monitoring team collaborate on the decision to go forward with the next deployment phase. To that end, you should circulate the agenda, summarizing the issues and the resolutions (or workarounds). The review meeting is not an open forum for debate—which should all be resolved. It is an opportunity to get everyone on the same page with respect to the status of the various issues, and the rationale for the choices made prior to deployment. Additional details for the preproduction review are discussed in Chapter 9.

Postproduction Review

This review can be a little more confrontational in that we want everyone's honest appraisal of how the prior deployment and operational period unfolded. Most of this will be factual and data driven. Some will be impressions. The goal again is to make sure everyone gets to voice their concerns and identify a course of action. In the event of an impasse, the PM makes the decision. The end result of the meeting is an actionable plan for the APM team (or consultants) to adjust the next deployment phase.

Data-driven characteristics include the following:

- Any errors encountered during installation
- Current Metrics Storage capacity and performance of the metrics collection platform
- Current visibility of the agent configurations
- Any operational incidents experienced
- How many alerts were generated
  - Availability alerts correlated with legacy alerting
  - Performance/capacity alerts

- Whether any incidents with the APM infrastructure were noted
  - Overhead, instability

Impressions include the following:

- Any requests for more visibility
- Any feedback on reporting and dashboards
- Growing or diminishing interest in APM by other stakeholders
- Whether we are on track (group consensus)

Install/Update Validation

Sometimes there is an internal process that formally validates an installation of technology that may potentially change the operation of a key application or service. I encounter this primarily with credit and trading applications and have a best practice module specifically for this situation. However, the certification steps are very dependent on the vendor technology implementation and are out of bounds for this book.

This activity can also be a benefit for stakeholders that are inexperienced with APM, and are uncomfortable with not being able to tell whether they are getting the appropriate level of attention for their applications. This is sometimes stated as, "We don't know what we don't know." So it is useful to be able to respond with something that is both comforting and productive.

For example, the phased deployment process will initially push out a default, one-size-fits-all monitoring configuration during each of the deployment phases. This is done because we know that we do not have time to individually tune and validate each configuration, and we do not want to risk putting out too heavy a configuration and creating a problem. In balance, you allow for an exception path where an application stakeholder can schedule a review of their visibility, which could result in additional visibility being configured. This is something that is essential for the long-term use of APM, but is a courtesy during the initial deployment.

In increasing visibility, we first want to confirm that we do not yet have sufficient visibility, and this takes two major forms, depending on the type of APM technology being employed: *call stack visibility* and *transaction definition*.

Call Stack Visibility

For instrumentation, we are concerned with the depth of the call stack and whether or not we are reaching components that indicate an exit from the monitored platform (see Figure 7-7). This will vary considerably with the complexity of an application, ranging from 2 to 25 elements in the call stack. What I prefer is to evaluate the percentage of gaps in the exits or lowest level of the call stack. If we can see 60 percent of the total transaction time, represented by the lowest components, and we have at least three to five levels represented, then we have a "good" level of instrumentation.

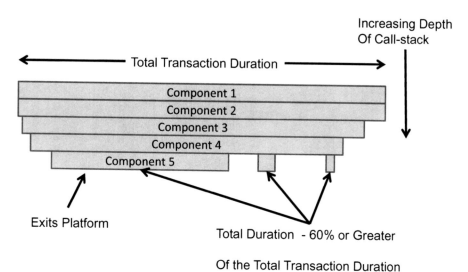

Figure 7-7. Call stack visibility

Can we provide "better" or "best" visibility? Absolutely. But it takes time and access to a preproduction environment with load testing, specifically the ability to exercise the use case of interest. For the APM initiative underway, "good" is enough, and you can log the stakeholder request for the APM team to address after the full deployment is completed. But if you cannot see at least 60 percent of the transaction time, in terms of the exiting components, then you are not in a position for effective triage. And this should be addressed and corrected during the preparations for the next deployment phase.

Sometimes a private framework or API is employed that may be missed by the default configuration. Once the culprit is identified, it is easy to add this nonstandard definition to the agent configuration. Very often this will impact a large number of applications, depending on how popular the framework is, so it is an important exercise to correct this missing visibility early in the phased deployments.

Transaction Definition

For real and synthetic transactions, we will have a similar exception process. The criteria are less complex (no call stack interpretation) and the "good" level of visibility is where we have at least one transaction that reflects the availability for the application or service.

When multiple APM technologies are employed, there is usually some overlap of capabilities. For example, all of the technologies have the ability to indicate availability. So, if I have availability confirmation via instrumentation, I do not consider it a defect to be missing an additional indication of visibility. And for the phased deployment and operational periods, I want to limit my remediation of missing availability, or more comprehensive visibility, until the deployment push is complete. I want the infrastructure in place before I start exercising some of the permanent and ongoing services. I do not want the implementation, which has the higher priority, to be distracted by the next stage of growth for the APM system.

The exception to this plan is synthetic transactions. We depend on these to give us availability information, off-hours, when there is no traffic that the instrumentation could use to assess availability. So, if we are missing a synthetic transaction, this is a higher priority than incomplete visibility. If synthetics are the only technology appropriate to achieve availability monitoring, then this is the highest priority.

For real transactions, additional visibility is a lower priority during the deployment. Again, it is not hard to do, but can be a distraction from growing the deployment and ensuring the overall stability during the operational periods. It is worthwhile to do some additional transaction definition, but I would limit it to the key applications for the deployment. It is an important process to practice, but let us make effort first for those apps that have the most attention, and schedule the others once the deployment dust has settled.

Updates

Often overlooked during the rapture of a first APM imitative coming online are the inevitable updates and major releases for the technologies, which seem to pop up at the most inconvenient times. Hopefully, the phased deployment will proceed without the need to update one or more of the components. It all depends on how long the phased deployment will be active. Typically, you will schedule 12 to 16 weeks of activities over a 6 month period for a large-scale deployment. About half of that time is used in the first 1 to 3 months, depending on the progress of concurrent activities (load tests, packaging, file transfers, etc.). If you were to schedule an 18-month deployment, you would be all but assured of incurring a critical update. This is another motivation for organizing your APM deployments as a sequence of short deployment activities.

Nothing is guaranteed, so I prefer to have a backup plan. And that plan involves doing some sort of upgrade along with the planned implementation. It does not need to be built into the schedule, as it is only going to come after the delay, but it does need to be understood.

In general, the impacts are as follows:

- *Major*: Change in vendor
- *Intermediate*: New Metrics Storage release, new real or synthetic transactions
- *Minor*: Agent upgrade

I find that agent changes can always be deferred, as most vendors will support a mix of agent versions. Some legacy platforms for which future support was denied depend on this capability. An interruption of the schedule occurs when a new platform needs to be recertified. Most clients do not account for this—but does anyone really think that a new release is not coming next year?

We present a scheme for managing releases later, but the basics are this: you should be continuously certifying new releases as they become available. For the actual deployment, you need to plan and fuss about when it is necessary or most appropriate. But as soon as the download is available, it should be in your lab and handling a small portion of your environment—similar to a preproduction or UAT model, but dedicated to the APM tools.

Alternate Agent Configurations and Versions

Alternate agent configurations can become quite complex and should be avoided where possible. It should never be part of an initial deployment because it simply adds complexity where none is appreciated. Our goal is to always become operational, over the full scope, as quickly and safely as possible. We are interested in proving our proficiency in realizing the APM implementation, not in managing a variety of exceptions.

You do, however, build the directory scheme, as well as many of the alternate agent configurations, to support the gold configurations. This is to accommodate different visibility objectives between development, QA, and production, as well as special configurations to support specific analysis. Memory management and Java garbage collection are two examples of these special configurations. All of this is academic until you actually receive the new release, so we will treat this as out of scope until you actually experience a significant delay and it becomes a reality. And if that happens, it will be an activity directed at the APM lab environment or at APM UAT only.

Alert Integration

Good project management is about scope, responsibility, and controlling external factors. The biggest risk we have so far suggested is access to QA testing. It's a different group, with a different agenda. It does not initially benefit from APM, and we do add a bit to their workload. But there is a more challenging group: the folks managing alert integration.

Many APM technology providers have a facility to export alerts to another system. That is the easy part. The other half of the integration—those who receive the alerts—is where things can become challenging. In my experience, this is because the receiving team is not really in the business of doing integration and the associated testing. Much of its alerting infrastructure is already long established. It did not really anticipate that other alerting systems would arise.

One such area of confusion is just the term "alerts." It seems that some organizations are overly focused on bringing all alerts to a central location. Since alerts are things that operations expects to action upon, this leads to an immediate conflict when it finds out that a performance degradation does not mean "reboot." For this reason, I try to introduce the term *notification* for anything coming from APM, especially performance or capacity alerts.

Also, part of the phased deployment process is creating a channel for notifications, separate from that used for alerting. This is specifically to manage the performance and capacity *notifications*, but this still leaves an opportunity for the availability *alerts* to be propagated to the alert management team. This gives the alerting team exactly what it expects, and also provides a validation that APM availability alerts may be trusted.

You may narrow the scope of the integration by focusing on notifications and establishing a separate channel, but you still need to realize the integration of the APM availability alerts. And this, very simply, is just beyond your control. The PM may push, but ultimately I find that the availability alert integration lags the schedule terribly. We will have full alerting capabilities via APM, for both performance and capacity notifications, and the availability notifications we redefine as alerts, via e-mail or other simple mechanism. Integration to trouble management or alert correlation will often fall just outside the initiative.

- Old-school:
    - External agent parses the Metrics Storage logs
    - System management tool provides log-parsing agent

- Autonomous:
    - E-mail alerting the monitoring team only
    - Just need access to an SMTP[3] server

- Typical:
    - Alert action script (command) invokes notification command for the target system (trouble or system management)
    - A bit more work to coordinate and test

- Combo:
    - Both e-mail action and command action
    - E-mail alerting today, action script in a week or so

In my experience, even when I have demonstrated alert integration as part of the initial or second phased deployment, a serious effort to complete the integration lags by 12 to 24 months. This is not a delay due to technology, this is concern for how many alert events will be coming, who gets to decide what is alerted on, and what the receiving team is going to do with them. The team has only ever worked with availability information, up or down. There will be a lot of concerns as to who decides what gets an alert and how the thresholds are maintained. Application information has never part of their role and the organization will need some time to adapt.

The above figure summarizes the various strategies and offers a definition of terms. They are not sequential and all may be present at one time. Many of my clients who completed the APM initiative with a secondary notification channel, and limited or no alerting into trouble management or equivalent began first by going "old-school" and parsing logs. This gave them a fully functional integration, but they alone decided which alerts to generate. They had control. This was then followed by the availability notifications, as defined by the application teams, and using a variety of

---

[3] Simple Mail Transport Protocol (http://en.wikipedia.org/wiki/Smtp)

action scripts to make sure they were assigned appropriate identifiers so that they could be routed to a responsible party.

As for the performance and capacity notifications, they have so far remained a future consideration. I do know that other clients have integrated them in a limited fashion, but I don't have any insights into their long-term progress and whether they got what they planned. They were following their own agenda, not what was prescribed by the APM best practices as exposed in this book.

Consider an automobile. When you're driving, a brake light ahead of you is something you need to respond to. You have to take action, which makes this an alert situation. A fuel warning on your dashboard is a notification, so you do not need to take immediate action. You need to plan when you can remediate and get more fuel—this quarter (next exit) or the quarter after.

Summary

Implementing APM is not just another deployment. The technology is quite easy to deploy. The challenge is with the supporting processes and the necessity to learn while doing, in order to establish an environment such that stakeholders may take advantage of the visibility, and to define practices for using APM consistently. None of this is hard or even unfamiliar; for many, however, it is unexpected.

No matter the size of your APM initiative, the questions and issues are the same. The sequence of activities is the same. The scope, duration, and level of effort are what vary. The duration and number of participants in your kickoff meeting will vary, and if the scope turns out to be more than expected, you can be confident that the techniques presented here have already been exercised for up to 10,000 applications and many millions of metrics under management.

Your scope may not include the establishment of a QA system, but you will know what to ask for when the time comes. You will find complete details for establishing a preproduction system in Chapter 8. I consider it the foundation for long-term success with APM.

Your scope will absolutely include triage, but how well you realize triage will be a direct reflection of the how much you can leverage your stakeholders to prepare information in advance, in order to accelerate triage and improve its accuracy. Which brings us back to preproduction, where folks exercise the application "for free!" We just have to help them get monitoring in place.

For the smaller initiative, Chapter 8 focuses on the essential processes you need to emulate. For the larger initiative, or those moving to a service bureau or COE organization model, Chapter 9 will finalize the definition of your service catalog. This will help you schedule activities to follow your initial APM implementation and incrementally expand the scope of activities you may support.

Essential Processes

Small projects need much more help than great.

—Dante Alighieri (1265-1321)

In the previous chapter, I covered a number of process activities that are part of a large-scale deployment. In this chapter, I take a step back and focus on the more critical processes that you need to enable a production deployment on a smaller scale. As you saw earlier, the scope of an APM initiative will vary widely, depending on monitoring and organizational maturity. A large-scale deployment is only possible with a mature organization. You need to fill the gap by focusing on the key processes that will protect the smaller initiatives from failure. However, a small initiative needs to keep the bigger picture in mind, even if some activities will be skipped over. You need to know what you do not know or what you are not yet capable of doing.

This can be annoying. If you have a list of "best practices" to guide you, why are they not being followed? Perhaps a modified version of Murphy's Law is appropriate here. It would state:

> *"... an organization will pursue a random-walk among strategies despite guidance or evidence to the contrary."* [1]

I cannot explain why it happens. I only know that it will happen. You need preparations to protect the APM initiative from itself when the sponsoring group is rocketing towards potential disaster. You need to get a few speed bumps into the road that the organization, in general, will support.

---

[1] I am certain that this is mine, even if it is in the style of Murphy's' Law.

This, too, is annoying. I have discussed a variety of mechanisms to accelerate the adoption of APM, and now I am telling you to consider some controls to ease that pace.

This advice is easy to accept if you know anything about small children. For example, a toddler, once they have learned to take a few steps, will plunge recklessly ahead in the sheer joy of being able to move of their own volition. They have no concept of failure or of pain. How much damage can you afford to let them incur? Instead, can you let them learn in a safer environment? Can you protect them from more serious injuries?

You will find that small initiatives have very diverse goals. This leads to a number of themes that may be followed. I find that these will usually fit into the following categories, with a few pithy comments:

- **The Monitoring Runbook**: The absolute minimum for success.
- **Pre-production**: We do not want or do not expect to get to production.
- **Operations**: We never considered anything but production.
- **Software Quality**: We expect that APM will improve our software—just by being there.

Your goal, from the implementation perspective, is to rein in these smaller initiatives so that whatever they achieve will be consistent with a larger initiative. You want to ensure that you can build upon, or add to at some later date, the processes that were set aside for the initial rollout—without redoing the whole effort.

Monitoring Runbook

The runbook is the answer when someone asks "Do you actually know what you're doing?" It may be a document cookbook, checklist, or website—whatever is convenient to allow a third party to independently check that your proposed deployment meets all of the criteria expected of a production application. Because it can mean so many things, runbooks are not very consistent from one stakeholder to the next. But runbooks are often the answer to getting an initiative back on track.

For example, when an APM initiative slips up and gets dismissed from production, the obvious goal is to get it back to production as soon as possible. Sometimes, the deployment fails because something was wrong with the monitoring configuration and no one was able to notice this until the application was active in production. Other times, the monitoring will be operating correctly, but a performance or stability incident will happen and the monitoring will be implicated and removed. The team deploying APM simply lacked confidence in the work they did and could not demonstrate (or be convincing or just bullied) that they knew what they were doing. What should they have done better?

There is a very simple rule for why runbooks are critical: "Last change, first blamed." When things go wrong, folks look to pin the responsibility on other folks. The production incident may have been completely unrelated to the monitoring technology. Your application may have been operating perfectly and as intended. If the lights dimmed, it must be the APM deployment! The real cause for the removal of APM is simply a lack of education about what the impacts of APM would be *if* it was contributing to the problem. The runbook is your tool to start educating the Operations team as to what to expect now that APM is in place. And sometimes the rollout may be completely messed up. The issue here is that no one can tell the difference. No one can defend the APM rollout. No one has any confidence that they understand what they are doing.

Many APM initiatives proceed to production with either blind ignorance or boundless naiveté. A first APM deployment has many onlookers; most of them are simply not friendly to the APM initiative for any number of reasons. You cannot expect to know all of these un-sympathetic stakeholders but they all know the runbook metaphor. They rely on it. So you must, too.

A runbook is your medium to communicate that you know what you are doing with APM. Those production stakeholders may not even actually read it but they have an uncanny ability to find any gaps that they feel expose them to operational risk. Their biggest gap is that they (in general) really do not know much about APM technology. You have to anticipate those gaps and address them in your runbook. You have to make an effort to educate those folks with the operational experience that you have some useful experience with APM—even if it is your first rollout.

My first lesson for the APM teams that I mentor is this: you simply never have an incident related to a production monitoring deployment. Every time you bring a new application under management, nothing bad happens that can be attributed to the monitoring configuration. Someday, someone will make a mistake, but it will not be any of the folks in my mentoring sessions.

To achieve this, you will practice deployments pre-production until you have identified every possible opportunity for a mistake. You'll practice until you know how to catch and remediate any mistake before anyone might notice—and certainly before it affects production. And you will document every one of these potential failures in the runbook.

The strategy is simple: do whatever you need to get a correct configuration. Test that it is working correctly. Then find a way to package it so that a minimal amount of typing or editing is required for each successive deployment. Finally, have somebody else follow your instructions until they deploy successfully. Note everything that goes wrong and how you figured it out. Repeat at least three times—or more, if no one seems to be able to get it right the first few times. You simply do not want your first production rollout to be the second time you configured an agent or defined and promoted transactions.

There are a few other issues. How do you know that the agent is working? How do you safely back-out the agent? Is there a fail-over configuration? How much overhead might be encountered? How much additional memory does the agent need? Is there any impact on the startup time for the application? If you take time to document how to answer each of these questions, then you will earn the confidence of the Operations team (or Production Review Board).

Figure 8-1 shows a high-level outline of a runbook for APM instrumentation. An example runbook is found as Ch 08 - Generic_Runbook.doc at apress.com.

Overview
    Establishing an Agent Configuration
    Determine the extension products to be employed
    Determine the type of instrumentation to be employed
    Prepare a DEPLOY directory
    Prepare the WLS Configuration Strings
    Validate Configuration
Launching the Agent
    Prepare the Agent Install (APM Admin)
    Completing the WebLogic configuration (WLS Admin)
    Recycle the Server Instance
    Confirm the Agent is Monitoring
    Agent Startup Problems and Resolution
Installing the Metrics Storage
    The Base MS Install (APM Admin)
    Licensing the MS (APM Admin)
    Starting and Stopping the MS
Configuring Users and Control
    Metrics Storage Tuning
Portability
    Transferring the Base MS Install (APM Admin)
    Transferring the Presentation Element Increment (APM Admin)
    Transferring Dashboards
Custom Tracing
Troubleshooting
    Monitoring the MS
    MS Startup Problems and Resolution
    Monitoring Browser-based

Figure 8-1. Runbook outline

This outline is sufficient for a small APM Metrics Storage component deployment, not exceeding 25-50 agents and representing 5-20 applications.

Pre-Production Practice

Using APM metrics earlier in an application life cycle is really the best way to leverage the benefits of APM. For a stakeholder who may not have mature practices and the discipline to use APM correctly in production, starting pre-production really eliminates all the trouble that a novice practitioner will encounter in an attempt to go directly to production. You also get to practice using APM without the pressures that come during production triage of a high profile incident. The following points summarize the typical goals of a pre-production implementation:

- Establish a well-defined process to validate an APM configuration suitable for production.
  - Validate the APM visibility.
  - Validate the monitoring configuration: agent configuration, thresholds and alerts, dashboards.
  - Validate sizing and capacity management for instrumentation and real transactions.

- Establish consistent practices.

- Practical Benefits

  - Enhance triage capabilities prior to production rollout.
  - Ensure suitable monitoring configurations are promoted to production.

The problem with this list is that it is far too general and it does not give any insights into how these tasks may be implemented. You have defined what you want from the practice but you need to turn these points into supporting skills and processes. In Chapter 7, you used the phased deployment model as a mechanism to help you implement a pre-production process. But if you have already deployed, that deployment-centric model is not quite appropriate. The incremental piece is Good (following Good-Better-Best), so you only need to rework (evolve) the process as summarized below:

- Good

  - Rapid Deployment (Agent)
    - Monitoring team provides the cookbook and management module.
  - QA Test Plan
  - QA Acceptance with Performance KPIs
    - Stalls, Memory Management, Response Time, Scalability and Stability

- Better

  - Baselines
  - Initial Triage
  - Agent Configuration Promotion
    - Tuning the Agent configuration (inappropriate tracing)
    - QA and Production (Dev to QA, QA to Prod)

- Best

  - Agent Validation
    - New gold configurations
  - Monitoring Configuration Validation
  - Application Audit

What is pertinent for your project manager, as part of the implementation discussion, is that this evolution will directly parallel the deployment plan that will ultimately fulfill the goals for the APM initiative. When you follow the phased deployment model, you know that during initial phase you really have no opportunity for sophisticated configuration tuning. It will be an effort just to get the 10% footprint deployed successful. Once that is completed, you have some breathing room. You can be confident that you can deploy without fouling everything up, so now you may devote a bit more energy to testing the various agent configurations, and during this second phase (30% deployment), push out a better tuned configuration.

During the first phase, you will go through the motions. In the second phase, they begin to have meaning and purpose. During the second phase preparation, you will contrast the operational experience with your testing efforts. You will see how the baselines capture the performance signature, even if the QA environment is vastly inferior to production. You will begin to believe what APM can reveal, if you know how and where to look.

As you appreciate the danger signs for over- and under-instrumentation, you will likewise become more confident in the sophistication and complexity of more advanced agent configurations. This is not just to show off your skills but to respond to those exceptions during the operational phase when the default configuration was not sufficient.

If you try to accomplish all of these activities into a single massive exercise by condensing the multiple, deliberately bite-sized deployments, you are really setting yourself up for failure. There are simply too many activities and too little experience executing them. About a year from this first APM initiative, you may well undertake a massive all-in-one deployment. It will be successful because you will have established and refined the processes that will ensure that you are prepared and practiced for the APM nuances. Please go to Chapter 11 to see the details for establishing a QA discipline with APM.

Let's summarize the benefits for a pre-production APM system:

- Helps ensure successful initial deployments of monitoring

    - Corrects management of metrics storage capacity
    - Confirms appropriate visibility
    - Eliminates un-safe or high-overhead configurations

- Deepens visibility into software quality in advance of production
- Leverages existing load-testing capabilities
- Provides a foundation to improve QA simulation accuracy by feeding back the upcoming production monitoring details

So you have a reasonable plan for how you may leverage the APM deployment to simultaneously evolve a QA discipline empowered with APM metrics and processes. You do not have to wait for a large-scale deployment to take these steps. The same activities may start at any time for an existing APM initiative. You may want to take months for each evolution, instead of weeks, and that is perfectly fine because you may have to wait for the right application to come along anyway. Just make sure your stakeholders understand what you want to do and what it requires. They might be inspired to help you accelerate the evolution. At the very least, they will have the correct expectations for what skills and capabilities you will be able to deliver and when they will be available.

Operations

Going directly to an operations environment is challenging but not impossible. In fact, I know of a number of practitioners who have done exactly this and were completely satisfied with their APM capabilities. Even if they were without a proper test environment to stage and practice their configuration promotions, they had appropriate skills and processes in place, and proceeded conservatively and patiently. They started first with a minimal configuration, and increased visibility as there was a need. This takes longer than validating a configuration via a sequence of load testing (days and weeks versus hours) but ends up with the same result.

Until I observed this conservative deployment best practice first hand, I was always going for the richest visibility configuration first. It's what was expected—for a software vendor to make sure that the prospect saw everything we had to offer. But it is difficult and potentially dangerous, especially when the prospect had a weak testing practice. For my firefighting activities, where the emphasis was on service and not product, this was the key to utter reliability for production deployments. I almost always had sufficient visibility in that first deployment to uncover performance problems and without going to the advanced configurations and extra features. After the most urgent problem was identified, and as time permitted, I could always add more visibility and start looking into other potential issues. With the pressure off, clients looked forward to each configuration change without any of the concerns they had with the initial deployment. As resistant to changes as most operations groups are naturally, once I had demonstrated that we could deploy safely and reliably, and quickly show value for the effort, their world was forever changed. This really is the model to emulate: Start small, add where indicated, and do not foul things up in that initial deployment just because you don't yet have appropriate processes.

A mature operations practitioner will also choose stable applications to start with. This avoids the doubt raised when working with unstable apps. Is it the app? Or is it the monitoring configuration? So they will roll out one to three apps, operate for a few weeks, and then follow with a larger rollout, and so on. This is exactly what you achieve with the phased deployments of Chapter 7.

Finally, mature pre-production system managers will first confirm the monitoring configuration with existing tools before trusting the APM metrics. Sometimes this leaves the Operations team a little near-sighted—they tend to stay with the metrics they are familiar with and do not really embrace the metrics they have never seen prior. This is not a problem because you can split availability and performance metrics in the future. The challenge is to get the tool into the hands of the application teams so that they can use those performance metrics.

However motivated the Operations team is to pursue APM, there are a number of gaps that will frustrate the initiative overall. The first of these is organizational. Operations will often assert that monitoring technology is their responsibility and thus take ownership of the tools exclusively, without acknowledging that other stakeholders will need access to the tools as well. This quickly becomes apparent when, under the pressure for triage and guidance into performance problems, the Operations team is unable to demonstrate any mastery of the internal component relationships that represent an application. They will be successful with triage of the resource outages, as they will benefit from the more timely availability of information. But performance information, including degraded responses, is not part of their traditional responsibility. The Operations role is simply not motivated to increase visibility once availability monitoring is confirmed accurate and deployed against applications that they were earlier unable to monitor availability for.

The biggest change for Operations is the access to detailed performance information in the form of dashboards. This is the part about APM that is most appealing to them because dashboards provide easy access to complex data.

Operations knows that they have a visibility gap and this is what they believe will solve that gap.

In many organizations, Operations will not actually be the primary consumer of dashboards. This is simply because most Operations teams will not themselves evolve to undertake the triage they think that they will be doing with these dashboards. Dashboards are actually for less technical users to understand performance information that they otherwise would not have access to. It will instead become the responsibility of the APM specialists to undertake complex triage on behalf of less technical stakeholders and deliver both the advanced analysis and more digestible content. And if the QA discipline is successful, the majority of problems will be uncovered pre-production, and the few operational dashboards deployed will fall away from memory. This is not an especially uplifting outcome, so what's the point?

The point is that the nimble, agile, and easily crushed nascent APM implementation needs a loud, stalwart stakeholder to target and satisfy. APM needs a bodyguard to survive the IT gauntlet and the initial deployment. You must appreciate and nurture the interest that Operations will have for dashboards because in the delivery of that capability, and with the rigorous testing and validation of the dashboards, you get to establish a QA role with APM that folks are generally less motivated to accomplish otherwise. As Figure 8-2 suggests, you simply do not have much of a chance to properly validate what goes into a dashboard without a large and foundational contribution from pre-production activities.

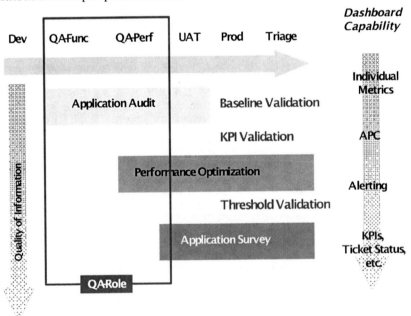

Figure 8-2. Dashboard lifecycle – QA role

The real challenge with dashboards is validation. How do you know that you have captured the right kinds of metrics and configured appropriate thresholds? As you can see along the right-hand side of Figure 8-2, dashboards evolve to the alert thresholds and KPIs those stakeholders are looking for. These are each validated via the primary APM competencies that you are trying to establish (refer to Figure 5-4 in Chapter 5).

And validation of thresholds is not just about dashboards. It is also a huge problem for teams that are employing synthetic transactions. They usually do not have detailed response information on which to base their thresholds. More often than not, this results in too many, or too few, availability alerts. When this happens, Operations loses confidence and the portion of the APM initiative based on synthetics transactions may flounder and be ignored.

As discussed in part 1 of this book, many stakeholders are under the misguided impression that the key to APM success is to deploy one technology at a time. And they pick the one they are most comfortable with—synthetic transactions. I have an APM survey to address this gap and to really understand what the response characteristics are. You need to collect real transactions before you worry about synthetics. And when you can't employ real transactions or instrumentation, then the mechanical elements of the assessment system will provide the information. It seems the obvious path but when I uncover the gaps, they have already been present for over a year. No one understands the big picture for APM so no one is able to correct the missing validation. As before, the problem with APM is not the technology but the absence of appropriate processes to employ the technology.

I would estimate that about half of all the clients I performed assessment service for suffered from an under-utilized synthetic transaction implementation—all due to poor practices in validating alert thresholds. Conversely, clients who were doing a good job with synthetic transactions fully understood the need for validation: doing a good survey up-front helped them establish and maintain appropriate operational thresholds. Furthermore, they understood the need for that survey to be accomplished with real transaction monitoring predominately and via manual assessment otherwise. Appropriate technology may make it easier, but appropriate processes ensure that whatever technology is employed will be done successfully.

Improving Software Quality

This is the latest strategy I have been discussing with clients to align APM best practices with the needs of the business. This software quality initiative is a pure business case that IT is being tasked to address.

Many organizations rely on third parties to develop and maintain their core applications. This model was established over the last 10 years during the push to outsource expensive capabilities (formerly in-house) on to partners who offered a comparable skill but at a vastly reduced cost model. I believe that this was initially attractive because the rigid silos of the application life cycle were conducive (even complicit) to being easily excised and transferred to the third party, leaving intact the interfaces between architecture/requirements and development, development and testing, testing and operations. By failing to collaborate and blend the scope of their activities, the organization made it easy to identify the boundaries and interfaces between the silos.

The disadvantage in this reassignment is that the accountability was not addressed. I have already discussed how a silo mentality is reinforced when schedules have a priority over quality. What was missing before outsourcing were effective metrics about application quality from the user perspective, in terms of performance and scalability, and not just the narrow functional testing or acceptance testing that allowed many apps to go forward despite performance shortcomings. Now that there is a contractual relationship between the third party and the client, and a perception that software quality is declining, management is looking for meaningful criteria to *proactively* identify performance problems.

In Chapter 5, I noted that moving from reactive to proactive management entails an entirely overlooked stage of *directed* management that establishes the process infrastructure to support proactive management. So you can be confident that looking at pre-production APM activities will give you some insights into what the relationship should look like in the outsourced model.

Your goal for *proactive* management is to prevent a problem application from getting deployed to production. You do not respond faster; you block unstable applications from entering the operational environment. That is the essence of what the business wants IT to manage, with respect to the third party relationship. To achieve this, you need to do the following:

- Identify problems pre-production.
- Allow teams to remediate and revalidate.
- Enforce performance criteria (it's not optional anymore).

You have to manage a whole assembly of processes and workflows. What does your organization want to take responsibility for? What will the third party take responsibility for? Figure 8-3 summarizes the application life cycle and highlights what may safely remain in the silo and what needs to be exposed to collaboration. In an ideal world, you would insist on collaboration across the life cycle. In an APM world, you need to revisit those boundaries and decide what you want to collaborate on, with the expectation that you will start small and then evolve to greater collaboration over time.

COLLABORATION

Dev	QA	Stress & Performance	UAT	Production

Unit Test	Functional Test	Performance Test	Acceptance Test	Trending, Alerting, Triage
Explore component relationships	Use case validation	Stability	Usability	Monitoring
		Scalability	Scalability	Incident triage
Assess impact of configuration changes	Smoke test	App characteristics	Stability	Capacity management
	Stability		Transaction characterization	Capacity planning
	Config errors			

Processes you need to be successful with APM	Key metrics thresholds
	Transaction characteristics

Baselines

Figure 8-3. Application life cycle

In each of the stakeholder areas, or silos, I have summarized the performance characteristics each silo is focused on. The APM activities are illustrated as bands crossing multiple silos. Each band relates a different type of performance information that would be shared as the software quality system evolves. The question for you, in your consideration of how you want to interact with your third party, is what type of information do you want out of this exchange?

Not surprisingly, everyone wants the "key metrics and thresholds." This is just what you need to performance manage your operational environment. Unfortunately, this means the greatest level of skill and effort on the part of the third party in order to deliver that information. You have identified all of the skills and processes that they need, but it will take quite a bit of time and investment to achieve.

A good compromise is to focus on the "transaction characteristics." This brings you back to the test plan, where each of the use cases would be identified and target thresholds assigned. This means more work for you, but results in a more mechanical process and validation for the third party. Many clients today follow this approach but are not at all satisfied with the results. There is an accountability gap in the difference between the definition of the test plan and the actual operational experience. The collaboration is simply not as effective because a large number of transactions need to be surveyed, regardless of their importance. And when a few critical transactions slip through the cracks, the potential for operational disappointment is high.

This leaves the "baselines" as the language of collaboration and a form of reporting. This is more flexibly divided among the third party and the stakeholder. For example, the stakeholder defines the baselines and the third party collects them. Or the stakeholder retests the application and determines its own baseline, independent of the third party, and then shares the findings.

In Chapter 5, I discussed the pieces, in terms of service offerings, that comprise this new relationship. What you will do next is arrange these activities, consistent with the outsourced theme, into a couple of examples of software quality programs.

Define Acceptance Criteria

This is what most stakeholders new to APM—or still planning for APM—are considering today: acceptance criteria. They simply want to know what the criteria should be and how to implement it. What should they expect of their third party supplier with regards to application xyz? If you engage stakeholders and suggest that they assess the applications so that you may more realistically make some recommendations, they resist. They do not yet appreciate that no two applications will have the same performance characteristics, so it is very difficult to come up with a useful list unless you have a program of measuring performance. Like baseball, which takes years to master, they do not want to do the work of training and playing in hundreds of games. They just want to swing the bat.

This is not to say that you can't come up with a reasonable list. It is just that it doesn't work. One size does not fit all when it comes to performance management. Someone has to do the work, not only of defining the list but making sure that the list is current and accurate as the application itself evolves.

Audit the Application

The audit is essentially the work of determining performance criteria, presented as baselines. Basically, you exercise the application under load, collect the different baselines (configuration, application, and performance), identify the key metrics and thresholds, and prepare dashboards and reports for stakeholders. The three big questions here are:

- Who owns the APM technology?
- Who collects the baselines? Who learns how to do it?
- Who builds and owns the test environment?

The ownership issues are probably the biggest challenge. Most technology licensing does not allow for re-assignment of licenses to a third party, especially off-premises. A third party software development organization is simply not in the business of making capital investments for licenses and hardware. This leaves you at an impasse. Perhaps different licensing schemes are possible but this is only speculation on my part. I suspect the only recourse is for a stakeholder to purchase the licenses on behalf of the third party.

Alternatively, either the stakeholder or the third party could purchase an Application Audit engagement from the vendor professional services organization.

Onboard the Application

The long-term alternative to using professional services to deliver the application audit is to undertake the audit with your own licenses and personnel. Here you will establish your own testing or UAT environment, deploy APM technology, and collect baselines. You will then apply your acceptance criteria and interact with the third party supplier for any issues. This route also allows you to prepare for production monitoring in terms of dashboards, reporting, and alerts.

I believe this is the best route for managing software quality. You may easily draft the production APM initiative and extend it to cover setup of the test environment, staffing, and procedures.

Supervise the Third Party Testing Process

Another approach is to delegate that responsibility completely to the third party and simply supervise their activities and perhaps act as an additional resource for difficult problems. This makes the stakeholder role more like a pre-production review, and the third party takes care of all the APM setup and baseline collection. The acceptance criteria would be shared and the third party would resolve most issues on their own. The challenge is to find or develop a third party with appropriate skills-sets and commitment to the overall program.

I have not observed any stakeholders operating with this program, nor have I seen any third parties. There has definitely been interest in the last year, but I do not yet see the demand for this kind of program.

Empower the Third Party to Deliver Proactive Performance Management

The final program idea is to turn over all the responsibilities for software quality to the third party. I envision a self-service subscription component, similar to how SalesForce.com manages sales information. This program would manage baselines and other software life cycle information. All of the test results, reports, pre-production reviews, operational incidents, and triage findings would be made available via a web interface. Users would self-train via built-in modules and follow cookbooks for detailed procedures. You could have approval workflows, escalation workflows, etc. and end up with a self-service portal for APM. It's a dream—but why not?

The ongoing debate for IT is how to cut costs, enhance performance, use the right technology, and cut costs. The mention of "cut cost" twice is deliberate. This is where all the pressure is coming from. Of course, I would prefer that you take the initiative to distinguish your group with a well-considered catalog of services and a strong value proposition for the business. Maybe that's not possible for your group, so a more capable third party relationship, or possibly a self-service portal for APM, is going to be your route.

Summary

I have covered here what I consider the essential processes for an APM initiative. Whatever you choose to do, at minimum it needs to borrow heavily from the process descriptions and goals in this chapter. The runbook is your primary artifact. Whatever environment you deploy to—QA , production, or both—a runbook is your best mechanism to preserve what you have learned so that others may use APM correctly the first time, without having to rediscover or prove again that the monitoring configuration is appropriate.

Much of the challenge in exploiting APM has to do with the rigid organization structures that you inherit and have to work within. These well-defined roles and responsibilities do not really serve the fast pace of distributed application deployment and management. I believe a change is coming that will dissolve the rigid IT silos in favor of the more agile and understandable goal of simply focusing on whatever it takes to improve software quality. Process is your ally in keeping APM activities on track and fostering collaboration. It seems that collaboration may be the route to removing the last vestiges of the availability-centric enterprise, dissolving the silos, and flattening the organization so that it becomes a performance-centric enterprise.

Essential Service Capabilities

When all you have is a hammer, everything looks like a nail.

No matter the scope or scale of your APM implementation, there are a few services with which you must be successful. In priority order, they are as follows:

- Triage
- Application audit
- Preproduction review
- Metrics capacity management

If you have any aspiration of growing your APM footprint, you should also consider the following:

- Solution sizing
- Capacity forecasting

This list, which I consider the absolute minimum for a successful APM discipline, is usually not part of your vendor product training. This is simply because the vendor is selling a software solution. You are expected to know how to use it. I find that most software products have this limitation where all of the vendors' training is focused on how to *operate* the software and not on how that software should be *employed* in your environment. I find that pretty much all software falls into this category. For example, you can purchase a really powerful word processor but there is no effort, on the part of the vendor, to show you how to write a book with it. You have to look elsewhere.

With APM, the problem is even more pronounced because it appears to be similar to other tools (profilers, management consoles) and also has a very broad set of use cases and varying objectives, along with additional responsibilities. Most of these similarities, if followed, can result in nasty anti-patterns for successful use of the APM technology. It is not that the vendors are unsupportive, it is just that the ease-of-use, on which many products aspire, did not address the full scope of users and activities. No one could foresee, at the outset of this industry, what the ideal practices would look like. No one could anticipated what the real education and mentoring needs of the end users would be.

When I conduct a mentoring session for APM best practices, I actually go in the reverse order, starting with a capacity forecast. The order here, starting with triage, is what clients are really interested in. However, the reverse order is really the way to address the longer-term use of the technology and build the stronger foundation. It is always hard to keep folks from just running off to play with their new tool!

Triage

If there is one facet of APM that almost everyone appreciates, it is the enhanced capabilities to triage critical operational incidents. Being able to quickly and easily visualize, via APM, the events leading up to a failure or alert condition—this is what folks have been trying to realize for years. Unfortunately, simply having additional visibility does not help you to triage more effectively. You very much need to know what you are doing, how to use the tool and, most importantly, how to communicate the findings in a non-inflamatory fashion.

Triage, however, is not limited to high profile incidents. It is a core skill employed by all of the stakeholders in the application life cycle. Everyone needs to know a little about how to interpret data. APM metrics are the language of cooperation in performance management. We use the APM technology to make it simpler to access the information in real-time via dashboards and reports. So the more understanding you have about the metrics and how they are obtained, the more effective you will be in your communication with other stakeholders.

When I mentor teams on how to do effective triage, I use lots of visuals of real situations to build up a vocabulary and a process of reviewing APM information. I also use real operational data in the form of archives and the APM technology itself. The great advantage of APM technology is the historical information maintained by the metrics storage component, which may be exported and reloaded into a separate instance of the tools. I receive these exports via FTP, load them on my local instance, and triage at my convenience. You do not need to go through these steps as you will have ready access to metrics. But they make for excellent mentoring materials.

For your APM discipline, you have to collect and preserve historical data to use in your own training and mentoring activities, so that you may continuously train and mentor new candidates in triage. You have to start this activitiy immediately. The easiest way to do so is to insist that every triage activity be documented with screenshots. After the dust has settled, you allow for a meeting to review the findings and discuss what went right, what went wrong, and what you can do better next time.

The APM best practice allows for three levels of triage competency, depending on the maturity of the client environment for load testing and access to historical information. These are as follows:

- Triage with single metrics
  - Simple navigation to examine individual metrics.
- Triage with baselines
  - Definition of normal and comparative techniques, using load testing or operational experience.
- Triage with trends
  - Analysis of multiple baselines and operational incidents.

Why are three levels necessary? For an APM team that is new to the technology, there is simply no historical information to use, and very often, no load testing environment. You have to be able to triage effectively with no prior information about the application and environment. You can do a much better job of triage once you start to get historial information digested in the form of a baseline, and you want to move to that model as soon as possible. You also want to make it possible for non-technical folks to quickly identify suspects, which brings me back to the collaborative goals for APM.

I have put more details on the mechanics of triage in the following chapters from the Practioner's Guide:

- Chapter 12 – Baselines
- Chapter 13 – ApplicationAudit
- Chapter 14 – Triage with Single Metrics
- Chapter 15 – Triage with Baselines
- Chapter 16 – Triage with Trends
- Chapter 17 – Firefighting

Triage is a big topic but you do not have to digest it all in a single effort. You want to plan to learn and practice in deliberate increments. You must appreciate your limitations. You do not get to do triage hidden away in a corner, with your favorite beverage, a clear schedule, and after a restful weekend. You do triage in the spotlight, and no one is going to be patient. Everyone wants to know before anyone else. And everyone knows where you are.

The goal of this chapter is to help you understand and plan for how you want your core APM service capabilities to evolve. A triage discipline is absolutely number one on everyone's list. There is just no easy way to teach you how to triage. You have to do it for yourself and you have to do it fairly frequently in order to exercise your skills and keep them fresh.

What I prefer to focus on are the exercises that you need to go through in order to practice and hone your triage skills. You do not want to wait patiently for a severity-

1 incident to occur so that you can rush in and save the day. You might get lucky, but my expereince is that you will have a very difficult time. In fact, you will likely do more to set back the APM initiative then you will to identify the root cause. You need to practice.

When I mentor a triage project, I review a number of different metrics and their normal and abnormal indications. This is a bit tedious, but I get through it and take some questions. Before the break, I ask for some names at random and list them on the board. Then I announce that, after the break, we will triage some real examples and these folks listed will be the first to stand up here and take us through the process. Usually, a mild panic ensues. I defer all further questions and try to clear the room, emphasizing that they *really* need to get a break now because the next section will be difficult.

I will admit to having a bit of a cruel streak because I think it is entirely appropriate that some folks will not come back to the meeting. Technical folks are not uniformly great communicators, so standing up front, leading the analysis of an incident that they have no prior idea about, and have no preparation or experience in doing this kind of activity is way outside of their comfort zone. So what is this exercise trying to accomplish?

First, I want to make sure I get a room full of folks who are more interested in learning how to triage than in hanging out passively for a couple more hours, listening to me talk. They have an expectation that it could be hard, and I will not disappoint them, but they have decided to incur some discomfort. They want to learn something. Second, the reason for their anxiety is that understanding simple metrics is simply not effective triage. They need a process to conduct the exercise, to communicate.

A recent study[1] that found learning was enhanced when you gave the exam *before* the lecture and then repeated the exam later. It reinforces what the student does not yet know and they will eagerly work to fill that gap. Discomfort or pain is a great motivator. Make sure you find some opportunities to exploit it.

When the break is over and a few souls have opted to return, I call out the first name and bring him up front. Sometimes I will simply grab the most eager candidate. Up on the display appears a screen shot of metrics presented in a dashboard, and away we go.

Metrics Storage Dashboard

The first application for a triage example should never be one that you actually understand or know intimately. While it is clearly more helpful to understand an application, you really need develop skills that are applicable to *any* application. The metrics storage components are also one of the more overlooked APM components. If the capacity and performance of the APM infrastructure are problematic, it is very difficult to access the performance data. This frequently impedes the overall success of the APM initiative.

---

[1] "The Pluses of Getting It Wrong" – Roediger and Finn, Scientific American Mind March 2010. Preview available at www.scientificamerican.com/article.cfm?id=the-pluses-of-getting-it-wrong

Remember, I do not often get involved with stakeholders who are new to APM technology. I get involved after things have not gone well, usually months (even years) after their initial product education. I have an expectation that a certain level of skill should be present, though often I will have already uncovered the fundamental problems during the Skills Assessement. So I am trying to make a few points. First, how can you expect to triage a complex application when you cannot yet triage your own APM infrastructure? Second, it is really hard to triage a problem if you cannot even confirm if it is normal or abnormal.

This leads me to my first tenet of triage: *How do you know that what you see is not actually normal?* When someone brings you an incident, points at application A, and asks you to figure out why there is a problem, how do you know that application A is not performing exactly as expected? There are no key indicators that anyone can refer to that will ever state, conclusively, that metric #46 is out of bounds. It is just not possible. The same metric #46 can have wildly varying values depending on the type of application and the configuration of the environment. Instead, you need to quickly survey all metrics and then look at the Top 5 or Top 10.

Basically, you will sort the metrics, largest to smallest, first for response time and then later with invocations (responses per interval, etc.). This will reveal which components take the most time and which components are the most active. For all but the simplest application, they will never be the same component. You focus on the Top 5 or Top 10 and then look at each of them in a historical window of two hours; 20 minutes after the incident and 100 minutes before. For the two sets of Top 5 (or Top 10) metrics, are the response time and invocations for each metric the same or different than the values around the alleged incident?

There are three possible outcomes at this point. The first two are simple: either there is nothing wrong with the application or there is a shocking deviation. If it is a deviation, then you pursue it with common sense, a hypothesis, and a hunt for the ellusive root cause. The third outcome, which I have not yet described, is a huge problem for a new APM user. If you do not see a deviation, is it because there is nothing wrong or is it because you do not have sufficient visibility?

The worst conclusion you can draw is to claim a problem with an application where no problem exisits. When this happens, no one is going to trust your conclusions the next time around. You can account for and excuse a problem of insufficient visibility but you have to set the stage for this kind of result, which brings me to the second tenet of triage: *You are not here to find problems. You are here to get visibility into the performance characteristics of the application.*

When an application fails, it is easy to decide where to start looking for the cause. When an application is degraded but otherwise continues running, it is a whole lot harder to know where to start looking. Your triage process has to take this into account. You need to understand your limitations and you need to avoid committing to "find" the problem. All you can ever do is attempt to get visibility into the performance characteristics. If you find something abnormal, you can pursue it. But if you do not find something abnormal, you have to take some extra steps to first confirm that there actually is a problem or then to question your visibility.

Most clients do not get themselves completely out of this question of visibility. The piece they are missing is that you do not want to wait until there is an incident to find out that you do not have sufficient visibility. How can you do that? You need to get a definition of *normal* before the incident or earlier in the application life cycle.

Pilot Findings

An opportunity to get that definition of normal may have already been completed during the pilot evaluation. I have worked on a lot of firefights and about 20% of the time I can actually refer to load tests and wrap-up results from a pilot 3-6 months earlier. Provided that the pilot was for the same application as the one experiencing the incident, this is a goldmine of help for your triage efforts. And even if it is a different application, there may be some helpful findings. Hopefully, the application was stable during the pilot but that's not a requirement. Perhaps you are thinking that the pilot environment and production are too different for comparison, such that the response times will be very different, for example, because of the performance advantages enjoyed by the production environment. So you don't look at response times, just like you don't look at CPU or memory or anything else that would be sensitive to the scale of the environment.

What you look at are those same Top 5 (or Top 10) components that you search for and sorted as your first activity. If you execute a login transaction, for example, the same sequence of components are going to be exercised no matter the environment. Yes, the response times will differ but the call stack should not[2]. This brings me to the third tenet of triage: *If you want to quickly find a problem, look first in the code that _was not_ tested.*

What you cannot be sure of is that the exercise or usage of the pilot application is actually representative of the production experience. This is more of a concern when only manual testing is employed, but when automated load testing is available, this will usually give good coverage of the app. I will talk more about the problems of test coverage when I look at the QA systems in Chapter12. If you see different components in production than what you saw during load testing in QA, you have a great opportunity in terms of problem solving but also a big problem in terms of test plan quality.

Invariably, when undertaking triage, bugs always manage to turn up in the code that was not tested. Experienced practitioners have been milking this reality for years. It is what makes us all look like heros and superdudes! All you are doing is taking advantage of visibility to prioritize your bug hunt, so start with the code you did not test. This is not actually a problem with the testing team. It is actually a problem of requirements for the test coverage. And, of course, sometimes you cannot test everything you need to.

---

[2] Just for completeness, you will frequently find differences in the call stack when the test applications are "stubbed." This means that instead of accessing a database or web service as part of the load test, the code simply returns "success." This is done because of difficulties maintaining or reversing the changes in the end resource that the test application is changing. Your result is actually a *Unit Test*, which is perfectly fine, provided that the stakeholders know that they did not experience an actual test of the fully integrated solution but only an isolated portion of the application.

What you must plan for is to review the production experience and feed back the unexpected component activity to the testing team, so that they can improve the overall test requirements.

Metrics Archive Triage and Presentation

An important and more extensive exercise to build triage skills is to assign a metrics archive[3] and have each participant independently triage and present their findings. Four hours is plenty of time, so you can assign this as an overnight project or maybe allow a week for completion. I prefer the short schedule simply because it is more realistic—and folks need to get used to it! Each participant will present their findings to the whole group and the group will offer supportive critique.

This activity confirms a wide range of basic skills, in addition to the findings presentation. You have to collect the archive via FTP. You have to install and license an instance of the metrics collection and workstation on your own laptop. You have to use a presentation tool. And you have to find a problem (or not) in an archive that may have 20-30 agents. It is a real trial by fire.

It is, however, more an exercise in getting comfortable with a rhythm for triage and presenting your findings than it is about finding problems. Some folks really believe that reviewing obscure and incredibly esoteric problems is the best path towards mastery of triage. But what is the point in learning about something that will rarely be encountered? I believe it is more useful to reinforce what you will be doing with every application. About half of the archives will not have any significant problems, which is actually harder to deal with than when there is an obvious problem. The first tenet of triage is going to slap you repeatedly!

For example, I reviewed testing for an application that was under-performing. I found that while everything appeared normal, the overall response times for the application were terrible. The memory was well-managed, the load profile was confirmed representative, the various resources were all confirmed operational. The client desperately wanted to know where the problem was and I had absolutely nothing to show. I confirmed that I had great visibility and nothing was being monitored that was inappropriate and might otherwise contribute to overhead. I also ran benchmark applications to confirm that there was nothing wrong with the hardware, and the response times were excellent. One area you can rarely have visibility into are the startup parameters for the JVM and application server. I fired up the projector, selected a big font, and with all eyes on, started going over each and every parameter being set and validating that it made sense. A couple of lines later, maybe a dozen parameters into it, we get to "debugFlag=true". With certain application servers, this parameter has a devastating effect on response time.

The moral of this story is that folks want to find problems with the application but do not really know what the cause is. The application is easy to blame. Somebody wrote code and that is just hard to get correct the first time. The triage job needs to be neutral but pragmatic. Triage tennet Number 4: *Trust nothing you cannot measure because everybody is mislead by their own agenda.* I actually derived this

---

[3] A *metrics archive* is a portable repository or database extract that can be fed back into the APM solution and then investigated.

from the TV show "House." His version is that "Everybody lies." They withhold information that might be embarassing because they think it is not germaine to their health problems, which only makes it harder for Dr. House to get to root cause. However, that pithy exclamation just does not fly in the corporate environment. You need to be firm but respectful.

Baselines

To advance your triage skills, the next evolution is to start using baselines, or summaries of application characteristics. You divide baselines into three types: Configuration, Application, and Performance. The process of baselining requires contributions from QA load testing and reporting over the APM metrics. To define the reporting, you have to identify groups of metrics that best represent Availability, Performance and Capacity (APC). And you may add in other single metrics of interest as appropriate for the application.

So you go again to the metrics repository, and armed with the metadata about each test (date, start, duration, load profile), decide which components and representative metrics for those components best capture the characteristics of the application. These decisions are represented as collections, and in the first interation of this exercise, you just navigate among the metric collections to discuss the salient features and why they are useful. The second iteration advances the presentation to a generated report; you focus on that content but also on the order in which the information should be presented and other considerations for how that presentation is structured. It should run about 15 minutes per person.

The source for these baseline exercises are the actual deployment candidates which had recent or ongoing load testing. If the client is unable to do load testing to support these exercises, there is really no point mentoring for this level of triage. The motivation to divide the mentoring over three sessions is to allow the testing organization to catch up in terms of being able to support APM activities. You have to manage the QA testing and help them work through issues in their execution before they become a reliable contributor to triage. But if your organization is never going to invest in appropriate test capabilities, there is no point in mentoring for techniques that you will not soon have a chance to employ and thus reinforce.

Characterization

With the baseline system established we can now move on to the last refinement for triage: Characterization. The motivation for characterization is from an early rule of engineering: *Two points do not make a trend*. If you have not yet noticed, I tend to do everything in threes. And here is where I bring that philosophy to bear. To correctly characterize an application, you need to repeat a test three times.

The resistance to this idea comes from the fundamental bias that if you test something once, and it was successful, then you do not need to test it again. Folks will repeat an unsuccessful test any number of times, but the first time it is correct, they say, "We're done here!" The challenge is actually something else. It is difficult to quickly determine if those three tests are similar. They may look similar but how do you really know? This is not just an academic consideration. When someone claims that an application is performing poorly, how do you really know that it is? How many comparisions do you think you can manage visually?

The way I accomplish it, and the full details are in Chapter 11, is to generate a report for each interval of interest. The report has a few metrics of interest presented as tables. Each report is saved in a .CSV or .HTML format—any text-based format will do. Then you write a script to extract the metrics of interest and present them in a small table. It seems trival. But try it with your software of choice.

Figure 9-1 shows a sample baseline report in table format for one of the load tests.

Baseline - Component Response

Component Response Time (overview)

Resource:Metric	Mean	Min	Max	MMin	MMax	Count
EJB|Messagge-driven:Average Method Invocation Time (ms)	1,284	9	106,942	0	607,856	12,775
EJB|Session:Average Method Invocation Time (ms)	1,851	1	279,491	0	1,369,006	9,693
JDBC:Average Query Time (ms)	950	0	37,218	0	83,313	28,214
JDBC:Average Update Time (ms)	79	0	13,093	0	200,896	4,221
JMS|Message Consumer:Average Method Invocation Time (ms)	57,109	567	143,981	2	716,873	66,412
JMS|Message Listener:Average Method Invocation Time (ms)	11,828	0	168,678	0	1,181,781	5,476
JMS|Queue Sender:Average Method Invocation Time (ms)	513	0	21,018	0	278,362	3,604
JMS|Topic Publisher:Average Method Invocation Time (ms)	36	1	32	0	179	36
JTA:Average Method Invocation Time (ms)	203	0	29,949	0	485,008	14,979
Servlets :Average Response Time (ms)	8,884	352	13,232	0	54,935	13

Start: 5/9/06 9:00 AM **End: 5/17/06 2:00 PM**

Metric Grouping: Component Response Time (ms)
Agents: ftbhvt01\|WebLogic\|wftf_srv_01

Figure 9-1. Sample baseline report

So imagine yourself with three such reports, which you will probably need to print out so that you can compare them.

Now here is a sample characterization with a slight twist. I got in my three runs but the cluster was not symmetrical, so I needed to analyze them individually.

"=========== EJB|Entity:Average Invoc. =========="	Avg	Min	Max	Count
PROD_1_060125_11.18-11.33_Test1	5	0	340	13470
PROD_1_060125_17.54-18.09_Test2	1	0	1003	9669
PROD_1_060125_18.23-18.38_Test3	1	0	151	6354
PROD_2_060125_11.18-11.33_Test1	5	0	266	10383
PROD_2_060125_17.54-18.09_Test2	1	0	137	9535
PROD_2_060125_18.23-18.38_Test3	1	0	146	6822

18.23 – 18.38 = 15 min test duration

	PROD 1	PROD 2	Avg	Diff	% Diff
Test 1	13470	10383	11926.5	3087	25.9%
Test 2	9669	9535	9602	134	1.4%
Test 3	6354	6822	6588	-468	-7.1%

Figure 9-2. Sample characterization

Now if you have done the little bit of math, you can see that each measured duration is 15 minutes (see Figure 9-2). The important part is the Count. This is the total invocations, over the 15 minute steady-state period, for a two machine cluster with the load generator directed at a load balancer. Usually, I prefer to have the test iterations in quick sequence. I guess lunch was important to this test team. Anyway, if you compare Test1(Prod1, Prod2) you can see that the cluster elements are not symmetrical (13,470 vs. 10,383). The smaller set of tables, in the lower left, calculates some statistics for each test. And if you compare the three runs, the number of invocations decreases later in the day. Clearly, something is wrong with this test evolution because we simply cannot reproduce the test and the number of invocations decreases with each test (13,470 to 9669 to 6354) . Remember, this is the same test across identical servers. The only difference is the time of day that the test is run.

So here is the point. If you needed to achieve 12,000 invocations in 15 minutes in order to go to production and you only looked at PROD_1 at the 11 A.M. test, would you continue on to production? If you looked at PROD_2 for that same test and noticed the 26% difference for an element that is supposed to be receiving the same load, would you be concerned? Finally, compare Test 1 to Test 3. Does a 50% reduction in capacity due to time of day affect your confidence in the test environment? Or do you decide to only run your tests in the morning?

Could you at least see what happens for a couple more days? Or should you just abandon testing altogether? Regrettably, this is what I believe is causing many organizations to abandon significant pre-production testing. These are real results and you will find problems with load reproducibility in the QA environment in four out of five different sites. It's not just a problem. It's an epidemic. When you are ready to address it, APM will give you the visibility—and then you are ready to get the full benefit of APM.

Characterization turns out to be much more than a mouthful of a word. It is a bit of work to do all the testing and summarize the results. But if someone is asking you to triage an application in QA, you actually have an obligation to ask if you are in fact really triaging the QA testing process, instead of the application. Characterization in production is a much more arduous process because you need three consistent samples, and production is always sensitive to time-of-day, time-of-week, or time-of-year differences. Basically, you need a minimum of three weeks of data and you should probably avoid the last week of the month.

Cookbook

The ideal time to undertake a characterization effort is when you've got enough time to do a thorough analysis. The reality is that you will use an incident to justify getting involved in a performance issue and then grab the characterization data from existing tests or during the initial audit of the application. Hopefully your triage will identify a code correction and you will get a regression test of the fix. That's where you will see the test plan and load profile.

1. Remember that you are only providing visibility into the performance characteristics of the application.

2. Get a description of the incident, what time it was observed, what systems were affected, and if a resart was ordered and when. Get a list of the APM agents employed, key transactions, and any log files or thread dumps.

3. Collect any pilot results, if available.

4. Collect any baseline results from a known normal production period or from QA stress and performance testing, if available.

5. Comment on the overall visibility of the monitored applications. How many metrics are being generated? What are the startup characteristics? What types of components are encountered? What extended or custom configurations are present?

6. Identify the Top 5 (or Top 10) components for response time and for invocations, ordered highest value to lowest value.

7. Comment on the apparent consistency (or not) of these components for the duration of the test or interval for the incident (2 hours).

8. Comment on the types of business transactions encountered, their response times, and consistency of useage.

9. Comment on the memory management. Is memory usage consistent? Rising? Massive sawtooths? Is the JVM or CLR well-tuned or in need of tuning?

10. Comment on the concurrency apparent in the application. Are any bottlenecks obvious?
11. Comment on the I/O characteristics.
12. Comment on the CPU consumption and other platfrom metrics, as appropriate.
13. Comment on the variety and response times for SQL statements and messaging.
14. Comment on the load simulation profile. Which metrics are sensitive to load and track load very closely? What metrics are independent of load?
15. Review the production visibility, contrasted with the testing visibility, among the testing and application teams and correct the test requirements and overall simulation accuracy.

Application Audit

If triage is the number one benefit folks hope to achieve from their APM investment, the App Audit is the most useful competency because it is essentially triage, but without the attention and headaches. Everything you need to know about the APM tool you are using is exercised during both the audit and triage. However important I know the App Audit it to be, very few stakeholders will independently make this realization. Even if they have been using APM for years, I have not yet encountered anyone who thought to use APM technology in this fashion.

The App Audit is actually an outgrowth of the APM pilot exercise. Long ago, when the technology was new and the clients suffering from performance problems, I and many others would be deployed to demonstrate the software in the client environment. These were pilots only in the sense that there was a legitimate performance problem, but there was just no actual criteria for an evaluation of the technology. All the client wanted was someone to come in and find the problem. They were clearly not really interested in buying anything. Those were the rules of the sales game at that time. The prospect would feign some potential montitoring initiative. We would go in to setup and demonstrate the software. Later that night the product would manage to find its way to production and the next day became very interesting.

It was a symbiotic relationship. The prospect got visibility into their performance problem. Sales qualified a lead. And we technical folks got an opportunity to practice our skills. Some of my system engineer peers went off to define the process and criteria for qualifying and scoping a bonafide pilot engagement that would result in a sale. I decided to reduce the pilot duration to two days. This allowed me to get two pilots per week and an opportunity to try a variety of strategies. There was, after all, no book discussing triage with APM. We learned that skill on the job.

I was also perturbed with the ethical conundrum of prospects feining interest in APM so that they could get access to the tools for free, as well as my feining to be interested in demonstrating APM so that I could get visibility into problem applications in a live environment. So during the pilot call, when it became clear that this was to be a bug-hunt and not a pilot, I would halt the call and simply offer to do the bug hunt for two days, rather than us both pretending to participate in a pilot for the remainder of the week. Thus, integrity was restored and I got frequent access to live production applications, which continued to validate the audit skills and processes.

Why Audits Matter

Aside from the bug-hunt adventures, once an audit service offering was available it was then incorporated in the scope call as an option for the initial interaction with the prospect. You could conduct a pilot following the guidelines in Chapter 6, you could commission a firefight, or you could commission an App Audit. This is an interesting scenario for the software sales process, which I will not not discuss here except to say that it is now possible to interact with a prospect who is not buying an APM solution but is otherwise interested in employing APM metrics and findings.

Referring back to the earlier discussion in Chapter 1, this is where the distinction between AP*Monitoring* and AP*Management* becomes apparent as you are no longer targeting an audience interested in tools, you are targeting an audience interested in getting better information about their applications. It changes the nature of the discussion and dramatically alters the value proposition. You are not asking for an investment that will be expected to return dividends later, you are delivering a service with an immediate value. It is no longer about monitoring. It's about software quality.

The folks interested in the App Audit proposition are focused solely on software quality. They are in a business model where they are responsible for managing the relationship with a software development partner. As code is developed and tested, it needs to be accepted (for folks to get paid) and someone needs to define the criteria. APM visibility provides this criteria, and with appropriate processes, provides a repeatable framework to collect the criteria as the project progresses.

The benefit of a mature audit process extends the acceptance criteria to providing specific recommendations to the developers. For the App Audit service, this is done by the consultant. Most clients are not interested in taking on this responsibility for specific recommendations, so the most you'll do for them, should they internalize the message, is to mentor project managers to oversee the audit delivery. This lets them establish some of the process guidelines and helps them get a consistent result, even if you are assigning different consultants. Audits in this fashion are generally done quarterly so it is a challenge to get the same consultant assigned each time.

The reason for bringing this up is that App Audits can be a unique offering, as part of your APM service catalog. As IT groups work to show value for the business, it is important to have service capabilities that map directly to business needs. Helping to manage the application life cycle is a means to distinguish your group from other groups when it comes time to divide the operational budget. It is not enough to be an APM operator in the current economy. Anyone can operate an environment. Delivering a valued-added service on top of the monitoring infrastructure is something that is difficult for a third party to step in and take over.

The following summarizes the App Audit activities:

- Test Plan

  - Agent extensions/configurations used
  - Duration
  - Use case characteristics

- Visibility achieved (configuration baseline)

  - Representative transaction traces
  - Benefit of custom tracing (if employed)

- Baseline report (application and performance baselines)

  - Metrics load
  - Performance characteristics
    - CPU, GC, response time, invocations
    - Potential scalability (if load to failure achieved)
  - Other components of interest
    - SQL statements, stalls, errors

- Alerting Strategy

  - Thresholds, if load to failure achieved

- Dashboard(s)

  - Which metrics best highlight the correct operation of the app and are predictive of failure?

This is all you need from the implementation perspective to understand the non-deployment activities of the APM initiative. Everything that is taking place to validate the gold configurations, assess the performance characteristics of the application, and validate the dashboards and reporting comprise the App Audit. At the close of the APM initiative, you not only have a functioning APM infrastructure, you have practiced and realized a core APM service capability that you can exploit to further grow the APM system. The full detail of how to conduct the audit are found in Chapter 13 – Application Audit.

Pre-production Review

Sometimes you cannot expect the ambition to employ APM tools under proper and effective processes. Perhaps someone has already completed the initial deployment and is readying a configuration for production monitoring. In this situation, you really only have a single opportunity to catch problems and enforce standards, and that will be just before the solution goes to production.

You need to intervene with the following goals:

- Assess if the release candidate is stable and scalable.

- Assess if the correct technology has been implemented for the target application.
- Assess what the deployment team has considered in terms of ongoing maintenance of the APM configuration and capacity of the metrics storage component.

Someone needs to get this information drafted as a document and signed off by the participating parties. You can host a discussion and then draft the minutes, or you can make it into a form and have them fill in the blanks. You have to make an effort to show that someone tried to restrain their deployment, if only via a cursory document.

Getting folks to sign is another bit of social engineering to help everyone understand their responsibilities and start to make activities more accountable. The absence of accountability is something I am finding more prevalent, especially for smaller projects, and it is poison for an APM initiative.

For the meeting where you present this list, simply replace "Assess if…" with "How do you know that…" and pull as much information as possible. Avoid being confrontational and simply note the response, even if it is nothing. Turn it around, and have them sign it. It takes five minutes at most. If they are uncomfortable signing, you can ask them what they would like to do to help address the gaps before taking this deployment to production. Whatever they reply with, add that to the form, even if it is a suggestion that cannot be addressed such as, "We would like to do more load testing but we no longer have access to the environment." It is not up to you, the project manager, to pass judgement on their efforts. It is up to you to act as a gatekeeper and attempt to enforce some minimum standards and accountability. And it is also an opportunity for you to establish rapport with the team by documenting their situation, their understanding of APM, and what they can do with the resources available to them.

If you can get that opportunity for more load testing (or even a first load test) then you are in a position to start defining minimum acceptance criteria. The following summarizes what I consider the minimum for consideration, in order of highest priority:

- No more than five stalls per operational day (8 hours)
    - A stall is any component response that takes longer than 30 seconds
    - No user-facing application should have stalls
        - This is a poor user experience
- Memory footprint that shows evidence of correct tuning
- No unhandled errors/exceptions
- Separation of batch and interactive processing
    - Poor candidates
        - 1 M transactions, 1 second or less
        - 10k transactions, 2 minutes or more

The stalls are the simplest metric to understand. Just imagine yourself on a book seller web site, shopping for books, and the search page does not come back after 30 seconds. How long until you abandon that site and move to another? To be reasonable, you have to exclude the startup period for the application because Java and .NET each have to compile classes and that can exceed the measure. During the operational day you may also allow a few but if you find dozens or hundreds, then there is something wrong with the app. Finding exactly what's wrong will take more work, but you need to set expectations that the operational experience will likely be problematic.

The memory footprint is a bit more subjective. But if you see a pronounced saw-tooth for the memory use, you actually have a default configuration for the JVM settings and very likely bad things will happen under load. A well-tuned memory profile is flat, even under load. For some GC algorithms, this is because the garbage collection is balanced between duration and frequency such that the memory needs appear static. The JVM configuration tuning should have already been completed during development and confirmed during testing. But if the testing was absent, then it is possible the configuration testing is absent as well. Java configuration tuning is a complex task but there is a very approachable reference that also embraces the application life cycle viewpoint in Haines[4]. There are many more memory management profiles to consider but this simple check will catch the big ones.

Having no unhandled exceptions or errors is a very contentious criteria. Very often you will have many 404 errors, which indicates a missing page. By many, I mean hundreds to tens of thousands. This usually occurs because the missing pages are simply not part of the test plan. That does not necessarily mean that there is a problem with the application; those missing pages will be found on the production site. However, when you start with a compromised test plan, you have to wonder what else is assumed to be present at production. Compromises tend to run in packs.

Initially, unhandled exceptions are usually very prevalent. This starts to change when you are able to count them and keep track of them. Again, there is no mandate for acceptance at this time so you just need to make a note and get a signature. Sometimes the issue resolves itself.

If you think this is unusually fussy, please bear in mind that a large number of exceptions, similar to a verbose level of log reporting, is going to consume platform resources. And anything that consumes platform resources is going to affect the performance of the application. No one really cared about this is the past because the only criteria was the smoke test—if it blew up, the app was not stable. If it did not blow up, it was ready for production.

When you talk about gold configurations for the APM agent, you are trying to generate a sense of quality about that configuration. And while you are assessing what makes for good visibility, and the balance between visibility and overhead, you want to also measure the things that folks have assumed were safe. It is as simple as running a load test with and without logging. Is it the same or different? In my experiences, the differences are stunning.

Acceptance criteria—defining it, establishing processes to expect it, and making it part of the organizational DNA—this is a long and arduous path. Project

---

[4] "Pro Java EE 5 Performance Management and Optimization", Steven Haines, 2006 Apress.

management is in a position to begin the evolution by simply making a few requests and documenting the results. The advantage of using a project manager is that they keep track of the project and they also maintain the artifacts for future, similar projects. If they understand the big picture for APM, then you have increased your opportunities for a successful deployment and laid the foundation for an evolving APM system.

"You're travelling through another dimension, a dimension not only of availability but of performance and capacity; a journey into a wondrous land whose boundaries are that of APM. That's the signpost up ahead—your next stop, the Pre-production Review!"[5]

Capacity Management of APM Metrics

The most common gap for a small APM deployment is in understanding the capacity constraints of the APM infrastructure. Unlike traditional systems management, which does not attempt to store data for any significant length of time, APM stores and manages massive amounts of data in comparison. As most technical teams are familiar with systems management, they will unfortunately assume that APM behaves much the same. Just this year, Gartner[6] released their analysis of the APM marketplace and put forth a five-dimensional model for defining the APM marketplace. The fifth dimension is focused on the "application performance managment database," which is considered a key area because all of the workflows around performance management need ready access to the performance metrics. Now, I prefer to refer to the workflows as "collaborations" but otherwise, Gartner is making a similar emphasis on the necessity of having good practices and capabilities around metrics storage and access.

A second gap is that every application is different. This means that the impact of a monitoring configuration will also be different, and so the number of metrics that an application generates will be different from any other application. With systems management technologies, you get the same dozen metrics, no matter what you are monitoring. With APM, your agent will vary between 50 and 20,000 metrics, depending on the type of application, depth of visibility, collection of JMX/PMI metrics, and the impact of any extension technologies (web services, etc.).

The trap for the small deployment is that they will usually be well within the capacity of a single metrics collection server, especially if they are the first to use the technology. This will not be the case for successive deployments, especially if they

[5] A shameless hack of the Twilight Zone opening, 1959 TV series Rod Serling. 1959. *The Twilight Zone.* tv series. Created by Rod Serling. Narrated by Rod Serling, Forest Whitaker, and Desi Arnaz. USA: CBS, 1959-1964

[6] "Magic Quadrant for Application Performance Monitoring", Gartner Incorporated, 18 February 2010 http://www.gartner.com/technology/media-products/reprints/ca/vol2/article5/article5.html

are following the Phased Deployment model. Their second deployment could be a 200% increase!

The solution is simple—another few basic questions from Project Management, as follows:

- How many metrics does your APM generate?
- How many APM agents will you deploy?
- What portion of capacity is available now in production?
- What portion of capacity will be available after your agents are deployed?
- In case capacity is exceeded, who is responsible for adjusting the agent configuration or getting another Metrics Collection server instance?

The challenge with APM is to get all of the stakeholders understanding the basics of the technology. Ultimately, you want to harness this collective knowledge for collaboration leading to better management of the application life cycle. You know that the language of collaboration is performance data, which begins with how many and what kind.

When I have a first meeting with a team that asserts they are using APM effectively, I give them all the rope needed to hang themselves. I invite them to describe what they are doing with APM. Then I ask them about the characteristics of the application, what types of components, how many packages define it, and various attributes about the application server. I get lots of details and information.

Then I ask them how many agents are deployed. How many metrics do they get from the agent? What components contribute the most metrics? How many metrics are they managing overall? I might get an answer to the first question but I won't usually get an answer to the remaining questions. They will have described how they monitor in QA and triage in production and a number of other things. That's the answer they expect someone wants to hear. It does not reveal anything about what they actually know or what they are actually doing.

Everyone claims they know what they're doing with APM, and yet no one can talk about what they are doing in even the simplest terms. They can do it for the application server but not for the technology monitoring that server. It is a massive gap and one that you have to bridge in order for APM to be successful in the longer term. You have to get in the habit of talking about monitoring with the same confidence as the rest of the application infrastructure.

Solution Sizing

Related to the overall number of metrics but appearing well before the start of the monitoring initiative is the issue of solution sizing. Once someone decides to purchase an APM solution, someone needs to procure appropriate hardware to support it. Ideally, the initial solution sizing is completed before the purchase order is cut, and sometimes it will be deferred until services does the scope call (if services are used). But when the licenses are drawn from a pool as part of an enterprise-wide licensing scheme, no gets assigned the responsibility to make sure that the deployments are sized correctly. There is also no coordination of sizing and access when the metrics storage servers are shared.

You know, from Part 1 of this book, how this happens and what to do to address it. And in Chapter 10, I will go into the details of how to do sizing. Here in Part 2, as a project manager, where you have just discovered that you are herding cats (multiple deployments underway), you have to take a different tack.

What you need to figure out is magnitude, frequency, and location. What are the biggest deployments, what are their deployment schedules, and in which business units are they occuring? Project management is a close community, so the email blast to various PMs is the first step to finding out who is running these other potential APM initiatives. The second step is to get ahold of the appropriate vendors and bring in their expertise. If you can bring the different pieces together, then you will make efficient use of their time and they will be highly motivated to ensure your success. If you cannot bring the pieces together, then you are probably going to need a services engagment to validate the sizing or conduct the pre-production reviews.

The third step is to bring together a recommendation of what can be done and what the risk of inaction will be along with some of the negative outcomes. Notify your management and then e-mail blast the level above. Then move on to your next task.

This is a difficult proposition. Everyone likes to stay within their scope of authority and certainly project managers have a lot to do already. But the PMs are the oversight for delivery of the project. They are the pilot on the tug boat that guides the super tanker (project) through the harbor and into the docks. You have be willing to take initiative and raise the flag. If management chooses to ignore it or elects to follow another path, that is their choice.

Capacity Forecast

This service is the foundation for really understanding an application and to undertake higher order analysis of metrics leading to service-level agreements (SLAs). I will take up SLAs and capacity planning later in the book. Here, you want to understand expectations about capacity planning and why you should not use that specific term.

Capacity planning is a well-established term from the early days of mainframe computing when hardware was really expensive. Those early client-server applications were ideal for analysis: you could make a few measurements around response times, count the number of users and estimate the number of transactions, and end up with a pretty good estimate of what sized environment you would need to support that application. These client–server and queuing models are still in use today; they are the foundation of modern simulation and modeling. The challenge is that they are not very useful for web-based, distributed computing. Simple web apps can benefit but something like a portal or other complex distributed application is really hard to simulate without making broad generalizations.

The problem with capacity planning is that it requires lots of data. As you are just now making available APM visibility and metrics to your environment, you do not really benefit from the types of analysis that the capacity planners are familiar with. There will certainly be some information you can use, but these will be about application servers in general as well as other resources. But since you have new applications, as well as new metrics from APM, you simply do not have any historical basis to make traditional conclusions about capacity. So how do you satisfy a stakeholder's request to plan for the capacity of a new application? You first replace "planning" with "forecast."

Application

A capacity *forecast* is something analagous to the capacity planning function except that it is not model-based, it is measurement-based. There are two reasons for this. First, you have no operational history. Second, and more significantly, most distributed applications today are simply too complex to be modeled with a discrete equation, as is possible with traditional client-server. The client-server model has three components: client, middleware, and database. You apply some queuing theory to this and you get an equation that you can simulate and explore the potential capacities of the application. With a distributed application, such as a portal application, you will have dozens of interacting services and resources. It is simply not practical to design a test plan to isolate each of the distributed components so that you could apply a client-server model. It is challenging enough to develop a test plan that will accurately summarize the performance characteristics in terms of direct measurements.

Provided that you have identified the dominant use cases for the application, what you need to forecast is a "load to failure" of its capacity and saturation characteristics. All the details are provided in Chapter 11 for this test plan. Basically, you increase load to the application over a period of at least two hours until the application reaches the first point, saturation, and the second point, total failure. A third point is estimated for the maximum safe load.

This exercise is crucial because it allows you to validate the warning and danger thresholds that will be used for alerting. And it also helps you to understand the characteristics of the application at saturation, which will be very helpful when you triage. However, you cannot expect to complete a capacity forecast without solid load simulation skills, and a solid App Audit. So what can you do to help establish and mature a capacity forecast system?

Monitoring Environment

The other area that depends on a capacity forecast, versus a capacity planning exercise, is the APM monitoring environment itself. For a group new to APM that has been unable to complete a capacity forecast for their application, you may still practice those skills on the metrics storage component. After all, it is just another distributed application. The only difference is in the availability of load simulation. Conventional load generation tools do not apply.

However, non-conventional tools may be available. Please consult your vendor. After all, they have to do testing themselves, at some point, before their product is released. All you really need is something that looks like an agent but otherwise does not require an application server to execute. You will need a few machines to host the robot agents just as you would with a traditional load generation tool in order to support a few hundred agents.

If, during the deployment, you find some issue regarding the hardware configuration, fail-over scheme, virtualization, or a direct validation of the project capacity of the solution, you should set aside a little time to build out the environment and then design a test plan to hit each server configuration with an increasing load until they fail over. You must have each instance running at the same time and on the same network so as to minimize any anomalies biasing the findings. If they are both running, the anomaly should appear at the same time for both servers. Ideally, you should have three instances of each target configuration in order to confirm consistency among the same servers.

The best time to think about this proof of capacity is during the initial sizing. For a large deployment (into the millions of metrics), you are going to need a fair bit of hardware. Your procurement arm is another group who may not appreciate the nuances of APM compared with traditional monitoring tools. They will look at the hardware order, emit any number of unusual sounds, and could very well demad you prove the need for that much hardware.

Summary

APM Tools are about monitoring. APM processes, which you assemble into APM services are about management of the application life cycle. If you expect to be proficient with APM*management*, then your APM discipline needs to be competent with these services and their underpinning skills and processes.

Of course, triage is the service that everyone expects from APM. The best triage will be built on a solid foundation of solution sizing, metrics capacity management, App Audit, pre-production review, and capacity forecast. If you do not have the time or resources to become competent in these other services, your triage will be Good—and maybe that will be enough. You cannot have an expectation of increasing APM maturity by spending more time with that initial level of competency. You simply have to master more essential services for your APM initiative to grow.

Practitioners

10

Solution Sizing

Anyone can sell you a hammer but how do you build a shed,
a garage, or a condominium complex with it?

Sizing is a fundamental systems engineering activity to determine the appropriate hardware (or costs[1]) and resources to support an application or service. In this case, we are concerned for the APM application and the collection of components that comprise your APM technology solution. How much RAM, CPUs, network, and disk capacity are needed to support your APM technology?

Directly related to these hardware questions are the appropriate capacities of the various APM components that may be supported by a given piece, or *instance*, of hardware. This will be in terms of metrics, transaction types, and volumes. How much capacity will you get for each instance of an APM component?

Finally, what are the characteristics of the application environment, or *workload*, to which you are applying APM technology. How many applications, databases, and web services will you support? How many defects and alerts do you expect to generate? What server models/vendors are you compatible with?

Aside from the technology concerns, sizing is just a medium complexity accounting exercise. What you need to be successful is a solid methodology and complete visibility into how you arrived at your recommendations.

Kick Off Meeting

Solution sizing is a variant of capacity planning. The essential difference is the absence of any historical performance information on which to base the planning analysis. While you may use a *capacity forecast* (see Chapter 18) for an application

---

[1] Gary Thomas, Christopher Miller, Ricardo Valerdi, "Systems Engineering Cost Estimation by Consensus," http://web.mit.edu/rvalerdi/www/SE cost estimation by consensus - paper.pdf

configured with APM technology, you have a greater challenge when the APM technology is not yet deployed. Basically, you need to estimate how much hardware is needed to support the various APM components. When there is no prior experience with APM technology, your sizing results may also be called into question, so you will need to invest time in educating your stakeholders, as well as completing the mechanics of the sizing analysis.

This somewhat pessimistic point—that the veracity of your results will be suspect—is simply because your recommendations are going to cause real money to be spent. And if you are forecasting a sizing over a three year period, for example, be prepared for serious pushback.

Classic capacity planning relies on four inputs:

- Understanding service levels.
- Understanding current capacity.
- Understanding the growth to be supported.
- Understanding the characteristics of the APM components.

Solution sizing will parallel these considerations so that you may not only address the initial deployment but also develop a process to handle future deployments. Those future deployments will bring you back to the goals of the classic capacity planning.

The inputs for solution sizing as follows:

- Deployment scope in number of applications

  - Specifically the number of JVMs or CLRs (instrumentation)
  - Number of business transactions (real and synthetic transaction monitoring)

- Solution architecture
- Application survey
- Capacity forecast
- Forecast of deployment growth

The essential question you have to answer is "Do we have sufficient monitoring capacity to support the deployment (monitoring initiative)?" The answer you need to provide is generally in terms of a hardware order. The only way to increase capacity with an APM solution is to order more of the APM components.

With an existing APM solution, you may sometimes avoid any new hardware by correcting an earlier APM configuration. There may be opportunities for tuning the monitoring configuration by reviewing the deployed agents and looking to reduce the number of metrics that they are generating, thereby recovering some capacity. This occurs in a small percentage of sizing activities. This situation has the benefit of more historical information and may follow the more traditional capacity planning steps.

Solution Architecture

With some ideas about the metrics capacity goals and growth, which you derive from the assessment activities, you can then move to considerations about architectures that will support the initial and follow-on deployments. There are a few considerations that are added at this point, related to access and fail-over capabilities, such as:

- Controlling access to the monitoring data

  - Partitioning by role and/or application
  - Where to get credentials (login, password) from
  - Failover capabilities
  - Routing and firewall issues

Of these additional points, failover considerations are perhaps the most contentious. Some folks are motivated to ensure that no metric will be lost and so hold the availability of monitoring data to some exceptional standards. I feel that this is a completely disproportionate response. If you never before had to manage APM metrics, why then would you require an availability target for those metrics, with exceptional 5-nines[2] availability, before you ever have operational experience with the APM technology? While anyone might appreciate the exceptional regard that such clients have for APM availability, it is totally out of proportion.

APM is nice to have, and even exceptionally useful, but it is not so critical to the business that you can't live without it for 30 minutes. All these kinds of exceptional failover criteria do little more than dramatically inflate the cost and administrative challenges of maintaining the resulting system. When these points are raised for an initial APM deployment, I must conclude that the proponent is trying to scuttle the effort.

You may not be able to avoid doing the work of architecting such an extreme availability, as an alternate configuration, along with your more modest and lower cost alternative. So you should undertake to really understand where these criteria are coming from, which monitoring systems today implement those criteria, and which applications depend on them. The cost differences are extraordinary, which all but ensures that they would never be selected—excepting, of course, when they are absolutely essential, which I have never seen implemented.

If you then limit yourselves to more reasonable solution architectures, there are four strategies to consider, as summarized in Figure 10-1.

---

[2] 5-nines availability, or 99.999% uptime, allows for less than five minutes of downtime per year, excluding scheduled maintenance.

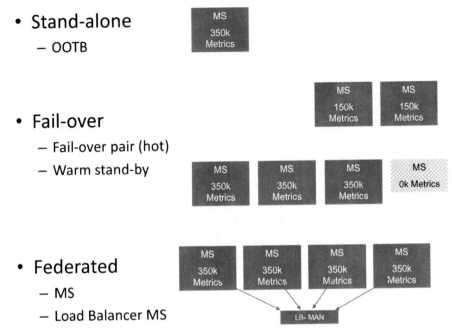

Figure 10-1. MS deployment architectures

For this discussion, the maximum capacity of a single instance of metrics storage is 350k. I also introduce here the concept of temperature for a standby system as being either hot (fully active and processing connections), warm (started and waiting for connections), or cold (ready to start).

Stand-alone

This is the simplest configuration and offers no failover capabilities or coordination with other APM resources. If the platform fails, it will take from 30 minutes to four hours to restore APM capabilities. During this time, no metrics are preserved and the various agents will simply drop their metrics.

Agents usually have minimal caching abilities, and some clients will want to explore how these caches could be expanded so that the metrics could be buffered until the metrics storage capability was restored. This is not a practical approach because the volume of metrics would require significant storage and this has the risk of competing with monitored application and possibly interfering with its correct operation. I don't know of any vendor APM implementation that would cache more than one minute of data in a failover situation.

Failover

True failover come in two forms: classic and spare-based. The classic model, where the resources are always arranged in pairs named primary and secondary, is the historical model for database and other applications. Usually, a failover agent on each platform monitors the heartbeat of the other platform and initiates a failover script when the primary becomes unavailable and a fail-back script when the primary is restored.

In the example illustrated in Figure 10-1, both primary and secondary are active. When failover occurs, all of the load (pending queries and metrics generated by agent and transactions) must move to the other platform. This requires that the metric load on each platform be less than 50%, so that the resulting failover load does not exceed 100%. In the classic case, which is typically hot/cold or hot/warm, the primary server is assumed to be at 100% capacity, so this requires the secondary server to be at 0% capacity.

In reality, neither of these failover schemes will be selected because no one is in a position to manage capacity to be always less than 50% and no one is going to be comfortable having a spare server just sitting around waiting for failover, consuming space and electricity.

You also may have noticed that I place a priority on testing failover as part of the phased deployment model (discussed in Chapter 7). In my experience, it is essential to establish that the APM solution is *failover-capable*, even if it will not be implemented later on. This is simply to put the APM solution is the best light. Some APM technology is inherently failover capable and will usually fail-over and fail-back with minimal additional configuration and zero cost. Compared with other fail-over initiatives that the client has experience with, especially their costs and administrative complexities, the APM solution will look like a rock star—so much so that the requirement evaporates as the client realizes that the APM failover capabilities will put their existing capabilities in a rather poor light.

Federated

Although classic fail-over is not really an interesting proposition for a small environment due to the cost, as the scale of the APM initiative increases, the number of deployed metrics collection servers will increase and the overall availability of the environment will become a concern. This is because you now have dozens or hundreds of users of the APM information, such that outages have a larger impact and thus there will be less tolerance for them.

That an outage will occur is a statistical reality. The more servers you deploy, the more opportunity you have for something to go wrong. If you have a cluster of metric storage servers, there are two strategies for enhancing availability: load balancing and warm stand-by. The warm stand-by is the classic solution. Each server periodically monitors the status of the other server. When one server fails, the other takes over after a few minutes.

The load balancing strategy introduces a *load balancing manager* to oversee the assignment of agents to metrics storage servers. This manager is directly related to the admin server of a cluster of application servers. Thus, the APM manager monitors the load of each of the collectors in the APM cluster and assigns agents appropriately. In the event that one of the collectors fails, then its agents are reassigned over the remaining collectors—exactly the same strategy as load-balancing over web servers, for example. You still need to have a portion of the capacity set aside for use during fail-over, called *head-room*. For example, if you have eight collectors in your cluster and you expect that no more than two collectors will ever fail at one time, then the total metrics capacity of the cluster cannot exceed the total potential capacity of the remaining six collectors.

The challenge is for presentation of metrics from a given agent. You have to go and find where the metrics are stored, because after failover, you will not have much control of where the agent is reassigned and where the metrics end up during the failed-over period. Fortunately, the manager knows where and when it reassigned the agents, so it's possible to construct a single view of the historical data, even as the agents move around to different collectors. This is called *federation*[3]: the manager federates access to the metrics, independent of their actual location. Federation is an object modeling design pattern, analogous to the access of data on the web.

For APM synthetic transactions, which are more concerned with generating alerts when transactions fail or are significantly degraded, there is simply less concern for any failover or federation capability. Synthetics transactions are issued at intervals ranging from 5 to 60 minutes, depending on criticality of the monitored app and synthetics component capacity. These are used for assessing off-hours service availability when there is little or no traffic present to confirm that key services have restarted correctly. Any alerts will go to a monitoring console. APM components for real transactions and instrumentation, which depend on transaction traffic, offer little or no visibility into this situation[4]. This first role is the ideal use case for synthetics; in this case, if the synthetics component were to fail, it would not be noticed until the operational day began. Any missing alerts will not actually be noticed for as much as an hour or two. And the priority will be to restart the failed service and not the APM synthetics transaction component. While it is undesirable to experience this monitoring gap, architecting a failover solution may not be cost effective.

The second use case for synthetics is the measurement of transaction response time during the production day. While this is certainly better than no visibility into response times, the intervals between synthetics, typically 5-30 minutes, results in significant gaps. So the expense of a failover solution cannot be justified; simply restart it when you notice it is missing, every 30-60 minutes. When you add the cost of maintaining the correctness of these transactions, which needs to be

[3] George Fernandez, Liping Zhao, Inji Wijegunaratne, "Patterns for Federated Architecture," www.jot.fm/issues/issue_2003_05/article4/

[4] APM instrumentation will detect the correct startup of the application server but it cannot confirm the correctness of a transaction and the availability of its underlying resources until transactions start to flow. Synthetics create that transaction flow for a single user. In the "Dashboards and Alerts" section of Chapter 14, there's an example of using APM instrumentation to assess server availability.

reconfirmed with every application release, you really don't have an attractive investment, considering that APM real transaction and instrumentation offer a much better fit if they are available for use.

There is no motivation towards federation because the first role of the synthetics is to provide availability status, which is shared via the alerting mechanism and not by sharing access to the underlying data. The second role for synthetics is to provide some historical context for the alert or degradation. This does involve access to the underlying data and you could potentially benefit from federation if there were any significant demand. In my experience, this second role is only marginally practiced and only as a stop gap until additional APM components become available.

Metrics Storage and Agent Capacities and Realities

This is a difficult section to discuss, given that vendor details will be omitted. The characteristics listed below will usually be addressed with the vendor sizing guide or via direct measurement:

- What platforms are supported?

    - Which mainframe UNIX or Windows versions are GA (generally available); you can usually focus this to the allowed operating systems for your environment

- Maximum metrics per MS

    - Maximum metrics per single instance.
        - Number and speed of required CPUs or cores.
    - Characteristics of minimum configuration.
    - Pilot maximum confirmed for the configuration you actually tested.

- I/O Characteristics of the MS data storage

    - Maximum throughput per single instance, for a maximum metrics configuration
        - Details of disk I/O configuration
        - Details of a SAN configuration (if used)
        - Steady-state I/O performance typical
        - Any periodic I/O demands, hourly, daily and what peak values are incurred

- Query Characteristics of the MS data storage

    - Maximum number of concurrent queries supported
    - Details for different use cases:
        - Historical Report Generation
        - Historical Dashboard Generation
        - External queries (if supported)

- Agent metrics capacity

  - Maximum number of metrics that an agent should not exceed
  - Typical agent metrics generation for different environments and applications

- Number of Workstations supported per MS (thick and thin clients)

  - Maximum number of concurrent thick client connections
  - Maximum number of thin client connections
  - Maximum number of concurrent external commands
    - Queries, reporting, maintenance activities, etc.

My preference is always for a pilot exercise in your environment and with your proposed hardware. It is very difficult for the vendor to test every possible configuration, so a direct measurement is the most reliable route. I will detail how this is conducted in the "Solution Certification" section later in this chapter.

In lieu of a pilot exercise, you will still get a good estimate using the maximum values for the vendor sizing guide and choosing a supported platform and configuration. Any severe deviation from this estimate will be picked up during the phased deployment model (Chapter 7) as you will have a number of partial deployments, followed by operational periods, to validate the sizing.

The I/O throughput considerations are important for a scalable solution. My preference is always with dedicated physical disk as this gives the best predictability and overall throughput. I have a lot of clients who are using SAN because of the advantage of the administrative model. It also seems to be more cost effective for the entire client environment. I do find that attempts to use virtualization successfully depend on a thorough knowledge of virtual machine configuration. This can be a very charged topic so you really need to lead with direct measurements, and not the vendor's experiences with applications that may have little in common with the performance demands of the metrics storage component. APM visibility will help you find and document the settings that make a virtualization effort worthwhile.

I do not find many vendors paying enough attention to the query characteristics of a fully loaded environment. When one or two APM specialists are using workstations, this is never an issue, as would be the case with a new or first installation of APM. This will change dramatically in a larger deployment supporting 50 to 100 users. Even if you can easily offer two tiers of service—typically thick client (full functionality) and thin client (reduced functionality)—a request for a historical view of a dashboard, for example, will result in a significant query load. If two dozen users do this around the same time, it will be like a bull in the "laws of physics" china shop—many functionalities are going to degrade.

When you certify a solution architecture, your test plan will include automation of reporting and other mechanisms to simulate how a varied user population will impact the proposed solution. It takes some work but it's the only way you can set expectations properly. It is also a very valuable exercise because it gives you some insights into how the APM solution will degrade under extreme circumstances. This is exactly the goal of the baseline processes (Chapter 13): to help you understand what is normal and what is becoming a scalability problem for the

APM solution. It would be unfortunate that as the APM initiative becomes successful that you must devote some effort to actually turning away prospective users and supporters. This is a survival technique that you would employ until you could consistently educate the new users on how to safely employ the system or until you come up with another scheme to allow casual users to observe the incidents and their resolution without crippling the efforts of the specialists to be able to access the APM data.

For the agents, especially with instrumentation, an inappropriate configuration can generate an incredible number of metrics that will almost certainly cause performance problems with the metrics storage components, as well as potentially steal resources from the agent. Some vendors will have a configuration point to cap or otherwise limit the number of metrics generated. There should be no reason to ever change this cap. If you are generating 20,000 to 50,000 metrics from a single agent, you are doing something wrong! With a target storage of 350,000 metrics, 14% of your capacity is consumed by a single agent, where you should be seeing 100-200 agents under correct circumstances.

Metrics Storage Sizing

Much of the mechanics for completing the sizing has already been covered in Chapter 3. I have provided some spreadsheets that summarize the survey and sizing results, available in the Chapter 3 Artifacts.

In this section, I will cover some of the more critical attributes of the sizing.

Application Realities

At the start of the APM initiative, you will find many applications jockeying for a good position in the deployment schedule. You need to temper that ambition by ruthlessly excluding candidate applications so that you can focus on defining an initial deployment that achieves many positive benefits and attention. You want to focus on important and stable applications before you take on less-important or troublesome applications.

You also want to establish the APM organization not only as the "APM specialists" but as trusted advisors for all types of monitoring. Sometimes the technology (Java or .NET) will be the major determinant. But what can you offer applications that you may otherwise immediately exclude? For the remainder of this section we will present a number of principles and examples, with some discussion and explore various application realities.

Not everything needs instrumentation monitoring

- For example, SSO (Single Sign-on) is important but otherwise the apps are stable/mature
- LDAP monitoring alone might be sufficient

The first rule is to identify which of your available monitoring technologies is appropriate for a critical system. The definition of a critical system is easy: if it isn't working, nobody is working! So, if business can still go on when this system is unavailable, it's simply not critical.

In this SSO case, there is also very little business process. If I'm going to instrument an application, I want to ensure that something significant is going on so that I can hide my instrumentation overhead. SSO applications and the underlying LDAP queries are extremely efficient. There is simply no place to hide instrumentation in this app. It also is not a protocol amenable to real transaction monitoring. You could do synthetics against the application but this would probably require a customized script to do sample queries against LDAP. In the end, perhaps platform monitoring of the LDAP platform is really all that is needed. To confirm, get a list of the last month's incidents and see what kinds of failures they are experiencing.

Not all apps need detailed application monitoring.

- Availability
- Down, Ready, Up

While you allowed more consideration for SSO as something that might benefit from real-time monitoring (likely using synthetics), this is due to its critical status. For non-critical applications, you only need to know when they become unavailable. So traditional availability monitoring is the right choice here. However, sometimes an SNMP agent is not available. You instead need to consider if there is a status command, log file, or maybe some type of synthetic transaction you could deploy against these applications.

Some apps need KPIs.

- Performance—Major components under threshold
- Capacity—Major components under threshold

Applications with mature performance monitoring needs are your second priority after the critical apps that were defined initially. These applications are stable (few incidents) and generate a number of valuable KPIs that the business wants to maintain easy access to. Provided they are of compatible technology, these applications will help to grow and sustain the APM value proposition. It is one thing to turn up metrics for an application; it is another to define the views, alerts, and reports for that application. Applications with KPIs will usually have all of these secondary roles and activities well defined; they really understand how to design and consume reporting. So it is a solid opportunity for the APM initiative to draft behind these applications that are already known to leverage performance KPIs for managing the application life cycle.

Not all apps function the same way.

- Some apps are CRITICAL
- Some apps are HIGH-VALUE
- Some apps RUN WITH KNOWN PROBLEMS
- Some apps have RISKY CONFIGURATIONS
- Some apps are OPERATIONALLY SOUND
- Some apps are near END-OF-LIFE

Above and beyond the architecture and component strategies, which dictate the type of monitoring technology you will employ, there's the basic question of stability. You want to know which applications get your top priorities when scheduling deployment. In a perfect world, you would only deploy stable applications. That is too optimistic to hope for but you may sometimes establish a separate production tier with a higher availability level where you can stack the deck in your favor and not get bogged down with applications that are causing problems most of the time. You try to cherry-pick the stable apps and avoid the problematic apps until your APM system is established.

More realistically, there will always be a number of exceptions such as extremely critical applications that the business runs on, even if they happen to be unstable. It is not a terrible problem to deal with these problem apps but you always want to have a cadre of stable apps to refer back to when the primary stakeholder for that critical and unstable app is out looking for someone to blame for their misfortune. A new APM system is much too convenient a target. Even if that critical/unstable app owner demands to be the first deployed, you need to push back and get two or three stable apps done first in order to avoid the "blame game."

Most apps have different monitoring requirements across the application life cycle.

An important part of the sizing calculators is to separate them out by environment. Just because you anticipate 750,000 metrics in production does not mean that you will have 750,000 in pre-production. The numbers will vary across the application life cycle. Occasionally, I work with a pre-production system that is so thorough that when they finally get to production they are only interested in a tiny fraction of the metrics they saw pre-production. Other times I will find a development environment that gets a very large number of metrics per agent but never has more than five agents deployed at any time. And I may find 20 agents in QA that become 400 agents in production.

The minimum adjustment I make for the environment is to scale the number of metrics that I expect for the different complexities of applications I will encounter. You can look at the sizing calculator spreadsheets for the details but it follows a simple model, summarized in Figure 10-2.

Environment	Metrics per agent	Agents per environment	Service availability target	Concurrent APM users
Development	10,000	4 - 20	weekly	1 - 2
QA/Pre-prod	3,000	10 - 100	daily	2 - 10
Production	1,500	50 - 1000	< 60 minutes	5 - 100

Figure 10-2. Environment differences

Environment plays a strong role in sizing. You need to pay careful attention if you are monitoring across the application life cycle.

Sizing Attributes

Very often you will have to give a sizing estimate as part of the scope call or maybe after a best practice discussion. Or sometimes you don't get the cooperation you need during the application survey. When the pressure is high, here are the most critical sizing attributes that you need to make a successful sizing:

- Number of distinct applications (see Chapter 3: "Application Survey")
- Number of JVMs or CLRs per application
- Number of gold configurations (see Chapter 7: "Phased Deployment")—this is to establish the level-of-effort.
- Number of thick and thin clients
- Metrics storage architecture (stand-alone, cluster, fail-over, etc.)
- Metrics storage hardware platform characteristics

Clearly, it takes a bit of experience to complete a sizing over the phone. Fortunately, whenever you forecast spending a large sum on hardware, they will always allow you the time to document the sizing in writing.

Deployment Strategy

The metric storage component does not present any unusual deployment challenges. For large deployments, you will benefit from the phased deployment strategy discussed in Chapter 7. Achieving your deployment footprint in manageable increments also allows you to pace out the expense of the hardware required for a large APM initiative.

After following the assessment activities discussed in Chapter 3, you will have an initial and follow-on plan for your APM initiative. This maps directly onto the required hardware but since many large-scale APM initiatives are for a three year period, it simply doesn't make prudent financial sense to purchase hardware and then have it sitting around for a couple of years until your deployment pace gets to that point. Also, priorities change and you may need to slow the deployment pace to better align with corporate spending objectives. A phased deployment supports all of these considerations, as summarized below:

- Procure sufficient hardware to support what you are ready to deploy and operate.
- Adjust APM capacity forecast to be with operation realities.
- Document the capacity utilization to further justify future purchases.
- Allow successive deployments to leverage newest available hardware.

It is perfectly acceptable to forecast the long-term expense associated with an APM initiative in terms of hardware and licensing. Accounting for how the investment has to be supported over the many quarters that the initiative is running will take some extra work. But it allows more management options, which is generally appreciated. It is a simple equation: if you get W dollars, you can deliver X capabilities by Y date, as part of a long-term initiative of Z dollars overall.

Ideal APM Architecture

Some of the difficulty in realizing an APM initiative is getting a meaningful hardware footprint in place. To be meaningful, you have to appreciate the APM benefits that would be desirable and build towards that in useful increments. Otherwise, you are going to be limited to the bare minimum, with the next increment in functionality being left to a separate project. This very often leads to narrow scope—usually just for the couple applications in the initiative.

You learned in Chapters 1 and 2 that an overly narrow scope can lead to a failure of the APM initiative and thus can require a specific investment strategy to stabilize the first initiative and improve the scope of the follow-on initiative. This is what is happening today but it is less efficient regarding the resources and effort required. If the circumstances are right, what would the ideal APM solution environment look like?

Figure 10-3 presents this vision. In this version, a centralized, corporate-wide initiative, you achieve a number of important goals. The easiest goal is having a separate server/cluster for each operating environment. This ensures that each environment has an appropriate capacity and service level. All the hardware could be centralized but you want to keep the traffic separate whenever possible. Behind these operational systems, and managed by the APM system, are two additional server/clusters.

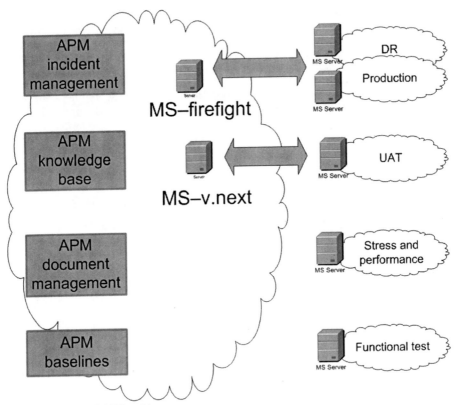

Figure 10-3. Ideal APM architecture

One of these is to support firefight activities for applications that are not actively monitored by APM but will use a rapid deployment of APM to get visibility into critical issues. This avoids any issues, capacity or access related, that would come up if you were to borrow some of the production capacity to conduct the firefight monitoring. The other is to always have the next APM version under ongoing acceptance and certification testing and being dropped into the UAT environment to take advantage of the live load and other operating characteristics of that environment. It seems that vendor releases come at a much faster pace than most clients can absorb them. That's not unreasonable. It is just when you really need to move forward to gain critical functionality or improved capacity that you find yourself needing 3-6 months to properly validate the new release. Having a platform to host these new releases simply lets you get an early start. And when you really need to move to a new release for all the other environments, you will already have experience with the new release.

As the APM solution grows, capacity problems will crop up, resulting in performance incidents or other advisories. Most clients will use e-mail and blast everyone who is allowed to use the APM technology. My experience is that this really shakes the users' confidence in APM, even if they are not actively using the product. My suggestion is to move the incident reporting to a "pull" model where the user can request the current status versus the "push" model of e-mail where everyone gets blasted with the status whether they want it or not. Having something as simple as an incident status web site addresses this problem. Integration with the existing trouble management system is also a possibility but this is limited by operations being more interested in availability issues that they can address, rather than performance issues that they can't address with a restart.

In larger environments, there is also a huge benefit to making things self-service whenever appropriate. Being able to check a meaningful knowledgebase for resolutions to common problems related to APM is the best choice. If you can defer direct interaction with your internal clients for all of the novice user issues, you have more time for critical activities. A knowledgebase is an easy mechanism to get internal users to self-train, which makes their future interactions with the APM system much more efficient.

In that same self-service theme is making the appropriate cookbooks, assessment activities, work requests, etc., available via a document share technology like SharePoint. This is really the minimum foundation to establish more a self-service culture. The benefit to you is that your future interactions will be among internal clients who have been thoroughly indoctrinated to your APM system.

The final element is collecting all of the test and incident information and baseline reports into a collaboration site. Baselines are the most important data to helping us accelerate triage and the accuracy of its recommendations. But you will not get that benefit if you have to go searching for the data. Likewise, if you want QA and operations folks to collaborate, you need to provide an environment for them to share and update the information they are using. This element is what I see as the logical conclusion for an APM initiative. It has many elements in common with logging portals, which exist at a number of client sites today, where you can access any type of application or platform log from a single page in a portal.

Monitoring the Metrics Storage

The motivation for monitoring the APM infrastructure increases as the solution gains acceptance, so I always consider interest in monitoring of APM as a strong indication of acceptance for the initiative. The more users become dependent on APM metrics and dashboards, the more they will expect rapid access to the APM workstations as well as consistent collection of the metrics.

There are the following options:

- Use the technology to monitor itself
- Process availability
- Log monitoring
- Synthetic transactions

Even if extensive metrics about the APM environment are available, if a portion of the APM environment goes down, you may not be able to access the platform in order to generate an alarm or visualize the problem. So process monitoring is the first truly external measurement of availability that many clients attempt. The main limitation of this approach is that it is really only an availability test. It cannot show any degradation in service. However, getting this first external measure implemented is important to establish a foundation for more extensive monitoring in future. It also makes a great object lesson. The client team is likely very familiar with this kind of availability monitoring and inclined to pursue it anyway. Later, when performance problems occur, I can always refer back to this and ask them if it is useful or not. When it is concluded to have limited applicability, I can then go to the real-time metrics and use the incidents as examples of how to use performance metrics to anticipate degradations in the APM service. This makes the lesson stick more tightly.

Even when the MS server metrics are accepted as being more useful in detecting degradation, there will still remain a strong desire to have some independent measure of the APM environment. You may then return to the availability script and add a few synthetic transactions to independently characterize the platform performance. This requires an appropriate command language for the APM platform that allows you to execute a small report or a query for some metrics every five minutes. I prefer a report because it exercises both the APM application file system and network. The script may be initiated remotely or the storage for the report may be remote, so this gives you an easy check of network connectivity in addition to exercising the APM reporting capability.

It is also possible to monitor the log file for the APM platform. Traditional system management tools have this capability and, depending on your vendor capabilities, you may be able to report these metrics back to the MS server. This approach suffers from the same limitations as the original availability script. The best route is to leverage both the real-time metrics as well as a script with synthetic transactions against the MS environment.

You could also use synthetics against thin APM clients (browser-based). My preference is always to go with the synthetics against a report interface or other process, analogous to the "ping" command. Do this via command-line (scripting) capabilities, as it results in a slightly lower complexity.

Why do MS Components Fail?

Figure 10-4 summarized the three major types of failures you need to alert on:

- Process failures
- Hardware failures
- APM release stability

I would estimate the relative proportion of these problems to be 70:25:5, corresponding to the A:B:C of Figure 10-4.

- **A: Process failures**
  - Rouge agents with excessive metrics
  - Rouge dashboards with excessive metric collections
  - Network stability (connectivity, throughput)
  - MS capacity exceeded
- **B: Hardware failures**
  - Network interface card
  - Disk controller card
  - Platform power supply
  - Storage subsystem
- **C: Software product quality**
  - Release stability

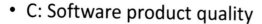

Figure 10-4. Why do MS components fail?

The APM best practices that I introduce in this third part of the book are really intended to help clients through all of these "class A" type errors. So you may also expect that any monitoring is also going to be focused on these same issues. You may not decide to actually put alerts on these quantities but you should realize that when you are looking at an MS capacity or performance report, these are the elements that will stick out when problems are looming. Excessive metrics or capacity utilization should be easy to observe and will likely have metrics continuously maintained. An item like "excessive metrics collections" will be a little harder to measure without some knowledge of the internals of the metrics storage application. Here you should probably plan to have the vendor's professional services do periodic HealthChecks of the APM environment as they should be expected to have more familiarity with those internal metrics.

Items such as "network stability" will usually require a triage effort to document normal and abnormal network states. You will triage the APM applications in just the same fashion as any other application that you might suspect of having network issues. Using synthetic transactions against the various points of the APM environment and sending these response times back to the MS server is the most direct scheme to document network problems and easily see everything aligned by time.

Communicating Sizing Results and Recommendations

Technical writing may not come easy to everyone who undertakes an APM sizing. This section is intended to give you a useful outline to follow, so that creating this document is less of a chore.

1. Executive Summary
   a. Why are you doing this sizing?
   b. What is the expected outcome?
   c. On what is the sizing based?
      i. Number and complexity of applications
      ii. Associated metrics and environments
   d. What did you find, in terms of number of metrics initially, and after three years?
   e. What solution scenarios were considered?
      i. Server platforms
      ii. Relative quantities

2. Requirements
   a. What applications and other factors are expected to contribute to the sizing?
      i. Number of workstation and browser clients
      ii. Specific applications or infrastructure

3. Constraints
   a. Summarize the sizing attributes for the target APM platform
   b. Summarize the storage technology and sizing attributes
   c. Summarize the thick-client sizing attributes
   d. Summarize the thin-client attributes
   e. Metrics Storage Component
      i. Minimum platform requirements and characteristics
      ii. Supported operating systems
   f. Archive component   platform requirements
   g. Thin-client component platform requirements
   h. Thick-client component   platform requirements

4. Terminology
   a. Architecture
      i. Definitions and sizing constraints for the following:
         1. Instance
         2. Stand-alone
         3. Fail-over cluster
         4. Federated cluster
   b. Sizing
      i. Definitions and sizing constraints for the following:
         1. Metrics

       2. JVMs
       3. Thin-client
       4. Thick-client
       5. Application complexity

5. Monitoring Capacity Assessment Tools

   a. Application Survey spreadsheet (see Chapter 3)
   b. Application Sizing spreadsheet (see Chapter 3)
   c. MS Sizing Tool spreadsheet

6. Sizing Process

   a. Good
     i. Estimate based on the total number of JVMs/CLRs multiplied by the expected metrics for each environment for a typical application.
   b. Better
     i. Estimate based on the total number of JVMs/CLRs multiplied by the expected metrics for each environment for a typical application, but including application complexity, extension products, and extension agents.
   c. Best
     i. Direct measurement of metrics from QA as part of an application audit.

7. Current Environments

   a. What environments are being considered for the sizing?
   b. Is the capacity for new applications or are existing capacity figured into the sizing?
     i. Dev/Integration
     ii. QA
     iii. Production

8. Proposed Environment

   a. Overall Capabilities
     i. Platform Support
       1. Describe the various target platforms considered.
       2. Summarize the number of platforms for the initial deployment and successive three years.
       3. Summarize the total surplus clients (if any) at each point.
     ii. Detailed Growth Forecast
       1. Your analysis process and suitable artifacts leading to your forecast

9. Alternate Scenarios

   a. Each scenario consists of a description of the hardware/configuration, the risk and benefits, risk mitigation strategy.
     i. Scenario 1 (Small Servers)
     ii. Scenario 2 (Large Servers)
     iii. Scenario 3 (Federated)

Process Considerations

Each of the following will benefit from a documented process, appropriate for your operating culture:

- What will it take to get a new MS provisioned and deployed?
- Considerations for different environments
- What is an ideal App Survey form?
- MS naming considerations, location
- Port numbering scheme for multiple instances
- New MS version validation and acceptance
- What environments?
- What duration for acceptance testing?
- Metrics archive migration/merge?
- Agent configuration promotion process?
- Can you make monitoring config changes outside of the normal application configuration change control?

Deployment Survey and Sizing

Unlike most other monitoring tools, with an APM initiative you have to spend some time estimating the impact of the proposed scope of application monitoring on the metrics storage infrastructure. Some months before implementation, someone will have to order the hardware platforms and configure the disk storage. This can be some real money and so no one wants to get it wrong. But if it is your first experience with the APM technology, where does the sizing information come from?

It comes directly from your stakeholders, so the more you can compel them to collect and validate this information for you, the more likely it will be accurate. It is also an opportunity to put a bit more process around this key information—the nature of the application to be monitored—because it is often very difficult to find the folks who really know what the applications needs and its role for the business.

The bit of collaborative process you employ here is called an *assessment*. It is basically an interview but can often involve direct measurements of an application. It provides a validated set of information with which you can forecast the impact of that application on the monitoring environment. It also gives you a mechanism to push a task back to the client, effectively assessing how committed they are to participating in the APM initiative.

For the sizing system, you will focus first on the application survey and then you will go into the mechanics of finalizing the sizing.

For the details of the assessment processes, please refer to Chapter 3.

Solution Certification

In additional to the document-based sizing analysis and recommendations, your organization may require a certification that the recommended platform will actually accommodate the expected solution capacity. The motivation for this is simply a lack of any experience with APM solutions. It will feel like a lack of trust but you need to set this aside and look at the big picture: nobody has any confidence yet. You need to help ease folks into the new reality.

Feel free to first point the folks asking for the certification to Chapter 1 so that they may understand how APM is different than any of their past experiences. Then follow up with a plan, after confirming with your vendor how you will load test a portion of the solution architecture.

What you need from your vendor is a capability to create hundreds of synthetic agents and send their metric traffic against a number of live metrics storage components. You are going to build a limited QA environment and the load generation will be these synthetic agents. A test plan will be developed to confirm the suitability of the solution architecture, hardware platform, and metrics storage configuration—and anything else your sponsors want to confirm. And you will need to tune this test plan down to something reasonable that will then fit in a 2-3 week period of testing.

One of the more frustrating points about APM is that as much as you expect that your vendor will know everything about sizing and have an example ready, this example is simply not going to be appropriate for your specific hardware and environment. Even if your vendor has a lab environment available, it will never be exactly the same as your environment. That means you have some exposure to folks who are looking for reasons to say no to APM. The one result that no one can take issue with, provided you followed a reasonable test plan, is a certification in your environment.

Test Architecture

For this example, you will certify an APM platform for a large metrics capacity of three million. As you learned earlier, the number of agents contributing to this total can actually vary quite a bit, so you will need to look at a typical and larger contribution. I like to keep a production agent generating about 1500 metrics. And I also know that some smaller percentage will be double, or even larger. However, you can limit the total number of permutations to "recommended" and "less efficient." You don't really want to prove how much you may abuse the solution; you just want to validate it towards your general recommendations. You will also conduct a "bake-off" between two competing architectures: native and virtual. In the end, you will end up performing a certification very similar to this one, in order to resolve the issue with "data."

		# Instances	Incremental Metrics Capacity					
			Scenario1		Scenario2		Scenario3	
			Total	Individual	Total	Individual	Total	Individual
Admin	anyOS	1	2,400,000.00		3,600,000.00		4,800,000.00	
Cluster A	Dedicated	4	1,200,000.00	300,000.00	1,800,000.00	450,000.00	2,400,000.00	600,000.00
Cluster B	vTier	4	1,200,000.00	300,000.00	1,800,000.00	450,000.00	2,400,000.00	600,000.00
	Total Agents	100			200		300	

	Each scenario		
# Agents	100	100	100
# metrics each	3000	1500	1500

Larger scale architecture

Smaller scale architecture

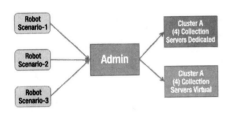
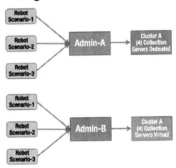

Figure 10-5. Metrics storage test plan

I find that the best way to keep track of the test goals and scenarios is to put it all in a spreadsheet, such as is summarized in Figure 10-5. This gives you a medium to vet the plan and solicit input. Your practical limit will be about two weeks to execute the plan that would be front-ended by building out the environment. While it is always desirable to build exactly what you plan to deploy, sometimes you will need to compromise in order to fit within the budget or available hardware. In this case, the most important aspect is that the two platforms must be physically and software identical, except for the native operating system and the virtualized analog.

Load Profiles

If you are not already well-experienced in the issues of load generation, here is where you can get a better appreciation for what the QA team has to manage. One difference here is that the duration of the test will be at least six days. The reason for allowing for two weeks to complete this certification test is because things never go as planned; something external will potentially compromise the test and you may need to repeat one or three days. I also find that running anything over the weekend is subject to some unforeseen interruption.

Your load evolution will follow the graph in Figure 10-6. Another immediate difference from a typical load test is that the ramp is occurring over the entire day—as much of the first 20 hours as possible, with 4 hours reserved for reaching steady-state prior to midnight.

Midnight is also a magical time—actually midnight until 4 a.m. All kinds of services may be rebooted, whole network segments disappearing, etc. This is all part of the normal routine. Most IT organizations will use this period for all kinds of urgent and/or scheduled activities. You can't control any of it so you need to allow a little extra time in your schedule to accommodate potential interruptions to the test plan and load evolution.

I find that a test plan is a goal toward which you make your best effort. You need to keep a log of the exceptions encountered and then make some decisions about whether that portion of the load evolution needs to be repeated. Most testing does not attempt to cover such an extended period of time, so you may find yourself facing problems that other folks have not had to deal with when they keep testing within traditional business hours.

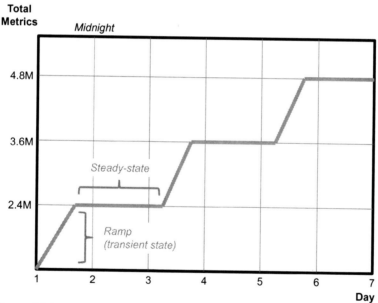

Figure 10-6. Metrics storage load profile

For the test architecture that you have planned, you effectively have eight probes into the environment. If all eight suffer some unexpected performance or connectivity problem, you can be extremely confident that the environment is to blame. If only one or two of APM servers have a problem, you can ignore it unless it becomes consistent.

Having the load evolution reach steady-state before midnight is critical. Some APM solutions undertake automatic maintenance activities between midnight and 4 a.m. while still collecting metrics in real-time. You want to make sure you capture these activities accurately in terms of their overall impact. These activities represent a type of transient processing, just like adding the agents, so you won't add any more agents until the next day. Some folks have a real problem with this because it increases the duration of the test overall. In fact, I've never had a conversation with anyone who was comfortable with the idea of doing continuous testing over a two week period. They may well know the problems with the environment and how it has frustrated test efforts in the past.

You really don't have an option. You know the types of scenarios you need to exercise, and despite any limitations in the environment, APM is a 24x7 application. You are going to find out the nature of the overnight and weekend issues eventually, so take this opportunity to get some real measurements. In particular, you need to know how sensitive a real-time application is to changes in load or responsibilities. This doesn't present an issue because APM software is designed to absorb all kinds of transient effects. You don't know yet how significant these transient effects are and a good part of the apparently "excessive test durations" is precisely to expose the transition between transient and steady-state periods of operation. I'll talk about this in the "Analysis" section, when I show some real results and provide some insights in how to analyze all this data.

Reporting

Most products will have a standard capacity or sizing report that you can leverage. The most important characteristic of the report is that is contains a table. If you generate this table report in a .csv (comma-separated values) format, it can be directed imported into a spreadsheet or processed via an analysis script. Figure 10-7 illustrates a typical .pdf formatted report, which looks better. However, a .csv is easier to import or process via scripts or external programs.

Sizing Parameters

Resource:Metric	Mean	Min	Max	MMin	MMax	Count
	130	123	138	103	151	9,297
Number of Agents	1	0	2	0	6	9,297
Number of Metrics	2,272	66	4,590	1	11,822	9,297
	2,259	57	5,437	0	17,137	9,297
Number of Workstations	0	0	1	0	2	9,297
	34	14	51	0	106	9,297
	6,788	3,561	7,302	0	22,439	9,297
	34	18	37	0	112	9,297
GC Heap:In Use (mb)	162	72	286	20	383	9,297

Start: 5/22/06 4:43 AM	End: 6/19/06 4:43 PM

Figure 10-7. Sample sizing report

For every Admin Server or Collector server that you are studying, you will need to generate a performance report for each 24 hour period. This results in (7 days) X (6 servers) = 42 separate reports. Building a script to auto-generate the reports is helpful.

Here is a cookbook:

- Using a spreadsheet, set aside a tab for each data collection day.
- Decide on an order for the files to be loaded and keep that same order for each day. This will help you later when you sort by metric name.
- Into the corresponding tab, insert all of the data files for that day. Make sure to use the same load order for each day.
- Delete anything in the merged file that is not useful. Only metric names and associated data should remain.
- You need to ensure that the metric names are unique as you will then sort the entire days worth of data. This will group all of the results for a specific metric in the order that you loaded the files.
- You then insert appropriate equations for the standard deviation and mean. If you have multiple instance of each configuration, you first want to check that they are reasonably consistent.
- Continue the analysis by organizing and looking at the Mean, Average-Max, and Maximum Max (worst case).

Doing this volume of analysis by spreadsheet is a little tedious. I use a dedicated analysis tool which does all the extracts for me, yielding the following result, shown in Figure 10-8.

```
==================================================

Metric::Metrics Storage: Number of Metrics

==================================================
```

{Server,20100107,20100108,20100111}
----

virtual	434966	501820	500288
virtual	434972	501839	500288
virtual	433452	501824	500294
virtual	433458	500405	500290
StdDev	874.1	711.4	2.828
Mean	$3.475*10^5$	$4.013*10^5$	$4.002*10^5$

{Server,20100107,20100108,20100111}
----

native	434978	509164	500293
native	433452	500398	500289
native	433458	503257	500292
native	434966	503242	500288
StdDev	875.9	3686	2.38
Mean	$3.475*10^5$	$4.039*10^5$	$4.002*10^5$

Figure 10-8. Extract via script

This tool extracts a single metric from every report file and generates a summary output. This is what you are bending the spreadsheet to accomplish. After you have confirmed that the individual servers are consistent, then those four values are reduced to a single value via the mean. In the analysis section, you bring together all of these mean values to generate a graph and reflect on the trends.

Analysis

There are many analysis strategies possible. However, while what you are doing is important, it will never make it to a research paper to be reviewed by peers external to your company. There is no Nobel Prize for IT load testing analysis. What you need to do is reduce the whole mess of results down to a series of numeric comparisons. Graphs are cool, but tables are always better.

Part of what your report needs is a demonstration of the basic concepts that most folks will assume to be operating in the artificial reality of your test plan. For example, some folks really get hung up on the concept of transient and steady states. Why are you ramping up for a whole day? Why are you holding at steady-state for another whole day? Can't you get all this done in a couple of hours?

Any injection of load is a dangerous event and Figure 10-9 shows exactly why. Here you have jumped 10 agents on a system that was running but otherwise had no agents. There is a corresponding increase in the number of metrics: (10 agents) X (3000 metrics each) = 30k metrics. The CPU responds pretty much as one might expect, with a surge to handle the incoming agents and then a drop back down. The response times of a few key metrics also appears to respond as expected but not quite. The response times look very similar to the ringing decay (peaks indicated) as if you struck a gong and then listened to the reverberation.

It's not every day that you get to see classic physics at work in your IT environment. Any complex application largely based on caching—which is really what the metrics storage component is doing—acts like a spring. If you apply a sudden weight (agent load), the metrics storage application "absorbs" that influx, and then persists the data and updates console and all kinds of other functions until that incoming surge is processed. During this processing, another wave of metrics data hits, and a smaller caching results. This configuration does not return to a steady-state for more than five minutes. And this is only for ten agents.

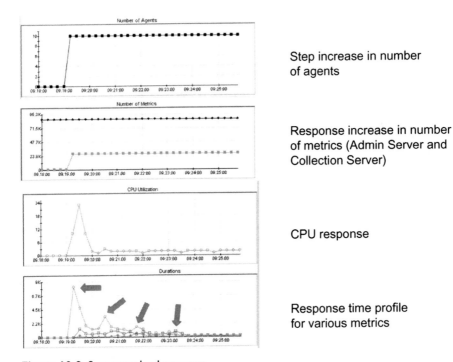

Figure 10-9. Step agent load response

While a *step function* (the mathematical term for this sudden increase in the number of agents and their associated metrics) will always have a "ringing" transient response, more complex responses are possible with more aggressive load scenarios.

One extreme scenario is an impulse response, illustrated in Figure 10-10. This is not a typical use case for APM—to have a surge in a number of agents that quickly reduces to a low level—but I had an opportunity to try something out in a full-scale environment.

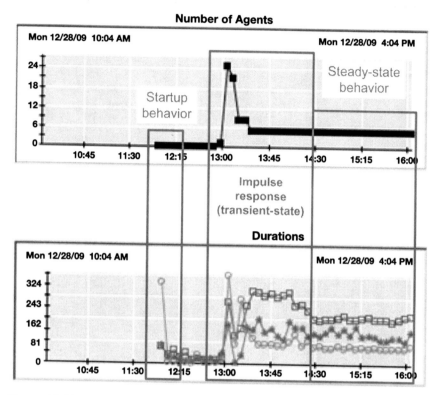

Figure 10-10. Impulse agent load response

There are three distinct periods during the test. The *startup behavior* is not surprising and clearly moves to a steady-state. At 1 p.m. the *impulse load* is initiated with a steep ramp to 25 agents and then a quick decline to 5 agents over a 30 minute period. This is not ideal; an ideal impulse would have a much shorter period, but it is definitely not a step response, as you experimented with earlier.

This results in a transient period of 90 minutes before steady-state is again established. None of this represents a problem with the APM application. It is simply the response characteristics of the application to incoming load. The point is that you could easily measure a significant transient at 10 agents, you could prolong the transient behavior by increasing to 25 agents, and you are going to your certification with 100 agents—you really need to spread this load out in order to get a valid test result.

I will talk a bit more about load generation in Chapter 12 and the effect it can have on the success of your test efforts. The first rule is to ensure a consistent load; one of the ways to ensure consistency is to always make sure you notice when a transient-state occurs and how long it takes to return to a steady-state. If you are always measuring in the transient-state, your results will not be reproducible.

For more practical analysis, you simply depend on the reporting that was defined earlier. This gives you tables of numbers which you may then process or extract into a spreadsheet, resulting in the summary analysis in Figure 10-11.

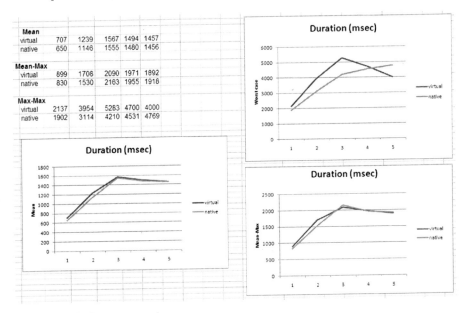

Figure 10-11. Summary results

One of the nuances with instrumentation is that while you see every individual execution of a component, you only deliver summary information about the metric. This consists of the mean, minimum, and maximum for each reporting interval. The mean is a coarse measurement; in performance monitoring, you also like to keep track of the maximum values encountered. It helps keep things in perspective. In a 24 hour report, looking at the mean of all of the maximum values encountered (at each reporting interval) lets you know how much you can trust the mean as being truly representative. If you are consistently finding maximum values per interval greater than ten times the mean, you know the mean is not actually representing a consistent performance. If the maximum of all maximum values is one hundred times greater than the mean, than that metric is a poor candidate for alerting or SLA definition.

In the results shown in Figure 10-11, you can see that there is a slight benefit of the native platform with regards to the mean. This increases when the max-max or "worst case" values are considered. Of course, there are other metrics and criteria that are being considered in the final determination.

I hope that you understood the strategies and mechanism of completing this analysis without getting to see the full metric names and other significant findings of this exercise. You cannot ever expect the exact same result anyway, which is why it is so important to be able to conduct this certification reliably. You will generate you own results and find your own conclusion—and hopefully one that you can be confident in—after considering how I have been doing it so far.

Competency

No surprise here—you need to size something! It will be a new MS deployment or incremental to an existing MS deployment. Can you support the new application? Will you run out of capacity? How much hardware will you need to purchase and provision?

Here's a cookbook for a new application (no prior instrumentation):

- Collect the App Survey
- Estimate the metrics volume
- Collect the current MS capacity
- Estimate the capacity consumed with this new app
- Size an MS platform to support 10 such "new" applications
- Prepare a recommendation that summarizes the following:

  - Characteristics of new apps
  - Metrics volume estimate
  - Suggested platform to support the 10 new apps

- MS Solution Architecture

  - Disk considerations
  - Number of instances
  - Thick and thin client support
  - Growth potential

Bonus Steps

- Perform an application audit against the target application.

  - How well does it align with your metrics estimate?

- Audit the application after it is deployed and operational for at least two weeks.

  - How well does it align with your metrics estimate?
  - How much headroom remains and how does this affect the longevity of the current APM platform configuration?

Artifacts

Metrics_Storage_Capacity_Test_Plan.xls

Summary

The sizing exercise is unremarkable but will often expose deep-rooted misunderstandings about APM as well as weak processes within the IT organization for soliciting meaningful contributions to the planning of the APM initiative. Of course, for a small initiative, all of this planning consideration is superfluous to the urgent goal of getting visibility into an urgent problem. The challenge is that multiple initiatives will see that same justification and continue to avoid meaningful sizing exercises. This puts the overall initiative at risk because these separate initiatives will remain uncoordinated and likely inefficient in terms of staffing, solution capacities, and capabilities.

I have countered this pessimistic view with a future state that illustrates what the end goal will look like for a mature APM initiative. You have explored some of the performance nuances that make APM technology so unique and interesting through a certification exercise. This also puts you on the path towards understanding load testing limits and the value in establishing a baseline, which you will later use for the application testing process. You've seen how to apply the assessments activities of Chapter 3 and arrive at a sizing recommendation that will be comprehensive and verifiable. What remains to be identified are just the initiators for the sizing exercise—demand and budget!

Load
Generation

To err is human—and to blame it on a computer is even more so.

—Robert Orben

This chapter discusses what is perhaps the weakest link in the application life cycle—automated testing, or *load testing*,[1] as part of the QA process. From my firefighting experience, I have found that the more I know about a stakeholder's QA practices, the easier time I will have getting visibility into their operational issues. Understanding their gaps in application testing often leads me directly to what is troubling them in production. Visibility is what I use to both confirm their suspicions and reveal issues they had not considered.

I have also noticed that reviewing what an organization thinks about the *value* of load testing, as well as the manner in which they conduct it, is a strong predictor of the overall progress with APM that they can expect.

For example, if the organization deploys directly to production, with no structured testing, the APM initiative will be to establish a pre-production process where the candidate application is given as thorough an evaluation as possible without the necessity of establishing a complete QA organization. It may be rudimentary load testing in support of a simple audit, or it may evolve into a full on-boarding effort. But it will likely never achieve the capabilities of a dedicated QA organization. It will be an improvement to the risky direct-to-production deployment even if true proactive management is simply not of interest. And there will be the production

---

[1] Wikipedia, "load test," http://en.wikipedia.org/wiki/Load_test

visibility benefit. In this example, Operations extends its capabilities a little but a bigger event will be needed to establish a QA organization.

If the organization acknowledges the need for testing but doesn't provide adequate investment, this situation will correct itself more rapidly as the APM investment proves its value with even minimal testing and acceptance processes. Any prediction of future performance will initially be set aside until those predictions are experienced in production. The emphasis here is to try it occasionally in QA but focus on the production deployment and use by operations. The production baseline process will actually become quite mature, which will be easily transferred back to QA when appropriate investment is realized.

If the organization has a robust testing process and a well-developed organization but struggles with performance issues, the goal is to improve collaboration. QA is already established and adding APM to that environment will not cause any major changes. Empowering the QA team to press the stakeholders for better test plans, this time validated with details from the production baselines, is where this collaboration is going. You have to ensure that you are testing the application in a meaningful way.

Simply stated, if you want to ensure client success with an APM initiative, you show them how to load test effectively to whatever level they can accommodate at the time. So you will also discuss how to establish and grow a pre-production (if they don't respect "QA") or a more capable QA system.

The discipline of *software performance testing* is itself an inexact science[2]. My goal in this chapter is to discuss the characteristics of a basic but completely capable QA testing system. And this is really to validate the APM configuration as much as it is to identify performance problems. Every application is different. If you want to ensure that you have set the correct alerts and thresholds, and that you have sufficient visibility to help identify performance problems, you need to evaluate the application under load before you get to production.

Kick Off Meeting

Much of the difficulties in becoming effective with APM technology can be attributed to poor preparation. This affects the deployment pace when an agent configuration fails, as well as the capability to triage effectively when stakeholders lack the background to understand the metrics. As you will see in Chapter 14, triage with single metrics involves understanding a lot of details and relationships. However, triage with baselines (Chapter 15) is relatively easy because it moves the focus onto the *differences* between normal and abnormal situations. This helps eliminate the distractions from the many thousands of metrics available—and keeps attention on what is unique about an application. Narrowing the focus helps an organization build up the pool of experiences more quickly.

---

[2] Wikipedia, "software performance testing," http://en.wikipedia.org/wiki/Software_performance_testing

So where do you get these baselines? You get them by summarizing the historical information about normal periods of operations. You will have a lot of history about the experiences in production but they are subject to interpretation. You have to accumulate a lot of production experiences before you can confidently define a baseline. This is because much of what goes on in the production environment is simply beyond your control. Instead, you look to the pre-production environment for the opportunity to have tighter control over the environment and load such that you can confidently identify and reproduce performance baselines. I will discuss the baseline process in Chapter 12 but the baseline process is utterly dependent on consistent or reproducible data. Load generation is how you get consistent baselines pre-production.

As much as APM technology is desgined to get visibility into the operational life of an application, I have consistently observed that success in production does not improve the application quality. AP*Monitoring, which is focused on the tools,* only reveals the nature of the performance problem and not the path to resolution. With AP*Management,* you focus on the processes around the use of the APM tools and are then aligned with resolving and eliminating the problems. In order to exploit APM visibility pre-production, you will need to understand load generation accuracy and how to structure a QA system to employ it.

Figure 11-1 depicts the impact on certain environments when problems are resolved across the application life cycle as testing maturity increases. This graph represents my on-site experiences as I moved from firefighting to mentoring in order to directly address the process gaps in employing APM technology.

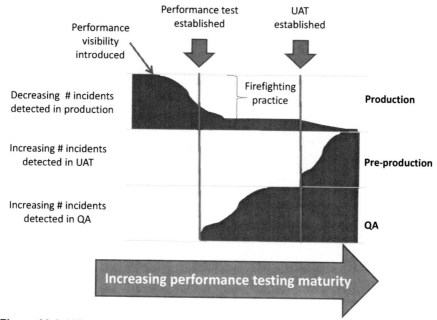

Figure 11-1. Where are performance problems identified?

What Figure 11-1 is showing is that the overall number of production performance problems is reduced more effectively with the introduction of a performance testing system. And that these performance incidents are further reduced only when a pre-production system is established.

- Doing it right might take longer.
- Doing it twice *always* takes longer.

A mature organization does not gamble that performance might be acceptable—it ensures that it will be acceptable.

Figure 11-1 also shows that firefighting, a triage activity discussed in Chapter 17, is something that is initially very active for an immature monitoring organization and is dramatically reduced as pre-production use of monitoring technology is achieved. The number of problems encountered does not change—you simply find them earlier and depend less on heroic efforts to uncover them.

Why Simulate Load?

I find many IT organizations avoid any significant load testing prior to production deployment. The primary reasons are lack of equipment to simulate the production environment and lack of expertise to design and execute a test strategy. Both of these are reinforced by a belief that testing is not worth the effort because they are never able to reproduce production issues anyway. This easily becomes a self-fulling proficy because without APM, they simply don't have the visibility to understand what gaps exist in their test environment and test execution.

While it is best to have an identical environment for test and production, it is simply not necessary if you have a reliable testing process. You do not have to test at a production load in order to uncover software defects. The goal of this chapter is to help you understand how to leverage APM during your test cycles and how to grow your QA testing system as you become more proficient at identifying performance problems prior to production.

If you already have a mature testing system, you can use these same techniques to introduce APM visibility pre-production.

Simulated load testing, in general, is very straightforward. Simply exercise the application to assess the following:

- Is the code deployable in a predictable fashion?
  - Staging
- Does the code execute as planned?
  - Functional
- Will it scale against a synthetic load?
  - Simple Load Simulation

- Will it support a variety of use cases?
  - Use case simulation
- Will it survive for one (or more) operational periods?
  - Stress or endurance testing
- What are its performance and capacity characteristics?
  - What monitoring configurations are supported?
  - What visibility is achieved?
  - What components and threshold values are appropriate?

These activities are arranged from the minimum activity (simply validating deployment) up to the fullest capability and benefits, which would be the application audit (see Chapter 13 for details).

Another excuse for not undertaking testing is that there is insufficient ability to generate a significant load. This may be due to license restrictions or the extreme efficiency of the application under test. The solution is simple: put the application on the smallest available platform. In other words, purposely undersize it. This is counter-intuitive because most folks are trying to certify a release at given load. With APM, you are instead interested to find out how the application performs when under extreme load so that you can use this information to help triage performance problems in the future. If you cannot simulate the volume of target users or transaction load, at least you will have better management and understanding of the application when it does come under stress. That is a valuable chunk of information that you can later use to justify increased investment in the QA test platform.

Types of Testing

There are a number of strategies for testing an application that I will summarize here. The first testing question: Which of these testing strategies can your organization deliver?

- Unit Test
- Functional Test
- System Integration
  - Packaging, Deployment, Availability
- Performance
  - Will it perform under load?
  - Will it scale?
    - Stability and response time
    - Throughput and utilization
- User Acceptance

Unit testing is completed by developers as they have code available and generally does not involve the entire application, just the pieces that they are changing. This is also an opportunity to employ APM because it is complementary to profiler technology and can offer some useful perspectives on performance. Sometimes unit testing is very limited and does not have enough complexity to justify the use of APM. Getting developers involved with APM is usually beneficial but it should remain an optional tool—not something that is manadated without first establishing that it will be useful.

Functional testing is what everyone acknowledges is a primary QA role. Some number of testers sit with the software and manually go through the various use cases in checklist fashion to make sure they are correct, or noting the defect. Sometimes this will be automated. This effectively becomes acceptance[3], regression,[4] or certification[5] testing, depending on the coverage of the test plan. Acceptance tests are usually associated with transfer of ownership. Regression tests aim to partially re-test after some modification of the code. Certification tests are limited to confirmation of certain characteristics, such as security or finance regulations. The benefit of using APM at this point is that you get a thorough audit of what code is executed for each of the test plans. This will be helpful later on when you determine baselines in QA-performance, UAT (User Acceptance Test),[6] and production.

The UAT is slightly different because often it is established as a subset of production that limits access to a small, highly qualified group of users whose role is to either exercise the acceptance test plan or to incorporate usage of the new system as part of their normal work day. It is a completely "live" environment with full production capabilities and performance, except for the limited population of users. For this reason, I always define UAT as a separate environment. It is generally more capable than the QA environment, which is supporting functional and performance testing, but it is not as rigorous as the full production environment because it expects that software will fail but with limited effect on the rest of the production environment. When appropriate, UAT becomes a test platform for the initial APM deployment.

Systems integration is where the functionally tested release is put through packaging and other integration considerations. There can be a large number of changes to the solution platform, including the latest software release. Assembling all of the latest components and ensuring that the application starts up correctly is the goal. This is effectively the first availability testing for the solution. It is also the last testing step before production deployment for some organizations.

When a performance testing environment is not available, some organizations will deploy first to a UAT or other limited production environment to avoid going directly to production. APM is very useful here because any load, even if it is

---

[3] Wikipedia, "acceptance testing," http://en.wikipedia.org/wiki/Acceptance_testing

[4] Wikipedia, "regression testing," http://en.wikipedia.org/wiki/Regression_test

[5] Wikipedia, "certification," http://en.wikipedia.org/wiki/Certification

[6] Wikipedia, "user acceptance testing," http://en.wikipedia.org/wiki/User_acceptance_testing#User_acceptance_testing

manual activity of a few users, it is going to be useful to establish a baseline. The challenge is the variability of the manual exercise, and the only way to address that lack of consistency is via automation.

Performance testing[7] is the exercise of an application under a particular workload in order to determine its performance characteristics. This more often involves an automated, reproducible test. You employ a load profile consisting of some number of synthetic users and some variety of use cases to simulate the exercise of the application as if it were being exercised by live users.

Once you have identified which testing strategies are available, you can then investigate what type of load generation is in use.

Load may be generated by any of the following methods:

- Manual
  - One or more users exercise the application.

- Batch
  - A file of transactions or messages is delivered to the application. This can be all at once, or a portion every 5 or 15 minutes.
  - The file of may be either pre-defined or captured interactions.

- Automated
  - A population of users and interactions is defined and a schedule of interactions is created.

The most realistic and reproducible interactions will be achieved via automated load generation.

While almost any type of load generation is useful, you have to be cautious and make sure you understand what you are not testing. I call these *visibility gaps*—characteristics of the application and environment that are not evident from the feedback that is received when following a test plan and a test scenario. The following is a summary of some visibility gaps and the actions that should be considered to understand and eliminate them:

- Is my monitoring impacting the test results?
  - Make an effort to test overhead

- Is my configuration tuning effective?
  - Compare test results before and after the change

- Are my load scripts accurate?
  - Compare the transactions tested with those experienced in production

---

[7] Wikipedia, "software performance testing," http://en.wikipedia.org/wiki/Software_performance_testing

- Is my test plan sufficient?
  - Are the findings scalable to the production experience?
  - Is there sufficient transaction variability?
  - Are the major transactions represented in the test plan?

- What are the differences between QA and Production environments?
  - Is a live data source employed during testing?
  - Is the network architecture comparable?

- If my app doesn't fail, does that mean it will scale?
  - What transactions need to scale?
  - What user load is experienced in production and what portion can you simulate?

- If my app fails, what components break first?
  - What are the characteristics of the application, prior to failure?

- If performance is bad, do I know which components are involved?
  - What components contribute significantly to a performance degradation?

Test Anti-patterns

So far, I have reviewed the correct or ideal testing considerations to hold and reflect on. You should not be surprised to find out that your testing organization has many visibility gaps. I attribute this to the erosion of confidence in the QA process that has occurred over many years. As applications became more complex, testing could not proactively identify performance problems. The time it took to test was thus considered a wasted effort. Without any meaningful visibility into the performance problems, there could be no useful guidance as to how to resolve those issues. Thus the time reserved for testing was compressed and ultimately cursory. There was much more to be learned simply by deploying to the production environment than there was by spending two to three weeks in the testing environment.

Coupling this confidence problem with the inevitable economic concerns in building and maintaining a realistic, end-to-end configuration (firewalls, routers, servers, and databases) or even an exact copy of the production environment, QA simply became too easy a target for cost-reduction.

There are a number of test anti-patterns that capture when the current state of QA testing is no longer contributing in a meaningful way:

- Performance Testing is left to the last minute
  - No allowance for reworking of unforeseen performance issues

- We don't have time for QA. It doesn't reflect the production environment anyway.
  - Why doesn't QA match production?

- Don't worry about that error message, it will not be active in the final build...

These are all simply excuses for avoiding the time and energy to conduct a test. A mature testing organization invests this time because identifying problems pre-production is simply the least expensive way to uncover the problems and still allow an opportunity to correct them.

Test Evolution

How a load simulation is delivered over time is called *test evolution* or load generation profile. This is normally specified as part of the *test plan*[8], which also includes details of the specific transactions that will be exercised during the test as well as any results criteria and reporting. The business unit that comissioned or maintains the application (the application owners) will have the responsibility for defining an effective test plan. The role of QA is to execute the test plan and report the results.

Figure 11-2 shows a typical test evolution, consisting of a ramp-up, steady-state, and ramp-down. This simple ramp pattern is crucial for consistent testing. As seen in Chapter 10 (Figure 10-9) during the solution certification of the Metrics Storage architecture, a sudden load against a dynamic system can actually cause a repeating surge for a significant period of time. This ringing effect is important because most test durations will be much shorter than the period of the ringing, and this will contribute to inconsistent results.

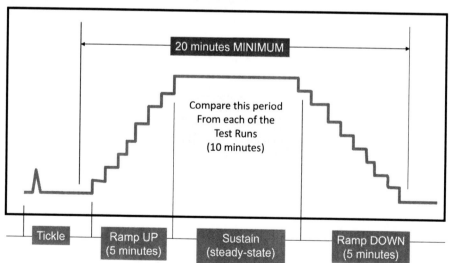

Figure 11-2. Ideal load experience (test evolution)

---

[8] Wikipedia, "test plan," http://en.wikipedia.org/wiki/Test_plan

The Tickle load is to force the initialization of the app server. You want all of the software components in memory that the application needs. This insures that the server is in a consistent state from one load test to the next, expecially if the server is restarted between tests. It is the smallest possible load that will force loading of the components needed for the load test. A single exercise of each of the target transactions (defined in the test plan) will be sufficient.

The Ramp UP is the addition of simulated users after some short delay. So you will choose a rate that allows you to go from zero to the target number of users. For a very large number of users, you will probably need to increase the ramp time to ensure that you do not end up with an impulse or step scenario (see Figure 10-9).

The Sustain (steady-state) maintains the target number of users for some duration. You want to be able to see the application at steady-state so that you get a good readout of the different component activities and performance. You may have scenarios where users are existing while new users are arriving. In this phase, we want the total active users to remain unchanged. This is where we will focus our measures in order to get the most consistent averages (response time, total invocations, etc.)

The Ramp DOWN begins to decrease the number of active users after some short delay. Simply halting the load will have the same impulse effect as suddenly initiating the load, resulting in an inconsistent state when a successive test is started.

You should always run your load tests for the same total duration. At the very minimum, ensure that you are maintaining the steady-state for the same duration of time or some convenient multiple of the time. This allows the results to be directly compared.

Maximum Load Considerations

Due to hardware or licensing limitations, you may not be able to increase the user load beyond the potential capacity of the application. This presents a problem when you are trying to forecast capacity for the application. In this case, you want to divide the available load into at least three steps.

For example, let's say you have an application that is known to support 5000 users in production, and your test platform has a comparable potential capacity. If you can only simulate 1000 users, evaluate loads of 10, 100, and 1000 users and note the average response time of a critical component for each load scenario. This result is summarized in Figure 11-3.

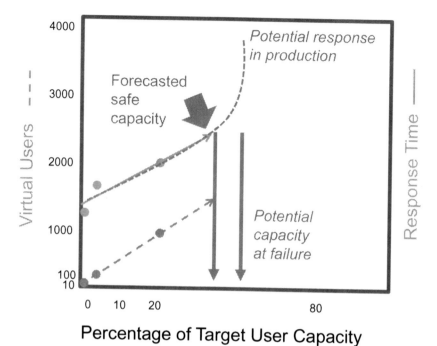

Figure 11-3. Potential danger of capacity forecast by extrapolation

This is potentially risky because it assumes that any performance degradation will be linear. In my expereince, it is never truly linear. Instead it will be linear to 60-80% of capacity and then rise exponentially, as indicated by the lowest curve. The arrow indicates the risk in that this curve may actually begin to rise at 2500 users. Every application responds differently and you will not really know until you get to production loads. This is why I emphasize the *forecast* of capacity which, like weather forecasting, is subject to some variation.

The motivation to do this analysis is to draw attention to the capabilities of the APM data for forecast purposes and to help justify improving the simulation capabilities in QA to get enough licenses to test properly.

Alternatively, if the test platform is known to be 20% of production capabilities, and you are able to load to 100% of that test platform, these results will be linear when extrapolated to the production capabilities. The response time at 80% of maximum load should be close to the real experience. The invocation rates should even be closer—simply multiply the invocations achieved in QA by five, in this case, to get the forecasted invocation goal.

The confirmation of the forecast by direct comparison to production is a critical step towards long-term acceptance of this forecast technique. So you should expect to bring that information back to QA and see what you can do to improve accuracy. After a few iterations, you will end up with a realiable and proven forecast technique.

Defining a Test Plan

In order to define a realistic test plan, you need to consider, at minimum, the following *usage characteristics* of the application:

- User population

    - Are there different types of users?
    For example: typical, expert, casual, high net-worth.
    - What proportion of the total are they? What transactions do they normally perform?

- Use cases and frequency of use

    For example: login, account summary, last month's transaction summary.

- Business Trends

    - Does the user population vary? Do the transactions performed vary?
        - Time Of Day
        - End Of Month/Quarter
        - Seasonal

- Adoption Sizing

    - How many users are there today, and what increase will be realized as the application is rollout and accepted?

From this test plan, you may then define one or more *test scenarios*[9] that will simulate a population of synthetic users according to the usage characteristics.

User Population

I have found that the user population has a variety of impacts on application performance and that this is especially useful during triage. When reviewing the test plan, note if the user population is proportional with any of the following characteristics, even if they are not part of the test plan:

- How many End Users?

    - Total Population
        - By roll-out phase, geography
    - Total Concurrent
        - By roll-out phase, geography

- How do Users connect to the application?

    - What is the authentication path
    - Are interactive and batch/semi-batch processes present at the same time?

---

[9] Wikipedia, "Scenario (computing)," http://en.wikipedia.org/wiki/Scenario_(computing)

- What does the physical deployment look like when the project is fully realized?
  - Server quantity and location

Sometimes a test plan can become too ambitious, leading to the rational deletion of one or more user scenarios. Having five extra user models could generate 15 additional test runs (3 runs for each model) and add days or weeks to the testing schedule. Paring down the test plan is not unreasonable but losing track of some of the usage characteristics will have a negative impact during triage.

Accuracy and Reproducibility

If a load test is automated, how can there be any opportunity for inaccuracy from one test run to the next? That's what I used to think when I reviewed testing results. If they were acceptable, as was often the case, neither you or I would be interested in re-running the test.

My first dose of a new reality came when I was evaluating the impact of adding an APM agent to an application. I asked for a short load test in order to confirm my agent configuration. The report came back after 30 minutes and indicated that performance had decreased by 20%, something I had never seen before. I could doubt my own configuration abilities but before going in and reviewing the settings, I simply asked for them to re-run the test. The second test result was a 3% improvement over expectation—the app ran faster than expected! We continued running tests for a few more hours. Every result was different and yet no settings were changed.

From my university experience, I recalled someone saying that "two points don't make a trend," so I would make it three—running the exact same load test three times in succession and seeing if I got the same results. The tests are each 20 minutes in duration: ramp up 5 minutes, steady-state 10 minutes, and ramp down 5 minutes. Sometimes I've added a fourth test.

The analysis is limited to the 10 minute steady-state interval in each test scenario. You want to indentify one or more active components and compare the number of responses and the average response time for each of the components. They should be the same or less than a 1% difference for the purposes of a load test. What you may find is that they vary from 10-20%. When the variance is large, it means that your findings are not consistent and your load is not reproducible. This is a significant problem. Very likely something external is compromising the test such as other processes on the test box, network problems, or resource problems. You've got to root that out.

APM visibility during the QA activities offers the promise of getting insight into configuration and coding differences. But you cannot expect to detect any subtle changes if the underlying test is already adding a 10-20% variation. It is not necessary to repeat every test three or more times, and then average the results. You should instead periodically evaluate if a single test scenario is actually reproducible and set expectations accordingly. Ultimately, you want to identify and eliminate the source of the variation, whether it is environmental or a result of too much variety in the users and their transaction profiles.

Process

Test Plans

In support of the baseline activities coming up in Chapter 12 you will summarize the load generation activities that will be necessary. There are three types of baselines and each *baseline test plan* will have different characteristics and goals. The configuration baseline has the most unique characteristics because it is very sensitive to your ability to reproduce a test. The application and performance baselines test plans should be familiar if your load testing discipline is already established. They are presented here for completeness.

Test Evolution—Gold Configuration (sequence of configurations)

This test plan is used to validate a monitoring configuration for a particular type of application. When this optimal monitoring configuration is identified, it is thereafter called a *gold monitoring configuration* or simply a *gold configuration*.

Agents can have a number of configurations that result in different visibility and potential overhead. Your goal is to document the impact of each configuration so that the application owner can select a monitoring configuration that best fits their goals.

Each configuration change requires a little coordination between the test team and the APM admin who is making a small change in the APM agent configuration file. This takes about 30 seconds, so close coordination via instant messaging is more appropriate than e-mail. Most of the changes will also require a restart of the application server. This is done to make sure that the starting conditions for each configuration change are exactly the same and that no side-effect from an earlier configuration is present.

The application under test should be stable and the application server should be already tuned for optimal performance. The duration of the individual tests is 20 minutes. The number of virtual users should be sufficient to generate a moderate load; 10 to 50 users is sufficient. All of the tests should be completed on the same day. With good coordination, the 10 tests will take five hours.

Depending on the variety of configurations that your application and the monitoring tool supports, you will have 7-12 tests overall. You will have fewer reasons to test if the load is not reproducible. The load profile is as discussed earlier in this chapter: tickle, pause, ramp-up, steady state, ramp-down. The first six tests are assessing the reproducibility of the test as well as the impact of any overhead from simply having the basic APM agent configured. Each of these tests may also need some external measures of the transaction response times in order to validate the response times independently measured by APM. This might be response time information from the load generation tool or transactions timings written out to a log file. When the load generation configuration is optimal, this will result in six runs (evolutions) with consistent response times.

If an external meaure of the application performance is not available, then you will omit the series of runs with NoAgent. The BaseAgent configuration, where instrumentation is disabled, will then become the testing control.

Each of these two initial configurations, NoAgent and BaseAgent, are evaluated statistically for consistentcy. Depending on the magnitude of the difference and the metric being evaluated, you can make the following conclusions, summarized in Figure 11-4. The details of the calulations are in the Test Plan Cookbook in the next sub-section.

Metric	Difference From Average		
	< 5%	< 10%	< 20%
CPU	•Overhead is not significant.	•Overhead is a potential concern.	•Overhead is a problem.
Response Time	•Test consistency is good.	•Test consistency is a concern.	•Test consistency is unacceptable •Environment is suspect.
Invocations	•Test consistency is ideal.	•Test consistency is poor.	•Test consistency is unacceptable •Load generation is suspect.

Figure 11-4. Evaluating load test consistency

If the test plan is found to be consistent among each of these first six runs, then each of the remaining test scenarios may be reduced to a single test run.

If there is a significant difference between the instrumentation-OFF (BaseAgent) and the instrumentation-ON, (BaseMinimum) then you will need to do three runs for each scenario and use the average values from the three runs in each scenario. And then you can again proceed with single test evolutions for the remaining configuration options.

If you still canot confirm the accuracy of the load reproducibility, then you really need to continue to execute three test evolutions of each configuration option, and then average the results.

The following sections lists the details of the tests plan with respect to the configurations tested and the number of runs required, assuming that the initial six runs will be consistent.

Test Plan Cookbook

1. Target Application
   a. The type of application is a Portal, with WebServices. This results in three agent configurations.
      i. Portal: Base-minimal
      ii. Portal: Base-minimal +WServices configuration
      iii. Portal: Base-maximum +WServices configuration

2. Three runs, 20 minute minimum, no agent deployed : NoAgent
   a. This is only possible if you have some external measure of transaction response times.
   b. Name as runA, runB, runC

3. Three runs, 20 minute minimum, instrumentation OFF : BaseAgent
   a. Update agent.profile on Portal JVM
   b. Restart application server, then initiate three runs in succession
      i. Name as run1, run2, run3

4. Analyze initial reslts for load reproducibility
   a. Calculate average for each set of three runs (runA, runB, runC vs. run1, run2, run3) for the CPU ultilization, response time, and invocation metrics
   b. Calculate the difference between the observed value and the average for each of the metrics. Where possible, use the response times and invocations for 3-10 different transaction types.
   c. If the difference is less than 5%, overhead is not significant and load reproducibility is good.
   d. If the difference is greater than 5% but less that 10%, overhead is a potential concern and test consistency is poor.
   e. If the difference is greater than 10%, test consistency is unacceptable and overhead may be a problem,

5. Three runs, 20 minutes minimum, instrumentation ON, Default-typical
   a. Update APM agent configuration on Portal JVM
   b. Base-minimal
   c. Restart application server, then initiate three runs in succession
      i. Name as run4, run5, run6

6. Analyze results for runs 1-3 vs. runs 4-5 as before. Here you are looking for any differences between the BaseAgent and BaseTypical monitoring configurations.

   a. If these are consistent, then the BaseAgent configuration is validated to serve as the no-instrumentation reference for the remainder of testing, all of which will be with instrumentation.
   b. If they are not consistent, then the following test cases must be repeated three times to have confidence in the comparison with the BaseAgent findings.

7. One run, 20 minutes minimum

   a. Base-minimal + WServices
   b. Restart, name as run7

8. One run, 20 minutes minimum

   a. Base-minimal, WServices
   b. Restart, name as run8

9. One run, 20 minutes minimum (optional, if a GC configuration is available)

   a. Base-minimal + WServices + GC
   b. Restart, name as run9

10. One run, 20 minutes minimum

   a. Base-maximum +WServices
   b. Restart, name as run10

Gold Configuration Review

The goal for the *configuration baseline* is to determine the appropriate monitoring configurations for QA and production environments. For instrumentation, the number of metrics has to be balanced with the permissible overhead. In general, the QA environment can tolerate much more overhead than what would be allowed in the production environment, so you will have at least two configurations. A developer environment can incur even higher metrics load, exceeding allowable overhead for any other environment. This is because many developer tools such as profilers routinely add 30-50% overhead, which is entirely acceptable within the developer environment. Sometimes the APM technology can be configured to provide deep monitoring comparable to a profiler, which can add considerable overhead, and again is perfectly acceptable for a developer. The challenge is to keep such a high overhead configuration from getting to the production environment. This is what the phased deployment model of Chapter 7 helps to control.

Even as the number of metrics is your guide, there is no absolute range to follow. A monitoring configuration for 3000 metrics may result in excessive overhead for a simple database application but poor visibility (and no overhead) for a portal application. Thus, each type of application needs to validate the impact of each of the potential configurations for suitability.

Any agent technology has overhead considerations, including SNMP, bytecode instrumentation, logging and polling instrumentation (JMX, etc.), and competes with the application for resources (CPU, memory, I/O). The *configuration baseline* is the process that will document exactly how much you can monitor without adversely affecting the application.

Number of Metrics

One of the first metrics to vary, as the different configurations are exercised, is the *total number of metrics* that the agent configuration generates. As you may know, bytecode instrumentation is dynamic and the actual number of metrics generated is a function of the application complexity and the visibility depth attempted. No matter how comprehensive an agent configuration, you will only ever get metrics if the specifc application code gets executed. If you were to simply startup a server, monitored by APM, you really would not see much until someone exercised the application.

And as you learned in Chapters 3 and 10, the number of metrics from each agent is critical to the sizing the overall APM solution, including those that come from the transactions and other forms of instrumentation (JMX, logging, etc.)

You will always want to report the number of metrics experienced with special emphasis if the number changes significantly. You can find some examples of the properties and thresholds for the total number of metrics for an agent in Chapter 13, Figures 13-6 and 13-7.

Load Reproducibility Review

For runs 4-6, you can get an immediate sense of the accuracy by looking at the highest invocation metric over the duration of the three tests, as in Figure 11-5. The invocation curves should appear similar. If they do not, as in the example here, you have a fairly significant problem with your load generation and should take steps to discover what the problem is.

Some of the potential limitations can include the following:

- The platform hosting the load generation robot is having problems or is shared with other CPU or I/O intensive activities.
- The network between the load testing robots and the application server is having problems or is shared with a process that can consume excessive bandwidth.

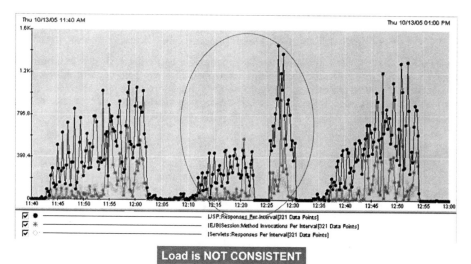

Load is **NOT CONSISTENT**

Figure 11-5. Example of inconsistent load

For an example of a consistent load, please look ahead to Figure 13-11. That example is from a production environment and was deemed suitable for determining a baseline.

Application Baseline

The application baseline is collected while you are evaluating the different use cases, as specified in the test plan for the application. I would like you to use my standard test evolution profile (tickle, ramp-up, stead-state, ramp-down) with a 20 minute duration but this will be subordinate to whatever the test plan dictates. Avoid any step-load increases (where there is no ramp) as this can cause inconsistent results, especially with short duration tests. Please refer to Figure 10-9, in Chapter 10, for an example.

The following activities contribute to the application baseline but would be managed by the APM practitioner. Some of these may be automated and require the execution of a script while the test is in progress.

- Survey more use cases at moderate load.
- User Experience Test Profile (Average Load).
- Employ transaction stack collection for 5-10 min during load test.
- Adjust visibility with CMTs as appropriate.
- Repeat test with each increment of tracing.
- Avoid any high invocation metrics.
- Survey transactions and get some screen shots of the more common or more interesting (5-10).

- Identify metric collections for APC: Availability, Performance, and Capacity.
- Identify metric collections for *heartbeat* and other interesting metrics.

Overhead is a concern whenever the invocation rate for a single component exceeds 20,000 per minute. This is the definition of a *high invocation metric* and the threshold for a potential overhead so you must evaluate the effect on CPU, memory, and response time. It does not mean you absolutely have overhead but that it is highly likely. This is just not something you want to leave to chance.

Heartbeat Metrics

Sometimes when you are reviewing metrics, you will come across metrics that appear to be independent of load. I call these *heartbeat metrics* because they indicate that the application is healthy. Figure 12-6 illustrates this relationship. The upper graph depicts the invocations that an application is experiencing over three production days. You can see that the load varies considerably. The lower graph depicts a number of candidate heartbeat metrics. They are largely independent of load. While you may uncover a heartbeat metric during a load test, it will be important to confirm it in production. Of the candidates identified earlier during QA testing, the best candidate is given by the trace starting at 2000 msec response time. The other candidates have some variation, which is appropriate only for confirming that the application is lightly used or not used at all. While these are interesting, I don't have much use for them because the invocation metrics alone do a good job indicating incoming load.

I prefer these heartbeat metrics for confirming availability of the application (component, not the whole service) because it will be more robust than agent connectivity or the number of metrics. It confirms that parts of the application are functioning as planned.

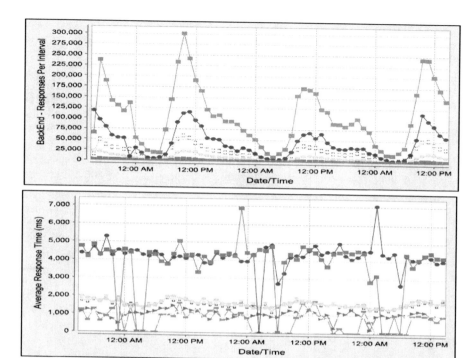

Figure 11-6. Heartbeat metrics

Performance Baseline

A stress test should be performed well before the application is authorized for promotion to the production environment. It should be completed as early in the testing cycle as possible but not before the application server configuration tuning is complete. Historically, stress testing, usually in the form of a *smoke test*[10], was used as the final acceptance test. If the application survived, it was deemed acceptable for production. In a mature testing organization, the smoke test would be followed with a stress test, which requires a lot more work to organize. With APM visibility, you get exceptional detail during the stress test, enough that you can conclude if it will scale, not just simply survive.

The duration of the test should be a minimum of 2 hours, up to 8 or even 24 hours. The test plan will dictate the duration as well as the *target capacity* in number of users or transactions.

The test profile is a little different from the baseline test profile. You will ramp to 75% of the target capacity in the first 30 minutes, and then slow the pace of new users, adding the remaining 25% over the next 30 minutes. While this is still a

---

[10] http://en.wikipedia.org/wiki/Smoke_test

ramp profile, and not a step load profile, there may be non-linearities, as you saw in Chapter 10. If a target capacity is unknown, then simply ramp to the maximum capacity of the load generation over two hours.

For the remaining hour, there are two schools of thought. The first is to continue to ramp to 125% of the target capacity, potentially driving the application to failure. This gives a comfortable margin of reserve capacity, should the application survive. The second is to hold for 30 minutes and allow the application to reach steady-state, followed by a final ramp to 125% over the remaining 30 minutes. This allows you to confirm that the non-linearities are not present.

If more time is available beyond the minimum two hours, I would first extend the pause to 4 hours and confirm steady-state, and then ramp to 200% over the remaining time.

Analysis of the results is focused first on the components with the highest invocation rates, as determined during the *application baseline*. Figure 11-7 shows the result for a initial stress test using a ramp to the capacity of the load generation system.

As the application becomes saturated, and performance degrades, the ability of the application to process the incoming events will be compromised and the requests queued, resulting in a widening swing of surge activity.

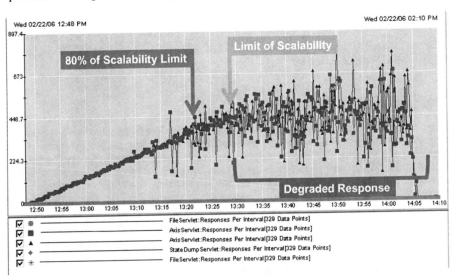

Figure 11-7. Stress load and scalability

There will be a point where the application no longer scales, the *limit of scalability* or the "knee" in the invocation curve. This is all your application should be expected to do without incurring a significant performance degradation. Looking at the response times at that point will indicate exactly how much degradation.

That the application may survive beyond this point does not mean it has "excess capacity." It means continued degradation in response times and potentially dangerous side-effects among other systems on the same server or network. The widening swings in the invocation counts are going to have unpredictable usage effects on the resources that are supporting these transactions. Ultimately, this means database or other resources may be impacted by continuing to operate this application while saturated.

What you should report is the *limit of scalability* and the number of users or transactions reached when the invocations are at 80% of the limit of scalability. This number is all that this application should be expected to support. You will adjust this recommendation for the differences between the QA and production environments, if known.

Load Reproducibility Analysis

1. Identify the steady-state period for the runs.
2. Generate a table report for each of the steady-state periods.

    a. Compare CPU and Response Time metrics.
    b. Duration and invocations should be EXACTLY the same.
    c. Summarize the response time and invocation metrics.
    d. A spreadsheet is the convenient tool.

3. Calculate the percent difference among the three runs for each configuration.

    a. Follow the analysis guidelines established in Figure 11-4.

General Acceptance Criteria

- Memory management when user load is a fraction of target load
- Instance counts (connection leaks)
- Stalls (>30 sec response)
- SQL Response time <4 sec
- MQ Response time <1 sec
- Error rate thresholds, by use case (transaction type)
- Exceptions
- Latency threshold (response time)
- No crashes (JVM recycle)
- Server resource utilization

    - CPU, RAM (no paging), minimal disk activity during test

Competency

Characterize your load reproducibility for a sample application. If you can't trust your load generation, nobody will trust your findings.

Artifacts

Generic_QA_Test Plan.ppt available on apress.com.

Summary

The QA discipline is a weak area in many organizations because it does not add much value for the time and energy required to develop and implement comprehensive test plans. APM visibility enhances the QA role by enhancing the value proposition for evaluating applications pre-production. And in parallel, the testing cycle validates the APM monitoring. As the QA system is restored, existing test strategies are vetted and refurbished, and you learn to focus on the critical aspects of the application because testing time still needs to be short in order to allow for an efficient identify-fix-retest cycle.

You can only become truly proactive in application management by preventing problems from getting promoted to the production environment. This simple goal means that the QA role will grow over time but not until it proves itself. Today, QA+APM needs to be quick, reliable, accurate, and unassailable.

Baselines

The last change is the first blamed.

Baselines are a key concept in maturing the use of performance information. With a baseline report you effectively take away the private view of the data presented in the APM workstation and share it among all of the application stakeholders. This is critical because access to the APM workstations is often limited both from a "needs some training" to a "we bought it, only we use it" perspective.

You also directly address the first question that arises during a performance incident: "What changed?" You achieve this by presenting evidence that suggests that the application, or one of its resources, is operating normally. This allows the triage effort to then focus on other areas. Conversely, you also know quickly if your application or resources are participating in the incident.

The simplest way to obtain baselines is to generate a report over a load test that is known to be acceptable and to compare that result with the same report template over the period of the incident. In this chapter, I will introduce how to determine what goes into that report as well as the different types of baselines and what they are used for.

Baselines are intended to be mechanical operations performed by anyone who can navigate the APM workstation and follow a technical cookbook. There are very explicit rules for what gets included in a baseline, as you'll explore here. Assessments about the quality of a result, be it a metric value or baseline, are reserved for the *application audit* in Chapter 13. Completing an audit requires experience and perspective—it requires skills. Generating a baseline just requires a little discipline.

Kick-Off Meeting

What are the performance characteristics for your application? This is an unfair question because everyone defines performance in slightly different ways. The concept of a *baseline*[1] is taken from the configuration management perspective: a point of reference. You want to be able to summarize and compare performance at two different points in time: during testing (or another good period) and during an incident.

The main reason I have found for establishing a baseline practice is to quickly answer the first question that comes up during an incident: "What changed?" In the IT world, the last change is the first blamed. It is all but unavoidable. The major change you are introducing, for the APM initiative, is a new piece of technology. So baselines are, in part, a defensive strategy—you need to show that you are getting the same result in production as you did when you tested the new monitoring configuration. Once that is established, the triage effort moves on to something else. This is unavoidable. A new APM initiative is pretty much always the last change in an operating environment.

As I collect baselines during a firefight activity, I also get to see what is "normal" for the application. In a firefight, I never know much about the application that is in trouble, so I really need to know what the application is like when it is not in a completely stressed and unstable state. The expectation here is not how helpful it will be, nor how pivotal the baseline process will be in helping organizations become effective with APM—it is about getting some clue as to where to look for problems.

Baselines are not configuration tuning. Configuration tuning should be completed before baselines and performance testing is undertaken. Changing an app server configuration effectively rebalances the overall performance characteristics and thus invalidates prior baselines. There is no universal baseline on which to compare any particular application. You have to generate baselines for each application that you will monitor. It seems like a lot of work, but you are already running the tests. You just need to structure them a little and generate the report.

Terms of Endearment

This section is a glossary of some important terms that contribute to the baseline process.

Configuration Tuning

This is the selection of settings for the application server that result in an optimal balance of performance and stability for a given application. While APM visibility can help guide and confirm app server configuration changes, the actual strategies are a significant and complex topic, and one that is outside the scope of this book.

---

[1] Wikipedia, "baseline," http://en.wikipedia.org/wiki/Baseline

What is critical to understand is that you do not want to define a baseline until the configuration tuning is complete. And if the app server configuration is changed at any time in the future, you need to re-run the baseline in order to determine if this balance has been enhanced or compromised.

Baseline

A baseline is a combination of settings and other runtime parameters that results in a specific response in terms of the quantity and variety of metrics. When such a combinations of settings is applied to an application, and that application experiences some exercise of its functionality, the characteristics of the response become a *signature* for the application. When the conditions of that exercise are controlled in terms of duration and reproducibility, the signature becomes a *baseline*. Thereafter, whenever you have a similar exercise of the application, you can assess if you have precisely the same response by comparing your new results to the baseline.

There are a variety of baselines that are appropriate when using APM technology, depending on your goals at the time. If you have a production incident involving multiple applications and resources, you want to compare each of the applications with their QA baseline to help you assess what is normal or abnormal and thus identify a suspect for the incident. If you have an idea for a configuration change to improve performance, you may easily assess it by comparing the performance of the new configuration with the earlier baseline.

Configuration Baseline

This baseline includes both the application server configuration (after tuning) and an APM agent configuration. This would apply only to APM instrumentation not to synthetic and real transaction monitoring. There may be multiple configuration baselines depending on the environment; dev, QA, and production settings, and would also include any optional monitoring configurations that are *validated*.

It is not necessary to collect a configuration baseline for every application that you test. But you will collect a configuration baseline for each *type*[2] of application that will be encountered and often for each monitoring configuration that you may employ. Once these different configurations are validated, they are thereafter considered *gold configurations* for that application type and may be deployed as needed without further consideration.

Sometimes you will want to assess the impact of the agent configuration on the application. This is something different and it's called *overhead testing*. You would evaluate the performance of the application with and without the APM agent. You should plan to do this overhead test at least once. It will give you confidence that

---

[2] Types of applications include J2EE, .NET, portal, etc. This is from the application survey information you would collect, to support planning and sizing activities, as discussed in Part 1 of this book.

the technology is working as advertised, and you will be able to refer to the findings for the next application you will be working with.

Application Baseline

The application baseline is all about the visibility achieved by one of your APM configurations in terms of transactions and the contributions from the underlying components and resources. As you exercise the various test scenarios from the test plan, you need to confirm that you are seeing sufficient detail about the transactions: how they are initiated and what components they use until the transaction completes or exits the application server. These components can also interact directly with the different physical resources that the application uses, such as databases, message queues, and web services. So if you want to be able to detect problems with the resources, you have to be able to see the components that manage those interactions.

Any exercise of the application will confirm visibility. Sometimes you will want to exercise individual use cases to make it easier to associate the specific transactions with specific components. None of this needs to occur at production user loads.

When you get to the portion of the test plan that specifies the proportion of user types and respective use cases, this is where you will increase the load. You want to ensure that each of the use cases is exercised enough to generate useful statistics and also to reveal which components are shared among multiple transactions.

I prefer to generate some moderate load (50-100 users) and then look at the top 5 or 10 components with the highest invocation rate and another batch with the highest response times. These two sets of components comprise the *application signature*: a unique combination of components and metric values. They also will represent the capacity and performance attributes of the application once you evaluate the application under load, which establishes the baseline.

You will also be looking for metrics that are independent of load. No matter the user volume, these metrics exist with a narrow range of values, so long as the application is functioning. These metrics will represent another availability attribute of the application.

All of these attributes are important for setting operational thresholds that will reveal the health and pain that the application is experiencing.

Performance Baseline

Once you have defined the application baseline, your next challenge is to validate that you have visibility into the key components when the application is stressed and that the thresholds are correctly indicating a problem, using the performance baseline. The performance baseline indicates the key components that best represent availability, performance, and capacity (APC) for the application. It is very easy to select components, assign thresholds, and create dashboards that represent what you *believe* are the critical points of the application. It is quite another to validate that the thresholds and critical components are representative of the application.

The only way to achieve this pre-production is with a *stress to failure* test scenario. You need to exercise the application over a couple of hours with increasing load until the application collapses or fails. This can be difficult for a number of reasons. You may not be able to generate sufficient load. The application may gracefully degrade service or otherwise handle the excessive load without incident. The resources available pre-production may not have sufficient capacity to support the high load of your test scenario.

Thus you may have to finalize the performance baseline when you reach production. This is not so bad because you will have completed much of the preparation via the configuration and application baselines.

Capacity Planning

Capacity planning is an analysis and projection of application growth based on *historical data*. For mature applications that have been deployed for years and have well-known user populations and use cases, this is a very robust discipline. Baselines are a form of historical data (a specific result at a specific time and duration) and sometimes come under the purview of capacity planning.

Capacity Forecast

New applications have no history on which to capacity plan so you attempt to predict the future capacity via a *capacity forecast*. When you simply do not have a mature application or understanding of the user population and use cases, you can still generate a projection of application growth based on *load testing*. When you have the opportunity to define the performance baseline, you will know the maximum capacity achieved when the application is loaded to failure. Simply moving to 80% of this maximum and correlating that with the number of active virtual users (from the load simulation) should give a completely accurate *forecast* of a sustainable capacity. You should not expect to operate the application at the maximum capacity revealed because you have already established that it will fail. Please review Figure 11-5 in Chapter 11 for an example.

The Fab Four

When I defined some key terms earlier, I hinted at some representations or views on metrics and transactions. The *Fab Four Views* are:

- Component bottlenecks or high response times
- Most active components
- Contributors
- Transaction perspective

Different APM tool vendors will have various techniques to represent these views. Here is an approximation starting with Figure 12-1.

What we have here is a sorted list, greatest to smallest, of response time metrics for various components which were experienced during a test. The values are in milliseconds, and the top nine components range from 2,149,362 msec to 7,741 msec, or approximately 2,000 to 7.7 seconds. Some are database calls and some are JSPs (Java Server Pages). All of them are pretty poor but you would not really be expected to know this until you have read Chapter 14.

All you really need to know at this point is that the top 10 metrics really capture all of the significant bottlenecks for this test scenario. As you will start to appreciate later, this is really all that matters for this application. Every other metric will be smaller, and until you address why you have 200 second database transactions and 118 second login pages, none of the other metrics really matter too much. When you correct these high response time components, the application will effectively rebalance its behaviors, so you will need to rerun this test and see that you have corrected the problem and that the new top 10 components are behaving better.

The test plan will detail what the acceptable response times should be. It will take a few iterations to root out these initial problem components until you get in the vicinity of those goals.

The ninth metric has been selected, and this results in the graph at the bottom. This graph is very typical for a response time in a Java system. The initial response time is very long and thereafter the response time is lower. I will review this characteristic in detail in Chapter 14.

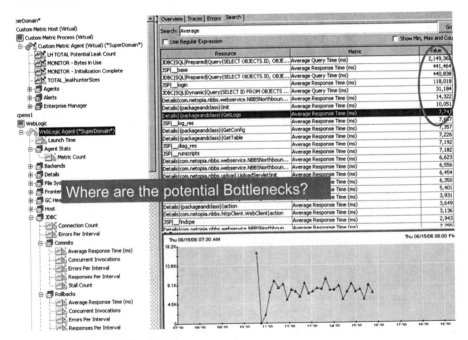

Figure 12-1. Potential bottlenecks

After identifying the bottlenecks, you issue a new query and select all of the invocation metrics, sorting as before and resulting in Figure 12-2. This generates a new list of components with counts ranging from 14 million down to 2 million. This is simply where the application is spending all of its energy. It also indicates that the agent has been misconfigured, which may or may not account for the unusual response times.

AP monitoring is a balancing act between visibility and overhead: how deep into the application call stack you can look and the overhead associated with doing so. So if you simulated 1000 transactions but found lots of metrics with millions of invocations, you simply have gone too deep in the application call stack and may incur significant overhead. This is what you see in Figure 12-2: components with total invocations in the millions for the test interval. When you examine the individual metrics, you see that it is consistently around 200k invocations at each reporting interval. As discussed in Chapter 11, an invocation rate greater than 20,000 per minute is the threshold for significant overhead. You are at ten times that guideline.

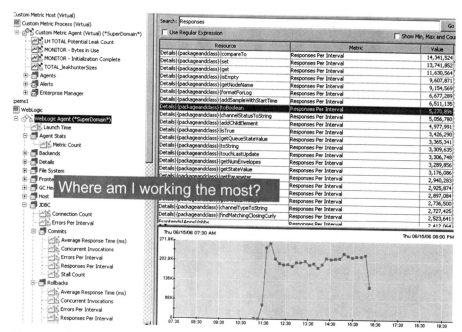

Figure 12-2. Most active

This overhead threat is something you really need to correct before going to further testing and certainly before going to production. But because the application is still working correctly, no one is really going to notice that the performance is degraded. This is nothing more than a process problem. Someone needs to look at the test results and see if this baseline results in a "normal" or "abnormal" response time. You need about two minutes to generate these first two views (Figures 12-1 and 12-2). Even if you know nothing about what this application is actually doing, you know the only thing that's important—that something is seriously wrong.

The third view, Figure 12-3, is to help confirm that the first two views are consistent. Here you look at some of the transactions that are being experienced and then drill down into the components that comprise the call stack of a single transaction.

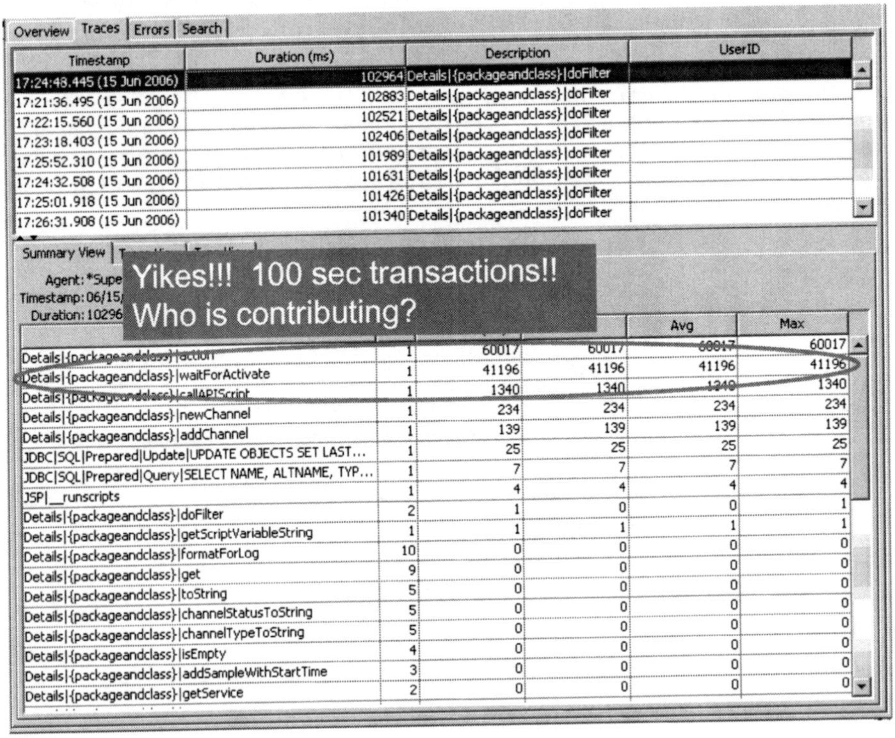

Figure 12-3. Contributors

Here you are looking at a number of the 100+ second login transactions. You only need to look at one of them, and in a similar fashion, find the total call time (response time) and sort on that value. This reveals many of the same metric names that you found when you took the invocations view. In this case, the top two components are responsible for 99% of the overall transaction response time.

You can often form another view of the transaction, one that shows the proportion of time that each component contributed (as in Figure 12-4) in what is called the *transaction perspective*. This view is what I use to confirm that I have sufficient visibility.

For each entry into a transaction, you need to have a few layers of the call stack exposed, down to the point that some component is interacting with a resource. And when you look at the lowermost component, at least 60% of the total transaction time should be represented.

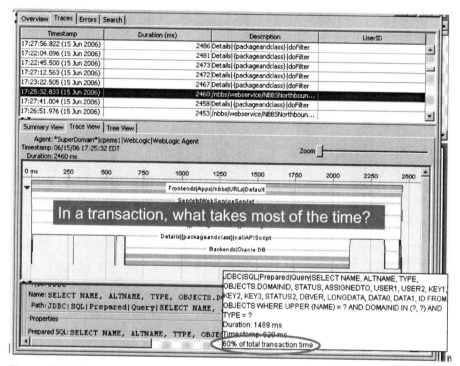

Figure 12-4. Transaction perspective

For this example transaction you therefore have "good" visibility. If I did not see this database transaction, or if I only had one or two levels of the call stack exposed, I would know that I had *insufficient visibility*, and must take steps to improve the situation. Conversely, if I had 50 levels of call stack, I would suspect I had *excessive visibility*. That would be confirmed via the invocations view, and it's also something that would need to be corrected.

In situations where only a few levels of call stack are present, or that none of the lower levels represents an interaction with an external resource, you know conclusively that you do not yet have sufficient visibility to reliably triage performance problems. This does not mean the APM configuration is wrong. It simply means that it is insufficient. You may still undertake APM monitoring even as the APM configuration is weak, but it is critical to know what limitations are present and to properly set expectations as to what you can do for triage.

With a single load test and a few minutes assembling the Fab Four Views, you are only scratching the surface of what APM can reveal. Your immediate focus is to confirm that you have sufficient visibility and that the APM configuration is appropriate for production use. That job is done. What happens if you have access to multiple baselines? How do you organize the metrics to represent APC (availability, performance, and capacity)?

Reporting

If the language of collaboration is metrics, then the forum for collaboration is the report. It just isn't practical for every stakeholder to be trained in, and have access to, an APM workstation. Providing casual access to dashboards and reports, via a browser, is attractive but I have found that many of these casual users simply don't understand what they are looking at. You simply have to do a lot more socialization of what the APM visibility means and this requires simple solutions. For many, the simplest route to establish collaboration and socialization is via e-mail.

E-mail is the starting point because it is ubiquitous and an e-mail thread takes on a life of its own. You can summarize the findings from a report and included as an attachment; for many stakeholders, that's all they need. If a questions pops up, the answer is seen by everyone on the thread. And the organization begins a slow climb out of the silo mindset and into a more collaborative environment.

There will be resistance at first. I find that many applications survive because no one really knows what is going on with them. APM removes many of the barriers to understanding the current state—and progress—that an application is experiencing. It is truly a double-edged sword because as much as you want to promote the application teams that are using APM visibility to manage the application life cycle wisely and with demonstrable success, you are also bringing to light the applications that are struggling and not quite on track to success.

As an APM practitioner, you don't get to choose which teams you work with. You simply have to establish and execute the processes that get visibility into performance problems. You have to defer judgment of any kind and allow the organization to adapt to the new visibility.

So why all the fuss and sensitivity? It's e-mail. Watch what you say and what others say. Keep it neutral and keep the caps lock OFF.

Frequency

How much reporting is sufficient? Figure 12-5 summarizes various reporting frequencies. The application team may want to get a summary of each load test but not too many other folks would be so motivated. When an application is ready to exit QA and be promoted to production, that's the time to socialize the baseline and other findings. That is basically *once* per release. This might be a little extra e-mail if all teams are on a quarterly release schedule, but this is what is needed to share the performance status and start educating all the stakeholders in how to communicate in performance terms.

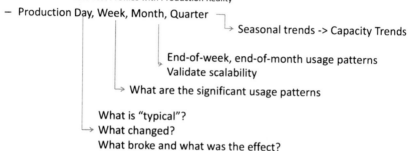

- Once
  - Key components
  - Operational thresholds (to be validated)
  - Startup Characteristics
  - App signature or profile
- Periodically
  - Across lifecycle
    - Track progress towards goals
      - More efficient, stable, scalable, etc.
      - Validate Test Profiles with Production Reality
  - Production Day, Week, Month, Quarter
    - Seasonal trends -> Capacity Trends
    - End-of-week, end-of-month usage patterns
      Validate scalability
    - What are the significant usage patterns
    - What is "typical"?
    - What changed?
      What broke and what was the effect?

Figure 12-5. Performance baseline—frequency

All *periodic* reporting is essentially a roll-up of the daily reporting up to annual reporting. While all of this data would be available in the APM database, any long-term report is going to impact the performance of that data store and limit the convenience of an ad-hoc analysis. Instead I prefer reports daily, and I take advantage of off-hours periods to generate the necessary reports and maintain them in a report directory. This keeps reporting activities minimal during the operational day and is always faster than reporting on-demand.

The time of day or even the day of the week you report on makes a lot of difference in the overall accuracy of your findings. For example, Figure 12-6 shows the production invocation metrics over two days.

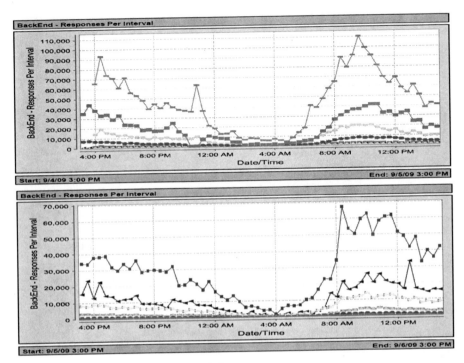

Figure 12-6. Production invocations variation

The overall pattern of activity during each day is similar but the day-to-day volume differences are almost double. Even if you considered the total invocations per 24 hour period, you might not appreciate the maximum load (110,000 invocations) if you only look at the total invocations. These day-to-day variations need to be documented and incorporated in test plans in order to insure that applications will scale as required. I always recommend picking a single interval (per day) on which to focus your analysis. In this case, 8 AM to noon would be the critical interval. This is what your business needs to manage in order to keep running, and any failure here is going to have a big impact. This is the area you need to understand the best.

Baseline

The baseline report summarizes the major components in terms of response time and invocations. Initially, your baselines should be limited to the key components, those top 5 or 10, that you have identified and established a metrics collection for. As the stakeholders become familiar with this type of presentation, you could extend this to the top 20 or 50. Initially, you want to keep focus on the key components. Otherwise, you face the risk of distracting the stakeholders from those key components.

Figure 12-7 illustrates the baseline report contents. Response time and invocations should be available from any APM vendor while the concurrency, errors, and stalls may have different names or require extensions to the agent. What is not present—CPU, memory, I/O—these tend to be a distraction from keeping an initial focus on key components. The report could handle these other metric categories as well but then that pushes it outside of the narrow focus you want for a baseline.

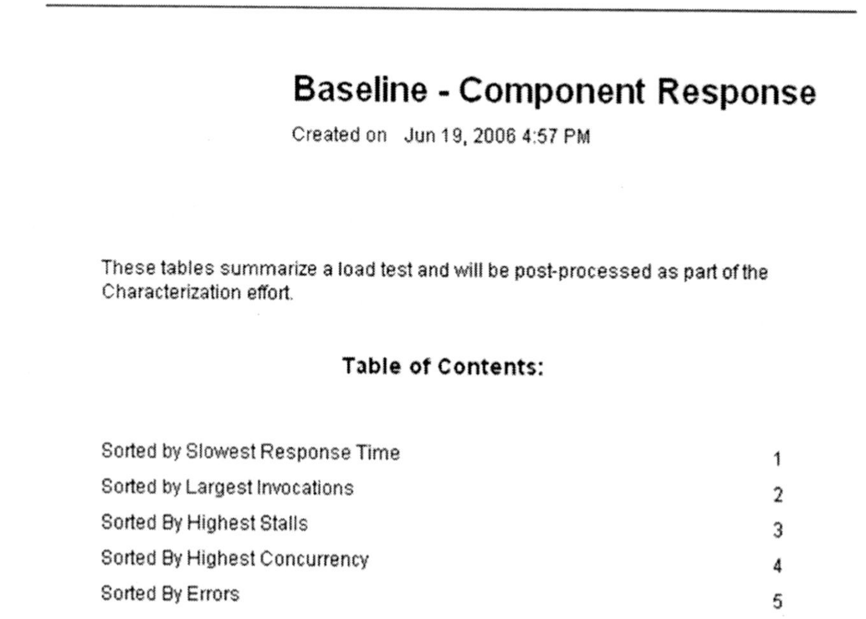

Baseline - Component Response

Created on   Jun 19, 2006 4:57 PM

These tables summarize a load test and will be post-processed as part of the Characterization effort.

Table of Contents:

Figure 12-7. Baseline report

Some stakeholders will prefer graphs instead of tables but it's simply not possible to make automatic comparisons of graphs. While a table, as in Figure 12-8, may reduce some of the flexibility in interpretation that a graphs supports, the goal for the baseline is to reduce the need for interpretation. The solution is easy: a report with some graphs for human use, and that same report in a *.csv file (which does not support graphs) for machine use.

In the baseline of Figure 12-8, which covers a four-hour interval, you can see that the main servlet was invoked 380k times and that this resulted in 168k errors. In other words, almost half of the invocations result in an error. This is a bad thing. There is nothing else about this application that you should spend any time on, no matter how interesting, until this error count is resolved. And that is the real goal of the baseline.

Some folks would suggest that more detail would allow a developer, for example, to be able to look at the report and figure out how to solve the problem.

322

Baseline - Component Response

Sorted by Slowest Response Time

Resource:Metric	Mean	Min	Max	MMin	MMax	Count
Servlets|WebServiceServlet:Average Response Time (ms)	503	15	2,656	13	3,277	383,260
Servlets|ACSServlet:Average Response Time (ms)	218	0	3,996	0	6,199	1.3M
Backends|Oracle DB:Average Response Time (ms)	23	0	1,775	0	2,048	4.4M
Servlets|FileServlet:Average Response Time (ms)	2	0	830	0	1,866	70,177

Start: 6/15/06 11:00 AM   **End: 6/15/06 3:00 PM**

Metric Grouping: Component Response Time (ms)
Agents: opems1\|WebLogic\|WebLogic Agent

Baseline - Component Response

Sorted By Errors

Resource:Metric	Mean	Min	Max	MMin	MMax	Count
Frontends|Apps|/nbbs|URLs|Default:Errors Per Interval	2,637	0	2,621	0	3,034	167,769
Frontends|Apps|/nbbs:Errors Per Interval	2,637	0	2,621	0	3,034	167,769
Servlets|ServletResponseImpl:Errors Per Interval	2,637	0	2,621	0	3,034	167,769
Details|{packageandclass}|getVariableList:Errors Per Interval	0	0	0	0	0	0
Details|{packageandclass}|getArray:Errors Per Interval	0	0	0	0	0	0
Details|{packageandclass}|initFromInform:Errors Per Interval	0	0	0	0	0	0

Figure 12-8. Baseline report details

This may be a nice idea but it's a dilution of the intent for the baseline. The baseline is a simple summary of what is significant for the application. Resolving problems that could involve any possible type of information simply cannot be anticipated and incorporated in the report. Of course, the report does not say that something is bad. Stakeholders already know enough to realize that errors are a bad thing. Nor does it say that something is good. The e-mail accompanying this report would simply say:

"A four-hour test was conducted and resulted in 380k transactions. A large number of errors were identified (168k) which merits further consideration as to this being normal or abnormal."

Simply sharing the fact that 162k errors were experienced will bring about sufficient pressure to see that the issue is addressed.

HealthCheck

After multiple rounds of generating baseline reports, addressing the issues that arise, and moving the application towards optimal performance and stability, the application will be deemed "acceptable" and eligible for production. Usually, there is a specific process to move to production and it begins with a review of packaging, integration testing, and a report on what the test plan achieved. A more comprehensive performance report than the baseline is called for, something I call a *HealthCheck*. Similar to a baseline report but with additional details to support additional measures of application viability, the HealthCheck establishes the characteristics for a healthy application. Here, the additional information is not a distraction because all of these measures now constitute a unique signature for the application. When using the baseline report, the characteristics of the application are still fluid.

The contents of the HealthCheck report are summarized in Figure 12-9. The important additions are the startup profile for the number of metrics (explored in Chapter 13) and the CPU and memory utilization. All of these are best represented by graphs.

The invocations are now divided over general, front-ends, and back-ends[3] to help correlate with other measurements. The response times are divided over general and front-end. The appearance of these "general" designations is simply a catch-all for anything that is not a front-end or back-end. If a stress test (load duration) was completed, I would use graphs in addition to tables for these numbers. Otherwise, I would wait until the HealthCheck was repeated in the production environment so that the hourly or daily variations were exposed, as illustrated in Figure 12-6.

---

[3] Wikipedia, "front-end," http://en.wikipedia.org/wiki/Front-end

HealthCheck - General View of the Application Under Management

Created on Jun 19, 2006 5:31 PM

HealthCheck - Overview of all the major components for the monitored application.

>

Table of Contents:

Metrics Count	1
CPU Utilization	3
Memory Utilization	5
Invocations	7
Invocations FE	9
Invocations BE	11
Response Time	13
Response Time FE	15

Figure 12-9. HealthCheck report overview

Summary

Both baseline and HealthCheck reports present the performance and capacity characteristics of the application. Only the level of detail and presentation differs. The output of a successful QA process is the definition and generation of the HealthCheck report that establishes the *normal* signature for the application. Once the application is promoted to production, the distinctions become less important as the narrower definition of baseline as the basis or reference for normal will be more readily used. Likewise, the HealthCheck report template, when employed over the period of an incident, becomes more associated with "incident" rather than HealthCheck. The report loses some of its neutrality in that it is now associated with an outage or performance degradation. It is no longer *normal*, despite the fact that the same metrics are being collected.

Process

Baselines are like hammers. They have a function that is easy to grasp and yet there are tremendous variety of applications. You need to be able to select the right one. There are four categories of baselines that present differences in both the duration of the baseline report and the frequency that it is used, as summarized in Figure 12-10.

The baseline characterization should have the fewest number of attributes reported. All the others are using the HealthCheck attributes.

Baselines	Duration	Frequency	Lifecycle
Characterization	10-20 minutes	Every use case, configuration, and code change	Dev, QA, Audit
HealthCheck	1-4 hours	Low	QA, Audit, Production
Incident	2 hours	Low	Audit, Production
Trend	1-4 hours	Weekly, monthly, etc.	Production

Figure 12-10. Baseline varieties

Characterization baselines are used to identify all the significant components (in a sorted list) that may then be directly compared to production.

HealthChecks include characterization baselines and other information that establish the normal operating parameters for the app.

Incident baselines are also a form of characterization except that there is a longer period and that you are contrasting the normal metrics with the abnormal metrics. This occurs first in the incident interval (two hours, typically) and then by comparing another production period with the incident period. Of course, a QA baseline may be helpful, provided that the relationship between QA and production environments is known for this application.

Trend baselines are really just regular reporting but will often use the same reporting template as the baseline.

Extra components appearing in production are initial suspects when a performance incident is evident.

Collecting Baselines

I follow a simple mantra to keep focus on the baseline goals:

> *We are not solving problems.*
> *We are characterizing the application under load.*
>> *What is the correct APM agent configuration?*
>> *Do I have sufficient visibility?*
>> *What is the performance baseline?*
>> *How do I know that something is different?*

If you can stick to this agenda (mantra), you will separate yourself from the diagnostic role. You want to provide consistent measurements for everyone collectively to make the diagnosis. Assuming that responsibility, in addition to making the measurements, means that you will end up with a poor result for both measurements and diagnosis.

Configuration

1. You must have a reproducible load test. Not sure? MAKE SURE.
2. Fire the same load three times in succession.
3. What is the variation in servlet response time, etc.?
4. Load testing should progress without significant errors; otherwise, the performance data will not be consistent.
5. Keep load test durations the same; otherwise, comparisons will be difficult.
6. Load test each configuration that you expect to use.
7. Pay particular attention to memory intensive extensions.

Application

1. "Warm up" the application by running a small set of users for 1-5 minutes before each load test or whenever the app server is recycled.
2. Make sure you can prove that initialization is actually complete before loading occurs.
3. Memory monitoring tools often indicate this directly.
4. Load testing should progress without significant errors; otherwise, the performance data will not be consistent.
5. If a slow ramp up in the number of users is not possible, do runs at 10, 50, and 100 users.
6. Keep load test durations the same; otherwise, comparisons will be difficult.

7. Use transaction trace/captures periodically.

    a. This helps characterize variety of use cases being simulated.
    b. Confirm appropriate visibility (depth and coverage of the transaction stack); otherwise, correct the instrumentation.
    c. Sample for any rogue transactions when the app is at steady-state.

8. If there are stability issues or memory leaks, get at least two successful runs at four hours or greater to document the extent of the leak.

Performance

1. "Warm up" the application by running a small set of users for 1-5 minutes before each load test or whenever the app server is recycled.
2. Ramp the load to application failure over a two hour (or more) period.
3. Keep load test durations the in multiples of 20 minutes; otherwise, comparisons will be difficult.
4. Use a transaction tracer periodically, as was done during the application baseline.
5. Look for a "knee" in the invocation rate.

    a. This suggests performance saturation.
    b. You also need to make sure the load generation wasn't itself saturated.
    c. Performance should sharply degrade.
    d. Other "interesting" correlations should be apparent.
    e. Components that change sharply around the knee are what should be monitored in production.
    f. Review Figure 12-5 for what the "knee" will look like.

6. Determine alert thresholds.

    a. Among your top 10 components, review their performance leading up to the knee event and select the ones that best capture the knee and also have a significant degradation.

        i. GREEN: 5% of the performance/capacity before the knee.
        ii. YELLOW: 80% of the performance/capacity before the knee.
        iii. RED: The flat portion where the app is no longer scaling.

    b. Assemble metric collections as appropriate for which the thresholds will apply. You should have one collection for each of APM: Availability, Performance, and Capacity.

7. If there are stability issues or memory leaks, get at least two successful runs at four hours or greater to document the extent of the leaks.

Competency

Evaluate your ability to reproduce load (see Chapter 11).

Evaluate a sample application and determine the configuration, application, and performance baselines.

Summary

The baseline is the fundamental skill for APM. It is a mechanical technique intended to expose a signature for the application to establish a framework on which detailed comparisons, called *characterizations*, can be made. In order to be effective with audits and triage, you have to have a reliable definition of *normal* for your application, which is simply what the baseline provides. There are a few variants of baselines that extend this simple technique. You will find use for these as your skill in developing the baselines improve and as you move closer to production and the inevitable operational incidents. It is these incidents that you are preparing for because APM will likely be the "last change" in the application configuration, and thus the "first blamed" should anything go wrong in production. The baseline is how you will establish that what you see in production is what you saw during QA testing. Once there is some confidence in the new monitoring configuration, you will be able to confidently pinpoint "what changed" in the performance of the application components, and set the stage for effective triage.

The Application Audit

Trust, but verify.

—Ronald Reagan

One drink ain't enough, Jack. You better make it three.

—George Thorogood

The application audit is what I consider the fundamental element of APM technology. It prepares and validates the monitoring configuration, dashboards, and alerts so that the APM tool is tailored to your applications. And it also establishes a foundation for more effective triage. If you learn to do nothing else with APM than to deliver this competency, you will not be disappointed.

An application audit does not result is a grade or score. It is more like a statement that you exercised due diligence[1] in evaluating the performance aspects of the application, much the same as if you were going to invest your money in a start-up opportunity. What is the technology like? How do they manage their resources? How can I promote the product? Do I know enough to keep them on track, if they get into trouble? You really want to know the same about your application candidate. What kind of resources does it employ? Does it manage memory and connections well? Can I determine the best metrics for availability, capacity, and performance that I might want thresholds and alerts on? Do I have enough visibility to triage performance problems once we get to production?

---

[1] Wikipedia, "due diligence," http://en.wikipedia.org/wiki/Due_diligence

To get all of this information, look to the APM instrumentation technology to get visibility into the component relationships. If that is not available, you can also survey the transactions or conduct an interview-based assessment, as with Chapter 3. Your best audit findings will come from APM instrumentation, where applicable.

Of course, you can do much more with APM technology, as discussed elsewhere. All of those higher uses ultimately depend on the information gathered during an audit. Doing a competent job here is the gateway to maximizing the benefits of APM when your organization is ready.

Conversely, if you do not have access to someone who understands how to conduct an audit, you have little chance of leveraging APM consistently in an independent fashion. Your circumstances may dictate reliance on professional services to set up and maintain your APM infrastructure, which is a perfectly valid business model (discussed in Chapter 2). Organizations evolve at their own pace. My goal is to simply inform you of what is needed to realize APM independently, should you have the opportunity.

If you are comfortable with load generation and baselines (Chapters 11 and 12), then you are ready for an audit. All you are really adding to those basic, mechanical skills is a scope, a process, and a report—and a little bit of subjective interpretation. You need to indicate honestly what you think the prospects are for this application in its current state. And you need some solid recommendations as to what should be done to improve the situation. This requires some experience and practice, which is what turns a collection of skills and processes into a valuable service offering for your internal clients. Your audit skills will also benefit from the *triage with single metrics*, discussed in Chapter 14.

Kick Off Meeting

An audit is an opportunity to compare and contrast observed performance. The challenge is to have some reference to compare and contrast against. I will discuss a number of reference strategies but the fundamental goal is to decide if the target application is ready for production. Even if you are limited to a QA system with APM, it's important to keep this goal in mind. So what needs to be done to confirm that the APM configuration is production-ready? If you think about how operations and triage teams need to solve incidents or understand performance, then you will have the right frame of mind to select the significant components, organize dashboards, and assign thresholds. From the thousands of metrics that may be available, you need to identify and manage the ones that matter. The first question you need to answer is "Do I have sufficient visibility in order to manage this application in production?" When you can say "yes" to this question, then you have completed the audit.

Once you have the metrics that matter, you can then apply your triage skills and decide if these metrics are exhibiting correct (or expected) behaviors. The second question is "Is the application stable for its intended use?"

Of course, if you can audit stability, it will not take long for folks to wonder if the application will scale for its intended use. Under the right conditions you can reliably forecast the capacity of the target application, but this has some other considerations. Having a capacity forecast is the best result for an application audit. Simply getting ready for production is a good result. Documenting evidence of stability or scalability is a better result.

Compare and Contrast

Much of the modern APM marketplace is focused on the real-time benefits of monitoring technology. What makes the application audit unique is that it is entirely *post-analysis*: all of the audit analysis occurs after the load testing (or production experience) has completed. A day, week, or month after the testing and you'll have everything you need to conduct the audit.

Comparing two or more events can be cumbersome and may not be directly supported. Since all of the data is present, it's necessary to exploit the reporting tools to get the data in a useful form for post-analysis. Some of the use cases I have considered include the following:

- Compare my best QA run to current production.
- Compare baselines of the last 5 QA releases.
- Compare all 12 production outages we had last month.
- Compare the Q1 and Q2 releases.
- Compare TomCat v4.x and TomCat v5.x.

I've thought a lot about the ideal user interface for answering these questions, and it's a lot of software to write—it would require quite an effort. Instead, I've tried to focus on the process and organization, determining that the baseline is the critical ideal. With a baseline, you are really only manipulating *metadata* about the test or outage. And this is much more efficient than always going back to the time-series data that is stored in the APM database. Metadata is like the card catalog at the library. You can look through summary data of hundreds of books without moving your feet. Or you can walk the stacks for hours to review the same information.

What to Look for

Of course, if you don't have the right metadata, you will constantly need to revisit the APM database. By extending the baseline concept beyond summary data about the test scenario and into the performance details that the configuration, application, and performance baselines reveal, you have what you need.

From the application baseline, you can determine the variety of components present and which of these are interesting, after sorting based on highest response time, and later by highest invocations. For the baseline report, the focus was to identify the top 10 components. For the audit, you will want to organize and review the metrics by the type of component. This broader organization of the metrics is called a *HealthCheck* report and contains the following categories.

GC/Heap

Garbage Collection (GC)[2] is an automated management of memory used by Java and .NET applications. Before GC was available, developers had to explicitly manage memory. As applications became more complicated, this memory management was often a source of performance-limiting errors. GC eliminates that general risk but introduces a new responsibility—tuning of the GC parameters. The use of memory is highly application specific. Coupling this with the large variety of tunable parameters and the high level of sophistication in understanding the fine points of GC and you still can have many serious problems related to memory management. Overall, I believe the situation is much improved but the depths of misconfiguration are more severe.

You are concerned for the following:

- The frequency of GC, full or partial, consistent or inconsistent.
- Any increase in the minimum memory maintained.
- Any increase in the heap size.

Figure 13-1 shows the major features of the GC or memory profile. This one is not terrible but a few problems are evident.

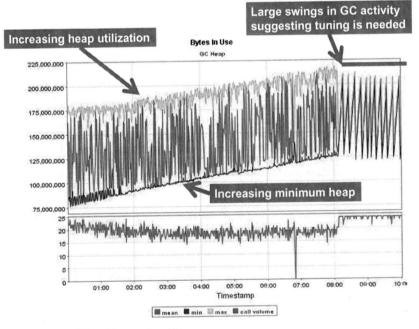

Figure 13-1. GC and heap schematic

---

[2] Wikipedia, "Garbage collection," http://en.wikipedia.org/wiki/
Garbage_collection_(computer_science)

EJB, Servlet, JSP

These are the front-end[3] components of the application and are the greatest contributor to the end-user experience. Most APM tools instrumentation, synthetic, and real transactions have a perspective on the front-ends. To contrast among them, instrumentation is considered deep-dive, as it shows details of the component relationships. The transaction view is more convenient for the business stakeholder but does not go beyond the Servlet or JSP in terms of revealing any component relationships.

You are concerned for the following:

- Degraded response over time.
- Unusually high response times.
- Degraded response consistent (correlated) with degraded GC.

Concurrency

Concurrency[4] is a feature of finely divided program control via individual threads of execution. Like the checkout at the supermarket, when the checkout line grows, additional staff are added to open more checkout counters, until the line dies down or no more checkout stations are available. When a component is capable of concurrency, multiple copies of that component may be executing at any time.

You are concerned for the following:

- Does concurrency increase with the load profile?
- Do concurrency counts plateau, indicating saturation of that thread pool?
- Do concurrency counts correlate with application slowdowns?

Stalls

A stall[5,6] is an unexpected delay in execution or failure to progress. From the software perspective, stalls may be recoverable, which makes them important indicators of saturation or bottlenecks[7] on a particular execution path.

---

[3] Wikipedia, "front-end and back-end," http://en.wikipedia.org/wiki/Front-end_and_back-end

[4] Wikipedia, "concurrency," http://en.wikipedia.org/wiki/Concurrency_(computer_science)

[5] A stall is a temporary thread block condition corrects itself after some arbitrary passage of time. For consistency, we consider such a thread to be stalled if the deadlock is in force for at least 30 seconds.

[6] Wikipedia, "stalling," http://en.wikipedia.org/wiki/Stalling_(gaming)

[7] http://en.wikipedia.org/wiki/Bottleneck

You are concerned with the following:

- Do stalls correlate with application performance degradation or slowdown?
- Do stalls plateau, which would represent bottlenecks?
- Do you find the stalled methods in your transaction stacks?
- Are a small number or a large number of stalls present?

Optional

Optional components are those which are not frequently part of an application or limited to specific classes of applications. Some examples include the following:

- SQL statements
- JMS (messaging)
- Web Services

Auditing Pre-Production

What you need for success is at least three reproducible tests under simulated load. If that cannot be achieved, the audit will be more difficult and you will have less confidence in the findings. All the details for quality load generation are in Chapter 11.

The real world is not often so cooperative, so many of the examples in this chapter are for unstable applications with unreliable load generation. There has to be some exercise of the application in order to conduct even a portion of the audit. And with APM visibility, there is a lot you can observe, even when the testing seems a waste of effort. Your first audit may not be perfect but an appreciation for what is needed will be firmly impressed. The audits following will be better.

Auditing Operationally

Collecting a performance baseline in production is hard. You need to get at least three samples when no outages are present and at the same time of day. So you need a minimum of three days of outage-free measurements. Outages have to be avoided because they unbalance the environment such that none of the performance characteristics can be expected to be consistent with non-outage periods. You may be tempted to compare outage periods but this is no guarantee of consistency. How do you know the outage #1 is attributed to the same root cause as outage #2?

An alternate approach to an audit via instrumentation technology, which gives you the deepest understanding of performance and component relationships, is to employ real-transaction monitoring technology. This moves the audit to more of a survey exercise but it will be very useful to help you document the performance issues and get a solid list of candidate applications to prioritize for an audit. It would also allow you to get a QA environment prepared, setting the stage for a reliable audit.

Whatever route you take to initiate the audit, the primary focus will be on the key business transactions. The better this list of transactions is identified, the more accurate the audit results will be, provided that you have a consistent measure of those transactions, real or simulated. Consistency leads to a reliable audit. Let's take an example application through the audit processes.

Configuration Baseline

During an audit, you will need to make a number of decisions quickly in order to maximize the value of the effort while accommodating the hard realities. Even if you carefully scope the project and set expectations as to the quality of load generation needed, you might still end up in a sub-optimal situation. For example, you may find that the load has poor reproducibility and that the app is unstable. Your host still expects you to work magic. How do you evaluate and document the stability of an agent configuration with a sub-optimal app and tools?

Project Scope

First, you will evaluate the APM configuration baseline and try to determine an acceptable APM agent configuration. This is a real-world audit exercise and with an application that is known to be unstable. The goal is to confirm if a specialty GC tool can be used in this environment. This GC tool has a couple of features that can dramatically increase overhead. Exactly how much, no one can hope to know without a direct evaluation. Your first job is to show if a suitable configuration can be validated as safe to use. Your second job is to determine if it can provide useful visibility and help you understand the nature of the instability.

The GC tool has both a minimum and full configuration option. The full option will generate detailed stack traces, which will be very useful for identifying the components contributing to any memory management problems. But this full configuration is known to have much higher overhead than the minimum configuration. The minimum configuration will be called "GC" and the full configuration will be known as "GC+ST." The "ST" is for "stack traces."

The basic agent configuration will be known as "BASE." The agent also has an alternate configuration for monitoring SLQ statements called "BASE+SQL."

Test Plan

There will be three configurations to evaluate in order to assess suitability: BASE, BASE+GC+SQL, and BASE+GC+ST+SQL[8].

---

[8] It would be desirable to test the SQL configuration on its own (BASE+SQL) but this example application was not functioning for most of the time that the test environment was available. When it finally started working, there simply wasn't much time left for testing. This is the reality of this particular example.

The load testing automation is limited, so you will have a suboptimal profile consisting of starting off with 10 users and then a ramp of an additional user every minute, for a total of 30 minutes and 40 users. Ideally (as described in Chapter 11), you would like a ramp from 1 to 40 users over a 5 minute period, followed by 20 minutes of steady-state behavior, and then a ramp back down to 1 user. This gives a total test time of 20 minutes per configuration and the possibility of finishing testing in as little as two hours. With the suboptimal profile, you will need four hours for a minimal set of testing.

Analysis of Results

Once the test runs are complete, you will then review the results and assess the impact on resource utilization during each test. Much of this is subjective, unless you have an outright failure of the application, which would suggest that the monitoring configuration (one or more) was incompatible.

Whenever you are working with an unstable or problematic application, you first want to assess if the introduction of an APM technology will be more than the application can support in its fragile state. Any measurement of the application is going to change its behavior in subtle ways. Whether or not these differences are significant is subjective. In general, if the application can still function, you may say that it is *compatible* with the APM technology. If there is a noticable difference in the resource utilization characteristics, less than 5%, you can say that the APM technology is *suitable* for production. If it is greater than 5%, you may recommend that it be *limited* to pre-production use (not production).

The *resource characteristics* include the following:

- Memory utilization
- CPU utilization
- I/O utilization/throughput
- Response times of key components

You will discuss how the load testing impacts each of resource characteristics in the upcoming sections.

Memory Utilization

You know that using the GC monitoring configuration will increase the memory needed by the application. To figure out how much, you perform one run with the basic monitoring alone, followed by a run with the BASE + GC + SQL. Figure 13-2 summarizes the difference in memory, which can be estimated from the graph to be 110MB. Considering the total memory for the base configuration was about 375MB, this represents a 30% increase in memory consumption, and well within the available memory.

Where this gets ugly is that the second run actually failed. Each of the runs in Figure 13-2 is indicated with a number (1-6). I will use this scheme throughout this section. The third run seems to do a little better but the configuration changed again. The fourth run failed more severely. The fifth run was pretty good. The sixth run was deemed completely successful despite that fact that runs 2 and 6, having the same configuration, look quite different. The application team was actually tuning the configuration on the fly, with each run representing both a new appserver configuration as well as a monitoring configuration.

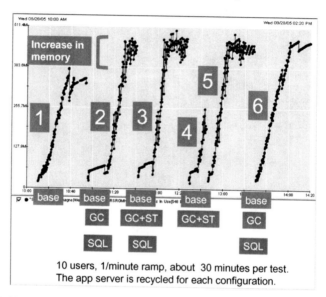

Figure 13-2. Memory profile

Kudos to the application team for tuning the configuration after four suspect tests and two outright failures. Given that the application was otherwise running as expected, you have not run out of memory, and the application is still functioning, you can conclude that the memory utilization of the alternate configurations is acceptable and you can continue your analysis to see what other effects the various configurations exhibit.

CPU Utilization

With the additional memory utilization determined, the next resource to review is the CPU utilization (as summarized in Figure 13-3). I don't normally rely on CPU metrics, but in this case they were able to confirm that despite the increase in memory utilization, the overall CPU consumption when comparing tests 1 and 6 increases only by a few percent. The additional witness lines on Figure 13-3 are there to emphasize that runs 1 and 6 have some differences. Their differences are not terribly significant compared with those of the ST configurations, so you can conclude that the GC+SQL configuration is acceptable in terms of CPU consumption. The configurations with the addition of stack traces (GC+ST) about doubled the CPU consumption. This was deemed excessive and the alternate configurations were deemed unsuitable.

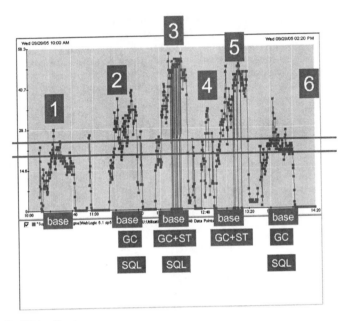

Figure 13-3. CPU utilization

I/O Throughput

The rates of data into and out of a computing system are *I/O[9] rates* or *I/O* for short. You will focus on disk and network I/O because each application has a *signature* or *pattern of usage* that is easily measured. Any performance impact on the application, created by the APM configuration, will be readily apparent with a reproducible load test, comparing runs with and without an APM configuration.

To evaluate the overall throughput of data through the application, you looked at the number of bytes traversing various ports. When ports are a construct of the operating system, they may be considered virtual. This is to distinguish them from the physical ports that allow a computing system to interface with the outside world (serial ports, keyboard ports, etc.) The GC+ST configuration is effectively a logging mechanism writing vast quantities to disk, or *disk I/O*. The SQL monitoring also will be impacted by the number of database calls, especially if the SQL activities are very simple transactions. Because the database is remote to this application, this becomes *network I/O*. Your visibility into I/O, however, does not make any distinction between disk and network I/O.

Figure 13-4 summarizes the throughput (higher numbers are better). What this figure shows is that there is contention for I/O between SQL and stack traces. The figure has two sets of comparison lines. The lower pair shows the contention for

---

[9] Wikipedia, "I/O," http://en.wikipedia.org/wiki/I/O

I/O when stack traces are employed in runs 3 and 5. The I/O activity is generally lower and more erratic than with runs 1 and 6. What is more surprising is that the throughput is best in run 6, despite it having a heavier monitoring configuration.

This outcome is really more evidence of the successful app server configuration tuning that was going on in parallel. However, the stack trace feature is not acceptable for the second time.

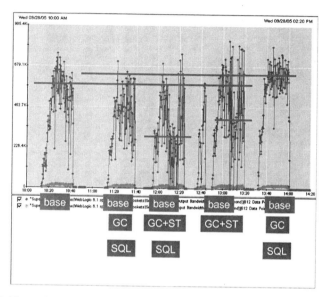

Figure 13-4. Throughput

I/O Contention

The third and final strike against the GC+ST configuration is found in Figure 13-5 by looking at the SQL response. First, you can see that there are some gaps in the test results where the SQL configuration was not deployed. Without that SQL visibility, there are no metrics to report.

In those tests where the SQL configuration was deployed, you find mostly uninteresting response times, with the exception of the GC+ST+SQL configuration where the SQL response time is degraded enormously. Without any changes in the transaction mix or the database resource, the only conclusion is that there is contention for I/O. There is plenty of memory, plenty of CPU, and a bottleneck when it comes to high disk I/O.

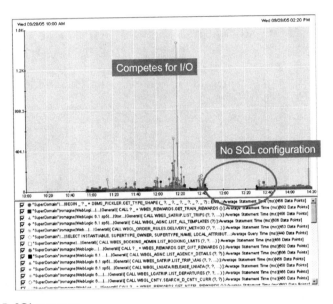

Figure 13-5. SQL response

Conclusions

APM visibility offers some powerful insights. This example, at the extremes of practicality with an unstable application and poor load generation, barely achieves a single test for each agent configuration variant—and yet you are able to have enough confidence in the result that the application team can plan ahead and with more visibility than they had achieved in the weeks before. It is not that this application team was stubborn or aloof. They simply needed the visibility so that they could get the project back on track.

This is not the ideal way to use APM technology. It is not reproducible—this was a one-time effort. It depended on experienced APM practitioners. It depended on some heroic efforts behind the scenes to bring the application under control. These situations are what a nascent APM system gets brought into. You might be the hero but you will more likely be the goat. These are situations to avoid until you have some APM experience.

This project was in deep trouble and turned completely around in just a few days—and four hours of testing. None of it could happen without this small amount of visibility. Once the APM configuration was validated, they could test independently, understand the performance impacts, recode and retest, and rapidly converge on a stable application. A couple of months later, a stable app was ready and the audit resumed with a new level of cooperation. The load generation was fixed. The testing time was increased. You were able to collect the application and performance baselines and define a basic set of testing processes. The app was ready and no one would doubt it.

HealthCheck

The configuration baseline exercise in the previous section is an example of information that can be a distraction for stakeholders. It is very helpful for the development and application owners who need to make adjustments to get the application stable, but once this exercise is complete, the detailed findings are subordinate to the conclusion: you can achieve good visibility with minimal impact to the overall performance of the application. That is all that the configuration baseline needs to deliver.

The ongoing performance information introduced in Chapter 12 is what you need to share. You can add other categories of metrics, like CPU and GC, and you can add more examples, such as increasing from the top 5 or 10 to the top 20 or 50 components in a metric category. But these will begin to get so numerous as to be confusing.

For the audit, you really need to distill all this information down to a simple pass/fail. So you can extend the HealthCheck report with a page that simply summarizes the behavior of all of the significant component categories, as in Figure 13-6. This presents both the response time mean as well as the total invocations for each type of component.

Baseline - Component Response

Component Response Time (overview)

Resource:Metric	Mean	Min	Max	MMin	MMax	Count
EJB|Messagge-driven:Average Method Invocation Time (ms)	1,284	9	106,942	0	607,856	12,775
EJB|Session:Average Method Invocation Time (ms)	1,851	1	279,491	0	1,369,006	9,693
JDBC:Average Query Time (ms)	950	0	37,218	0	83,313	28,214
JDBC:Average Update Time (ms)	79	0	13,093	0	200,896	4,221
JMS|Message Consumer:Average Method Invocation Time (ms)	57,109	567	143,981	2	716,873	66,412
JMS|Message Listener:Average Method Invocation Time (ms)	11,828	0	168,678	0	1,181,781	5,476
JMS|Queue Sender:Average Method Invocation Time (ms)	513	0	21,018	0	278,362	3,604
JMS|Topic Publisher:Average Method Invocation Time (ms)	36	1	32	0	179	36
JTA:Average Method Invocation Time (ms)	203	0	29,949	0	485,008	14,979
Servlets :Average Response Time (ms)	8,884	352	13,232	0	54,935	13

Start: 5/9/06 9:00 AM	End: 5/17/06 2:00 PM

Metric Grouping: Component Response Time (ms)
Agents: ftbhvt01\|WebLogic\|wftf_srv_01

Figure 13-6. Minimum HealthCheck report

I've separated out this particular report for the audit as it may not be possible using the standard capabilities of your APM tool to summarize these quantities automatically, as you would want during the baseline process. If that's the case, this summary can still be achieved but you will need to print the list of components into a spreadsheet for each category, and do the summary and averaging there. This type of analysis can really eliminate the need to present the more detailed baseline information, which can be a distraction.

For example, for the application in Figure 13-6, the following conclusions are evident. The first analysis is to look at the mean values, where you see that the EJB times are a little long and that the SQL times are reasonable. The JMS times seem excessive, but this is a characteristic of a message listener where the time spent "listening" is actually part of the response time—even if nothing is being done. The JMS send is a little long at 513 msec. The JMS topic publisher is quite good at 36 msec. The Servlet is a bit of a concern at 8.8 seconds.

Now if this last discussion of appropriate values for various metrics left you a little lost, you have crossed the thin line between the mechanical process of executing and collecting the details of the audit and the deeper knowledge about what the normal values should be. This is a gap that many stakeholders have; bridging this gap will take some time and effort. There really are no hard and non-subjective values for metrics. The value depends on the type of component and application. This also reveals the beauty of the baseline process on which the audit is based. With baselines, you are always focused on what has changed—this is all you really need to communicate among our stakeholders. Ultimately, someone has to decide if the change that you detected was a help or a hindrance towards optimizing performance.

If you are familiar with these components and how they work, you already know what reasonable response times should be like. I will cover the normal range for many of these components in Chapter 14 when you learn *triage with single metrics*.

The second pass of analysis is to consider the Max value. APM agents are reporting metrics at approximately one minute intervals, which allows for a high resolution plot of the different behaviors that a component experiences. Within this *agent reporting interval* are a number of real-time measurements. The total number of measurements is the *count* or *invocations*. The *mean* is calculated over all of the measurements in the interval. And the *max* and *min* are the largest and smallest values of the measurements in that interval. My experience with the relationship of the max to the mean values results is a simple *rule of thumb*[10]: if the max is ten times or more than the mean, then this metric is unsuitable for setting a threshold. Conversely, if the max is appreciably less than 10 times the mean, it is a good candidate for a threshold. I call this the *rule of 10*.

Alerting and thresholds are directly connected. If you set the wrong threshold, you will either fail to alert or you will alert too frequently. Both situations will cause the operations team to lose confidence in the APM initiative. The quickest way to excessive alerting is to select a component that has too much variation. Of course, there are other settings available to help tune the trigger before an alert. When

---

[10] Wikipedia, "Rule of thumb," http://en.wikipedia.org/wiki/Rule_of_thumb

you have no other metrics, then you will need to resort to those tunings. Until then, find one that does not violate the *rule of ten.*

Reviewing the max values and applying the *rule of ten*, you find that there are only a few candidates for alert thresholds: JMS Message Consumer, JMS Topic Publisher, and Servlets. Don't feel bad! Feel happy. If you picked the JDBC or EJB, you could very well sink the APM initiative. Here we don't play favorites or go with our gut instinct[11].

The third pass of analysis is to consider the MMax value. Every agent reporting interval has a max value, so every report duration between the start and end times for the report has a maximum of all max values for that duration called the *maxmax*. I have a similar rule of thumb called the *rule of hundred* that says if the *maxmax* is 100 times greater than the *mean*, it will be a poor candidate for an SLA. SLAs (Service Level Agreements)[12] are a more important threshold because when they're crossed, you will likely have to pay a monetary fine. The trend in IT is to move more towards SLAs for management goals. But when a thresholded metric violates the *rule of hundred*, you have a strong chance of losing money on the SLA.

In this example, EJBs, JDBC-update, and JTA will likely break your SLAs. You are left with the JMS metrics as the best candidates but these would be poor choices on which to base an SLA. The front-end component, the servlet, would be the better candidate for an SLA, if it were working at an acceptable level.

After the mechanics of executing test plans and collecting baselines, which is 90% of the audit work, you need to tie all of your findings together. You will summarize the accuracy of the load generation and the suitability of the test plan in helping you define the three baselines: configuration, application, and performance. You will note the key metrics and other interesting characteristics of the application in the HealthCheck report. You will then make your subjective analysis in the three passes outlined:

1. Are the major categories of metrics operating within normal values for this type of application and test plan?
2. Have you identified suitable candidate metrics for thresholds following the rule of 10 or was this not possible?
3. Have you identified suitable candidate metrics for managing an SLA following the rule of 100 or was this not possible?

With these three analysis steps (passes), you then determine what portion of metrics would meet the criteria in three levels: Most, Few, and None. It is then possible to construct a type of lookup table to help you select an appropriate adjective for your audit conclusion (see Figure 13-7).

---

[11] Wikipedia, "extrasensory perception," http://en.wikipedia.org/wiki/Extrasensory_perception

[12] Wikipedia, "service level agreement," http://en.wikipedia.org/wiki/Service_level_agreement

Analysis Step	Most Metrics Meeting Criteria	Few Metrics Meeting Criteria	No Metrics Meeting Criteria
Average value Is the app performance consistent with similar apps?	False •Servlet is a concern •EJBs a slight concern	**True** •JMS Publisher – quite good •SQL is reasonable	False
Max value – rule of 10 Are the thresholds consistent?	False •JDBC unacceptable •EJB unacceptable	**True**	False
MaxMax value – rule of 100 Is the performance predictable?	False •EJBs •JDBC-update unacceptable •JTA unacceptable	False •Servlet would be a candidate once performance is improved	**True**
Subjective Conclusion Is production deployment advised?	0/3–Suspect 1/3–Weak 2/3–Stable 3/3–Solid	0/3–Problematic 1/3–Significant Risk 2/3–Moderate risk 3/3–Low risk	0/3–Inconclusive 1/3–Tuning likely 2/3 –Tuning needed 3/3–Unacceptable

Figure 13-7. Subjective conclusion matrix for audit

To employ the matrix, determine which of the categories in Most, Few, and None best applies to the findings for each analysis step. Each step can only result in one of the categories being true. The last row is the subjective conclusion. Simply select the term that accounts for the number of true conclusions in each column. For the current example, this results in *Suspect, Moderate risk, Tuning likely*.

Thus, your conclusion for this application is that it would be at low-to-moderate risk for the production environment. It is going to cause some problems and you should really look to improve the performance of the Servlets, JDBC, EJBs, and JTA components.

Dashboard and Alerts

The goal for the audit efforts are to identify metrics that best indicate availability, performance, and capacity, and to build those collections. The next step is to apply thresholds against those collections and incorporate them into dashboards. This avoids the navigation and lagging interpretation of the metrics by encapsulating into both the threshold and collection all of the knowledge about which metrics are useful and what values are acceptable.

This brings you right back to that uncomfortable realization that you may not know the appropriate threshold value for a given metric or collection. And again, you would be correct. Assigning thresholds requires good evidence and attention to detail. If you do it wrong, you will annoy a great many stakeholders with meaningless alerts. It's not really your fault. The problem is your stakeholder's expectations. You may not have added a sufficient simulation resulting from your test plan, and yet your stakeholders are expecting to see dashboards and reports and all manner of monitoring conveniences. You really will not know the correct thresholds until you get operational experience—until you get to production.

Fortunately, the audit process will bring about much of what you need for reliable thresholding. And with better data, you will get 100% of your stakeholders requirements addressed (assuming that those are reasonable). You need to deliver some dashboards. You need time to validate your techniques. To be successful, you just need to limit the scope of that initial delivery to something that you can be very sure of while minimizing the impact of any poor threshold settings. The sure path is to focus on availability metrics for this initial release of functionality.

To show how all these pieces come together, let's work through an example for availability. Figure 13-8 shows the metric count for a production application over three days. The total number of metrics varies from 4000 to 5300. There is a startup period where the number of metrics starts low and then grows quickly. If there were any other restarts, the process would repeat.

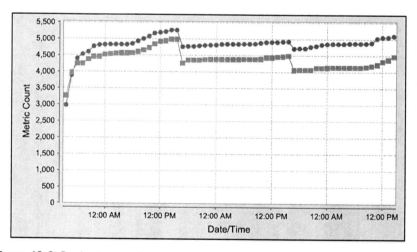

Figure 13-8. Production metric count

That the metric count varies a bit should not be a surprise. Byte code instrumentation is dynamic and only the code that is actually executing will contribute to the number of metrics. If different mixes of transactions are experienced, you will see different metrics being generated. JMX and logging instrumentation tends to be more static in quantities of metrics generated.

So how does the number of metrics represent availability? Anything below 3000 metrics suggests that there is problem for this application.

Note that the resolution of Figure 13-8 is a little low due to the three day reporting interval. Also, you don't have a lot of detail about what contributed to that first data point at 3000. At this resolution, every point represents 24 minutes of data. Let's look instead at Figure 13-9, which shows a two hour period and higher resolution. Here you can see the detail of the startup of the application. I've added some lines to indicate where the thresholds are set and I've labeled the regions to reflect the alert state that would be indicated.

What is interesting here is that you can effectively capture the startup success of the application server prior to that actual startup of the application.

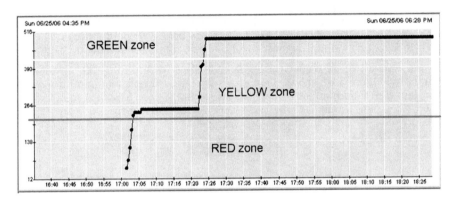

Figure 13-9. Availability thresholds for number of metrics

Typically, availability monitoring only indicates the state of the platform from the perspective of the operating system. If the platform is functioning, the platform is assumed to be available. Sometimes this is extended to include specific monitoring of the application server process that is running on top of the operating system. If the process is absent, it means the application server—and the application it hosts—are not available.

With an APM agent, you can measure both the operating system and application server availability, provided that the application server actually started. And you can further measure the start of the application and indicate if it was actually exercised, which would suggest that the application is now fully functional. Of course, if the application is receiving traffic, you would look to the performance and capacity thresholds to indicate if the application were truly available. And if you have APM synthetics available, you can certainly employ that technology to achieve the same thing. The advantage with this metric count approach is that it is reporting continuously—you do not have to wait until the APM synthetics start firing.

I've included a portion of a high-level dashboard that reflects the progress of the application, from initial startup to indications of performance and capacity, in Figure 13-9. This is the minimum that you will prepare as part of the application audit as it can only be completed if the audit was successful. Each of the indication lamps is, in effect, a validation point for your audit investigation.

The Connectivity lamp, which represents an agent that has managed to start up correctly and connects to the metrics storage server, is pretty easy to establish. If there is no agent, this value will be dark or red, depending on the APM solution. If it's yellow, the platform and agent are suspect and perhaps the app server has not started correctly. This will be confirmed by the Availability lamp, to be covered shortly. If it is green, this represents the good connectivity among the platform, agent, and metrics storage component.

The Availability lamp represents the progress of the application server becoming active, reflected in the metric count for the agent, following thresholds defined in the graph above the dashboard. This is also fairly easy to do as they will be a metric that contains the current total. Deciding where to set the thresholds is the only effort because every application will generate a different number of metrics at the initial, middle, and ready stages of its startup.

The remaining Performance and Capacity lamps will take a bit more work. Here you need the baseline process to help you identify the top 10 components that have the highest response time and the top 10 components with the highest invocations. From these, you will select the best representatives, assign them to a metric collection, and then assign a threshold to that collection, following the same technique as you did for the Availability lamp.

For most load simulation systems, this is going to be very subjective. You may know that your QA environment is only a fraction of production. You may also know that you are not testing a representative sample of your actual production use cases. So how do you validate that the thresholds set for performance and capacity are accurate? You can't. You can make a recommendation and set some initial thresholds, but do not under any circumstances hook those thresholds into the alerting mechanism. You might get lucky but you will more likely end up sending excessive and invalid alerts. This will compromise your APM initiative. The connectivity and availability thresholds are the only thing that you can validate while in the limited environment. Initially, these are all you can reliably alert on. Validating the performance and capacity thresholds is something that can only occur in the production environment. This is what the operational period of the phased deployment specifically accommodates. Get a minimal dashboard into production, operate for a couple of weeks, validate the thresholds for performance and capacity alerting, and deploy the full dashboard in the next phase.

Managing Alerts

One of the bigger blows to the acceptance of an APM initiative is when spurious alerts are generated—alerts that suggest a problem when in fact there is no problem. When this happens, it's very hard to have folks trust the alerting ever again. It happens because everyone expects alerts to come from APM monitoring, even as the APM team may not yet have sufficient experience to define the alerts correctly. The solution is simple: only propagate the alerts that you can trust and put all other alerts on a separate alert channel until they are validated.

This alternate channel is simply to use e-mail among the APM team. If you get too much e-mail, you are sending too many alerts! It is really very effective. Even if your APM solution does not support it directly, you can easily subvert the alerting mechanism to redirect the APM alerts.

The Connectivity and Availability thresholds will be the most reliable part of the configuration since the number of metrics will not usually change dramatically in the production environment. And this has the benefit of giving operations an alert that they can respond to with their normal procedures. If there is an unexpected increase in metrics, this will not usually affect the Availability threshold. If a threshold at 200 metrics indicates that the application is functioning, getting 2000 metrics has no affect on that result.

There are two major reasons why the number of metrics can change dramatically in production. The first, promoting an inappropriate APM configuration, is frequently encountered because no one checks if the configuration is actually safe. You can fix that with appropriate processes. The second has to do with the differences between the testing environment and production. Very often the database and test plan used is simply not as rich as what is encountered in production. You may test five representative transactions but encounter 20,000 different transactions in production. Each unique select statement will generate a number of metrics, so the total count gets significant quickly. It is not that too many metrics are a problem. It's just destined to become a bad habit and one that wastes APM capacity.

The Performance and Capacity alerts are sent initially only to the application team, with the realization that the thresholds are yet to be validated. It will take a few days to a few weeks to complete the validation. But the APM monitoring will be delivering Availability alerts all during this period when encountered, so the operations team will begin to see that APM alerts will correlate with their existing availability monitoring tools.

As you found earlier, this hooks in nicely with the phased deployment model in the Implementation section. You will put out a default agent configuration with the minimal alerting, as discussed here. After a couple weeks of operational experience, you will revisit the alert thresholds and adjust them to better fit your production reality. Even a weak QA system can put out a successful initial monitoring configuration when you allow for a validation step, once the dashboards and alerts reach the production environment.

Getting Production Baselines

This is probably the most difficult path for defining baselines, as you do not even have an initial set of thresholds from any QA testing. As seen in Figure 13-6, the production day can have quite a bit of variation. Figure 13-10 shows a production week, this time with an application that is degrading daily.

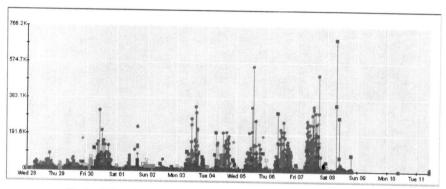

Typical::Servlets: 0.5 to 5 secs, JSPs:1-3 secs, EJBs:0.5-3 secs

Figure 13-10. Production response times for one week (very poor, compared with typical results)

As the week progresses, response times begin to erode. The weekend is less trouble but the new week is showing a slowly increasing level of disaster. I've noted the generally acceptable response times for various components below the graph. It appears that even a good production day will find the average response times 20 times greater than acceptable. The worse case time are hitting 500 seconds—an incredibly poor response time. That the problem is getting worse is evident. That the problem was allowed to go to production with 30-40 second response times is the bigger issue.

It's not that you can't collect baselines from production; it's simply that it takes a long time to get consistent results. What the QA process gives us is an opportunity to control the load and thus work exclusively with consistent load generation. What takes a couple hours in the QA environment is going to take days to weeks in the production environment.

Figure 13-11 shows an example of a production baseline opportunity and some of the compromises. You're looking at a JDBC-Invocations metric, which is frequently a good candidate to represent the capacity of the application. You have managed to find four days of consistent invocations. Note that the earlier period actually has much higher invocations. The fourth day of the selected area of the graph is a weak candidate, so the prior three days would be the best. At a higher resolution display, even those three days might not be attractive. This is the difficulty of determining the production baseline.

The choice of the JDBC-Invocations metric merits a little more discussion. As outlined in Chapter 12, searching for high invocation metrics and then sorting them, largest to smallest, is always the correct approach. It simply doesn't assume anything about the app, and keeps you focused on the significant performers. All you have done here is select the more consistent metric from those top 10 or 20 candidates. Historically, a JDBC metric wins the honor of representing capacity, but that will not always be the case. The first consistent metric is always the correct choice, even if it is not a JDBC-related metric. It simply reflects that you don't have a pure database application.

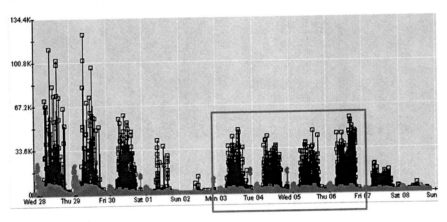

Figure 13-11. Consistent production period suitable for baseline

Back to Figure 13-10, how do you get consistent results during an audit for this type of performance degradation? You don't. There is going to be nothing consistent on the platform, save for unacceptable response times. There is no normal period on which to form a baseline. Instead, you need to reduce the scope of the audit to those activities that are going to help with bringing performance under control. Then you can address the manageability of the application.

Working to define alert thresholds is the first activity to be skipped and so the performance baseline is eliminated. Likewise, the configuration baseline, with respect to the agent configuration, is unnecessary at this time, provided that the current configuration is safe—no excessive invocations or large metric counts. This leaves the application baseline and the focus on the transactional perspective. Simply find the most active transaction type and get all attention focused on it in order to correct and optimize its performance.

APM monitoring at this stage will probably not lead you to the exact component causing the problem. It will help you confirm the direction of changes with the application server configuration and code changes. And it should help identify what is different, day to day, in the mix of transactions that are being experienced. Until the application is stabilized, you don't have much chance of getting a consistent baseline upon which to build the remainder of the monitoring configuration.

Process

Conducting an audit consists of the scope call and then the execution. For the scope call, you want to ensure that you have a suitable application and that there is some facility for load generation. You need to reliably exercise the application in order to complete the audit. Auditing in production is possible and it takes a lot of time to get consistent results on which to make your analysis. Do not try a production audit until you have completed a few audits pre-production.

Scope

These are the talking points for the conversation with your sponsor. You need to set their expectations as to what you can do, how long it will take, what potential blockers may occur, and what the report will look like.

- A single application is best

    - You get better control over interactions (load and response).
    - The application should be stable but you should be prepared for the worst.

- Must have some load generation capability

    - Manual exercise
        - This is the least preferable but you will be able to get some usable findings.
    - Batch file
    - Load Generator
    - Ability to load to failure
        - You can skip this but you will not be able to forecast capacity otherwise.

- Duration

    - 2 to 5 days, depending on availability of load generation
        - Actual work: 4 to 10 hours

- Wrap-up Presentation and HealthCheck Report

    - What was done
        - Agent configuration
        - Visibility achieved
        - Type of load generation and accuracy
        - Initial dashboard
        - Baseline report template
        - HealthCheck report template
    - Findings
        - Key components
        - Suggested thresholds and alerts
        - Concerns and recommendations

Necessities

During the scope call you need to validate the environment. The details will vary depending on the capabilities of your APM solution.

- JVM or CLR to instrument
    - If this isn't present, consider using the real-transaction monitoring APM component and surveying the key applications and transactions.
- APM database (metrics storage)
    - No firewall or other connectivity issues
    - At least 30k metrics (or 15%) headroom on metrics storage server
- Load Simulation
    - One to three tests to confirm *configuration baseline* for APM agent
        - You can identify default configurations for common environments.
    - Two to three tests to confirm visibility for the *application baseline*
    - Three tests to confirm *performance baseline*
        - One point does not make a trend
        - Thresholds need validation under load

Load Generation

To simulate exercising the application consistently, you need to employ load generation technology. Chapter 11 covers this in detail. To summarize, you need a 5 minute ramp-up, 10 minutes at steady-state, and 5 minute ramp-down. If possible, exercise each use case (set of transactions) separately but whatever combination of use cases comprises a realistic test is always acceptable. All of your analysis will be focused on the 10 minute steady-state intervals of each test.

Production-Only Situation

- You need at least three samples, preferably more, of production operation *without* outages.
- If complete days are not possible, make sure you compare the same daily intervals.
- Be sure you know and record all of the events that occur during production operations.
    - JVM parameter changes
    - Restarts
    - Timestamp of app slowdowns
    - Timestamp of user complaints/issues

- External resource issues
  - Database CPU utilization
  - Network availability
- When resources became unavailable and when they were restored.

Once peak processing periods are identified, collect transaction stacks 20 to 30 minutes prior to peak load and at peak load in order to catch rogue transactions.

Transaction Definition

Ideally, the definition of the critical use cases, which are implemented as one or more transactions, would come from the test plan. If these definitions are inadequate, it's unlikely that the simulated load will have much accuracy when compared with the production experience, and the audit should not be used to forecast scalability or suitability. You can still use the audit process to confirm stability for the transactions that you are able to exercise and leave the rest to hope and luck. (I don't mean that seriously but more to set your expectations.)

If load simulation is not available, it will be more useful to survey transactions, either by capturing real-transactions or by having the application owners define a proper test plan by identifying what they expect to test. An audit is not a replacement for a repeatable testing process.

Acceptance Criteria

As the QA testing and application owners mature their processes, a critical interface or checkpoint forms between pre-production and production. To cross between environments your application should exhibit minimum acceptance criteria. The variety of these criteria increases and becomes less negotiable as the management of the application life cycle matures.

1. Runs continuously for at least two hours under moderate load.
2. Presents evidence of correct memory management.
3. Does not consume more than 30% CPU at any time during the two hours test.
4. No more than five application stalls per hour, after the application has been started.
5. No component response time greater than 10 seconds measured 30 minutes after the application was started.
6. No errors message detected 30 minutes after the application was started.

Reporting

- Overview presentation

  - Overall configuration employed
  - Monitoring Configuration used
  - Load Profiles employed and what they looked like

- Findings

  - Startup characteristics
  - Stability
  - Is the application server configuration optimal?
  - Code coverage
  - Recommendations

- HealthCheck Report

  - Metric count, CPU, and memory profiles
  - Response times
    - General, front-end, back-end
  - Invocations
    - General, front-end, back-end
  - Stalls
  - Errors
  - Other metrics of interest
    - Messaging, SQL transactions, web services, etc.

- Visibility—sample transactions via screenshot
- Summary of thresholds defined, alerts, and dashboards

  - Focus first on APC (availability, performance, capacity) and add additional dashboards as time allows.

Competency

For your application, undertake the audit and collect the following baseline:

- Configuration Baseline

  - What alternate configurations are appropriate?
  - What is the impact on APM database capacity?

- Application Baseline

  - What are the most active components?
  - What components take the most time?
  - Are additional tracing or extension agent configurations needed?
  - Is sufficient visibility achieved?

- Performance Baseline

  - Are there stability and/or performance issues
  - Startup characteristics
  - What is the evidence?
  - What are the participating components?
  - What are the KPIs and appropriate thresholds?
  - Can you forecast the potential capacity of the app?

Summary

The audit is the fundamental process for APM. It brings together all of the basic skills in installing that agent, navigating the workstation, identifying components of interest, assembling metric collections, assigning thresholds, defining dashboards and reports. And in this assembly of techniques, it allows you to show value in using the tool. Right now, this is limited to deciding if the application is acceptable or problematic, but along with this exercise you also end up with a fully validated production monitoring configuration. If you cannot deliver a consistent audit, you have to admit that you really don't know how to use the APM tool to its fullest potential. When you can deliver a consistent audit, you have established a foundation on which your APM discipline can continue to improve.

Triage with Single Metrics

A single tree doesn't make a forest.

—Chris Bradford

The ability to triage is what almost everyone believes will be introduced or enhanced when they undertake an APM initiative. If you dig for a bit more detail, you will also find that IT folks tend to treat triage and root-cause analysis as the same thing. They are not. While they both depend on processes to augment the various tools employed, *triage* is what you do to eliminate suspects during an incident, and *root-cause analysis* is what you do to understand how the incident occurred—after triage has confirmed your suspect. In reality, there are four levels of triage capability that an organization will achieve as APM becomes established. You need to understand their goals and limitations so that you can manage the expectations of your stakeholders and keep your APM imitative on track.

Triage is the foundation for any significant IT initiative that depends on quantitative data, such as root-cause analysis, service-level management, monitoring integration, and governance. Each of these is an example of a higher-order use of the visibility that supports effective triage. If you don't have a plan to get sufficient data to support triage, it is unlikely that you will be successful in getting data to support these other higher-order initiatives. In this sense, triage capabilities become a gateway to these higher-order initiatives.

As discussed in Chapter 9, there are a number of tenets for triage, summarized here:

- How do you know that what you see is not actually normal?
- You are not here to find problems; you are here to get visibility into the performance characteristics of the application.

- If you want to quickly find a problem, look first in the code that *was not* tested.

There are some basic skills that you need to establish before advertising that you are ready to triage. The first is an accurate scope. You cannot hope for success if you cannot control the situation you are being drawn into. The second is the rapid deployment of your monitoring technology. There is little advantage to doing triage when you cannot even trust your own installation. The third is collecting and reporting on baselines. If you cannot describe a normal application, you will have little success trying to describe an abnormal one.

Triage is also an Essential Service Capability, as discussed in Chapter 9, and so a critical part of your Service Catalog, if you are following that organizational model. Because you know that triage is difficult to do well, you need to allow for an orderly development of skills and you will find the justification for this approach as the chapter unfolds. My strategy in developing a triage practice is to focus on the fundamentals and defer the responsibility of actually identifying the source of a problem. Instead, this strategy calls for helping to prepare what the triage experts will want to look at in order to make the best use of their time; in other words, to do 95% of the job without the attention that comes with delivering the conclusion. To pull this off, you need to understand what the triage expert is trying to do. You need to fully understand the job of the triage expert and then assume the responsibility for the role.

The Program

Chapters 14-17 of this book present the complete realization of a triage system. There are four levels of triage that I mentor. Each level builds on the prior.

1. Chapter 14: Triage with Single Metrics covers how to interpret the response times, memory patterns, invocation profiles, etc. that help you understand when something is suspect.
   a. Delivering an Application Audit is how you assess competency at this level

2. Chapter 15: Triage with Baselines shows how to utilize QA and production baselines or application signatures to identify and triage operational performance problems.
   a. Delivering a performance optimization is how you assess competency at this level, and it involves both QA and production.

3. Chapter 16: Triage with Trends covers how to prepare for and manage Service Level Agreements (SLA) and root-cause analysis (RCA).
   a. You assess this level of competency with a lifecycle management/visibility audit.
   b. You also look at the integration of other data sources to enhance your overall visibility.

4. Chapter 17: Firefighting explains how to use monitoring data to manage and resolve critical IT incidents.

    a. You assess this level of competency with an audit of the firefighting practice and at least three "live" incidents.

Some folks prefer a more narrow definition of triage that excludes trending and firefighting, both of which I find are utterly dependent on effective and reliable triage. Trending encompasses a broader scope than a single application or transaction, but if you do not have basic visibility, you cannot trend effectively. You simply don't have the necessary information to undertake analysis in support of SLA definition and RCA. Trending is about integration and correlation, as you will see in Chapter 16.

Likewise, firefighting is sometimes considered separately from triage even though it is also completely dependent on the triage findings and capabilities. You are potentially capable of using whatever triage skills you possess for firefighting but conducting a firefight reliably is a skill unto itself, as you will see in Chapter 17. Firefighting is really about managing expectations as to the types of problems you can expect to address, depending on your skills and visibility.

This chapter will be a little long due to many graph examples. The remaining chapters, which all build on the techniques here, will be shorter.

Kick Off Meeting

Motivation

As discussed so far, process maturity is the real gap that keeps organizations from realizing APM. So, the first part of the triage process that you need to understand is what it is not. The outcome of a successful triage exercise is the consensus of where it would be most profitable to look, not what caused the incident. This consensus is achieved by contrasting a normal baseline around the time of the incident and comparing historical information in order to exclude the normal behaviors and focus on the abnormal.

Why Triage is Difficult to Master

The marketplace is a bit to blame for why triage is hard to master. The emphasis is on tools, not processes, and the tools are marketed as "rich in visibility," "quick to deploy," and "easy to use." They may even suggest that they "enable" or "facilitate" root-cause analysis, which is simply not the same as telling you where the problem is and what to fix. The challenge for any monitoring tool vendor is that the information leading to the root cause may simply be outside of that particular technology. That's the situation a triage specialist has to face—understanding the nature of the problem and figuring out if they actually have visibility into it. In other words, you really need to understand your limitations. Let's look first at triage and save a discussion of root-cause for Chapter 16.

Regarding limitations, what I really mean is that triage has to eliminate suspects even when you do not have direct information about those suspects. You will not always have the luxury of a "smoking gun."[1] You will have to use inference to direct efforts onto profitable areas, resulting in something actionable. And that's a risky proposition. You want to avoid, whenever possible, potentially designating a resource or system as a suspect without a solid line of reasoning.

Once you move away from the application server, for which APM tools have incredible visibility (when compared with other monitored systems), you really never have comparable real-time information from any other resource or component. But if you understand what the application is trying to do and its relationships with other resources, then you may successfully *infer* what contribution those resources have and whether that behavior is suspect, even if you are not directly monitoring that resource. This requires a strong background in every type of system, resource, development strategy, application design, etc. The difficulty with triage is having a sufficient background to reliably bridge these gaps in visibility.

Figure 14-1 shows the differences between Availability Monitoring and Application Monitoring. In it, you can see what you are asking of the various stakeholders.

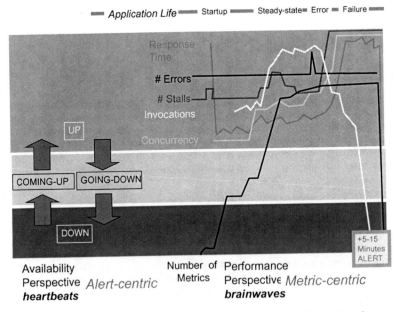

Figure 14-1. What is the practical difference between availability and performance?

---

[1] A type of evidence that is directly associated with a crime. Here, I am associating the *crime* with a performance incident or outage and the *evidence* as the performance metrics directly associated with the incident. http://en.wikipedia.org/wiki/Smoking_gun

APM tools not only provide information on availability and platform performance, they provide details about the relationships of the software components among themselves and their supporting resources. So not only are you asking the triage team to have a deep understanding of how to navigate among the various metrics being collected, but you want them to appreciate what the normal range is, what the inflections may indicate, and ultimately what historical trends among these metrics mean for successful management of the application lifecycle. The real complexity here is not actually the richness of metrics and visibility, it is the variety of ranges and relationships that may exist because, essentially, each and every application you will encounter will behave differently.

For example, let's consider a simple metric like heart rate among a population of disparate applications (people). What is a normal, resting heart rate? For an average adult, it's 60 to 100 beats per minute (bpm); it varies according to developmental age. If you consider Figure 14-2, is a heart rate of 155 normal?

Resting heart rate (normal)	bpm
Newborn infants	100-160
Children 1 to 10 years	70-120
Children over 10 and adults (including seniors)	60-100
Well-trained athletes	40-60

Figure 14-2. Resting heart rates[2]

According to the data, your only choice is to propose that if the subject is a baby, then this is normal, but if the subject isn't a baby, it's suspect. So you'll concede that it is suspect. But what does it mean that it's "suspect?" And keep in mind, this is all the information you have at the moment!

---

[2] Adapted from www.nlm.nih.gov/medlineplus/ency/article/003399.htm

This is what triage teams are expected to answer and this is not what monitoring tools are designed to do. The only way to understand this metric is via experience and training—which follows a process. Continuing the physiological example, if the application is tuned (well-trained) and under heavy exertion, a heart rate of 145 bpm is also normal and expected. If the application is an adult who just experienced a surge in traffic (a walk up a couple flights of stairs), then you would conclude that the adult is not scaling (he is out of shape).

This is what I call *triage with single metrics*. It attempts to assign normal ranges for key metrics and then uses these ranges to exclude a suspect. Thus, if the message queue has a response time of 250 msec, and this is within the normal range, then the message queue is not suspect. This continues until you are left with a manageable pool of suspects (even better, a single suspect). You would then grab all of the available information until you have eliminated all suspects or identified a potential root cause.

In order to do effective triage, you must have background about the application under duress as well as a deep understanding of how various types of applications will fail. Just like a medical doctor, you need to have a patient's history, diagnostic tests, and observations in order to recommend a treatment plan. The challenge is that most organizations simply do not have access to resources with the appropriate level of expertise. These resources are short in supply and expensive to acquire. The best practice approach is to utilize your existing staff and structure, both in how they accumulate experience and how the organization can support their efforts with meaningful history and observations.

The most important piece of history is called a *baseline*. At some point, either in production or pre-production, someone collected metrics on the application when it was performing normally and generated a report of graphs and tables about the key metrics. (For what the key metrics are and how to find them, please look at Chapter 12.) This baseline report is essentially a signature of what the application. It's what most folks long for when have an incident but they lack ready access to historical information. They are trying to compare what they are seeing in real-time with what they remember about the application when it was performing normally. A baseline eliminates the subjective memory and replaces it with a historical snapshot of performance characteristics.

Provided that monitoring is active, you can obtain a baseline of performance data from last week or last month. The subjective part is to have someone decide what is normal. For firefights, I often exploit the findings generated during a pre-sales pilot (which is incidental to installing and exercising the monitoring tool as a demonstration) as a baseline for a production incident. Prior to the engagement, this baseline allows me to quickly identify suspects. Of course, several years of experience helps me to appreciate how far I can trust what the baseline says about performance. Invariably, I am able to triage effectively with data as old as three months.

For a new triage team, you want to improve the odds for success. The easiest way to do this is to have baselines collected during pre-production testing. And this is where the organizational process comes in. Hopefully, someone is doing testing, so you simply need them to enable monitoring and pass judgment on the results ("test was successful"); this will supply all the baselines you could want. But the monitoring has to be enabled. When you're able to collect and exploit normal baselines to assist your triage, it's called *triage with baselines* and it's covered in Chapter 15.

Triage with Single Metrics

You first need to decide how you're going to navigate among the metrics of interest. I will review a number of techniques. The important evolution in capabilities is the ability to organize and identify an arbitrary *collection of metrics*. These collections then form the basis for more consistent views into applications as well as dashboards and reports.

Navigation Among Single Metrics

This is where everyone starts. You hear about a problem, you get an idea of where to find it and you navigate to that metric and evaluate it over the last few minutes or hour. Metrics navigation is often hierarchical, similar to finding a file on your computer. You start at the top and drill down through the hierarchy until you find what you want. When you have the time and date for a specific incident, you want to position a two hour window of 1.5 hours before and 30 minutes after the incident. This lets you appreciate any trending up to the point of the incident and any recovery after the incident.

While this is the intended use of the interface, I find that the navigation capability is more of a distraction. You tend go in the direction of your personal preference or bias. This is not a problem for an experienced user but I find that novice users can easily get distracted and end up without a consistent way to evaluate the incident.

My preference is to use the *Fab Four Views*, which were introduced in Chapter 12. By searching for the loudest metrics (those with the greatest response time or greatest invocations), you are limiting your navigation to those key metrics that are actively contributing to performance. And those key metrics are the ones that will likely be impacted the most when performance degrades.

Organization via Metrics Collections

After you have some experience with a particular application in appreciating which metrics are significant and which contribute little, you can assemble those metrics into a collection. This way, instead of navigating around to find your key metrics, you can instead define and name an arbitrary collection. Whenever you need to view those key metrics, you simply navigate to the appropriate collection.

Again, my preference is to use the *Fab Four Views* to guide me as to which metrics to include in the collection. In general, I am trying to populate at least three collections, those of APC (availability, performance, and capacity). Into these collections I will place the very metrics that I find when I do the initial search. Once these are established, I just navigate to the collection and my key metrics are ready for my consideration. If I don't find something interesting after looking at the collections, then I go back to the search technique and see what new metrics may have stepped into center stage. If a new metric is interesting, I will add it to the appropriate collection.

Presentation via Dashboards

Even the use of metric collections still requires navigation around the APM workstation interface. For some consumers of the APM data, especially casual users, this may still be too much to handle reliably. A graphical representation is one answer, as depicted in Figure 14-3.

This example, what I call the *survey dashboard*, was the cornerstone of my APM practice for many years. I came to APM in much the same fashion as anyone else. I simply have the advantage of using it every day. Although it's a natural progression (from single metrics to collections to dashboards), it's not terribly useful. It still requires interpretation and correlation.

A better example is Figure 14-4 because it simply tells you what part of the architecture is having the problem. With this simplicity comes a lot more work because someone had to figure out appropriate thresholds for all of the devices in the architecture.

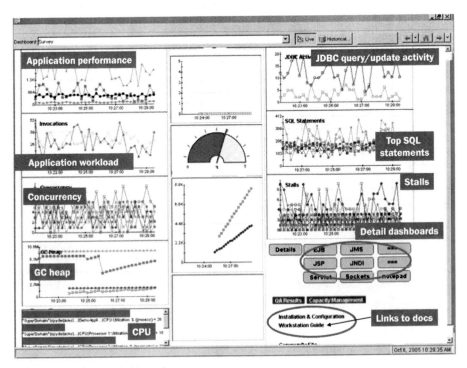

Figure 14-3. Survey dashboard

The navigation concept is still used because it is possible to drill-down through the architecture, probably ending up with a more complicated dashboard, as in Figure 14-3.

I don't have any more space for dashboard topics but if you follow the progression (identifying critical metrics, assembling them into metric collections, establishing thresholds and planning for hierarchal dashboards), you'll have all that you need. The most important phase of dashboarding, which is also the simplest, is to set up the APC metrics with thresholds. Once you can complete that process reliably, the architecture dashboard (shown in Figure 14-4) will be achievable.

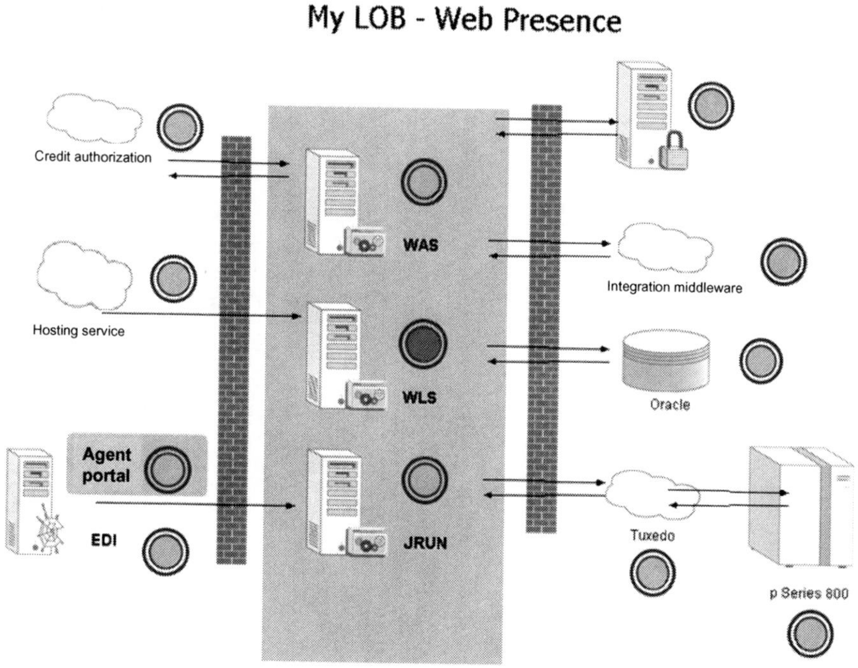

My LOB - Web Presence

Figure 14-4. A sample of single application architecture

Presentation via Reports

The other use for metric collections is to support reporting via tables and graphs, resulting in .pdf or .html documents. I also consider gathering together screenshots as another type of report. Both have the advantage of avoiding direct access to the APM workstation, which means less software to deploy, less training, and fewer issues associated with the absence of training.

I prefer reporting over the APM workstation as it is the basis for more open collaboration and easy dissemination of the findings. It will need a patient pace of introduction to help socialize the terms and the expectations. Initially, reporting has to be simple, concise, consistent, and self-explanatory. In order for the APM initiative to be successful in the long term, you need to have a large population of report consumers.

In Chapter 13, you will find some examples of reports in Figures 13-6 to 13-8.

Metric Categories

Beyond the basic skills with navigation within your chosen APM user interface, what you need to begin triage is an understanding of the normal and abnormal behaviors for the different categories of metrics that you will encounter. The profiles of various metrics, in terms of the curves presented on graphs, can be classified as follows:

- Constant or static
- Periodic or repeating pattern
- Increasing or decreasing

The relationships among metrics can be classified as follows:

- Correlate with load
- Independent of load
- Limited to a specific use case

If you construct taxonomy of metric types, they would be assigned across four major areas as follows:

- Configuration
    - Static, meaningful at startup
    - Generated by the operating system and JVM, and republished by APM
    - Examples:
        - Vendor-defined JMX and/or PMI
        - GC Parameters

These are not especially useful for triage but helpful to confirm and document any configuration-related performance issues.

Platform metrics are dynamic in that they respond continuously to changes in how the application is interacting with requests and resources.

- Platform
    - Dynamic and process-centric
    - Generated by the operating system and republished by APM
    - Examples:
        - CPU
        - I/O (network and disk)
        - File system (disk space, mount points)

They are useful as secondary metrics to help confirm a situation that you assert from primary metrics. Some folks are totally focused on CPU as this is the classic performance measure, especially in the mainframe world. With distributed systems, it has much less meaning because you have deeper visibility into the components that are consuming the CPU. If the only metric you have is CPU metrics, triage will be difficult. In general, process metrics only give you availability, not detailed performance information.

- Application server or container
  - Dynamic and instance-specific (can be multiple processes)
  - Generated by the vendor and republished by APM
    - Sometimes instrumentation may be applied against the app server
  - Examples:
    - Thread pool
    - Database connection pool

The application server presents a lot of interesting metrics that are clearly useful for tuning the application server configuration. They have little value in triage, except as a starting point to effect a configuration tuning that was not completed earlier. Major changes in the app server configuration will invalidate your baselines.

- Application-specific
  - Dynamic and instance-specific
  - Generated by instrumentation and real transactions
  - Additional metrics may be defined by the developer via JMX or PMI, and republished by APM
  - Examples:
    - Component response times
    - SQL response times
    - Invocation counts and rates
    - Counts
      - Specific object instances
      - Stalled components (>30 seconds)

These metrics are the most significant for triage of performance problems, especially when performance degradation is encountered but does not lead to a total application failure. These are the metrics that you need to have some experience interpreting, so I will devote the remainder of this section to doing exactly that.

Other metric categories are possible but these are vendor-specific capabilities and will be ignored here. This does not imply that they are of limited value, so you should certainly plan to take advantage of them when they are available.

The order in which you evaluate metrics is critical because the component that you initially see as out of bounds is very often affected by another component or setting. You need to fix problems from the top down, rather than the bottom up, or what I call "fixing the loudest problem first." Addressing the loudest problem will very often cause the entire application to rebalance, and what was initially a suspect component simply vanishes. Ignoring this advice leads you to a complementary position of chasing your tail, where you continue to chase the components with poor metric values without actually making any progress.

For example, you audit an application and find that the response times are completely unacceptable. If you take the worst performing transaction and try to figure out why, you will be *chasing your tail* and finding nothing to fix. Every metric you see is bad or otherwise *out-of-bounds*. The enlightened approach looks first for the *loudest problem*—the initial configuration—and reviews all settings, especially the ones that are not visible to the instrumentation; you'll find that the debug mode is still in effect. Changing the debug setting and rerunning the test will result in normal response times, with the exception of a poor response time on a different transaction than was initially identified.

In general, the top-down approach is to evaluate configuration, platform, application server/container, and then application-specific, just as I have outlined in this section so far. Depending on your APM technology, you may not have metrics addressing each of these categories or they may have different names or terminology. The remainder of this section presents the details of each category so that you can choose appropriately.

Memory Profile

How an application uses memory is perhaps the best perspective on the overall stability and scalability of the application, if you have sufficient resolution and effective presentation. Java systems employ dynamic memory management so it is a very accurate reflection of what the application is actually doing over time and how well it manages those resources. In my experience, I have found that 30-40% of performance problems are due to inappropriate configuration of the memory management. In Java applications, this is called *garbage collection* or GC. Whenever an object completes its task, its memory resources are marked for collection. Periodically, the GC mechanism activates, clears this marked memory, and makes it available for reuse. Unfortunately, all of these capabilities may be adjusted. This is important in order to accommodate the specific needs of a given application. Setting these parameters to match the needs of the applications is called *configuration tuning* or *performance tuning*. Making these adjustments correctly is challenging and it invites two major sources of problems: changes that were ill-advised or arbitrary, and no changes at all (running with the defaults).

Tuning the JVM for performance is a big topic and I recommend *Pro Java EE 5 Performance Management and Optimization* by Steven Haines (Apress, 2006).

Some of the questions to consider when reviewing memory management graphs include the following:

- Are memory settings correct (limited to GC frameworks)?
  - Initial and max heap
- Is the server initialized?
  - When is the server idle?

- Response to load?
- Successive tests returning to baseline?
- Memory Abuses

Figure 14-5 summarizes what a GC profile (specifically, *bytes in use*) will look like for a reasonably healthy application. It gives you a clear demarcation among the initialization, idle, and the period of the load test or exercise of the application. In this example, the app server configuration and the JVM settings are not optimized. This is evidenced by the characteristic saw-toothed curve in the graph; an optimized configuration would instead be flat. This is not cause for alarm; it simply means that the configuration has not been tuned. However, if you see this during stress and performance testing or in production, it is cause for alarm!

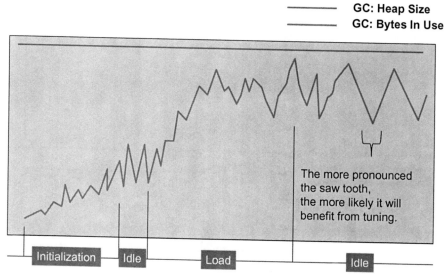

Figure 14-5. Typical initial memory profile

Another useful metric to confirm the absence of configuration tuning is the *heap size*. When a Java application needs more memory, it makes a request to the JVM. If additional memory is available, the JVM will then increase the heap. This happens automatically. The problem is that it also has a fair expense. When the memory is insufficient, the GC runs frequently, effectively stealing cycles from the application. This continues until a balance is struck between memory size and decreasing the activity of the GC mechanism[3]. Most folks will assume that this is all buried in the startup period of an application, which is always doing some variety of expensive tasks that only occur at initialization. My thinking is different. When I see an unmanaged heap, I wonder what other settings were undersized or left at the default value. Figure 14-6 shows what an unmanaged heap looks like in terms of not setting an appropriate initial size.

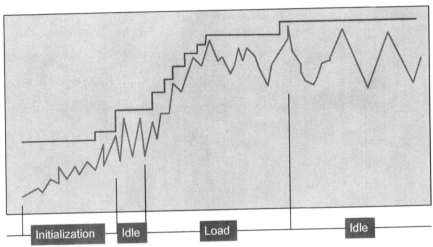

Figure 14-6. Insufficient initial heap

"For many applications, the default heap size is too small. There are several factors which suggest an increase of heap size. For example:

- OutOfMemory errors
- Frequent garbage collections
- Generally slow application performance that cannot exclusively be attributed to other factors like IO or CPU."

"Tuning Heap and Garbage Collector " http://fedora.fiz-karlsruhe.de/docs/Wiki.jsp?page=Java%20Heap%20%26%20GC%20Tuning

"Large server applications often experience two problems with these defaults. One is slow startup, because the initial heap is small and must be resized over many major collections. A more pressing problem is that the default maximum heap size is unreasonably small for most server applications." Java SE 6 HotSpot™ Virtual Machine Garbage Collection Tuning http://www.oracle.com/technetwork/java/javase/gc-tuning-6-140523.html#generation_sizing.total_heap

"If the initial heap size is too small the garbage collector runs almost continuously." Java Memory Tuning Tips http://publib.boulder.ibm.com/infocenter/iseries/v5r3/index.jsp?topic=%2Frzamy%2F50%2Fadmin%2Fprftunejmem.htm

The final value of the GC:HeapSize +10% should be the starting point for many applications, depending on the types of object collections in use and the type of collector in operation. Change the app server configuration to reflect the new value and rerun the load test. Unless you have production experience, which is never a good sign, you must adjust the HeapSize with this load test and confirm procedure in a pre-production environment.

Knowing that an application initialization is significant and noticing that it has not had time to complete is one of the earliest triage contributions you can hope to document and resolve. Many production apps are restarted every day prior to any load being applied to them, until a few hours have passed. When an app gets started mid-day, it will often be hit immediately with a full load. Figure 14-7 illustrates this point.

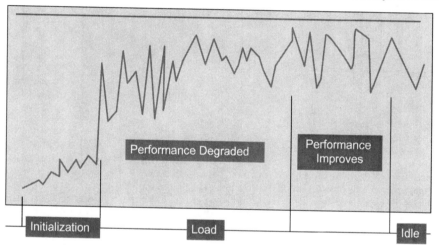

Figure 14-7. Server initialization not complete

The load (synthetic or real) has started before initialization is complete. This will often result in poor performance for 30-60 minutes, after which the performance "suddenly" improves. If you do not understand the initialization requirements for your application—and every app is different—you will have production issues.

For example, some financial trading apps require over two hours to initialize. If a server comes online, how do you know when it will actually be ready for requests?

Another frequent offender that GC metrics will identify is the memory leak, the classic flavor of which is illustrated in Figure 14-8. In this example, the saw tooth pattern is evident, indicating configuration tuning is required, but it is also increasing and bounded. This is a software defect—some component is not releasing memory correctly, so with every successful use of the application, the lost memory increases. This is called a leak because the memory cannot be recovered by the JVM; it has leaked outside of its control.

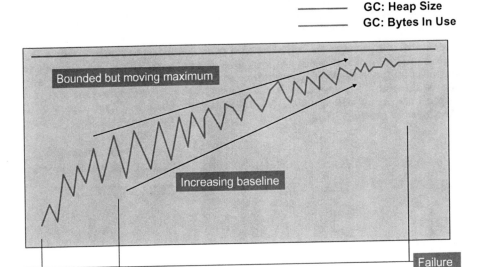

Figure 14-8. Classic memory leak

An historical view is essential because some leaks are only evident after many hours of production load. This creates a real challenge for the test environment, where a load test may take 20 minutes or an hour. This is easy to overcome; I discuss how in Chapter 13 as part of the baseline practice. A memory analysis tool will often help identify some of the data structures responsible but these are not yet available from all vendors. Detecting that a memory management problem exists is what I will focus on here.

An advantage of APM is ready access to the historical data. If you organize your load testing correctly, you will easily detect all but the most subtle leaks. Figure 14-9 illustrates how this may be detected over a sequence of load tests. The only coordination with the testing team is to avoid any restart of the application server between tests.

While this may seem obvious, I find that many load test plans require a clean restart of the application server between tests. I've never received a straight answer as to why this is being done, other than it is the standard practice. If you want to catch memory leaks, don't let anybody restart the server.

There is another test plan strategy called a *soak test*, which is specifically designed to catch slow acting problems like memory leaks. I discuss test plans in Chapter 12.

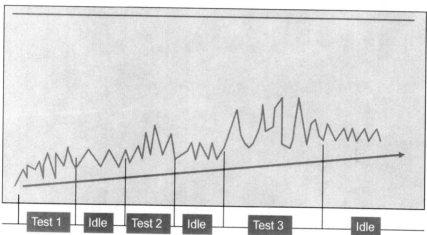

GC: Heap Size
GC: Bytes In Use

Figure 14-9. Classic memory leak—QA

When the load generation or selection of use cases is not sufficient to see the historical growth in the memory usage, as shown in Figure 14-8, you then need to exercise the application server by running multiple load tests and allowing the server to go idle between each test, illustrated in Figure 14-9. Do not restart the server in between the tests.

You can actually approximate the Mbytes/hr lost by calculating the slope of the bottom portion of the GC curves. It's likely unsuitable for production at 5MB/hr or greater. As long as you know the MB/hr that you are losing, you will be able to decide which applications get fixed first. It's often unrealistic to hope that all leaks will be eliminated. But with a proper measurement, you will be able to focus on those apps that are having the greatest difficulty.

There are a number of other leak types that are not as easy to uncover. One of the nastier ones is a *connection leak*, as illustrated in Figure 14-10.

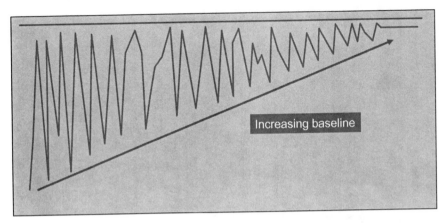

GC: Heap Size
GC: Bytes In Use

Increasing baseline

Figure 14-10. Connection leak

A connection leak occurs when a handle to a resource is referenced in a wrapper class, such as a DBMS Connection Manager. The application marks the wrapper class for cleanup but the object cannot be removed because the resource object and not been released—it still has a valid reference. The wrapper object will never be released and a chunk of memory is lost. This is how the baseline grows. The application then allocates a new wrapper object, which requests a new resource connection object, and the pattern repeats itself when that new wrapper is again marked for cleanup.

The span that the GC is traversing between *memory full* and *cleaned up* is actually resulting from an attempt to throw more memory at the problem. Even if the configuration was properly tuned at one time, earlier attempts to identify the memory leak failed. In order to keep the application running in production, the total memory was increased until the application could survive for a business day. But all this excess memory actually unbalanced the configuration again, resulting in the saw tooth. Once the application was stable for the production day, attentions turned elsewhere. When a successive release became available, more memory was added again. Fortunately, at least for procurement folks, 32-bit operating systems have a limit of how much memory can be made available to the JVM. Once this limit is hit and the application is no longer able to survive for a production day, you no longer have any choice but to fix the underlying problem.

A memory analysis tool is not useful in this scenario because it will focus on the generic data structures. Here, the data structure is the client's own code; with these kinds of connection leaks, instrumentation alone is useful is identifying the issue.

Not all memory management evidence is related to mismanagement of data structures. This next example, Figure 14-11, looks at how thread locking and other types of application stalls can affect the GC profile.

GC: Heap Size

GC: Bytes In Use

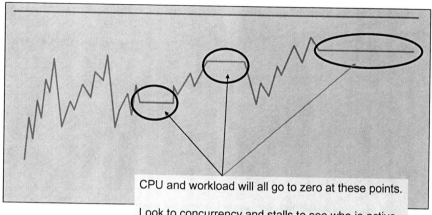

CPU and workload will all go to zero at these points.

Look to concurrency and stalls to see who is active.

Figure 14-11. Thread lock and stalls

Here you see a complete stall in the progress of the application in that objects are no longer being created or destroyed. If a CPU graph were overlaid, it would likely show 100% CPU activity or saturation at these same stall periods. If you look to the views of concurrency (number of active threads for a specific object) or stalls (method calls that take longer than 30 seconds), they will put you on the track of what use cases and components are participating. A historical view will have some potential to correlate suspect components once they hit a certain threshold. Prior to the threshold, the system will look normal.

That this kind of problem gets past the testing process is the real defect with the application. In this case, they simply never tested the app at realistic loads and thus went to a large-scale deployment completely unaware of a serious limitation, but it could just as easily have been the result of a hardware consolidation, making several lightly used instances into a single heavily-used instance, again without the benefit of a meaningful test. There are many different routes to end up at the same GC behavior.

Another common impact of poorly tested code is the OOM (Out of memory) exception. As you can see in Figure 14-12, this exception can occur at any point in the GC cycle, which puts it in an apparent conflict. How can there be an OOM exception if you still have loads of memory left?

GC: Heap Size
GC: Bytes In Use

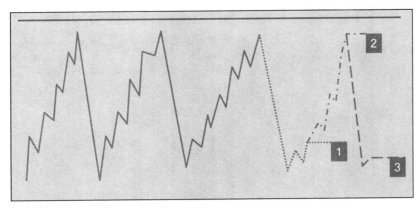

OOM exception received at different points in the apps evolution,
while sufficient memory is still available.
Each number illustrates the point of failure where multiple runs are superimposed.

Figure 14-12. Out-of-memory (OOM) exceptions

What the OOM exception really means is that a *request* for memory was received that could not be fulfilled. This is very often the result of an extremely large result set in response to a database query. This is more often encountered in a production setting where one or more use cases are responsible for the error. It was not detected in QA either because the use case was never exercised or it was exercised in isolation (no other use cases were present). This sometimes can be the result of a *rogue user*—someone who is performing an action that is both unanticipated and ill-advised. Finding this individual among the dozens or hundreds of users can be a challenge as the damaging queries will only show up at irregular intervals. Interviewing that user is critical for correctly engineering a solution to prevent that usage from occurring, especially if it is a defect in training or understanding. Application behavior may become unpredictable after an OOM exception is generated, even if the application appears to recover.

This situation emphasizes why it is important to have a realistic distribution of use cases while in QA; it also demonstrates the absolute value of monitoring directly in production. Look to see who is active in the SQL statements. Very often it's a lightly used query.

Response Times

Pretty much everyone appreciates response time metrics. If a 2 second response is expected and a 20 second response time is experienced, then there is a problem. Unfortunately, there are many different types of components that themselves have response times that may directly or indirectly contribute to the response time experienced by the user. Here are some simple requirements for response times:

- Web applications in general should not have Servlets, EJBs, or JSPs response times in excess of 2-3 seconds.
- Response times should be consistent across the duration of the test. If not, there is a bottleneck or the app is otherwise saturated.
- Response time degradation will often correspond with large GC activity.

In Figure 14-13, you can see why response times are relative. In a Java environment, the first time a component is accessed, the response time is very poor. This is because compilation is occurring (which is expensive in some JVMs). Thereafter, any access of that component will be very fast. So you simply can't say "No response time greater than 2 seconds" without adding a qualifier: "after the application has been running 30 minutes."

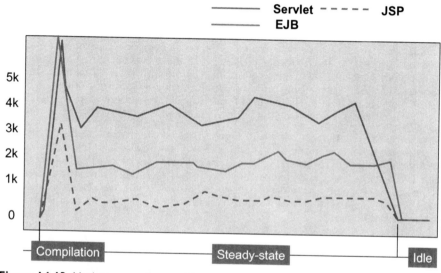

Figure 14-13. Ideal response time profile

In general, a Servlet response time will always be greater than a JSP (Java Server Page) response time, which will always be greater that an EJB (Enterprise Java Bean) response time. In practice, these values can be anything from sub-seconds to minutes, depending on the architecture of the application. So how do you know when a response time is inappropriate? You don't. This is one of the limitations of trying to triage with single metrics.

Figure 14-14 is an example of a response time that seems immediately suspect. After all, who wouldn't cringe at a response time of 35,000 milliseconds?

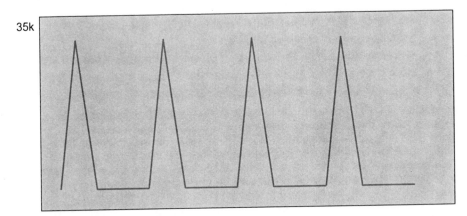

Figure 14-14. Heartbeat or periodic

This is a heartbeat or periodic characteristic. Some components are asleep or idle and then wake up to see if there is processing. If there is processing, they complete it, but otherwise they just wait around for a while and then go back to sleep. It appears that they take a long time but, in fact, they are doing nothing (or very little). Very often this is the result of starting a transaction that returns when either data is received or a timeout period is reached.

Another extreme situation, shown in Figure 14-15, is a long duration degradation of response time, best observed via a historical view over 2-8 hours after an OOM exception has been received. This is a strong confirmation of the observation that OOM exceptions may leave the JVM in an unstable state. When we talk about software quality as a driver for an APM initiative, these are the kinds of small, easily dismissed blemishes that frequently add up to an application that is simply unstable.

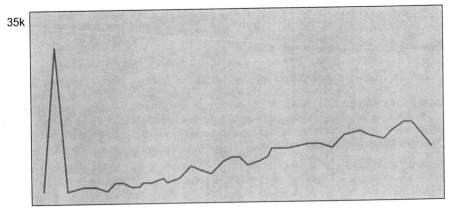

Figure 14-15. OOM: Degradation

Another response time situation is the classic processing bottleneck, shown in Figure 14-16. A response time of zero, which seems ideal, is in fact very bad—especially when processing loads are known to be consistent at that time of day. When you encounter a situation where a value goes to zero, then you have to look to another metric, typically CPU, to confirm if the application is idle, thrashing, or worse. As you find yourself building tables of other metrics to consider and what the values might be for the different situations, you should start to realize the futility of the situation.

This is the *visibility gap*—knowing what the performance characteristics for any given application will be but with no prior knowledge of the application. I don't know of any technology today that can achieve this.

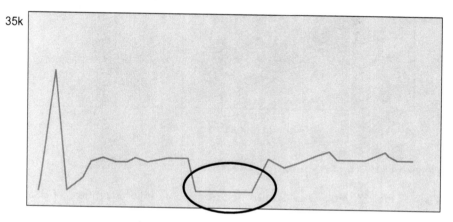

Incoming requests can't get started.
No work is getting done.

Figure 14-16. Bottleneck

To finish off this discussion of response times, consider Figure 14-17. Here the response time behaves unexpectedly and any numbers of explanations are possible. It may reveal contention for some resource. It may be due to an absence of traffic (incoming requests). The next question you have to consider is how many invocations of the component contributed to this response time? Was it a single invocation, which means more of a rogue use case, or were hundreds of invocations all reporting the same excessive response time?

You may continue to navigate ad-hoc among the available metrics, building collections of interesting metrics and searching for the longest duration and most active of the running components. It is a fairly easy skill to acquire, provided that you have enough time with the workstation to master its interfaces and usage. This is not the real world situation, however. In the real world, you may have months between triage events, which makes it very difficult to keep all of the rules about one type of metric, such as the response time, clear in your mind. The only way to break this *infrequent usage pattern* is to use APM outside of basic, reactive monitoring and during QA testing and for production reporting. This ensures that you have much more experience accumulating data and are more likely to be moving towards triage with baselines. Everyone becomes familiar with what the metrics mean and what is normal, so they can eventually focus on the overall characteristics of the application via the baselines, as you saw in Chapter 12.

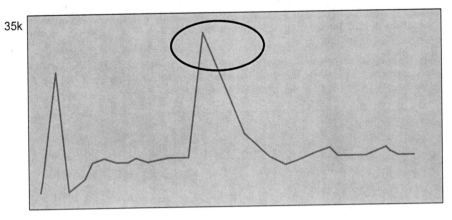

Current requests are stalled.
No work is getting done.

Figure 14-17. Contention or stall

The question of how to evolve an organization to take advantage of this APM information is the real point that begs addressing, as you found in Chapter 5. I know that triage with single metrics is easy to start out with but it will not be the technique in use in the long term. Most stakeholders need something more streamlined and reproducible. It is not helpful if only a single individual can alone interpret the metrics. This is what I will establish with *triage with baselines* in Chapter 15, and also with the *application audit* in Chapter 13.

Concurrency

If response times are the most recognizable type of metric, concurrency may be among the least. Different from the batch and process-centric computing of the recent past where all your work was performed a single transaction at a time, modern component software expects to operate many multiples of transactions at one time. This is called distributed computing and its major attribute is *concurrency*, which means that a number of components associated with one or more threads are ready to run simultaneously. This is different from traditional computing where transactions are processed sequentially. Depending on the supporting platform, any number of components may be active, each starting and stopping independently of the others. This is different from parallel computing when each component moves exactly lockstep with all others. Concurrency is like commuting: everybody leaves for work at the about same time and arrives about the same time, but many different routes are employed.

Concurrency shows a number of things, including:

- Who is active?
- Who is stuck waiting on resource?
- Configuration issues.

Figure 14-18 shows an idealized concurrency curve. Here, a concurrency of zero means that only a single instance is running. A concurrency of one means that a pair (two instances) are running but not necessarily in lockstep with one another. As long as the concurrency can increase to meet the incoming load, we say that the application *scales*. And if the application then reduces the number of concurrent instances as the load is decreased, we say that the application is *managed*.

These nuances are necessary because concurrency often maps onto one or more threads. However, threads are usually very expensive to create, so threads are created once and then explicitly reused but without giving up the total number of threads. For example, a workflow system may allocate 15 threads for processing. These 15 threads are always indicated as available until they are used, at which point the number of available threads decreases. At all times, the number of threads is constant but they move between the available and in-use states.

When threads and concurrent requests are the same or less, things are predictable. But when the pending requests outnumber the available threads, things can get bad very quickly, depending on how well behaved (managed) the concurrent objects are. Typically, the requests are queued, which is normal, until the queue size becomes excessive and the application can become unstable. How that instability occurs is an issue for the developer. The APM specialist simply needs to indicate which concurrency strategies are successful or not.

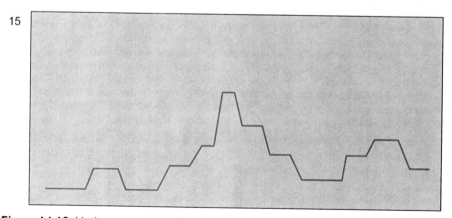

Figure 14-18. Ideal concurrency

As to how threads, concurrency, and batch processing one transaction at a time have all gotten mixed together, this is the "legacy" of legacy applications. An original design for batch computing got ported to a modern process-based architecture, which then moved to distributed objects and threads, and then moved to component-based computing and concurrency. The most visible parts of the application are the most modern (especially the front-end interfaces), but many parts of the application and its resources never evolved past their original implementation. Many modern applications today employ every conceivable type of software engineering model and computer architecture. In general, the developers employ the best tools and process available at the time. But this is only applied to the functionality they are working on; it leaves many other portions untouched.

As sub-systems are repurposed or move into use cases for which they were not originally designed, interesting things are observed, as shown in Figure 14-19.

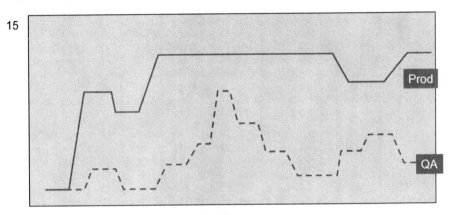

Figure 14-19. Concurrency: insufficient threads

Here you see that the QA testing revealed a concurrency curve that is comparable to the ideals but failed to scale once it got to production. Depending on software architecture, threads may even be shared by multiple components, with one set of components pushing out the other. The end result is an inability to scale, which points again at a weak test plan (insufficient load). The resolution may simply be to increase a configuration parameter or it may require more extensive software changes; regardless, it's something that would have been detected pre-production with the right plan.

One other variant on thread saturation is *thread deadlock*, as shown in Figure 14-20. There are sufficient threads available but another resource or code section locks and you end up with a plateau curve.

15

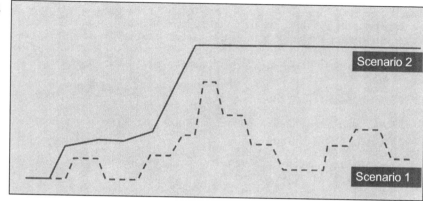

Figure 14-20. Deadlock

Deadlock issues will also show some sensitivity to increasing load; however, given that multiple threads are involved and the threads are identical, you have to look to the software components and the triggering use case to get a meaningful suspect. Identifying concurrency problems is the responsibility of APM. Solving the problems and understanding the details of how they are manifest is a separate topic. I recommend *The Art of Concurrency – A Thread Monkey's Guide to Writing Parallel Applications* by Clay Breashears (O'Reilly Media, 2009) for the full story.

This brings me to the more useful type of metric that's directly related to the thread and concurrency: the application stall count.

Stalls

Rather than working from the bottom up, starting with the thread doing the actual computation, the stall count allows you to work from the top down to isolate the entry point and use case. This is a more meaningful identification, and along with transaction tracing, reliably points you in the direction of a solid suspect.

A stall is counted whenever a monitored component does not complete within a pre-defined interval of time. The time interval is arbitrary but for web facing applications, a stall threshold of thirty seconds is appropriate[4],[5]. An increasing stall count is significant because the overall throughput for the application is potentially degraded. It may be limited to a single transaction, which is often a minimal impact, or it can be a characteristic of many transactions.

---

[4] Industry web site response times can average twenty seconds normally (2005). www.websiteoptimization.com/speed/1/

[5] An example of a stalled component thresholds is 15 sec from "Detecting and Resolving Stalled and Stuck I/O Issues in SQL Server 2000 SP 4" 2005, http://technet.microsoft.com/en-us/library/aa175396%28SQL.80%29.aspx

A stall count is complementary to a response time. But the response time cannot be determined until the transaction completes or is abandoned. The stall count gives you earlier notice of a long transaction and is a unique measure if the transaction never completes. You not only see that a transaction is stalled but you may also get details of which components contributed to the transaction that stalled.

Here are some stall count characteristics:

- Any instrumented method that takes more than 30 seconds to complete.
- A quick test of web app quality.

  - For example, if you have more than five stalls per day in UAT, you may not deploy to production.

- It's usually indicative of bottleneck or resource issues.

The ideal number of stalls is exactly zero but this is also unrealistic. The more realistic situation is when there is some stall activity at startup or maybe during peak loads but the application otherwise recovers. When the stall count for a component plateaus, it will usually correlate with a problem.

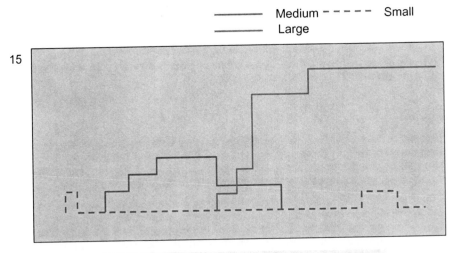

If stalls decrease, the app will survive.
Otherwise, the app will hang (run out of resources).

Figure 14-21. Spectrum of stalls problems

The magnitude of the problem may be roughly apportioned as shown in Figure 14-21. If you have a few stalls, it's a small or inconsequential problem. Because of the compilation time required when an object is first accessed, you will often encounter a few stalls. Infrequent use cases will account for those well after startup. If you encounter a surge in stalls correlated with a surge in processing load (number of users or transactions), this is indicative of an application in stress, but if it recovers, then you simply note it as a medium concern. If you find a sudden surge up to a plateau, this is generally acknowledged to be a large problem that usually requires a restart of the application server. An application in this state is often "hung" and no further processing will occur until the application is restarted.

SQL

There are a number of SQL metrics that APM will collect of both response time and invocation metric types. I prefer to treat them separately because there are simply no standards for what is an acceptable response time or query load—they are both completely application dependent. Here are some SQL characteristics:

- SQL response times should generally be less than 200 msec.
- SQL response times greater than 2-4 seconds can be problematic.
- SQL response times greater than 10 seconds suggest that the app is unbalanced between interactive and batch. You should consider partitioning the app onto a different JVM and/or using a workflow solution.

Realistically, I have seen SQL response times anywhere from 1 msec to 10 minutes. The problem is when you have this spectrum of response times occurring in the same application.

Early in my own computing education I recall an instructor admonishing us students to "keep your transactions short." I have found that when you mix extremely short transactions with extremely long transactions, you can never successfully optimize the application server and JVM configurations to suit either one. And when you get a whole spectrum of SQL response times, all with high volumes, you can end up with a very unstable application.

The solution to this type of architecture problem is to perform a *workload partitioning*. I like to say that you can't do workflow in a lottery ticket application. So what does that mean?

Workload partitioning is a concept from the mainframe era, now repurposed for virtualized operating systems, where you desire to divide a resource fairly among competing applications. At the coarse level, this means separating a database from a web server from an application server so that each runs in its own virtual environment. They all fit on the same box but through the magic of virtualization, they appear to be running in isolation.

My fastest transaction is the lottery ticket. There is no business process; you simply enter a number into a database, and at the end of the week you find out if you picked good numbers. My slowest transaction is workflow. I start a task, set it aside, come back to it in an hour or so, and repeat until it gets finished. When someone issues a request and waits synchronously for the 10 minutes it takes to complete, this is workflow, compared with the blazingly fast lottery ticket transaction.

When I am waiting for that 10 minute transaction to complete, I am holding on to memory, connection pools, and any number of other resources. These are the same resources that my lottery transactions will use. As the volume of my workflow transactions increase, the amount of resources available for the lottery transactions will decrease. Eventually, I will no longer be able to process lottery tickets because all of the resources are committed to doing workflow. Workload partitioning allows you to separate these two extremes and many other intermediate transactions so that you can properly configure the resources for optimal usage. Thus, you end up with one JVM for workflow transactions and one JVM for lottery transactions.

As before, the challenge is first to realize that your composite legacy application has these negative characteristics and then to re-architect the solution so that the workloads may be shifted. In the following process section, you will learn how to quickly assess the high response time and high invocation metrics. When you see different SQL statements appearing for the largest invocations (the most frequent statements) versus the highest response time, then the workloads are unbalanced. Ideally, you want 95% of your transactions to be one workload and the remaining 5% the other workload.

Process

There are two fundamental processes you need to establish. The obvious one is the mechanics of doing *triage with single metrics*. More important is to *scope* the activity that you are being asked to undertake. A *scope* is a conversation with the business owner, application team, or Operations to detail what the application environment is like, how APM technology might assist, and what you can personally deliver. This is a simple exercise with very significant ramifications for how the triage activity will be received. This is where you set and manage expectations. And expectations are ultimately what is going to help or hinder the APM initiative.

Scope

- How will you be engaged?
    - Scope document
        - Assess what you can do to improve visibility into the application.
        - Collect information as to the nature of the problem and what result is expected.
            - Never commit to finding a problem.
            - You can only attempt to enhance visibility into the nature of the problem.
        - Environment
            - Can they test in QA?
            - Metrics Storage requirements and connectivity.
            - Is there a centralized Metrics Storage server reserved for triage? Is it a new server?

- Rules of Engagement
  - Who to contact
  - Duration of monitoring
  - Time to respond with initial recommendations
  - Chargeback policy

Triage with Single Metrics

The goal of triage is to summarize the visibility and indicate normal and abnormal findings. You are providing evidence to the other stakeholders. Those stakeholders need to decide what to do with the information. Resist any opportunity to declare the root cause.

Single Incident

1. Note the characteristics of the incident.

   a. Has it happened before?
   b. Are there seasonal or time-of-day/week/month/quarter considerations?
   c. Which platforms were affected?
   d. What is the duration of the incident/outage?
   e. Were any other applications affected?
   f. What alerts did systems management receive around the incident?

2. Note the monitoring parameters.

   a. How many metrics are being generated?
   b. What types of software components are present?
   c. Were there any abnormalities in the data collection?

3. Generate a historical view for a two hour range around the time of the incident; 90 minutes before and 30 minutes after.

4. Collect the top 10 metrics with the highest response times.

   a. Review each metric.
      i. Does it correlate with the incident?
      ii. Does it represent an external resource?
      iii. Is the component shared with other transactions?

   b. Take a screen shot of anything interesting.

5. Collect the top 10 metrics with the highest number of invocations.

   a. Review each metric.
      i. Does it correlate with the incident?
      ii. Does it represent an external resource?
      iii. Is the component shared with other transactions?

   b. Take a screen shot of anything interesting.

6. If this is a clustered application, are multiple agents employed?

    a.   Does each agent give similar performance degradation around the incident? Or are they independent?

7. If transactions stacks are available, do they contain any of the top 10 components?

    a.   Which transactions were impacted by the incident?
    b.   Do the transactions have appropriate visibility?

8. Review the memory utilization.

    a.   Are there memory management changes around the incident?
    b.   Are any memory utilization trends evident?

9. Review additional platform metrics as appropriate.

10. Reporting (presentation format)

    a.   Where appropriate, use a screen shot and annotate it with notes and arrows that highlight your observations.
    b.   Summarize the incident characteristics (1 slide).
    c.   Do you have visibility into the incident?
        iv. What metrics identify the incident unambiguously?
        v. What software components or resources are implicated?

    d.   What metrics indicate normal (or abnormal) behavior?
    e.   Summarize any alerting that correlated with the incident.
    f.   Show any dashboards that captured the incident.
    g.   Recommend any thresholds that would have allowed early warning of the incident.

Performance Test

Reviewing a performance test has two flavors: initial and ongoing. *Initial* is if the application has never before been configured with APM. *Ongoing* refers to anything else that should have baselines available—data and reports about the earlier testing—because the monitoring will have already been established. A report is a consistent mechanism to review performance information. Before performance criteria are established, you will tend to focus on baseline reporting. This allows the greatest flexibility until you determine the unique signature for your application. Once the criteria are established, your emphasis will be on HealthCheck reporting. This puts more structure into the reporting (less flexibility) and also adds in non-APM data sources as appropriate. Chapters 12 and 13 have examples of both types of reporting.

Initial

1. Treat the test initially as a *single incident* and follow the previous cookbook, but focus on the duration of the test (typically 20 minutes) with particular emphasis on the steady-state portion of the test.

2. Find an appropriate metric that tracks the test scenario. This will be an *invocation metric*. Generate a graph of this metric to document the overall load profile. Note any anomalies.

3. Prepare metric collections that summarize the major components, in terms of APC: availability, performance (response time) and capacity (invocations).

    a. For availability, I always start with the number of metrics. If you have some load-invariant metrics, add these to the availability collection.

4. Prepare additional collections for stalls, concurrency, and errors, if these are available.

5. Prepare a baseline report that presents the following, each sorted greatest to lowest, for the duration of the test:

    a. Slowest response time (performance collection)
    b. Largest invocations (capacity collection)
    c. Highest stalls
    d. Highest concurrency
    e. Largest errors

Baseline Report Available

When baselines reports are available, someone has already done the work of getting the performance characteristics defined uniquely for this application. This limits your role to confirming some of the basic characteristics, reusing the existing report templates, and then making some discussion about what has stayed the same or changed since the last test.

In Chapter 15 you will do quite a bit more for triage with baselines. At this stage, you simply do not have the tools and strategy, but you can still do a commendable job making the comparisons among two sets of tests. The challenge is that two tests can quickly become four or five that you need to compare, which requires a different kind of preparation.

1. Collect the metadata about the test.

    a. Agent configuration used
    b. Test plan
    c. Test profiles used
    d. Duration of test, plus start and end times
    e. Descriptions of any anomalous behavior with the application or the environment during the period of the test

2. Review the existing metric collections and report templates for the application.

    a. Set up an historical view of the test period and see what each of the metric collections looks like in that period.
    b. Search and compare the greatest response times and invocations with those defined in the metric collections, and note any differences.

3. Generate new baseline reports focused on the steady-state period of the test.

4. Compare and contrast the differences between the new and old baselines.

HealthCheck

A HealthCheck report has a fundamentally different goal than the baseline report. Instead of simply presenting your findings, you need to render an opinion as to the scalability and stability of the application. Practically, you need to consider more than a single test in order for your conclusions to have any weight.

The format of the HealthCheck report should follow the test plan, including key transactions exercised, response time targets, and stability goals. Not much interpretation is needed for these points. The scalability conclusion will require a bit more finesse. The quality of your conclusion will be a function of the user load that you were able to generate during QA testing. The better and more realistic the load, the more confident your scalability forecast will be.

QA HealthCheck

Most of the load testing will have progressed with small loads and short durations. You can then generate a baseline for each of these tests and then review them for anything troublesome.

Any stress testing will unfold over a couple of hours so there will only be one or two tests to consider. If you were able to stress the application to failure, simply use 80% of the maximum load achieved when performance degraded to unacceptable levels. If you could not stress the application to failure, use the approximation technique discussed in Chapter 12.

Whatever path you choose, make sure to define what "forecast" means and how it still needs to be validated via the production experience. Once validation is achieved, acceptance of the technique is possible and less time will be spent defending it in the future.

Some areas of concern for any of the test results are excessive response times or stalls and poor memory management. You need not worry about making a recommendation to defer deployment—no one will allow that to happen initially. You simply want to express your concerns and show the evidence supporting them. Your goal is to make everyone aware of your techniques and findings because when you get to production, you will repeat all of these findings.

Production HealthCheck

The difference between the production and QA HealthCheck techniques is simply the source of the data. Your minimum report interval should be two hours and you should avoid looking at intervals longer than a production day (8, 12, or 24 hours). Off-hours activity, in particular, will significantly lower the averages and counts, making direct comparison with the QA findings difficult.

You should look at daily and weekly views for historical trends, but don't use these intervals to generate tabular data because of the rounding down that will occur off-hours. In general, when comparing two different historical periods, make sure they are the same day of the week and same hours of the day. It doesn't matter if it is a peak or a quiet period. It just needs to be a consistent period.

Competency

Assessing competency for triage means going out and doing it. Theory is fine but the real learning occurs when you are configuring agents and navigating the APM workstation—while several frustrated folks are breathing down your neck. The ideal situation is to have a repository of APM database excerpts. This is what I use to great effect. It is hard to schedule a real problem to occur for a competency exercise.

What I call *remote analysis* is exactly that. Someone with a problem sends you an APM database with little more information than what you have right now. Loading, reviewing, reporting, and making recommendations is completed in about four hours, and is wrapped up in a presentation file. Someone else actually delivers the presentation. This is what you want to practice, at least three times, before you attempt to do an application "in the wild." Just deliver the presentation to your peers, defend your approach and findings, and keep it simple.

- Remote Analysis

  - Install, configure and test the APM software on your desktop.
  - Download and unpack the Metrics Storage archive in a separate directory.
  - Modify Metrics Storage properties to point to the new archive.
  - Start the Metrics Storage component, open a workstation, and explore the data.
  - Is there a problem?
  - Describe the problem (or why it appears normal).
  - Prepare a presentation that summarizes your process, observations, findings, and recommendations.
  - Present and discuss your findings in front of peers, who then constructively critique your delivery.

- Rapid Deployment

  - How you deploy and configure an APM agent is highly vendor-specific. You want to be able to do this, reliably, in 30 minutes. Two hours is acceptable, but the faster you can deploy, the more time you will have for analysis.

- Practice *rapid deploy*ment in a QA environment. Three separate installs (different applications) with zero errors is what you will need for maximum confidence. Every time you make a mistake, you reset the count. If you cannot get three successful installs in a row, leave the rapid deployment to someone else.

- Metrics Storage Server Analysis

  - This is one application for which you can always practice interpreting metrics. Simply triage your APM database and server. The APM environment is just another application in your IT environment and, like most other applications, you probably don't know anything about it.
  - If you can't triage your APM environment, you are not going to have much success with a business application.

Artifacts

SampleTriage.ppt

Triage scope Template

- Application:

  - AppServer|POJO ___v_ on OS ____v_ with ____ JVM
  - # JVMs
  - What does it do?
  - What problems were experienced to date and how were they resolved?

- Platform for Metrics Storage component
- Extension products needed
- Access to restart servers
- Access to generate load
- Suitability of testing scripts
- Target start date
- Expected duration

Summary

Triage with single metrics is challenging. There are a great variety of metrics available and many of them will not be familiar to you. The APM workstation is designed to make this triage more efficient and easy to learn. What is more difficult is navigating the different internal motivations for employing APM. Knowing the problems to solve and the processes to follow is often a problem for organizations that are desperate to improve their situation, so much so that they reach for any tool that seems appropriate.

You can eliminate and simplify most of the monitoring use cases that you want to support by using techniques that I will introduce in the next few chapters. These techniques will require planning and process development; you will only appreciate them after you have some perspective on the differences between how the APM tools are designed to be used and what you really need APM visibility to do for you.

Bear this in mind while you practice navigating among the metrics, discovering key components, and developing reports and dashboards. Now that you can find and understand relationships among components, how does this help you manage the application lifecycle? What would be better information?

Triage with Baselines

Kick Off Meeting

Motivation

The most important piece of history is the *baseline*. At some point, either in production or pre-production, someone collected metrics on the application when it was performing normally, and generated a report of graphs and tables about the key metrics. For what the key metrics are, and how to find them, please look at Chapter 12. This baseline report is essentially a signature of the application. It is also what most folks are attempting to compare to when they have an incident but they just don't have ready access to historical information. A baseline eliminates the subjective memory and replaces it with a historical snapshot of performance characteristics.

Provided that monitoring is active, we may always obtain a baseline from the last week or last month of performance data. The subjective part is to have someone decide what is normal. For firefights, I often exploit the findings generated during a pre-sales pilot which are incidental to installing and exercising the monitoring tool, as a baseline for a production incident. Even as I will know little more about the application than what I learn on the scope call, prior to the engagement, this baseline allows me to quickly identify suspects. Of course, I have the benefit of a few years experience that helps me to appreciate how far I can trust the baseline, in as much as what the baseline says about performance. Invariably, I am able to triage effectively with three month old data.

For a new triage team, we want to improve the odds for success, and the easiest way to do this is to have baselines collected during pre-production testing. And this is where the organizational process comes in. Hopefully, someone is doing testing and we simply need them to enable monitoring and pass judgment on the results ("test was successful"), and we will have all the baselines we could want. But the monitoring has to be enabled. So when we are able to collect and exploit normal baselines to assist our triage, we simply call this *triage with baselines*.

As the organization matures and becomes comfortable with monitoring in general, and with some process changes as appropriate, we will be getting baselines from both pre-production and production. In fact, it will be hard to keep baselines from showing up during unit testing and being digested by capacity management teams. This takes us later to the next stage of triage called *triage with trends*., in Chapter 16.

Triage with Baselines

This is the second level of triage, where we move away from single metrics and start instead to work on summary reporting of the tests and production experiences that we encounter. We introduced some of the cookbook to guide the mechanical part of the process, in Chapter 12. In this chapter we want to be able to confidently compare a known baseline, with a representative production period, and look at some techniques for interpreting this information.

Why is working with baselines a separate topic? It is because I simply see very little evidence that anyone is actually using APM for anything other than *triage with single metrics*. Making comparisons among different baselines and trying to use today's APM tools to support that activity is really cumbersome. It simply doesn't align with what folks want to know.

Here is a summary of the high level activities that APM tools should directly support:

- Basic comparisons
    - Compare to a *baseline* of acceptable performance
    - Compare my best QA run to current production
    - Compare baselines of the last 5 QA releases
    - Compare all 12 production outages we had last month
        - What do they have in common?
        - What is unique for one incident, from all the others?

    - Compare the Q1 and Q2 releases
    - Compare application server release: TomCat service pack 2 vs. TomCat service pack 3

When preparing to review baselines, define a list of criteria on which to compare and contrast specific findings:

- For each run/day:
    - How is memory used?
    - What is the user load throughout the day?
    - Which components are stressed?

- Are the top 10 performers, each component, consistent from run/day to run/day?
- Are there situations where different performers are active that are not part of the top 10?
- Are stalls present?

The bulk of our analysis comes from the baseline report which has established the following attributes about an application from our earlier triage with single metrics:

- We know 5-10 high response time components
- We know 5-10 high invocation components
- We know if our SQL is consistent or in need of partitioning
- We know 5-10 high response time SQL statements
- We know 5-10 high invocation SQL statements
- We know the memory profile for the application
- We know the variety of components expereinced
- We know the characteristics of key transactions

Some of these elements we can put into tables after generating a report. This report is then something we have the potential to compare automatically as well an manually (via a spreadsheet). Others will remain graphics, as screenshots or charts, and will still require manual and visual comparison.

Reporting Conventions

When we can output the report as a *.csv (comma-separated values) format, this file may be opened directly into a spreadsheet. You can then divide and sort according to the type of component. I will put each component in its own tab/worksheet and then create a new tab to hold the analysis and other observations, as shown in Figure 15-1. All of the data is in a single *.csv file, so you will have a bit of copy-and-paste to get it in a reviewable format. This is a slightly painful, manual process, which can be endured because it accommodates any variety of data formats.

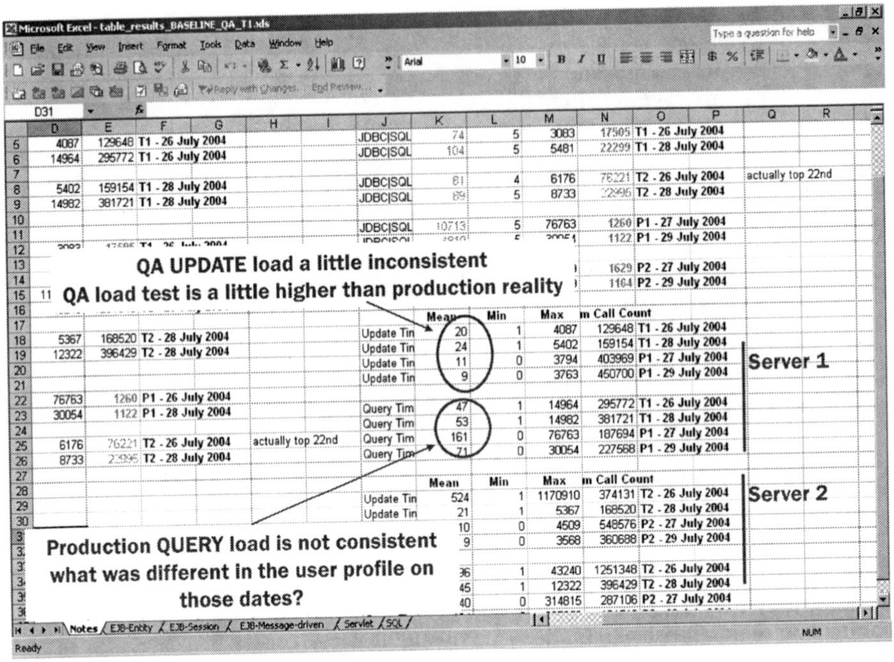

Figure 15-1. Summarize Results

Achieving Consistent Results

In order to summarize results accurately, we need to know what factor exists between our test period in QA and a comparable period in production. I tend to focus on a two hour period (120 minutes) around an incident (1:45 before and 00:15 after), so that is a good point to start. In QA, I tend to try for a 20 minute test of which 10 minutes is at steady-state. Thus, if I multiply my QA invocation totals by 12 for my top components, this should be comparable to my production experience for the same components over a two hour period.

If the numbers are not within 5-10%, then I will calculate a scaling factor to increase the QA value and check with the remaining values of my top components. If my load profiles were accurate, the final counts should be within 5-10%.

Component Analysis

When you are deciding which components to focus on, sorting the metrics, largest to smallest, as shown in Figure 15-2, always ensures that you are looking at the significant components first. All metrics contribute to visibility and give some assurance that if an unexpected error occurs, some metric will correlate with that event. But until that unexpected event, the only metrics that matter are the ones that are being exercised the most, or contribute the greatest response time.

Addressing these components first offers some real potential to improve performance overall. Once they have been addressed the application will effectively rebalance, revealing some other bottleneck.

Thus Figure 15-2 emulates the same capability you may have in the APM workstation, as we illustrated earlier in Figure 13-1 and 13-2. Using a reporting scheme lets us bring more data into perspective where before we needed two searches to get the response time and invocation results.

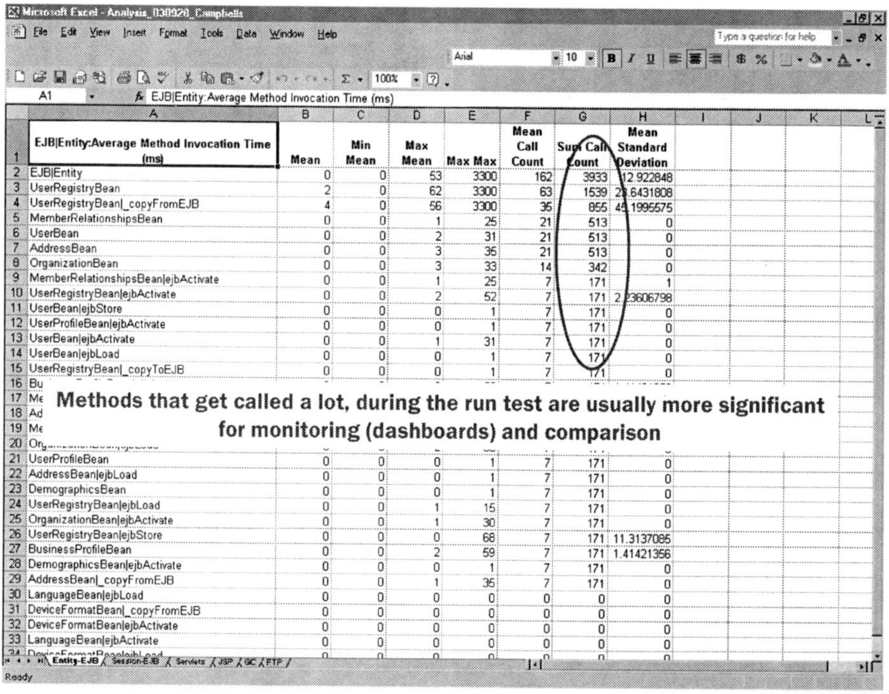

	EJB|Entity:Average Method Invocation Time (ms)	Mean	Min Mean	Max Mean	Max Max	Mean Call Count	Sum Call Count	Mean Standard Deviation
2	EJB|Entity	0	0	53	3300	162	3933	12.922848
3	UserRegistryBean	2	0	62	3300	63	1539	23.6431808
4	UserRegistryBean|_copyFromEJB	4	0	56	3300	35	855	45.1995575
5	MemberRelationshipsBean	0	0	1	25	21	513	0
6	UserBean	0	0	2	31	21	513	0
7	AddressBean	0	0	3	35	21	513	0
8	OrganizationBean	0	0	3	33	14	342	0
9	MemberRelationshipsBean|ejbActivate	0	0	1	25	7	171	1
10	UserRegistryBean|ejbActivate	0	0	2	52	7	171	2.23606798
11	UserBean|ejbStore	0	0	0	1	7	171	0
12	UserProfileBean|ejbActivate	0	0	0	1	7	171	0
13	UserBean|ejbActivate	0	0	1	31	7	171	0
14	UserBean|ejbLoad	0	0	0	1	7	171	0
15	UserRegistryBean|_copyToEJB	0	0	0	1	7	171	0
16	Bu							
17	Me							
18	Ad							
19	Me							
20	Or							
21	UserProfileBean	0	0	0	1	7	171	0
22	AddressBean|ejbLoad	0	0	0	1	7	171	0
23	DemographicsBean	0	0	0	1	7	171	0
24	UserRegistryBean|ejbLoad	0	0	1	15	7	171	0
25	OrganizationBean|ejbActivate	0	0	1	30	7	171	0
26	UserRegistryBean|ejbStore	0	0	0	68	7	171	11.3137085
27	BusinessProfileBean	0	0	2	59	7	171	1.41421356
28	DemographicsBean|ejbActivate	0	0	0	1	7	171	0
29	AddressBean|_copyFromEJB	0	0	1	35	7	171	0
30	LanguageBean|ejbLoad	0	0	0	0	0	0	0
31	DeviceFormatBean|_copyFromEJB	0	0	0	0	0	0	0
32	DeviceFormatBean|ejbActivate	0	0	0	0	0	0	0
33	LanguageBean|ejbActivate	0	0	0	0	0	0	0

Figure 15-2. Call Count Analysis

This brings us to another important consideration. A high response time is significant when it is being exercised significantly (high number of invocations). For example, a component that has a response time of 200 seconds is not significant if it is only exercised twice a day. It does not mean that it is unimportant but from the triage perspective, you only want to focus on the most active and worst performing components first.

Initial Automation

Manual techniques can be limiting but what can we do for automation? The first step is to simply go into the each report_nnn.csv files and pull out metrics of interest so they are follow one another. The format for the outputted data is [filename avg min max count], for the example in Figure 15-3. The header line shows the component and the metric type.

```
=========== "Servlets:Average Response Time (ms)" ===========

msydor_051105__qa_0_1405-1535  2499    10      193972   10815
msydor_051106__qa_0_2300-0222  39148   10      9614068  24018

=========== "EJB|Session:Average Method Invocation Time (ms)" ===========

msydor_051105__qa_0_1405-1535  3504    0       1661461  19032
msydor_051106__qa_0_2300-0222  7440    0       504462   62939

=========== "JMS|Message Listener:Average Method Invocation Time (ms)" ===========

msydor_051105__qa_0_1405-1535  3641    16      71645    3003
msydor_051106__qa_0_2300-0222  5669    13      522139   5677

=========== "JNDI|Context:Average Method Invocation Time (ms)" ===========

msydor_051105__qa_0_1405-1535  293     1       14409    698
msydor_051106__qa_0_2300-0222  114     0       4091     1210

=========== "JSP:Average Response Time (ms)" ===========

msydor_051105__qa_0_1405-1535  5039    12      404951   5421
msydor_051106__qa_0_2300-0222  17624   13      3745361  17432

=========== "JDBC:Average Update Time (ms)" ===========

msydor_051105__qa_0_1405-1535  44      0       9090     26034
msydor_051106__qa_0_2300-0222  61      0       19851    84201

=========== "JDBC:Average Query Time (ms)" ===========

msydor_051105__qa_0_1405-1535  2433    0       1647963  17687
msydor_051106__qa_0_2300-0222  38      0       11903    49658
```

Figure 15-3. Output of the Characterize Script

It should seem like a trivial exercise to have this information available but I have not yet found an APM workstation that can directly compare two baselines in this fashion. An alternate technique, shown in Figure 15-4, is to specify the metric of interest and then feed it a list of files that are to be examined.

```
test -runlist runlist.txt -csv -metric "ServicePageDisplayServlet:Average"

============== CAPAqa1_060206_12hrs_0800_2000.csv =

    728    7    9933   4    58737   2908

============== CAPAqa1_060207_12hrs_0800_2000.csv =

    717    41   8445   3    33808   2429

============== CAPAqa1_060208_12hrs_0800_2000.csv =

    630    574  8638   4    32736   3603
```

Figure 15-4. Output for Single Metric

These tools, which comprise what I call *characterization*[1], are just simple perl scripts that operate over a directory of *.csv files. All they need are consistently formatted reports, which are just the baselines we have been talking about in Chapters 12 and 13. The example baseline report in Figure 15-5 used summary values for the different components. Some components have multiple sub components. For example, an EJB[2] (Enterprise Java Bean) has messaging and session varients. There may be dozens of messaging beans but sometimes it is sufficient to look at all the messaging beans in aggregate, rather then report them individually.

---

[1] http://en.wikipedia.org/wiki/Characterization_test

[2] http://en.wikipedia.org/wiki/EJB

Component Response Time (overview)

Resource:Metric	Mean	Min	Max	MMin	MMax	Count
EJB|Messagge-driven:Average Method Invocation Time (ms)	1,284	9	106,942	0	607,856	12,775
EJB|Session:Average Method Invocation Time (ms)	1,851	1	279,491	0	1,369,006	9,693
JDBC:Average Query Time (ms)	950	0	37,218	0	83,313	28,214
JDBC:Average Update Time (ms)	79	0	13,093	0	200,896	4,221
JMS|Message Consumer:Average Method Invocation Time (ms)	57,109	567	143,981	2	716,873	66,412
JMS|Message Listener:Average Method Invocation Time (ms)	11,828	0	168,678	0	1,181,781	5,476
JMS|Queue Sender:Average Method Invocation Time (ms)	513	0	21,018	0	278,362	3,604
JMS|Topic Publisher:Average Method Invocation Time (ms)	36	1	32	0	179	36
JTA:Average Method Invocation Time (ms)	203	0	29,949	0	485,008	14,979
Servlets :Average Response Time (ms)	8,884	352	13,232	0	54,935	13

Start: 5/9/06 9:00 AM	End: 5/17/06 2:00 PM

Metric Grouping: Component Response Time (ms)
Agents: ftbhvt01|WebLogic|wftf_srv_01

Figure 15-5. Baseline Report Table

While Figure15-5 is obviously a graphical depiction of a page from a baseline report, this same report would have been saved in a *.csv or *.html format in order to support characterization.

Process

In order to undertake any significant *triage with baselines* you will need a consistent source of baseline reports. You can do this on demand but this results is a rather hectic rush to gather details of the important QA test runs and operational incidents. And once you have gathered all of this test and event metadata you will then need to run quite a few reports. This takes time – 30 minutes to a few hours, depending on the scope of the analysis.

Instead, if you have been collecting baselines after each test, generating a report for each incident, and keeping filenames consistent, then you need only run the characterization script – which will complete in seconds.

Triage with Baselines

1. Prepare metric collections appropriate for the key components in your application

   a. APC (Availability, Performance and Capacity) are ideal, if you have had time to validate that the collections are accurate.

   b. Summary metrics, when available, make excellent candidates for a summary of the application, when you don't have the time for validating the actual key components.

2. Prepare a baseline report with the metric collections

3. Generate a baseline for each successful test or operational period

   a. The operational period may be 2-4 hours, while the test period is only 10-20 minutes.

   b. The test period should be focused on the steady-state performance.

   c. The suggested format of the report filename should have the following details:
      i. Application Name [APP1, APP2] (something appropriate)
      ii. Environment [QA, PROD]
      iii. Date [YYMMDD]
      iv. Duration [10, 20, 120]
      v. Start [hhmm] (24 hours clock)
      vi. End [hhmm] (24 hours clock)

4. Create a runbaseline.txt file, for each application, to contain the names of the baselines you want to trend or compare.

5. Prepare a script that will extract the component names for each of the baseline filenames in the runbaseline.txt, and output the results to the screen or file.

   a. Whether you target the screen or file, be sure to use <TAB> between the output fields in order to support use by a spreadsheet.

6. Compare, contrast and discuss the salient features.

Summary

Baselines are an important foundation to more accurate and rapid triage. We can eliminate much of the focus on how an APM workstation is to be used, who is entitled to use it, and the training and experience required, by enacting a process to generate a simple report with all of the key information. An APM specialist will define that report, but a simple script is all that is necessary to execute it and exploit the APM visibility.

Once baselines reports are readily available, there is great potential for automation of the analysis. This further eliminates requirements for spreadsheet skills and patience and simply brings the metrics data to a point of direct comparison. We reviewed a couple of strategies to enable this next generation of post-analysis but there is much more that could be done.

Triage with Trends

Opportunity is missed by most people because it is dressed in overalls and looks like work.

—Thomas Alva Edison

The third level of triage is to consider the full perspective of APM by exploiting historical metrics from other sources; this is called *triage with trends*. Trending is the consideration of data over some period of time, usually via statistical techniques; it's something that IT is trying to do for all types of availability and performance problems, not simply those that have the benefit of APM visibility. The challenge is to bring together all of these disparate sources of data into something on which correlation techniques may be applied.

Historically, this integration effort is what folks are trying to do for all types of IT performance problems. The challenge has always been with the timeliness and quality of the trend information. For example, logfile information can provide much of the same transaction information and details as APM, when the application has been designed to log all of the necessary information. But it does so at a much lower resolution (hourly or daily), so you find yourself delayed anywhere from 2 to 12 hours before you can access the information. Bringing together all of these disparate sources of information so that trend analysis may be performed is also a significant integration challenge. The APM initiative becomes a natural integration point.

A more rigorous definition of this third level of triage as it correlates to APM is the collection, dissemination, and use of accurate and reliable quantitative data. In the language I have defined so far, this becomes a *trending process* and it covers data and report integration, correlation, RCA, and SLA definitions. Much of what you are considering so far for triage is still ad-hoc—you investigate performance problems as they arise, and you know now that preparation makes the triage more effective. Now you are asserting a greater perspective and building visibility into how the enterprise conducts business rather than the earlier focus on a key application or transaction. These business decisions, defined as SLAs, are based on the same metrics you are collecting to support triage—you simply have a higher-order use of that data.

The first two triage levels, described in Chapters 14 and 15, are designed to provide consistently summarized information to enhance the trending process and to make this information available in minutes. But this is only the first part of the bigger integration problem. Within the APM domain you have ready access to performance data. But how do you get data from the other types of monitoring technologies? This is an important consideration because as you becomes successful with the APM initiative in delivering a more accessible collaboration among performance information, you'll find a number of other IT focus areas that would benefit from this same level of collaboration, which would help to further enrich the visibility for the enterpise overall, including availability and capacity management. When you combine the coarse-grained availability metrics with the much finer-grained APM metrics and compare actual performance with baselines, as shown in Chapters 12-15, you have all the tools and processes that support *service level management (SLM[1])*. Pursuing triage with trends establishes the foundation for SLM; indeed, you can't have effective SLM without strong triage capabilities.

The broad perspective that triage with trends will provide is leveraged to help you undertake some sophisticated analysis, including definition of the service level agreement (SLA) and determination of root cause[2] for a performance incident or outage. Application management becomes efficient and effective when you distill numerous measurement points into key performance indicators (KPIs)[3] that management teams can track and influence to meet business objectives.

Trending helps determine root cause for a performance incident. Root cause determination, which I often characterize as something to avoid for an emerging APM discipline, is what most folks associate with triage and firefighting. They want to find problems and fix them, somehow bypassing the process gaps that allowed the problems to occur in the first place. For example, the accepted definition of *root-cause analysis* (RCA)[4] asserts that RCA is a *reactive process* that becomes *proactive* after you gain experience incrementally. I prefer to state that RCA is a post-analysis process (after the incident) that can be incrementally improved by collecting performance baselines proactively. This is, of course, more consistent

---

[1] Service Level Management (SLM) is an ITIL discipline, in the service delivery section, and is focused on the relationship between the consumer of the service (client) and the provider (IT) as define by a service-level agreement (SLA) Wikipedia: Service_level_management

[2] Wikipedia, "root cause," http://en.wikipedia.org/wiki/Root_cause

[3] Wikipedia, "key performance indicator," http://en.wikipedia.org/wiki/Key_performance_indicator

[4] Wikipedia, "root cause analysis," http://en.wikipedia.org/wiki/Root_cause_analysis

with the evolution of triage techniques already established, and still allows you to accomodate the big exception: How do you do RCA when there is no opportunity to collect baselines or incremental experience? I will address this topic separately in Chapter 17: "Firefighting."

Another approach often confused with triage with trends is *forensic performance analysis*[5]. The difference is that trending is information gathering that is built up over time in anticipation of a triage activity, while forensic analysis is a detailed review of logs and other data sources in response to an unexpected event; it is completely reactive. You can allow for a forensic approach with APM but this is really more to expose the full nature of a performance problem, as discussed in Chapter 17.

Kick Off Meeting

Motivation

When the organization is comfortable with baselines, audit and basic triage, you will start to notice that performance suspects are being suggested in systems that are not directly monitored by APM. This results in a visibility gap and requires identification of existing performance information, followed by integration within the APM environment, in order to be useful for triage in the future. Each visibility gap is an opportunity for a small integration project, filling in the monitoring gaps and resulting in more effective management. Integration progress is a trend. The data and reports being integrated very often contain performance trends, or via APM techniques will become important evidence of trends.

Trending is another magical term where everyone knows what it means but no one seems to have anything actionable (something they will contribute) to facilitate the definition and the interpretation of the trend. The emphasis here is to fill that gap and provide you with something actionable—specifically, how to address visibility gaps and leverage baselines to define SLAs and undertake RCA.

Types of Trends: Correlation

Much of the science of trend analysis is focused on statistics for data being collected. Statistics are important when your data is noisy, or is otherwise being interferred with. That's not the case with APM where you have direct measurements with little opportunity for error (within the limitations of the timebase for the measurement). The noise is something that is added to a measurement through electronic instrumentation, not software instrumentation. This does not mean your measurements are always consistent. The quantity being measured, like response time, is quite variable from one invocation to the

---

[5] Forensic performance analysis is more frequently associated with network management. http://en.wikipedia.org/wiki/Network_performance_management

next. But whatever value you get, you can be confident that the measurement is quite correct[6].

The reality that a measurement quantity may vary from one minute to the next means that you will attempt to reduce the variation by structuring the load or test plan for that measurement. Otherwise, you have to live with whatever range of value you may get. As you found in Chapter 15, this variation ultimately decides if the metric is suitable for a threshold.

When it comes time to compare metrics, you have two approaches to consider. In the QA enironment, you will minimize any variation by limiting the use cases explored and structuring the load to be reproducible. In this case, you can average the metric over the steady-state period and arrive at a single number that can be directly compared with a previous test or test varient. When you get to the production environment and the conditions are reproducible, you will likewise be able to identify a steady-state period on which to calculate the average and make direct comparisons with another single metric value.

More often, in the production environment, you will find it difficult to identify a consistent, steady-state period over which to caluclate the average. You will not be able to reduce the comparison to a single averaged number. Instead, you will need to assess if any trends are present in order to compare metrics over different intervals. This is where the time-of-day and time-of-week considerations come in to play. To get consistent results, you need to discover what the optimal frequency of baseline collection should be in order to identify significant trends.

With APM and the conditions of direct measurement and selecting a suitable period for comparisons, the emphasis will be on *correlation*[7] among various metrics. The observations on corrllation that you will make for a given metric A and its baseline B include the following, summarized in Figure 16-1.

---

[6] Within the accuracy of the time base on which the measurement is made. See Wikipedia: accuracy_and_precision.

[7] Wikipedia, "correlation," http://en.wikipedia.org/wiki/Correlation

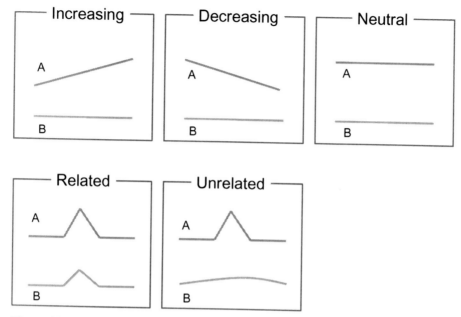

Figure 16-1. Types of correlations

Initially, and for the near future, these correlations are determined by inspection. Of course, each of these features, as well as the comparison, could be calculated statistically. But that remains for a future generation of APM software designed to automatically identify the critical components and trends. Today, you need to conduct correlation via human intervention, and you need to be careful that the data sets are consistent for the interval you are comparing.

Trending Scenario

Trending is the greater perspective on an application or service. It's where you bring all the seemingly disparate pieces of performance information together into a cogent realization and ensuing plan of action. If you look back at the first two levels of triage, they are a bit narrow. *Triage with single metrics* is extra-ordinarily narrow; it only considers the metrics as isoloated bits of information. *Triage with baselines* only considers the performance of an application in the context of a single test or related group of tests or operational expereince. Triage with trends is the perspective over the application lifecycle to date and could also include experiences from other independent applications or resources.

Let's look at an example scenario that expresses the scope and evolution of a performance problem:

An application has just been released by development into QA. It integrates a new framework that provies new user interface capabilities and has a different app server configuration to support the new functionality. This will be the first test of this new framework. QA is unaware of the nature of the changes to the application. They see it as a scheduled update of the application.

The first round of testing is conducted and the application has some difficulty. It is unable to complete the standard load test and suffers from a poor memory utilization profile. It appears that the new version of the application consumes much more memory than the previous versions. Application and performance baselines are generated for the current version. After comparing the failed test run with the prior acceptable application and performance baselines, it is confirmed that transaction response times are unacceptable and that the memory usage pattern is also problematic. The top five components, representing response time and invocations, are found to be significantly degraded from the earlier baselines but no new components were identified. QA contacts the developers, explains their findings and their lack of visibility into any explanation for the degradation. After some discussion, development reveals that they are using a new framework. They were not able to fully exercise this new functionalty during unit testing, because they didn't have the real database available. Instead, they just used a "sham" database call, one that issues a query, and returns after some delay, without actually hitting the database. It was determined to restore the earier version of the data persistence layer and retest the application.

The second round of testing is conducted after the developers identified some of the class names of the new functionality they had built so that the data persistence layer could be changed as needed. This information is added to the agent configuration and a short test is conducted to confirm that there is now visibility into this new functionality; a new configuration baseline is established. The performance testing is able to conclude without failure but a large number of stalls are detected and attributed to the new functionality. The stalls are attributed to the use of stubs. If a real database was present, the stalls would be absent; so goes the explanation offered by development. With no other concerns for the app, it goes forward to production packaging and deployment.

The deployment takes place over the weekend. As load increases during business hours, the application is significantly compromised, resulting in two high severity incidents (SEV-1) being logged. After the second SEV-1 incident, it's decided to remove the application from production; this decision takes place Monday evening. The same stalls are being experienced, except this time extreemly long response times were noted and the persistence mechanism was implicated. The release is sent back to development for a fix. They have about 6-8 weeks to implement a fix and retest the application before the next production deployment window.

Now four weeks later, the parent group is re-organized. Deployment schedules are frozen while the overall portfolio of applications is reviewed and prioritized. As part of the reorganization, the business sponsor has brought in a new Director of Development and four of that new director's former direct reports. There is a high expectation that they will be able to turn around the overall development effort. The new team has no monitoring experience but has really strong experience with persistence frameworks from their former project. Two weeks later, the problematic application is back in production, the apparent benefit of a steamlined approval process and developer expertise.

After ten days of production operation of the new app, and all without any significant incidents, a catastrophic string of incidents occurs, taking out multiple applications in addition to the newest app with the persistence framework. The result is two days of significant service outages. Monitoring is enabled throughout the production environment but none of the prior monitoring team (those with any

APM experience) survived the re-organization. None of the new team, as mentioned earlier, has any experience with APM technology and processes. The new Director of Development is getting a lot of attention and pressure, and is scrambling for some resources who can use the existing APM information.

This is the point where your phone is ringing, e-mails are surging and you are beginning to lament ever coming back from vacation! But this is what people expect from an APM expert. They expect you to sort out this whole mess—not just to isolate the offending code but to identify what went wrong during the application lifecycle that allowed the major outage to occur.

My personal preference is to be the firefight specialist who just needs to isolate the offending code (put out the fire). I always appreciate some history into how the problem evolved, because it makes the firefight really easy, but I don't have to deal with the politics of avoiding these problems in future. I can avoid the new Director of Development, the new developers, the code base from another project. Your reality will be different and you will likely have to assume responsibilities for these details that I can brush aside.

Back to the example, there are a few trends you will need to establish. The application lifecycle is well documented but you really need to know what the new development team was doing in their prior roles. What was unique about their applications? How did they developed their expertise? What kinds of issues did they encounter? That's what you currently don't have visibility into. You also need to get a perspective on the other applications that were affected. Your application is the "last change" so all the focus is on your app but how well do the other apps get along with each other? Maybe your app was just enough to upset the balance. You need to understand more about the app environment or you risk chasing your own tail. You might find that it has nothing to do with your app at all, despite its checkered past.

The ease with which you can get this other information will be a function of how prepared these stakeholders are to fulfill your request. The ability to understand and undertake trending is another perspective on collaboration. Baselines are focused on your application to the exclusions of other things, and sharing baselines is how you foster collaboration through APM. Getting these other stakeholders to understand how to baseline their own systems and environments and how to interact with your triage activity is the next level of collaboration. They will not have the same tools and technology but they can understand what you will need and they can plan to be prepared. Achieving this level of cooperation is challanging and it's what makes triage with trends, leading to RCA, out of reach for many practitioners.

Taking care of trending is the executive management part of APM. It is understanding and documenting the development constraints, the testing short-comings, the misdirected responses and fixes so that you can confidently recommend organizational and process changes that will improve the situation. The apex of these goals are the measurements that support SLA and RCA, so your ability to manage successfully is directly proportional to the accuracy with which you can undertake SLA and RCA.

Preparing for Triage with Trends

So what do I do to mentor a triage candidate in order to deliver *triage* with trends? I focus first on the integration of the non-APM performance data sources and tools. Once some of the critical integrations are initiatied, you turn back to APM and look at techniques to precisely increase visibility with more sophisticated instrumentation strategies. The customization and tuning of APM instrumentation is quite vendor specifc and propritary, so I will not cover that here. This is also requires the definition of real transactions, such as those definitions focused on specific content types. You will need to add those details on your own.

Data Integration Strategies

As introduced in Chapter 3, there are a variety of technologies that contribute to APM, although they are not typically considered APM tools. These include log analysis, database analysis, SMF Records, and packet capure and traffic analysis where stand-alone tools will be employed. Agent APIs and scripting make up more flexible approaches.

Before instrumentation techniques were established, log files were the most flexible way to get performance information for an application. There are a couple of limitations. The first is that you have to be able to modify the application code in order to utilize logging and to identify an appropriate metric. The second is that over-reliance on logging can negatively affect application performance because significant resources may be needed to accommodate increasing levels of logging. The third point is that analysis of the log becomes complicated as the log file increases in size and quantity.

That said, logging is useful when you're started APM, and because it a well-established approach, there is a good chance that some important system that would provide valuable information during triage will be making some use of logging. These are the types of opportunities you look for when you are establishing a foundation for trending, in addition to instrumentation and real/synthetic transaction monitoring. Analysis of the log file data can be achieved through some free tools[8].

You will uncover opportunities for triage via logs when you are completing the visibility assessment described in Chapter 3. It is then important to get a sample log and see what kinds of information it collects. Ideally, if you can get logs from an incident, you will be able to evaluate if the logs can correlate with your other monitoring and thus contribute to triage. This is something you want to try in advance in order to confirm the log as useful.

---

[8] Wikipedia, "web log analysis software," http://en.wikipedia.org/wiki/Web_log_analysis_software

Sometimes the source log file will not be in a convenient format. In this case, use an ELT[9] (Extract – Transform – Load) tool to convert the data to a more consistent format.

Database Analysis

APM will often have evidence that a database query is suspect. Verifying this presumption requires a database administration tool[10] to execute suspect queries, try alternatives, and make changes to the database configuration. While this tool is not often a source of performance information, it is important to confirm a query or database problem.

SMF Records

While much of APM is focused on distributed applications, mainframe applications or resources can contribute to APM. The System Management Framework[11] (SMF) is designed to collect performance information to aid in the tuning of mainframe applications.

Again, you need to evaluate how useful SMF records will be in correlating performance incidents that you detect with other technologies. Processes for getting the recording configuration enabled and transferring the data need to be established well in advance of a triage event.

Packet Capture and Traffic Analysis

An emerging focus of real-time analysis are the network protocols[12] used by various applications. This extends APM into non-HTTP client-server applications; it also allows for troubleshooting complex network configuration issues. You will take advantage of this technology when you are defining transactions for use with real-time or synthetic transaction monitoring.

Agent APIs

Some APM solutions allow you construct your own agents. You are supplied with an agent API, which takes care of all communication with the metrics storage component, and you supply the code that makes the measurements and generates the metric. If you have something to measure (such as interactions and data via some other application API), this is a very efficient mechanism to accomplish the integration with only a few lines of code. The benefit is that the metrics are available for triage and correlation, just as from any other agent in your APM solution.

---

[9] TalenD is an example tool for ETL
www.talend.com/index.php

[10] TOra is an example tool for database administration.
www.osalt.com/tora

[11] Wikipedia, "SMF_120.9," http://en.wikipedia.org/wiki/SMF_120.9

[12] WireShark is an example of a network protocol analyzer.
www.wireshark.org

Scripting

A non-programming alternative is to use existing commands to get the status or performance metrics for various systems and applications. The commands can be provided by operating system, such as vmstat or netstat, or your target application may have a command interface that can be invoked. Your script will parse[13] this command information and publish it as metrics if an agent API is available. Otherwise, you can simply generate a timestamp and output the data to a log file. Interacting with an application by simulating a user issuing commands is just another form of a synthetic transaction.

Scripts can also issue a ping[14] command to confirm reachability or as a coarse measure of network efficiency.

Extending Visibility

After additional metric sources have been integrated, any additional customization of the transactions or instrumentation falls into the category of *extending visibility*. Often, the default set of transactions or instrumentation is focused on those elements that closely follow industry standards. When you have evidence of gaps in your visibility, such as missing transactions or inadequate transaction stack depth, there will be an number of remedies depending on the capabilitiies of your APM solution.

For transaction definition in support of real or synthetic transaction sources, packet and header analysis, as discussed earlier, will be your path to greater visibility.

For instrumentation, you will need to have some conversations with your developers in order to uncover any functionality that does not closely follow interface standards. This is often the case with a custom or third party (purchased or open-source) framework that provides functionality for the application. You will want to review the component architecture where requests are initiated, find out what resources are involved, and then refer back to the transaction call stacks when possible. The call stack adds a visual component into the extent of the visibility gap that can help the developers quickly understand what you are looking for.

After you have identified the missing functionality (classes and methods) you will add this to the APM agent configuration; exactly how you do this will vary for each vendor. Once the changes have been made, you will then exercise the application by basically repeating the application baseline process in order to confirm that the visibility gap has been filled. Usually one to three iterations will take care of most visibility gaps.

---

[13] "Scrape" is another term often used to describe the process of extracting metric information from the output of these commands. "Screen-scraping" is this same approach but applied to a user interface, often a legacy device. You open a session, send commands, and then scrape the resulting output form metrics.

[14] Wikipedia, "ping," http://en.wikipedia.org/wiki/Ping

I prefer to focus on common frameworks first because any work done here will easily be amortized across multiple applications. This fortunate circumstance happens frequently, so creating an opportunity to correct visibility is a key goal captured in the phased deployment methodology, discussed in Chapter 7.

Reporting Integration

Rather than building interfaces and agents to collect data for APM, you may sometimes find opportunities to work with summary information in the form of reports. Reports are often text-based and thus their data is readily extracted. Keep in mind that much reporting is of the daily and weekly variety and not at all the same resolution as real-time monitoring. But if you want to be successful in triage with trends, you need to find examples of successful, trusted reporting.

The first objective is to validate that the real-time monitoring is seeing the same trends. A new APM initiative is always being challenged to prove that the APM view of the world is just as good as the current reporting practice. Of course you expect it to be even better, but until you establish that it is just as good, no one will have confidence when you start to show them things that the current reporting cannot do.

There is much to emulate from application teams with established reporting (format and frequency), especially in how they gather the data and how they share the results. You second objective is to help ensure the long-term success by getting these existing report consumers to build APM information into their view of the world. Providing the same information as another report is a poor value proposition; you have to show them something new and more interesting.

You should already have experience in extracting metrics from existing reports. Triage with baselines, covered in Chapter 13, depends on this technique. Getting the reporting data into a useful form will often involve a combination of techniques, such as a script issuing SQL statements against a data warehose or an ETL tool to collect and reformat the data for you.

The Future of Monitoring Integration

It should be clear that the foundation for triage with trends is based on integration of various monitoring tools and technologies. And today this is painstaking work because many of the integration targets, however valuable, were originally designed as *stand-alone*[15] (reserved for a small goup of people and in a limited role). Integrating these data sources requires skill and creativity in order to have them seamlessly support the trending activity. The monitoring tool industry has long recognized this impediment and has developed a number of different integration strategies[16]. There have been architectures supporting point-to-point

---

[15] Wikipedia, "stand-alone," http://en.wikipedia.org/wiki/Stand-alone

[16] Wikipedia, "enterprise application integration," http://en.wikipedia.org/wiki/Enterprise_application_integration#Integration_patterns

integration bus and lately *federation*[17] of the underlying data sources. Of particular interest for APM are the ideas of the configuration management system (CMS) and the configuration management database (CMDB)[18].

The goals for CMS and CMDB are to federate access to the underlying sources of data about the IT environment, present this information as needed, but more importantly, focus on establishing and maintaing the relationships between the abstraction of the business service to the underlying physical IT infrastructure. The federation means that access to the underlying management data repositories (MDR) is transparent with the data remaining in place and not replicated. The APM metric storage server is one such MDR. Any other monitoring tools effectively reduce to some sort of MDR. Provided that all of the participating vendors subscribe to the CMDB model, the integration problem becomes reasonable.

Of course, all of this is only an idea and there are few examples of a successful CMS/CMDB effort today. I believe it is a problem of scope. Following a CMS/CMDB strategy requires an enourmous effort before any benefits might be realized, akin to boiling the ocean to get out the dissolved gold. But I also believe that APM tactics—small incremental efforts, focused on key applications and services—is the way to get the benefits of CMS/CMDB earlier and more reliably.

There are a number of use cases that CMS/CMDB is intended to support. Two of these, RCA and SLA compliance, are specifically what *triage* with trends is targeting. If you can reach these two use cases, then you will have enough integration achieved so that you may understand the relationships among the physical infrastructure and complete the mapping to the business abstraction. It will also be tractable for validation of that portion, rather than dozens or hundreds of applications.

The next sections will look at this integration question in more detail, including some example applications of how the CMS/CMDB would be leveraged.

Integration Strategies

As the CMS/CMDB strategy is a big step, I will look first at the more typical integration options and service management goals, and build up to the CMS/CMDB. For an example environment I will consider the following:

- Three APM vendors: MDR-X, MDR-Y, and MDR-Z
- One LDAP mapping directory (MD) that maintains platform IP addresses and platform names.
- One application versioning system (AVS) that maintains application name and release numbers.

---

[17] "Future CMDB" by Hank Marquis
www.itsmsolutions.com/newsletters/DITYvol6iss29.htm

[18] Wikipedia, "CMDB," http://en.wikipedia.org/wiki/CMDB

- One inventory management system (IMS) that maintains the dollar value of critical business transactions.
- One mainframe (MF) that logs transactions to a file.

Your integration goal for triage with trends is to integrate the mainframe performance data and generate baselines for each of the applications manged by their respective MDR. When the integration is established, you can deliver RCA and define an SLA.

Your service management goal is to present a single view of the critical business transactions automatically enriched by the current values of the IP addresses, application names and versions that are executing, and assigning a dollar value lost when the application is down or degraded.

What does triage have to do with all of this? Triage is the tail wagging the dog. Your stakeholders want a single view of the business service. Your attempts to do RCA or to define SLAs as part of a triage event highlight the integration gaps and allow you to methodically identify and resolve those gaps—to the benefit of the service management goal. But if you don't make progress with triage, you won't make progress with service management. That's my big assertion as to why service management is not yet delivering on its promise—most folks are weak in the triage department.

Let's look at the different integration strategies and see how they make progress towards service management.

Point to Point

In this strategy, illustrated in Figure 16-2, every MDR is connected directly to every other MDR to share the data that each holds. This is so that each MDR, which is actually an APM component, can assemble a single view of performance data from its perspective. Each MDR has a single view, which is not especially useful. Few, if any, of the MDRs would enrich that single view with the other configuration information from the MD, AVS, and IVS. The MF is integrated via an extension agent, and this technology is only available from a single vendor, in this case. This necessitates the integration among MDRs so that the other solutions can get access to the MF data. Because the MDRs do not offer a service management view with enrichment, a separate application was developed to host the service management single view. Remember, you are not moving data from these MDRs to the true single view. You are only moving information about what components have agents and which MDR hosts those agents. This will allow you to drill down from the business abstraction and into the appropriate MDR in order to veiw a response time or alert status.

In the absence of a standard interface for the interchange of enrichment data, you end up with an increasingly fragile solution as the number of unique MDRs increases. In this case, with 3 MDRs plus several enrichment sources, you will have 15 interfaces to maintain and 6 independent application lifecyles. Any application change could potentially affect the integration at multiple points, so what you really end up with is a fragile solution that will be very difficult to update and maintain.

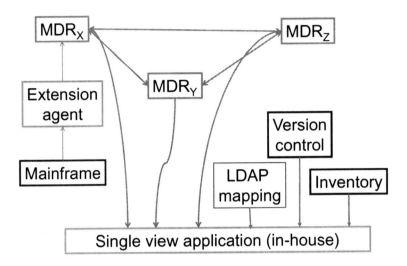

Fifteen integration points to maintain and
six different application lifecycles.

Figure 16-2. Point-to-point integration

This situation is pretty much unsolvable as a point-to-point solution architecture
and I believe that this difficulty accounts for the absence of this kind of solution for
service management. It would be acceptable for a closed system with infrequent
changes. That is simply not the case in a competitive monitoring marketplace.

Integration Bus

You can eliminate more than half of the integration points by moving to an
integration bus architecture, illustrated in Figure 16-3. This approach standardizes
the interface between an MDR and the bus and eliminates the need for MDRx to
support interfaces to MDRy and MDRz, as was done prior. You will still have a
challenge to propogate changes between the bus and the connected resources. The
bus will have its own lifecycle for bug fixes and new functionality, as will each of the
participating resources (MDRs, etc.). At best, you could hope for updates on a
quarterly basis, but an annual pace is more likely. This is fine for a mature
technology but APM—and service management in particular—is still on an rapid
pace of innovation and that means releases at intervals of six months or less.

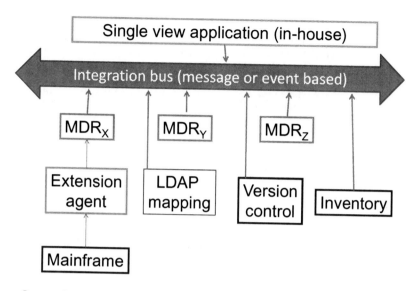

Seven integration points to maintain and
six different application lifecycles.

Figure 16-3. Integration bus

The technology for the integration bus is a big consideration. You could use
messaging or transactional middleware to build your own solution, or something
more capable like event-driven middleware available from multiple vendors. The
problem is that this technology has been around for 10 years already and yet no
one has stepped up with a commercial monitoring or system management
solution-based event-driven middleware. Maybe the licensing cost is too
expensive for a viable product or maybe, as I suspect, the cost of maintaing the
seven integration points is still too risky.

Mediation

This next integration pattern, illustrated in Figure 16-4, represents a very rare
case of a single vendor solution for monitoring and service management. This is
the pattern employed by many monitoring products today for the relationship
between the agents and the monitoring workstation. Rather than having each
agent report to the workstation independently, a mediator (called the manager
application or the metric storage component) accepts all agent connections on one
side and supports some number of workstations on the other side. While any
vendor dreams of this situation—to be that single vendor—such a scenario does
not meet the needs of the IT organization. The problem is two-fold. First, the pace
of available integrations always seems to lag a bit and your organization may
need a particular technology that your monitoring solution just doesn't support. A
smaller, more focus vendor will always be able to innovate at a quicker pace than
a larger, established vendor. The second point is that the protocols for agent-

manager and workstation-manager are unique for each MDR (manager) and this represents a serious impediment for integration into higher-order uses of the agent data, such as SLA management. The service management initiative is an example of an innovation that today is still not part of the default APM capabilities and still is changing at a rapid pace, despite being available for some 15 years already, as is the case with ITIL. It's not that the integrations can't be built; rather it's because they only work within a single vendors' product line. Your IT environment is simply not a single vendor solution and so the mediation pattern doesn't benefit your heterogeneous collection of monitoring and service management technology.

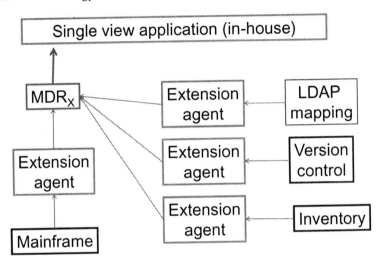

One integration point to maintain and
four extension Agents to maintain;
six different application lifecycles.

Figure 16-4. Mediation

The benefits of the mediation pattern are clear. There's only a single interface to maintain. There is a little more work for the extension agents because as the source applications change, the data being transferred may also change, but this is not a big concern. The real concern is whether you will always have an extension agent available for any of the upcoming enrichment sources. When you don't, you have left open a door for a competing vendor to enter and provide that capability.

When you hear folks talking about the consolidation of IT tools, this is the vision they have in mind. Things will be better if there are fewer integration points to stress over. Reduce the number of vendors and the whole maintenance of the integration becomes more tractable. You simply have to set aside competitive innovation and hope that your selected vendor will be innovative through their own ambition. Historically, this rarely happens.

Federation

Up to this point, you have seen that a integration bus and a single vendor are important patterns in reducing the overall complexity of integration. In isolation, neither of them are successful in the marketplace. Taking the best of these two patterns and merging them into a solution is what the federation pattern provides, as illustrated in Figure 16-5. Here you get the simplicity of reduced integration points coupled with the single interface standard that you would get as with a sole vendor. If you use a standards body to define the interface, all vendors benefit from the interface specification and can avoid writing their own standard. This offers the possibility of true interoperability amongst incumbant solutions and still allows for innovation to integrate without being disruptive. This preserves the relationships among the agents and their respective managers because those details are now abstracted away. When you need to access metrics from both manager-A and manager-B, the *federation service* would collect the information from each manager and present it to the single-view workstation, which no longer requires a direct connection to any of the managers. Thus, enrichment metrics from agent-A and agent-B would be seamlessly available to the SLA application, for example, and the goal of seamless service management is achieved.

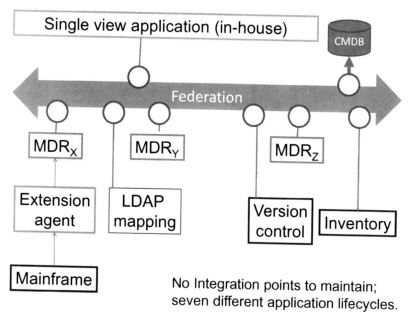

Figure 16-5. Federation

In the upper right-hand corner of Figure 16-5 is a repository called the CMDB, which is a standards initiative called the configuration management database that implements this federation service by employing web services for the interface definition and intends to automatically keep configuration and enrichment information up to date.

If you take a very narrow view of the service management application as only supporting drilldown from the business abstraction and into the physical implementation of the managed service, APM doesn't offer much valuable information. APM will provide details about the agent, the monitored platform versions for operating system and application server, and other tidbits. That is what the strict defnition of configuration information allows. But if you instead focus on data for enrichment, the scope quickly changes to include response times, alert status, transaction flows, etc. If the other resources, such as inventory management and version control can contribute to enrichment, why not APM? Why not use this index of details about the IT infrastructure to federate access to baseline reports, triage findings, and other information that today is otherwise difficult to manage and keep current?

APM-Specific Applications for CMDB

This next discussion is to present a few use cases that I have been considering as CMDB applications. A lot of energy on the standards side of things is focused on getting information into the CMDB. I think that exploring a few scenarios would help you appreciate the value of this technology and understand how your current technology can support these use cases or where enhancement should be directed.

The architecture for CMDB is simple (see Figure 16-6).

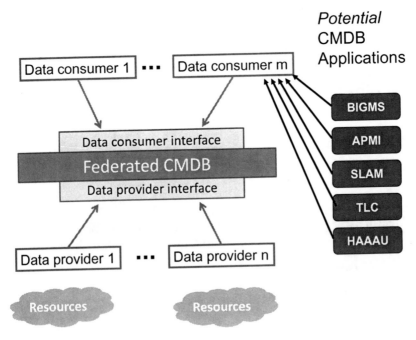

Figure 16-6. CMDB architecture

One implied element is some kind of framework on which to implement the CMDB applications. There are a number of vendor-specific frameworks and some emerging independent and open-sourced frameworks to pick from. I will not dwell on this point but instead will discuss what some of the example applications need to accomplish and how current tools can struggle a bit to achieve these use cases today.

BIGMS

It doesn't take too long to realize that the APM database or metrics storage (MS) component is something that has to be carefully managed. If your metrics can't be reliably persisted, you will simply be unable to do any significant analysis. What you may not appreciate is that the APM-MS database can easily become the single largest application in your environment. How much will you really know about it? Can you get alerts when capacity or performance is compromised, as you would for any other major application?

BIGMS is using the CMDB to provide a single view of all of the APM-MS resources. It reports on the available capacity and generates a map of what agents comprise any of the monitored applications. Many large applications will have multiple instances of that application running at the same time. When there is a problem, you want to quickly compare all of the instances for a single application and see which ones are having problems. If you have 20 APM-MS databases, what steps do you have to do in order to generate a list of agents that correspond to a single appliction? And for bonus, what would you have to do to find all of the agents that participate in a given transaction? A CMDB directly supports these questions by iterating a query over each of the indvidual APM-MS resources and presenting the result.

For a bit more of the use case details, you can apply the good-better-best concept and phase in the capability.

- Good
  - Configuration Information
    - Host IP, MS port, OS version, etc.
  - Capacity Information
    - Current number of metrics and workstations

This is really basic information and it's the original intent of the CMDB specification: to focus on the basic configuration information and simply provide a reporting mechanism to gather and present the results. Since this information doesn't really change that often, it can be considered *static configuration data.*

- Better
  - APM Information
    - List of hosted agents, per APM-MS
    - Key component response times
    - Alert status

This level of information is much more dynamic but you aren't asking the CMDB to hold all of this information. You are only making a request to the underlying data provider, which can be an APM component or other monitoring device, to give you the current information or that of some prior historical period. I consider this to be little more than requesting a report, which is generated by the data provider, and a link transferred to the data consumer via the CMDB. Can your current APM solution define reports to cover these requests? Can they be automated? This is just a simply request-reply interaction and something that the CMDB specification anticipates.

- Best
  - List of the web services
  - List of key transactions

This final level of information is to be used to populate a list so that the analyst can then pick from the list and initiate requests for more details, which are then directed back to the data providers. This request-reply-request-more-detail interchange is not something that the current CMDB specification anticipates. You have to be able to populate the GUI list control with the current transactions and services. You need to make it easy for the analyst to find the transactions of interest. But this results in large number of transactions between the CMDB and the data provider, and this is not a use case that the CMDB authors had in mind initially.

APMI

While BIGMS is initially focused on the platform configuration, it sneaks its way up to something that is meaningful for APM. This next use case of APM Integration (APMI) goes immediately to the core of the challenges with monitoring technology. The use case is as follows:

Application X is covered by multiple monitoring technologies. Provide a single view of application X.

Some folks think this is the holy grail of performance monitoring. You know that you have multiple tools gathering performance information. When there is an incident, you want to see what each of the tools has visibility into, and you want to do it quickly and easily. So you want all of the information to appear on a single screen. The CMDB has the potential to provide this single view into all of the available data. You have an interface into each data provider. You simply issue the appropriate query to each data provider and then organize the data for presentation with APMI.

There are two levels of information that you want to gather. The first is for availability because almost every tool existing today will do availability monitoring. No vendor has yet provided such a single view in a vendor-neutral fashion. CMDB, which has an interface into every major vendor, is the mechanism to finally construct this single view. In this case, it's simply a single verion of the availability truth: Is one of my monitoring tools indicating a problem or are all of them indicating a problem?

The second level of information is for performance. As you have already appreciated, APM monitoring technology has a scope of applicability. I have discussed three of these: synthetics, real transactions, and instrumentation. The other major component is the network itself and often the authentication service. When you have a performance alert, you simply want to confirm that the transaction and component response times are not being impacted by a network problem or an authentication problem.

I can usually infer the network or authentication component response by transaction and deep dive monitoring but that depends on having accurate baselines. Getting production baselines quickly is all but impossible—unless you have a couple of weeks time. But if I can directly correlate my network throughput with my transaction response, then I need only put together about two hours of history to establish a trend. A CMDB application lets me avoid having to open multiple screens and eyeball the correlation. It also provides some historical capacity in the event my network monitoring tool does not preserve history on the throughput.

SLAM

Another important CMDB application is *service-level agereement management* (SLAM). I will show you later in this chapter how to use APM for SLAM based on a largely manual process. The bulk of this labor is for defining the SLA but the monitoring and reporting about the SLA is just not something you can get out of the box. The main impediment is the definition of the operational period on which the SLA will be managed. Many monitoring tools simply do not support a definition of your operational day. So I think you can depend on a CMDB application to host and manage this time-of-day (TOD) constraint and then automate the reporting by generating the required reporting intervals.

Once these reports are generated, you can then initiate a process to audit the SLA for the appropriate operational period: How much time was in violation of the SLA? The holy grail here would be to then track the SLA performance on the last 20 weeks and see whether things are improving or not.

Ideally, this type of reporting and analysis should not involve any more keystrokes than your going online to check your investment protfolio performance. In the simplest terms, that's all the SLA is about. Are you making money or paying penalties?

TLC

This CMDB application is *track license consumption* (TLC). It is just one of the facts of life. Unless you build all of your own software, you have to account periodically for what elements you are using from third parties. Unfortunately, there is no consistent license scheme but this is something that the CMDB should be able to resolve for you easily, rather than the very painful auditing that you may conduct quarterly or annually. It's really a lot of work.

Just the presence of the data provider interface is the necessary mechnism to at least establish what technology you have deployed and are actively using. The second level of queies would to tally up the number of CPUs or concurrent users or whatever attributes your vendors require.

I think the industry overall would benefit if each vendor was required to supply their own CMDB-TLC app in order to remove the drugery of completing the license audit. It makes for good governance to always know exactly where you stand.

HAAAU

This last CMDB application really pushes the model: How about an automated upgrade (HAAAU)? If you already know where every APM agent and configuration detail lives, why can't you get an automated upgrade, subject to your own criteria (when and which systems) so that you can eliminate the drugery of keeping your monitoring software current? I'll admit that I'm really getting spoiled watching my productivity software update itself. Sometimes I don't even need to reboot or restart the application; my phone and my browser periodically find out if there is an important update or release. The remote database that they interact with sounds very much like a CMDB application, or at least what I think a CMDB application should be doing.

Root-cause Analysis

This activity is also known as the *smoking gun*, which goes along nicely with another anology where many stakeholders have an expectation that APM will be their *silver bullet*, something that can kill most monsters (or address any problem). Pragmatically, your stakeholders don't really care about your process or your tools. They simply want to know what to fix and how much it will cost. Frankly, it is a little unrealistic to receive an alert, spin a few CPU cycles, and discover a root cause. But it's an important goal for the industry. It's the ultimate in user-friendly APM.

When I talk to stakeholders about root cause, I give them a simple thought-experiment. I start by claiming to have a software system that delivers RCA. You ask how it works. I say it is an expert-based[19] system that uses experience about application management along with an inference engine to arrive at a single outcome and conclusion or to draw conclusions when two or more outcomes appear equally probable. You ask how I trained this expert system. I say that it's based on years of performance data, gathered from hundreds of operational environments across all major industries. You say that sounds unlikely because it presupposed some standard way of describing performance incidents and cataloging them, and also having standard mechanisms for triage, communicating findings, and tracking remediation. You say I would need access to the entire application lifecycle to collect all the meaningful data and interactions that demonstrate the manifold ways that stakeholders interact in the resolution of a problem.

---

[19] Wikipedia, "expert system," http://en.wikipedia.org/wiki/Expert_system

And you would be right. Truthfully, I and a few others practice RCA from time to time. That's about it. We usually don't get to root cause because of gaps in the data—missing visibility—which reinforces the points I have made so far about pulling together all of these disparate sources of metrics. Just because it's rare to get root cause doesn't mean you have failed. It simply means you have to take the recommendations on faith. I can't prove the recommendations will be successful—only probable.

For the efficient APM practitioner, it's quicker to make a change, retest, and hope for improvement then it is to take care of all the integration necessary to support RCA. But that does not abate your stakeholders' desire for you to find the *smoking gun*. That's why you have to keep an eye out for opportunities to chip away at the visibility gaps. When you push for RCA but encounter a visibility gap that leaves root-cause just beyond your grasp, if you can address it, you bump out the limits of your visibility. You bring more and more of your environment under APM. The next opportunity for RCA will get a little further.

And that's also why this book isn't called "Perfecting APM" or "Mastering APM." The epic story has only started, even if the marketplace is over a decade old. For many APM users, getting the technology to do something useful is still just beyond their grasp—until this book. At least now everyone can consistently categorize incidents, collect baselines, make correlations, and detect trends. You have some standards for how to categorize APM activities consistently. You have a means of tracking progress and effectiveness. It will take a few years for someone to be in a postion to finally build that expert system for RCA.

Implementing the Fix

Even when root cause is identified, real fixes take time. Most times, you simply do not have that luxury of time and so the remaining options will be very familiar: reboot, scale horizontally (add more CPU or servers), or degrade the service (slow down the incoming users and transactions so that the system survives).

Sometimes you will encounter a big problem that gets resolved with a minor change in a configuration. Such a quick fix is not root cause. The bigger problem— and the true root cause—will likely be found in the process that allowed the application to go forward with that incorrect setting or code. This same root-cause problem will have the potential to occur on the next release or with some other application because the fundamental process is broken. If you find a quick fix to a performance problem, be thankful. But make sure you do not get deluded into thinking everything is better. You need to continue RCA and identify the process defect before you really get jammed.

This is the limitation of becoming dependent on firefighting, which I take up in the next chapter. Firefighting is all about creating an environment to uncover a quick fix. Once the fix is confirmed, the firefight is over and the team disperses. Firefighting is not RCA, no matter the outcome. Just like real firefighting, preventing future fires depends on fire inspections, building codes, homeowner education, and manufacturing standards for items that homeowners purchase.

Given the incremental evolution in your RCA capability, as you fill in the visibility gaps, you will identify trends that can be used to enhance management of the application. When you can take a suspect to confirmation, immortalize it with a custom dashboard. The next time that situation comes up, you need only confirm it via the dashboard. This is very significant to marshal stakeholders into realizing that the only way to eliminate a recurring problem is to make the investment to fix it. Moving the recurring confirmation onto a dashboard makes it accessible to your non-technical stakeholders, which will eventually lead to the management team that can make the fix happen.

Service Level Management

As organizations mature in their service delivery to customers and trading partners, and when everyone is delivering the same capabilities, the only opportunity for competitive differentiation is in the quality of delivery. An SLA is a document that defines the measurements of that service as well as the penalties that will be applied if the service-levels are not met. All parties agree to this document; it's a serious commitment that involves all aspects of the business. While IT may not initiatie these agreements, the capability of IT to respond, both with the appropriate metrics and operational capabilities, means that the business may establish a competitive advantage. Conversely, you also need to inform the business when a given SLA is going to put the company at risk because the IT infrastructure cannot support it. You need to know where the service is weak so that appropriate investment may be made in order to meet the SLA.

This chapter is to help you prepare for that meeting with the business where they talk about the SLA they want to pursue and you respond with what your service management can deliver. This is a critical point in the evolution of an IT organization. It's an opportunity to show the business that you are not just an operational function but that you are a valued partner in helping to grow the very nature of how your enterprise competes and is profitable. Your capital is your intimate knowledge of your applications and infrastructure that APM is providing. Of course, you still need to make decisions about how to address performance problems but simply having performance information is good enough to differentiate your group from other competing interests. Ultimately, the IT function, being standards-based and using off-the-shelf systems and applications, is relatively easy to swap out for a lower-cost but comparable service. The group that can do a better job managing that collection of technology is the one that will maintain the role. Being able to define, accept, and deliver against an SLA is how you will differentiate your service management capability from all the others.

One caveat for the "A" in SLA. As discussed in Chapter 1, historically the "A" means availability. And while service-level *availability* is a recognized and valuable activity, it depends only on availability information, which I have shown to be inferior to performance information. In the definition of a service-level *agreement*, which is how I use the "A" here, modern SLAs are based on the user experience, response times, and other performance-related attributes of the business relationship and is no longer limited to availability information.

Defining the SLA

An SLA is an agreement to provide a business service or capability within strictly defined criteria. The most common metric is that of availability. Is the service available over the contracted operational period? However, this is too coarse a measurement because you know today that business transactions and end-user expereince may experience significant degradation without affecting the availability criteria. So the business is looking for other criteria about the delivered service, which they may promote or enhance so that they can ultimately be more profitable.

The challenge for IT is to provide metrics that may be mapped to the business goals. The business will describe their goals as "improve customer retention" or "increase cross-selling opportunities." Sometimes you will get lucky and they will want to target a specific transaction or service within a portal. More often, you may not be entirely sure what they are asking you for. The challenge is that the business and IT do not share the same language. I will introduce some mapping between the language domains but it will not always be possible to resolve the busines goal onto an IT operational metric. You will need to be creative.

What I can do is help you understand the process of defining an SLA so that you can ensure that you are collecting the right kinds of information. Ultimately, your ability to meet an SLA is going to be strongly correlated with your overall software quality. If you have adopted the practices for collecting baselines (Chapter 12), developing runbooks (Chapter 8), and auditing key applications (Chapter 13), then you already have much of the infrastructure to manage software quality, so you can expect to contribute meaningfully to the SLA initiative. But you should also expect that you may not be focused on software quality, so I will also discuss how to get contributions from real and synthetic transactions in order to provide a minimum understanding of the service characteristics.

What you need to get are consistent measurements across pre-production and production so that you may then analyze, interpret, and incorporate within the SLA. Visibility plus reporting leads directly to an SLA. APM will give you the visibility but the fundamental capability you need to establish is reporting.

Operational Day

Before you can address reporting, you have to define the primary characteristics of the target service. The most significant of these is the operational period. What portion of the day, week, month, quarter, or year is the SLA going to govern? Look at Figure 16-7 for some examples. Are there different service levels depending on on the operational period that are significant? Because SLAs usually have a penalty associated with them, you will have the opportunity to define precisely when that penalty may apply or maybe even to have different penalties for different classes of service.

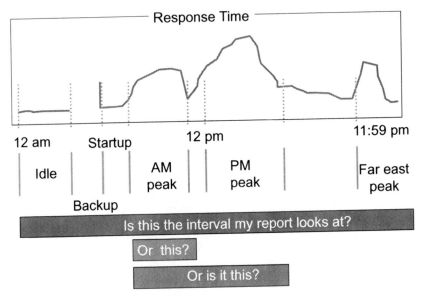

Figure 16-7. What constitutes an Operational Day?

For example, an online tax preparation service could have a different SLA for the month that tax returns are due, the three months prior, and all other times of the year. A financial services company could have an SLA for all transactions and a separate SLA for high-value clients. Every industry has its own conventions. You need to be sure that you understand your own. This should not be difficult as availability monitoring has already defined these periods. You may use them directly or with some additional refinement.

Conversely, you also need to know when you may relax the SLA in order to perform maintenance, upgrades, or new releases. Sometimes there is no such period as the service is expected to be operational 24/7 (24 hours a day, seven days a week). This has obvious implications for a high availability architecture.

There may also be SLAs for holidays, vacation periods, and even the period after a major sports or entertainment event. Telecommunications and network providers have lots of experience with SLAs, so you should follow their experiences closely and employ some of these strategies to ensure that you will meet the SLA requirements. In the next sections, I will present some examples of SLAs.

Chargeback

The evolution of KPI-based management of IT systems and services, from the business perspective begins with the concept of *charging back*[20,21] for the systems and services consumed. This is an internal mechanism to recover the costs associatiated with obtaining and operating the computing platform. I find that many organizations will treat chargebacks as something completely different than SLA definition and management. They certainly have different levels of participation but they are both dependent on the performance measurements that APM will provide, especially those metrics that support a metering of the service or activity.

Types of Metrics

The foundation for the SLA are those metrics that may be measured accurately. As you improve visibility, you get access to a greater variety of metrics, which will then support a greater variety of SLA strategies. There are four general categories: configuration, platform, application server/container, and application-specific.

Prior to APM technologies, platform metrics were the basis for many SLAs. Responsiveness was assessed with stop watches. Workloads were characterized by file size or call volume. You can find some example SLA for this scenario in the sources mentioned in these footnotes[22,23,24].

As the concept of instrumentation evolved, configuration metrics became available for auditing the size of a application platform and confirming that sufficient resources were made available to the application or service. This is also when efforts to chargeback for the platform cost began to be implemented. Platform-based chargeback, in terms of CPU consuption, has been around since mainframes were first available. The API for technologies like JMX was also exploited to report internal performance metrics, which was a bit more convenient than relying of logging information alone.

The real flexibility in defining and managing SLAs comes with the availability of performance metrics, which includes all of the metric types now available. As APM technology matured, the frequency at which updates to the metrics were available increased to essentially real-time. Here is a summary of what is now available as real-time metrics:

---

[20] The Organizational Implications of Chargeback Systems – March 2010 - http://wikibon.org/wiki/v/The_Organizational_Implications_of_Chargeback_Systems

[21] What is.com, "IT chargeback system," http://whatis.techtarget.com/definition/it-chargeback-system.html

[22] Knowledgeleader.com, "Service Level Agreement Sample Template," www.knowledgeleader.com/KnowledgeLeader/content.nsf/Web+Content/SAMServiceLevelAgreementSampleTemplate!OpenDocument

[23] TechNet, "Establishing a Service Level Agreement, http://technet.microsoft.com/en-us/library/bb124886%28EXCHG.65%29.aspx

[24] "Information Technology Service Level Agreement Template" www.purdue.edu/bscompt/Projects/SLAs/SLADraftTemplate_111901.doc

- Real-time
    - Platform
    - CPU, GC Heap
    - Response time (component, SQL, message, etc.)
    - Invocations per interval
    - Concurrency
    - Stalls
    - Front-end and back-end metrics
    - Errors
    - Transaction traces
    - Specialty
        - Number of instances in a collection class (data structure)
        - Number of object instances

Not all of these real-time metrics are directly useful in defining an SLA. Sometimes an arbitrary function of these metrics will be employed to obtain the KPI. Others will be used internally as part of a charge-back model. Unlike mainframes, distributed systems can't easily associate a given web application with its CPU consumption and implement a mainframe-like chargeback for CPU. Instead, invocation metrics for specific servlets give an exact measurement of how many times the web application was invoked. Thus, when multiple web application share the same server, the cost of each may be apportioned according to the number of invocations throughout the operational day. An example of this more performance-centric SLA can be found at here[25].

The final type of SLA metrics are those for the timeliness of the response to an outage: time-to-respond and time-to-resolve. APM does not provide any direct measure of this duration. Instead, it's the responsibility of the trouble-ticket or trouble management system to record these times and compile appropriate statistics. While these metrics are appropriate for managing the support organization or help desk, they do not offer any true visibility into the customer experience with the managed service. When the support organization experiences poor performance or there is an excessive number of help requests, this does indicate a significant problem but you don't have any guidance as to how to resolve the problem. As discussed in Chapter 1, when the help desk is your best indication of poor application performance, as evidenced by the increasing frequency of incidents, you really need to consider moving to APM technology to address that visibility gap. An example of this type of SLA is here[26].

---

[25] Sun Blueprints, "Service Level Agreement in the Data Center," www.sun.com/blueprints/0402/sla.pdf

[26] Ideabyte, "SLA Benchmark Metrics," http://www.scribd.com/doc/8532482/Ideabyte-SLA-Benchmark-Metrics

Natural Business Units

All of the metrics discussed thus far are what I call IT-centric: they mean a lot to IT folks but are confusing for less-technical stakeholders. Figure 16-8 shows some examples of *natural business units* for various applications. Your challenge is to find the metrics that relate to these kinds of business units and to understand the frequency that these parameters might change. The frequency of change will dictate the type of monitoring technology will you choose to collect those metrics.

Application	Business unit
Email	Number of users
eCommerce	Number of orders
Telemarketing	Number of calls
Checking account	Number of customers
Inventory	Number of stock lines
Rental car	Number of vehicles
Stock exchange	Number of shares traded

Figure 16-8. Natural business units [27]

Let's use the e-mail application as an example and respond to a request for "needs more monitoring" for this application. Many e-mail systems simply don't present a lot of performance metrics. It's either working or it's down. A common capacity goal from the business perspective is the number of users that the system supports. This alone doesn't tell you very much because each user gets a different volume of mail. You would want to consider the largest and smallest mailbox size, and the average, largest, and smallest message size. That's the way IT-centric metrics come about—trying to anticipate what metrics might be useful.

These are not metrics you are likely to find, unless you are developing the e-mail system from scratch. Instead, you may only be able to measure the total volume of mail incoming each day, which you could infer simply by watching the disk space utilization. And for the number of users, well, everybody is on e-mail so you just need to count the total staffing of your company. You can then approximate the mail per user by dividing the total daily volume by total population.

[27] Table adapted from "Capacity Planning for Web Performance", p 255, Menasce and Almeida, Prentice Hall 1998, ISBN0-13-693822-1

You could continue to define additional business metrics based on what your team dreams up, but it's actually simpler to first understand what the business user expects the e-mail system to achieve during the normal operation and future growth. Do they expect bigger messages? More frequent messages? Is there a new attachment that needs to be supported? Will the new workflow system be making use of e-mail for notifications? Are they planning to use an e-mail service provider? Are they about to merge with another company? Each of these is a business concern for which you need to indentify one or more IT metrics that would allow you to get visibility into the performance of each concern. When that is not possible, you then need to indicate that you don't have visibility into that specific concern, and you begin to realize that this e-mail application is not very manageable.

While business requirements are sometimes vague and imprecise, even improbable, working through the definition of the business objectives and then mapping them onto the available IT metrics or finding a way to collect new metrics is a collaborative exercise. The business needs to know where the visibility gaps are. You need to share what is possible and what needs investment.

Process

Triage with Trends

Triage with trends consists of three major activities; planning, implementation, and triage. Ideally, the planning and implementation activities will be completed prior to attempting triage and RCA. If you can not accommodate such forward-looking plans, you can at least use these activities to explain why you are unable to find root cause. That will be an uncomfortable situation, but if your stakeholders expectations are already inflated, you will need to use these opportunities to explain why and marshal support for addressing the gap.

Your actual process will be subject to the extension and integration capabilities of your selected APM tools, as well as any additional tools available in your enterprise. The process outlined here should be taken only as a template onto which your specific activities will be detailed.

1. Survey what tools are available, end-to-end, for the transactions you are interested in. Figure 3-16 has an example of an end-to-end catalog. That spreadsheet is also available on apress.com. This survey is best completed prior to an attempt to triage with trends.

   a. Identify the source of visibility and time duration that it's useful, according to the following scale:
      i. No visibility
      ii. On-demand tool
      iii. On-demand command
      iv. On-demand status display
      v. Logfile

       vi.   Real-time, current time only
       vii. Report, current time only
       viii. Real-time with historical
       ix.   Report historical

   b.   What type of metrics will be available?
       i.   Availability
       ii.   State[28]
       iii.   Queue depth
       iv.   Performance
       v.   Capacity
       vi.   Transaction summary

2.   Prior to attempting triage with trends, extend visibility from your basic monitoring configuration to address the gaps uncovered during the survey. A period of 2-6 weeks is considered the minum for worthwhile trending. There will be up to three passes of extending visibility.

   a.   Full alert integration
       i.   Performance and capacity thresholds established
       ii.   Performance and capacity alerts integrated within existing availability trouble management
       iii. (optional) Service-level management and SLA definition

   b.   Optimal instrumentation configuration
       i.   Visibility into propritary and third party frameworks[29]
       ii.   Integration of logs and commands identified during the tools survey

   c.   Report integration and normalization
       i.   Identify useful reporting and subscribe to the distribution
       ii.   Post-process the report to extract useful metrics for future correlation

3.   When an incident calls for RCA, evaluate the following:

   a.   Triage if the monitored platform (application server), a participating resource, or an independent resource is suspect.
       i.   If the application service is suspect, use the enhanced visibility to identify root cause.
       ii.   If root cause cannot be confirmed, identify the gap and schedule remediation.

   b.   For the suspect resource
       i.   If the resource is suspect, do you have visibility to identify root-cause?

---

[28] Wikipedia, "state," http://en.wikipedia.org/wiki/State_(computer_science)

[29] Wikipedia, "framework," http://en.wikipedia.org/wiki/Framework_(computer_science)

    ii.   If you do not have sufficient visibility, does a stakeholder have something that would be helpful?

       1.   If that contribution is useful, plan to integrate that dataset later on.

       2.   Identify the visbility gap for future efforts to enhance the monitoring of this resource.

  c.   For the suspect independent resource

    i.   If you do not have sufficient visibility, does the resource owner have something that would be helpful?

       1.   If that contribution is useful, plan to integrate that dataset later on.

       2.   Identify the visbility gap for future efforts to enhance the monitoring of this resource.

Competency

The failure to achieve root-cause is often due to a lack of visibility. You cannot trend if you don't have visibility. The triage process helps you to identify visibility gaps that, when solved, will enhance your capability for RCA. Given that the motivation for RCA is infrequent, the activity you need to show competency in is solving visibility problems. When a gap is identified, how do you get visibility and resolve that gap? You will want to address this as the first stage within the capabilities of your selected technology and extend the agent configuration to reveal any framework interfaces, for example. If not already initiated, you will also want to integrate alerts defined for thresholds managed by APM. Sometimes you will have additional reporting mechanisms based on alert activity, so getting alerts that you initiate into this other tool will help you evaluate how effective they will be when it is time to triage.

The second stage would be to integrate something outside of instrumentation or real transaction monitoring technologies and bring those metrics into the APM environment. A logfile or command, where you scrape the result to generate metrics, is a frequent point of integration. Use these easier sources before attempting something exotic. Whatever path you pick will exercise your scripting abilities but you will get a number of scripts to help jumpstart any other integrations at this stage.

The third stage would be to integrate an external report. Your APM technology may allow for direct import of the report or its metadata. More often, I end up using an ETL tool to extract metrics of interest and write these to a simple logfile. Then I finish the integration by following the second stage approach. You will leverage your scripting here to process the reports on their schedule.

Artifacts

Given the complexity of this topic and the difficulty that you might have in finding suitable source material, I have enclosed a selection of the external materials I often share with clients to get them started with SLAs. This is all freely available on the Internet though some sites may required registration. Although some of the material is sponsored by a monitoring technology vendor, the appearance of any vendor here does not constitute an endorsement or certification as to fitness of use.

Avoiding Seven Common Pitfalls of Service Level Agreements: Gaining Greater Value and Reducing Costs – Hayes www.clarity-consulting.com/AvoidingCommonSLAPitfalls.pdf

A Framework for Service Quality Assurance using Event Correlation Techniques – Hanemann, Sailer http://whitepapers.zdnet.com/abstract.aspx?docid=166907

From Service Level Management to Business Management - www.oblicore.com/resources/white_papers.php

The Best Practices Guide to Developing and Monitoring and Monitoring SLAs www.heroix.com/aspscript/wp_sla_form.asp

Summary

It should not have been suprising that triage with trends comes down to the same requirements as the monitoring initiatives that came before. IT management is about getting visibility into the operational environment. APM technology simply makes the work of trending and analysis a lot easier, provided that a meaningful integration of availability and performance information is available. And that is the real challenge. Everything that APM can easily monitor is composed of newer technologies and solution architectures. Everything that IT is currently operating is a much broader set of technology, reaching all the way back to when dinosaurs walked the earth and the world needed "at most five computers"[30].

Striving for RCA, exposing the visibility gaps in your monitoring architecture, addressing those gaps, and bringing all of the disparate metric and reporting resources together can be a lot of work. You can achieve much of the same benefits by narrowing your focus to your more modern (and APM-compatible) services with a *service management* initiative. Here you can craft your initial SLA around any major visibility gaps and still prioritize integration tasks that will result in a tighter SLA over time.

---

[30] Attributed to IBM chairman Thomas Watson in 1943. "I think there is a worldwide market for maybe five computers." Referenced in "Microchip fabrication: a practical guide to semiconductor processing," Peter van Zant, McGraw Hill Professional, 2004 ISBN 0071432418, 9780071432412

Firefighting and Critical Situations

*Facts are stubborn things; and whatever may be our wishes,
our inclinations, or the dictates of our passion, they cannot
alter the state of facts and evidence.*

— John Adams (1735 - 1826)

Dependence on *firefighting*, the rapid application of technology to an urgent IT
incident, is characteristic of an immature monitoring discipline. It is a purely
reactive response to a problem, usually lacking deep understanding of the issue. It
is certainly not done with an eye towards preparation for proactive management.
You will use the firefighting techniques discussed in this chapter to basically get
Management off your back. Management is struggling with a large number of
problems throughout their business management life cycle, and they need you to
quickly uncover what is vexing their efforts to deliver a successful service. They
couldn't care less about the correct use of APM.

During the course of the firefight, they will also have the expectation that you will
help them prove the value of APM monitoring tools, along with any number of
additional goals. It will seem as if your firefighting event, if successful, will usher
in a new age of rational and reasonable management of the application life cycle.
And if you fail, the IT organization will likely slide of the face of the earth. The

expectations are often simply unreasonable. Kill ten birds with one stone—and let's see if you can "borrow" the stone.

Firefighting could be considered an anti-pattern of a successful APM discipline. The more successful the APM implementation, the less you will come to depend on firefighting. The more time you spend firefighting, the less time you are spending establishing a robust and scalable APM system. But until the APM discipline is established, you had better plan on a robust firefighting response. Reliance on firefighting is a substitute for actually planning to manage performance. It is a form of IT co-dependency. To break this dependency, you need to leverage these urgent situations to give a glimpse of what the correct use of APM will look like and get stakeholders refocused on that goal. When that happens, your stakeholders will finally begin to plan an APM initiative and eliminate firefighting as the sole response to a performance problem.

Kick Off Meeting

The most important part of a firefight event is what happens before you engage the problem. You need to have some control over how a decision to firefight is made through what is called the *scope call*. This is a conference call or a meeting where you checklist what is needed and set expectations about the results of the firefight activity. Among the participants, it needs to be a formal declaration that all other means have failed. It's also a time to review what was done to date. And the definition and necessity of the scope call needs to be comunicated to the app teams well before they are in a position to invoke it. So before you even initiate a scope call, you need to define and communicate the following:

- How does a new application team interact with you?
- Under what conditions do you provide critical issue support?
- How do you leverage existing technical resources to help your monitoring organization to scale?

This is just a small bit of process but it functions as a filter to ensure you only get pulled into situations where the app team is committed to understanding the problem. Otherwise, you are just another resource being tossed at the problem while the app team is off doing something else. You will rarely have any history or deep understanding of the application, so if you don't have someone knowledgeable at your disposal, you have all but eliminated any chance of success.

The details of the scope call are in the "Process" section of this chapter.

Firefighter, Smoke-jumpers, Triage

The next element for a successful firefight is simply the gut-check[1]: do you have the fortitude to step into the quagmire and be the target for pent-up frustration and

---

[1] Merriam-Webster, "gut check," http://mw4.m-w.com/dictionary/gut check

dispair? If you think you want to fill this role, then you really need to want the problems that no one else wants to address. You will be at the center of attention trying to improve on a situation that everyone else has determined is too hard and too difficult to sort.

Note Firefighting is a rapid response to an urgent IT issue, generally involving a production outage or a performance problem with an application in UAT. It is delivered by Firefighting Specialists with the goal of accurate triage and diagnosis of the major contributors to the outage/performance issues as quickly as possible.

To be successful you need to have a broad understanding of distributed computing, mainframes, networks, security, and software development. You need to work fast. You need to have limitless patience. You should not be easily swayed or distracted by more powerful personalities. You need to be an effective communicator.

I can add some processes to help make the execution of a firefight predictable. But you have to be able to "weather the storm" where everyone else is looking for someone to blame for their problems.

After you have passed the gautlet of the first couple of firefight incidents with even minor success, you will quickly establish a reputation of being calming and insightful. Eventually, stakeholders might appreciate when you get involved with their problems even if they are neutral towards your efforts overall. "It can't hurt..." is perhaps the best opinion you can hope for. The other opinions are much more negative.

Often the resistance to firefighting is very pronounced. It's not simply that everyone is concerned about resolving the problem quickly, especially if this has been going on for a while. There is a strong possibility that someone will be implicated as being responsible for the problem. That is never the goal of firefighting but know that it's foremost in the minds of your stakeholders. You have to be the moderator of this volatile situation AND you have to get visibility into the nature of the performance problem.

Before You Jump

A big part of achieving a calming and insightful reputation is to carefully avoid those situations where you probably can't do anything meaningful. Folks are in a panic because they don't know what to do. You will bring your experience—at first limited to the rapid deployment and correct configuration of the monitoring technology, and later as the neutral perspective on the application life cycle—and you will explain exactly what you are going to do. And then you need to execute that plan, hopefully without any surprises. In the scope of your plan, you need to address the topics in the following four sections.

Do You Have the Right Tools?

It's a simple question, but if you don't have visibility into a system, you are pretty much left with voodoo and tea leaves as your primary diagnostic tools—or more realistically, log files and crash dumps. If logs and dumps are all you have, this is not firefighting. You can't respond quickly because you will need hours and days to analyze the results. You are "panning for gold" and hoping to get lucky.

When you do have an appropriate tool and you are attempting to apply it against a new application (one that has not been instrumented prior), the real test of the firefight response is to simply get the tool installed quickly and reliably. This is the *rapid deployment* process that I introduced in Chapters 3 and 5. You should strive to get an agent deployed in 30 minutes or less, to bring up a new environment in 4 hours or less, and to complete any configuration testing and deploy to production in 6 hours or less.

Figure 17-1 summarizes the decisions and actions leading to effective triage of a performance incident. If you have already used APM against the application, then you are looking for baselines and ending up with *triage with baselines* (Chapter 15) or *triage with single metrics* (Chapter 14).

If this application is new to APM, you need to deploy APM rapidly. Confirm you have sufficient APM-MS capacity, qualify an agent configuration, and you're ready for triage with single metrics. If you don't have sufficient MS capacity, you'll need to setup the appropriate environment.

If time constraints do not allow for a rapid deployment, no firefight is possible. Perhaps the application team might then consider scheduling an *application audit* (Chapter 13) so that the monitoring visibility may be confirmed and the initial baselines generated. This can proceed at a more relaxed pace. Otherwise, you are left with an *application survey (Chapter 3)* and/or *outage analysis* to determine the most appropriate tool and future course of action.

You will also notice that firefighting is only possible when you can rapidly deploy an APM component. Currently, this is limited to agent-based APM (Java and .NET). Synthetic and real-time transactions do not meet the criteria for rapid deployment (6 hours or less). Of couse, this does not precude adding additional transaction definitions to an existing installation but that is simply triage and configuration tuning; monitoring is already in place. Firefighting is the urgent deployment of monitoring where none existed prior—and as an apparent unplanned deployment.

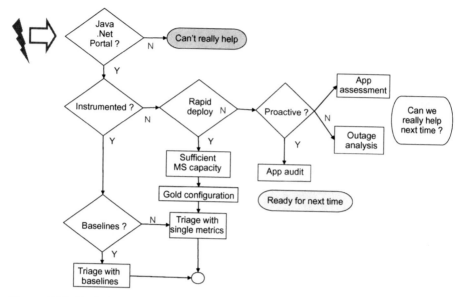

Figure 17-1. Firefighting: qualifying what may be done

Do You Have Potential Data?

Even when you have an application monitored by APM, it doesn't guarantee that you actually have visibility into the problem. You need to gather the evidence from the application team that indicates a problem. What time did it occur? What systems were alerted and when? Who was affected? Were other applications affected? Is this a recurring problem? If they already do not see some consistent evidence of a problem, you should not expect APM visibility to fill that void. It might, but you are gambling. Falling back to an *application audit* would be more prudent if there isn't consistent evidence of an issue.

You need to ask several important questions. How reproducible is the problem? Does it occur at the same time each day? Is it reproducible back in the testing environment? What have they tried to reproduce the problem? Anything that can be reproduced can be exposed via incremental efforts and via different tools and different strategies. In time, it will succumb to the right blend of tools and visibility. The advantage of a reproducible problem is that is usually excludes the environment as a contributor. The problem is in the application. You just need to find it.

Problems that are not reproducible are really difficult because their apparent randomness does not exclude the environment outside of the application. This is where you need to look to other complaints such as other applications having similar problems at the same time. In the event that your target application is not amenable to APM, then one of these other apps might be a better candidate.

In Chapter 16: "Triage with Trends," I discussed the necessity of this larger perspective. Often a problem is intractable because you are too close to what folks suspect is the area of the problem—except they are completely wrong!. You always need to take a few steps back and validate those earlier opinions. Once you are confident that you have idenitfied a suspect application or resource, then you can apply the process outlined in Figure 17-2 to tighten your focus on unusual metrics.

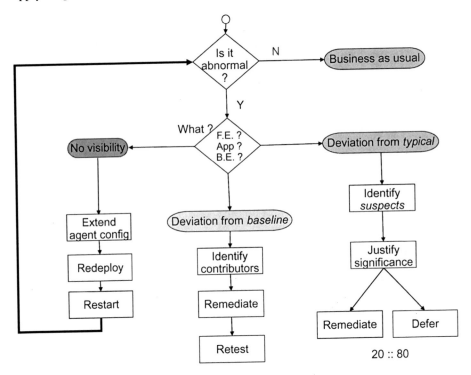

Figure 17-2. Firefighting: what you observe

As before, the technique is slightly different depending on the availability of baselines. If you only have triage with single metrics, then you apply conventional response times and usage characteristics and arrive a some number of suspects. Most often (about 80% of the time), very few of these suspects can be acted on directly because there simply isn't enough compelling evidence. One point does not make a trend. A small portion (about 20%) can lead to something that may be modified or remediated.

When you have triage with baselines, there isn't much opportunity for a deferred change. You *know* that the suspect component is part of the problem because it deviates from the baseline. The only circumstance you have to watch out for is when *all* major components of the application are equally degraded. Then you look to the shared resource, very often a configuration setting (debug-enabled, for example) or network issue.

Do You Have an Appropriate Environment?

The bulk of firefight requests arise from production issues. And getting a monitoring configuration into production quickly is what everyone expects. Approximately 80% of these production incidents will be associated with a recent deployment. The remaining 20% will be something unexpected with an otherwise stable application.

While the production environment seems like the right place to start, it is something to avoid, unless you already have significant deployments and experience operating with APM. You need to consider when problems are being introduced in the application life cycle to really be efficient in rooting them out. Code and configuration changes occur long before deployment to production. Why are they not tested as soon as they are made? Invariably, this is due to gaps in load generation and test plans in general. Turning production into a test platform simply because you don't make the effort to simulate load or test configuration changes is simply immature.

The one important exception to this rule is when you have an application with multiple JVMs or CLRs, called *multiple instances*. If you have four or eight instances of the application, then you can confine your activities in production to a single instance. This will absolutely NOT help you in uncovering the performance problem but it will help you to establish that the APM technology is deployed safely and configured correctly. After a couple of days of *operational experience* you can then extend the monitoring to the remaining instances.

When a test environment is simply not available, try to install first on some application server that is not part of the production cluster and manually exercise the app. This will at least confirm that the agent configuration is appropriate and, if this is your first deployment, insure that you have one round of practice before going to production. You will usually need to restart the server in order to enable the agent. The more restarts you request, the more confidence will erode in your ability to help the situation, so you should attempt your initial install where the frequency of restarts will not draw attention.

Getting visibility into the problem does not absolutely require a production deployment, because 80% of these incidents were occuring during pre-production. No one had appropriate visibility at that time. As much as you would prefer to avoid the risk of blowing something up in production, by attempting an untested monitoring configuration, you sometimes have to play into this gambit because ultimately you don't want to find the problem too quickly.

I call out this gambit because the application team may already suspect that they missed something. And if you go in, pre-production, and find out something that they missed, it looks very bad for them. It means they didn't do a thorough job for an important application. They would much rather risk you deploying an untested configuration (or unproven technology) into production, under enormous pressure and attention, because it deflects scrutiny away from them. No matter what the application does next, they can always blame you first. And if you identify some suspects in production, they will accept it willingly because they never had production monitoring with APM before and so their integrity remains intact.

So what you want from the pre-production environment is a single load test. Even a manual exercise is appropriate at this point. It will be enough to confirm that your starting agent configuration is safe but not quite enough to identify any but the most henious problems. And then you move onto production and hopefully collect enough data to identify some suspects.

While you are monitoring in production, keep testing going forward in pre-production. APM visibility will often give insights into the test configuration and procedures that will lead to an overall improvement in the testing process. Even as all eyes are on production, you want to take opportunities to replicate your production findings with the pre-production environment. This is an important step to helping your stakeholders appreciate that production firefighting can be avoided when APM technology is available pre-production.

Have You Set Appropriate Expectations?

Even if you have outstanding tools, supurb skills, and excellent processes, there is almost no way to dig yourself out from unrealistic expectations. This firefight outcome is effectively determined at the scope call.

- To set expectations
    - Summarize what you have done in prior situations
    - Summarize what is different about this situation
        - What are the risks?
        - What is unknown?
        - What is out of scope?

- Summarize what you will do and the approximate time required

    - What access is required?
        - Test scripts, environments, changes to the application configuration

    - What resources need to be available?
    - Describe how you will know that you are making progress and when you are done

- Describe what you might find

At the conclusion of the scope call, everyone should know precisely what to expect from your efforts. You have established a social contract: if they give you appropriate access and support, you will get them additional visibility, subject to the risks and unknowns you outlined. No one knows where this additional visibility will lead them but everyone will be in agreement to undertake this next step.

Why Do Applications Fail?

In Chapter 3, I looked at how applications fail by analyzing the incident reports. This was to help you understand what visibility gaps existed and how a monitoring initiative helped address those gaps. Normally, a portion of those incidents were resolved only by APM. Here, I will focus on this limited set of incidents—those where the stability, performance, or capacity of the application failed to meet expectations.

When stakeholders hear about an application failure, their first thought is to suspect the underlying code. And about 30% of the time, they will be right. The mission for APM is to identify the most probable source of the problem. Getting evidence that the code is the root cause is frequently difficult to document unambiguousely. Moreover, I find that a *broken process* is responsible about 60% of the time. The critical process here is called *change control*. Someone didn't implement a configuration change correctly—these can include firewall ports, memory settings, database settings, and broken packaging (wrong application component installed). The broken part of this process is that no one tested or confirmed that the change was made as intended (typo) or that the change was demonstrated to actually be effective (flat out wrong idea). These are also much easier to document because there will usually be a dramatic effect on the application and one that is easily identified by comparing with the baseline or performance prior to the change.

Two other modes of application failure are due to hardware (5%) and just simple bad luck (5%). These will also be evident by comparing current metrics with baseline or historical, but frequently the server cannot start or operate at any level, so you really cannot count on metrics being available. However, these modes are relatively rare compared to process and code defects.

A broken process can also be divided into "too little process" and "too much process." Too little process is usually associated with a bad configuration change or inadequate testing, as described earlier. Too much process comes about when folks are circumventing process controls because they have become too cumbersome. This is a direct result of too much division of responsibility, often in conjunction with too much emphasis on keeping the schedule. And as you saw in Figure 17-2, the majority of the time you will end up with a recommendation that will be set aside because the correction process is simply out of scope for the application stakeholders—it will miss the scheduling window. Without any chance of remediation, you can only focus on restoration, resulting in *management by restart*—scheduling a restart periodically in order to avoid the failure.

What May Firefighting Achieve?

Without exception, invoking a firefight exercise is the absolute last resort when it comes to triaging a critical application problem. When you are employing APM correctly, your need to firefight will decrease, as shown in Figure 17-3. Firefighting *does not* fix your application code or repair/replace your hardware. Firefighting *does* help you to achieve the following:

- Enhance operational visibility
- Triage the nature of the problem and resources involved
- Document efficacy of incremental release and fixes
- Clear and unambiguous recommendations on how to proceed

In short, firefighting will eliminate any individual agendas and get everybody on the same page, working in one direction and with a single version of the truth. This is absolutely critical when the customer is managing multiple vendors as part of the overall solution. Otherwise, you will end up with a cycle of finger-pointing among the vendors (or their sponsors) which will get you nowhere near a concise recommendation.

Resistance Sounds Like...

When experience with APM technology is limited or negative, there will be a number of objections to employing the technology. How do you know it will not make things worse? How do you know it will actually solve the problem? How do you know the monitoring technology actually works? How do you know that the performance engineers will bring anything new to the table? You have to have a solid response for each of these concerns. For example:

- There is always a possibility that APM might have an unexpected effect on the application. You need to describe what that might look like and how quickly you can detect it. You will also describe how the tools are configured and backed-out in the case of difficulty. Your best path is to do this pre-production with a limited test. If that isn't possible, then you should deploy a very conservative configuration. If you are really lucky, you can reference a similar application and the steps you took there.
- You are not here to solve the problem. You are here to apply APM technology and to see what additional visibility you can obtain. This new information may, or may not, help to resolve the application performance issue. You simply will not know until you try. All you need is a couple of hours.
- Even with an 11 year history of successful monitoring in QA and production, APM is still an unknown quantity for many stakeholders. And applications are always different and they change to take advantage of new technologies. APM is an established tool; this is an opportunity to show if it is valuable for the application at hand.
- What the performance engineer brings to the table is a conservative and reliable process to get additional visibility into the application. The more time you can spend with the application, the more you will learn about it. This may or may not result in a root cause determination simply because you may not get enough information during this firefight. But you will get

additional information that you may never before have had an opportunity to consider.

It's never enough to simply repeat these statements. You have to build confidence in your stakeholders that you will actually deliver. And you can never realistically hope to achieve this delivery for a firefight unless you have attempted it a few times prior. If you expect to firefight, then you need to use the process a few times. You need to have your own story about what you've done and what you have found with earlier exercises. No one wants to see if you can get lucky on your first real use of the technology. That's what your stakeholders are trying to avoid.

Success Sounds Like...

When firefighting is conducted successfully, the tone of your stakeholder conversations changes remarkably.

"... you always knew what to do..."

"... we always knew what you were doing and when it would be ready..."

"... you understood the impact and benefits of your tools..."

"... it was much less painful then earlier methods..."

"... we really got something out of the exercise ..."

From the initial scope until the final presentation, it is up to you to manage expectations. These comments will only occur if you have carefully addressed each of the concerns of your stakeholders. They will always have the same concerns unless they have recently experienced a successful firefight recently. As the number of successful firefights increases, there is the potential that the organization as a whole will come to understand and embrace the methodology, benefits, and limitations. That ambition is actually contrary to your recommendations, especially if you have had any success uncovering issues pre-production. The real measure of success for firefighting is when it is no longer necessary.

Firefighting is Temporary

I have reviewed the many benefits and challenges of a firefighting system, but it's important to realize that this activity is a temporary one. Firefighting is a necessary response to weak processes during the management of the application life cycle. In Chapter 11, I introduced the concept that as you increased your performance testing maturity, you also decreased the frequency of unresolved problems in production and increased the number of defects that were identified and resolved during pre-production. I reprise that concept with some additional emphasis on the change in production in Figure 17-3.

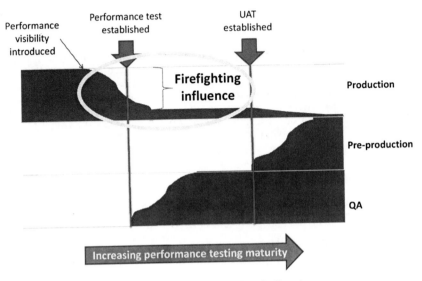

Figure 17-3. Where are performance problems identified?

Clearly, firefighting is important to help with the initial categorization of incidents. But as you increase your performance testing capabilities and move the realization of visibility into performance problems earlier in the application life cycle, there will be less for the firefighting discipline to do. A successful pre-production APM system will put a firefighting discipline out of business.

This is not to say that all firefighting will cease. It simply takes less heroics and stress—and more process—to achieve the same diagnostic result. There is always a new application in the wings, waiting to take center stage and demanding all attention in order to get it stable. With an improving pre-production system, you simply end up with fewer production firefights. That's the sign of a mature APM discipline. APM practitioners just don't panic. They deploy resources and follow well-known practices that all the stakeholders understand and expect.

For those organizations with a dedicated APM discipline, the initial teams vary from 10-20 individuals for an enterprise-wide discipline. After two years, these teams are generally reduced to 3-6 persons. It is not due to performance problems suddenly going away. It's just that the organization has moved from crisis mode to APM. I find that most mature APM systems (those established for more than 5 years) will only have about 3-6 people in them and at least one of whom is management! The expertise has not been lost; it's been spread out into the enterprise, and the bulk of it is focused on pre-prodution use of APM. And through the mentoring philosophy of the APM best practices, you will actually have about 50 to 100 persons competent with APM technology and following the various cookbooks for its rapid and consistent usage. This also sets up the potential for a rotation of staff into and out of the APM team.

Until a pre-production use of APM is acknowledged and supported, firefighting is a necessary reality for most organizations. It is up to you to decide just how long it's going to take your organization to employ APM pre-production in order to determine the appropriate level of production fire-fighting investment. As the organization matures in its use of APM technology, the need for firefights will decrease. Visibility will reduce the urgency of production incidents simply because it will be obvious what the problem is before getting dozens of people involved. More people will know how to use the information and thus will be less dependent on firefight experts to help them understand the data. The overall number of incidents related to configuration problems or software quality will be reduced because the problems were identified and addressed pre-production. And so goes the age of the firefight.

Process

There are a couple of processes to establish in order to support firefighting. The most critical is io define to what level, if any, you want to support firefight activities, in terms of what you promote to your business sponsors. This would be a document of what your *firefight process* will do and how it gets invoked. But if you do not have the correct personnel and experience, you really should push these requests back to an *application audit* activity. The audit covers the same ground as a firefight but does not have the same emotional context (rapid and urgent problem diagnosis). You will give them better visibility. You may find some unusual things and everyone will benefit from the exercise of deploying the technology and experiencing what APM brings to the life cycle.

If you decide to make firefighting a service, you need to have a scope process to help ensure a successful engagement. A template for that document is included in this section.

There is also a cookbook for conducting a forensic analysis with APM.

The final bit of process is to address how to grow a firefighting system. This presumes the following:

- That you do not today have a strong pool of candidates to take on the firefighting role.
- That you anticipate the need for a competent system.
- That you will have time and access to APM in order to grow your skills.

Firefighting Process Documentation
Scope document

- Assess what you can do against the app.
- Collect info as to the nature of the problem and expectations.

- Environment
  - Can they test in QA?
  - Are multiple production instances in use?

- Is sufficient metrics storage capacity available?
  - Metrics storage requirements (longevity) and connectivity (firewalls)
  - Centralized triage MS? New server?

Scope Template

However you conduct the scope call, the following is a list of topics that you will need to over in order to insure your firefighter has a chance at a meaningful contribution. This template is for a Java application. You can find a sample document following this template on apress.com.

- Application
  - AppServer|POJO ___v_ on OS ____v_ with ____ JVM_v
    The prior shorthand is as follows:
    - What application server and version?
    - Or is it a stand-alone java process?
    - What operating system and version?
    - What JVM provider and version?

  - # JVMs
    - What does it do?
    - What problems were experienced to date and how were they resolved?

- What platform for Metrics Storage is required or available?
- Any extension products needed (APM vendor specific)?
- Who provides access to restart servers?
- Who provides access to generate load?
- Who can confirm suitability of testing scripts?
- Target start date?
- Expected duration?
- Rules of Engagement
  - Who is the primary contact to ensure the effort progresses?
  - What duration of monitoring is expected?
  - How much time to do you have to respond?
  - Does a chargeback policy apply?

Rules of Engagement (internal to the firefight organization)

The following are the processes you will implement in order to establish a firefighting response.

- Who gets contacted, who qualifies and assigns the degree of response?
- Who defines and maintains the scope document?
- What gets communicated about your firefighting capability to your stakeholders?
- What is your definition of firefighting?
- What do you allow for firefighting to achieve?
- How do you qualify a firefight engagement?
- What staff undertakes the firefight? What credentials or experience do they have?
- What fees are associated?
- What does the firefight deliver, day by day?
- How to contact the team if you think a firefight is necessary?
- How do you certify a firefighter?

Forensic Analysis

This process is something that firefighting can support once you have collected enough information. You want to have a detailed analysis of not only how the problem was identified but what defects in your internal systems and processes, if any, contributed to the problem. A single firefight engagement will not support effective forensic analysis. You really need to have a couple of events, often firefighting in combination with application audits (both production and/or QA), and you need to reach out to other data sources, as discussed in Chapter 16: "Triage with Trends." You could also gather sufficient data during a performance optimization exercise, which would be undertaking a series of configuration and code changes and using APM visibility to ensure that progress was being made.

As opposed to RCA (root cause analysis), which looks simply to identify the problem and is willing to accept an "ah-ha" moment for expediency, a forensic analysis is about getting evidence. You need a solid, unreproachable timeline to lay out the issues that led up to the performance incident. And each issue will be confirmed by suitable evidence. Your process is as follows:

- You *really* need well-established baselines.
  - Appropriate instrumentation established
  - Monitoring already in place

- Look for metrics that are unexpected.
- Look at stalls and concurrency.

- Look at transaction traces if the outage has a reproducible scenario.
- Sporadic outages may need days to reproduce.
  - Get the baselines done in QA while you're waiting!

The emphasis on evidence is because a structural organizational problem cannot be resolved with a simple fix. Change can happen quickly but a lot of elements will need adjustment in order to reach the new organization, which requires significant executive support, which in turn requires unequivocal evidence.

Establishing the Firefighting Discipline

It is never too early to introduce a firefight capability provided that you have clearly communicated the scope of what you may deliver. Your firefighting skills will improve as you master the three levels of triage. If you stay within scope of each level of triage, then you may reliably deliver that capability even during a firefight. If you go beyond scope, you might get lucky but it is not worth the risk of failure until you have appropriate experience managing expectations.

If you have an active APM discipline with small deployments ongoing along with a couple of application audits or similar activities pre-production, then you really have enough going on to be able to let someone with appropriate background and experience with APM technology focus on a triage role. They can be fully capable in about three months just by focusing on the competency exercises. If you are only in your first deployment, and no one yet has any significant experience, then a triage role is six to twelve months away. Here is what a practical path to a firefighting role would look like, starting from this first deployment, and what you might reasonably hope to deliver.

Get Visibility

This initial phase of a system is very conservative in what it may offer in a firefighting situation. You will commit to nothing more than successfully deploying the APM technology, which has the obvious benefit of getting additional visibility into the problem. Of course, it has to be a compatible application technology—something that you have the technology to monitor. You can't commit to do anything else. You also need to be honest about your installation expereince, especially if you have not yet installed successfully against the target application server or resource technology. This is especially important if you are being asked to deploy into production but have not yet achieved that result three times.

Checklist

- Do you have an APM component that is compatible with the target application in order to get some visibility?
- Will you deploy into a pre-production environment?

Audit the Production Experience

A production audit is similar to a pre-production audit except that the source of load is real user transactions, not simulated. Thus, you need a minimum of three production days of monitoring to get anything useful in terms of a statistically significant result. Fourteen days would allow for a much better result as this would allow you to detect if any day-of-week activities were significant. Please refer to Chapter 13 for more discussion on the application audit. Here is your process:

1. Install APM on one instance of the application unless you have significant install experience.

2. Find the most significant invocation metrics and assess how consistent these metrics are for each day.

    a. Are there time-of-day peaks or surges?
    b. Are there examples of invocation metrics that are complementary?
        i. A complementary pair of metrics is where metric A is low when metric B is high, and vice versa.

3. If the invocations are consistent for each day, audit the major applications (following Chapter 14).

    a. Do you have appropriate visibility?
    b. What are the representative transaction profiles or traces?
    c. What are the key metrics that best represent preformance and capacity?
    d. Generate a two hour baseline of the key metrics for each major application, if they have a normal period of operation.
        i. These baselines should be consistent over the three day (or longer).

4. Review any operational incidents

    a. Focus on a period with 90 minutes before and 30 minutes after each incident.
    b. Find metrics that correlate with the incident as indicated by any consistent increase or decrease that is outside of that captured in the baseline.
    c. Look for correlations with error and exception reporting, if available, prior to the incident.

5. Summarize your findings.

    a. Do you have sufficient visibility? What efforts did you undertake to improve visibility?
    b. What are the baseline characteristics for each of the major applications? (Look to Chapter 13 for more background on baselines.)
    c. Which incidents were you able correlate with changes in the key metrics?

Audit the QA Experience with Recommendations

This follows the same cookbook as the *Audit the Production Experience* with the exception that you can replace "day" with "test." This is the advantage of a testing environment compared with production: things can go much more quickly when you have precise control over the load and use cases.

Aditionally, you're able to present detailed recommendations, depending on the reproducibility of your testing, along with a summary of the observations. The process is as follows:

1. Conduct the audit as before, generating an initial set of observations.

2. If the application is unstable, attempt to correlate among the key metrics to characterize the performance as the application fails. Drill down through the key components to the underlying components or transactions to prepare a list of suspects and discuss with the developers for remediation. Don't forget to consider the application server and virtual machine configuration, which may be contributing to the problem, and what changes might be beneficial there.

3. If the application is stable but underperforming, look first for configuration changes that have potential, following each change with a load test to confirm the benefit, if any. Follow the configuration tuning with discussions with the developers for opportunities to ehance performance.

4. If the application is stable and performance is acceptable, apply your acceptance criteria (see Chapter 8) and prepare to *promote* the monitoring configuration to production. This entails completing the assignment of thresholds and preparing suitable dashboards and reports. See Chapter 13 for details.

Competency

Before you attempt to firefight you really need to be fully proficient on mechanics of deploying, configuring, and interpreting the APM technology. It doesn't matter if you have someone else assisting you and taking care of getting the APM tools in place—you need to know if they got things correct, even if they don't know themselves. You must have the experience to render such judgement. If you don't, none of the problem triage and analysis is going to make sense.

To make the road to firefighting more achievable, I break down the skills into four competencies. Each of these needs to be successfully demonstrated before a candidate can move on to the next level.

Rapid Deployment

This is vendor specific but entails everything necessary to get a monitoring technology successfully deployed. This requires verification of sufficient capacity for metrics storage, confirming that compatible technology is available, packaging the agent configuration, and enabling monitoring. Rapid means thirty minutes or less from notification to having metrics generated.

Analysis and Presentation

You will have a good understanding of the techniques in Chapters 12 and 15 (baselines, triage with single metrics) and some experience presenting your findings in front of a pessimistic audience. You need to review what you did to enable monitoring and how you know it is safe and giving useful visibility—never assume that everyone knows what you did. Review the firefight process, depending on production or QA. Then review your observations, simply indicating anything unexpected as "suspect." Finally, summarize the significant observations and findings and supply recommendations as appropriate.

Application Audit

I find that three separate audits are a powerful predictor of firefighting prowess. Full details are in Chapter 13, and you will also want to be familiar with Chapters 11 and 12 (load generation and baselines). All of your practice audits should be completed pre-production. Depending on stakeholder interest, this is also an opportunity to hone those presentation skills.

Performance Tuning

This last competency is for support of the remediation life cycle—what it's like to coordinate with developers and bring a fix back for confirmation testing. Any *performance tuning* exercise is effectively two or more application audits followed by configuration or code adjustments, resulting in a verifiable improvement in performance via APM, of course. Usually, a configuration change is much more a practical tweak than an update of the code, but it's useful to find out how fast a code change can be implemented if the opportunity presents.

Summary

Firefighting is a response to weak processes across the app life cycle. Initially, it will serve to justify an APM initiative because of the rapid benefits of additional visibility into performance problems. Later, it will become more infrequent as proactive APM processes become established.

Preparation will lead to reliable firefighting. You have to practice getting APM deployed and configured quickly as well as uncovering and presenting observations and recommendations. Careful management of stakeholder expectations is key to a successful firefight and acceptance of the results. What you undertake as part of a firefight is often the first time stakeholders are seeing APM technology at work. You need to get it right the first time and every time.

Index